PRAISE FOR *THE WOMAN IN THE ROOM*

"Long before the gender revolution in the professions, L. Jane Hastings was one of a few pioneering women who challenged convention and made their own way forward. Entering architecture school in the 1940s, she later built a successful Seattle practice, first as a sole proprietor and then as leader of The Hastings Group. Along the way she showed extraordinary generosity—mentoring younger professionals and providing professional leadership locally, nationally, and internationally. In this detailed and well-illustrated personal account, Jane shares her story and vividly shows us what a life in architecture can be."

Jeffrey Karl Ochsner, FAIA
Professor, University of Washington
Editor/co-author Shaping Seattle Architecture: A Historical Guide to the Architects

"The Woman in the Room documents how a singularly independent woman built an impressive decades-long career in architecture despite the obstacles placed in her way. Jane Hastings not only shattered the glass ceiling for women architects, she dismantled its structure and showed her male colleagues that it was superfluous from the start."

David Martin
Northwest art historian and author
Cascadia Art Museum, curator

"In *The Woman in the Room*, Jane Hastings generously brings us along on her journey as she navigates the challenges of becoming an architect. Never fazed by her male-dominated profession, Jane treats the barriers placed in her way as 'puzzles' to solve, thriving as she defies the doubters and deftly builds a celebrated career."

Eugenia Woo
Director of preservation services, Historic Seattle
Co-founder, Docomomo US/WEWA

THE WOMAN IN THE ROOM

❖

A MEMOIR

L. Jane Hastings, FAIA

TANDEMVINES MEDIA
Seattle, Washington 2023

Book Editors: Kate Krafft and Denise Clifton | Copy Editor: Julie Hanson
Book Design: Tandemvines Media | Photo Production: Jennifer Nerad

Unless otherwise credited, all photographs and illustrations are from the author's personal collection. All images used with permission.

On the cover:
Jane with fellow University of Washington Architecture School graduates, June 1952

Dedication:

To my wonderful family, my dear friends, my clients, employees, students, and colleagues who have been part of my story.

I thank you all.

CONTENTS

LIST OF ARCHITECTURAL WORKS

Selected works of L. Jane Hastings that appear in photographs and plans in this book:

THE COLLECTED WORKS OF L. JANE HASTINGS: The majority of L. Jane Hastings' project records are held by Virginia Tech, Blacksburg, Virginia, in the International Archive of Women in Architecture (IAWA):

> Special Collections and University Archives, Virginia Tech
> L. Jane Hastings Architectural Papers (Ms-2004-004)
> Series III: Project Records, 1959-1998, n.d.
> Summary of Project Records (project list)

Selected photographs and drawings from projects by L. Jane Hastings and her practice, The Hastings Group, are held by University of Washington Libraries, Special Collections. These records cover ten projects that were recognized by the juried AIA "Home of the Month" program and featured in a monthly column published by the Seattle Times. This collection also includes photographs of two additional award-winning projects: the Karrow Residence and the Johnston-Hastings Residence. The collection is not digitized at the time of publication.

> Jane Hastings Seattle Times AIA Home-of-the-Month Photograph
> and Drawing Collection
> UW Libraries Special Collections
> PH Coll 1604

FOREWORD

NEARLY FIFTY YEARS AGO, I was so fortunate to walk into a room and meet Jane Hastings. It was a classroom at Seattle Central Community College; she was there to teach, and I was there to learn. At the time I knew she was a well-established and highly successful architect, but I knew little about the crucial role she had played in creating the academic program I was enrolled in. Nor could I imagine how much she would shape my own subsequent career and the lives of so many others who were lucky enough to cross her path.

After pursuing an extraordinary list of professional and personal accomplishments, Jane has spent the last several years examining and recounting her path from a nurtured childhood in Seattle's Fauntleroy community through challenging years of academic work at the University of Washington to a remarkable architectural career and loving marriage to Norman Johnston. That path is filled with extensive world travel, hard work on her architectural jobs and for various professional and women's organizations, and lifelong friendships. Today, I realize more than ever how fortunate I was to have been at her side in that classroom, as well as later at the drafting board and at the end of a measuring tape, in snow houses above Snoqualmie Pass, in symphony halls, and in dining rooms at her marvelous Laurelhurst house and art-filled Horizon House home. I am still learning from Jane.

Her positivity, level of energy, determination, and focus continue to be astonishing—even now at the age of ninety-five. Jane is the daughter and granddaughter of two women who were both highly skilled seamstresses and tailors; they instilled her with a creative spirit and love of construction, albeit of a more structural nature. Comprehending how hard she worked to follow her dreams—to build a career in which she designed more than five hundred projects while pursuing a life of adventure—is both fascinating and exhausting.

Jane's life is full of serendipitous events, and you will find a wonderful throughline along her path. As we prepare for the publication of this memoir, she is preparing to move once again. Horizon House is planning to construct a new tower on the site of her comfortable west wing home, so she will soon move to a new unit in another existing tower. Thus, we recently found Jane drawing up floor plans and busily measuring rugs and cabinets in order to create her newest home. And as is her way, she is doing that with enthusiasm in between an active social life with her many friends and loving family, chorale practice and events, a devotion to the university, and meeting with curators as she continues to donate more of her marvelous book, art, and antique collections.

Jane's whole story is a captivating and compelling adventure she generously shares with all of us. And this memoir is a wonderful metaphor. Since her childhood, Jane has had a fascination with bridge construction, and her own path is itself a bridge and the story of connections across nine decades through the city of Seattle and around the world. In sharing her story now, she continues to build bridges, connecting her rich past to our present, thanks to her extraordinary memory and boundless enthusiasm, as well as the marvelous collection of letters she wrote to her family during her time in Germany that are among her remarkable personal papers and her professional records.

Thank you, Jane, for sharing your story and inspiring all of us to pursue our own paths by following our dreams, facing our challenges with determination, and making connections.

Kate Krafft
Cultural/Historic Resources Specialist
and former employee of L. Jane Hastings
July 2023

Jane's father took this photograph of Grand Coulee Dam under construction, c. 1938.

PROLOGUE

I **WAS NINE YEARS OLD** when I knew I would be an architect.

It was 1937, and my father laughed when I announced this. I didn't know anyone in my West Seattle neighborhood who was an architect. No one in my immediate family had yet graduated high school, let alone university.

But the foundation was there, laid when I was very small, visiting my grandparents' home on the north side of Seattle's Queen Anne Hill in the early 1930s. The George Washington Memorial Bridge (now better known as the Aurora Bridge) was under construction over the Lake Washington Ship Canal—it would be taller than the Brooklyn Bridge, the newspapers said—and while my brothers chased each other around the yard, I sat on the front steps transfixed, watching these guys dangling off the skeleton of this bridge. *Building* it.

From then on, I was fascinated with anything that had to do with construction. I was in every garage and doghouse ever built in my neighborhood. I still have a photo from a family trip in the 1930s to the worksite for Grand Coulee Dam in Eastern Washington—a beautiful lacework of steel in the sky. When my father hired a carpenter to build a garage in our back yard, I was at his side every day, like a surgical nurse with the right tool in hand before he asked for it.

My interest was clear, but I don't fault my father for chuckling at my fourth-grade aspirations. Washington state had licensed its first woman architect in 1923, and in 1953, I would be only the eighth.

But my mind was set and by high school I had a plan: My first goal was to get my architecture degree. My second was to get licensed, and my third was to see Europe. When I got that far, I figured I'd have more goals.

To their credit, my parents never tried to reroute my ambitions. That was left to schoolteachers and potential employers, and the barriers they set before me became my puzzles to solve.

There was the chairman of the University of Washington Architecture Department who told me I could not work and attend school at the same time. Of course I could. I could not afford the five-year degree any other way, and I figured I could graduate in seven years if I worked part-time. I was the only woman in my freshman class of 200, and I finished in six and a half years.

After I graduated in 1952, the U.S. Army Corps of Engineers told me they didn't hire women architects for work in Europe. "It's dangerous," the man said. "The war's over!" I pointed out. "Well, we know that," he replied, "but you have to work with all those *men*." I thought, "Fella, what do you think I've been doing?" But never mind. If I couldn't go to Europe as an architect, I'd go as a recreation director running programs for U.S. troops overseas. What mattered was, I would go. I would see the grand European landmarks I had studied. I would solve the puzzle a different way.

When I began my architecture career in Seattle in the early 1950s, there were more puzzles: The contractors who didn't want to work with a woman architect. The auto-insurance companies that did not insure a never-married woman over the age of 25. The banks that wouldn't extend loans to women.

I didn't dwell on the puzzles, I just solved them. And I had one advantage: It never fazed me to be the woman in a room full of men. I had two older brothers and six older boy cousins, and I did everything the boys did: playing ball, fishing, and skiing. I climbed over logs, baited my own hooks, cleaned my own fish. All my life, my backpack was just as heavy as any carried by a guy.

Being the woman in the room even brought some unique opportunities, including the first and smallest job of my career. In 1943, drafting instructor Fred

Gorton received a request for a design of a storage locker for the West Seattle High School girls' gymnasium. Because I was the one girl in his class and I could easily go into the gym for measuring, it became my assignment. Fred Gorton was probably the only teacher I ever had who didn't see any reason why I couldn't be an architect. Just nine years later, I was working on my largest-scale job: the hangar and production facility at the north end of Boeing Field that would house four or five B-52s.

Even when I was an established architect and running my own Seattle firm, some acquaintances couldn't comprehend it. At times, I avoided telling people what I did because they did not believe me or would think I was involved with some type of an arts and crafts project. In the 1950s, women just *didn't* design and build homes. But I did.

Of course, there would be firsts in a career spanning seven decades: I was the first woman hired as an architect at a large national firm, in its Seattle office; the first woman president of the Seattle chapter of the American Institute of Architects; the first woman to be honored as Chancellor of the College of Fellows in the national AIA; and the first person ever to be awarded the Northwest and Pacific AIA Region Medal of Honor. These accomplishments brought me a good deal of press coverage over the years but being "first" was never that significant to me. At the time, I simply focused on doing.

Throughout my career—my life—my head has ruled. In my winter ski-school racing days, skiing with control meant I could finish the race upright; thus, I was consistent. I have never let anyone's "no" keep me out of the sport, the education, or the career that I chose.

Now from the vantage point of my mid-nineties, I look back over an extraordinary life built on a simple and steadfast decision made by my nine-year-old self. I have had experiences she never could have imagined. If I could go back, I would tell her, or anyone: Don't accept "no." If you really want to do something, there is always a way—even if it takes longer, even if it requires solving puzzle after puzzle, even if some people don't believe in you.

And I would tell them: I would certainly do it all again.

L. Jane Hastings
Fellow of the American Institute of Architects (FAIA)
January 2023

The Hastings kids with their mother, Camille, and the Stearns-Knight

1 | JANE ANN

"Saturday's child works hard for a living ..." – *traditional nursery rhyme*

A **TWELVE-YEAR-OLD GIRL,** visiting friends of her mother's, admired the family's black-haired, blue-eyed baby girl. "When I grow up, I'm going to have a little girl that looks just like yours and I'll also name her Jane Ann," the girl said. Baby Jane Ann's mother looked closely at the girl, noting her brown hair and hazel eyes. "I certainly would be careful about the daddy you select," the infant's mother said. At the time, my future mother did not think much about this.

About twenty years later my mother awaited the birth of her third child. The first "Jane Ann" had instead been James Calvin, his middle name in honor of President Calvin Coolidge, who was also born on the Fourth of July. Naming the second "Jane Ann" was more difficult; the parents finally agreed on Harry, for his father, and Arthur, his grandfather's middle name.

With her two young sons in tow and very pregnant, my mother accompanied my father on a visit to his former employer in downtown Seattle's Colman Building. Father was very outgoing, and that day, he stopped to talk with Pete Arcodares, owner of the lobby shoeshine stand. Arcodares, as our family knew him, was aware that my parents wanted a baby girl. All eight grandchildren on the Hastings side so far were male: my two brothers and six male cousins. The next time my father saw him, Arcodares told him not to worry, this baby was a girl.

While giving birth on March 3, 1928—"a Saturday's child"—Mother overheard the nurse say, "Doctor, you have just performed a miracle." My parents had planned on a larger family, but after the difficult birth, Mother was informed: no more.

Father was always a good tease, and when he next saw Arcodares, he told him how disappointed he was that the baby was another boy. Not possible, said Arcodares. He had seen me before I was born, and the baby was a girl with black hair and blue eyes. He said the next time Mother was downtown, she should bring me by so he could see "his little girl." I had dark hair and blue eyes, as my mother had foretold, but I was not to be "Jane Ann." Father convinced my mother that they should name me Lois Jane in honor of my mother's younger sister, Lois Belle Pugh. But from the beginning, I was always "Jane."

One day on the way to a doctor's appointment, our whole family stopped to see Arcodares. After admiring me, he said to my mother, "When you are at the doctor, have him look at my girl's hip. Something is wrong, and I don't want her to be crippled." As I hadn't started to walk, no one had noticed any possible problems. At my mother's request I was examined and found to have a hip disorder. This examination and treatment were not routinely done at the time, and several children my age wore one shoe with a wooden block under it to make their legs equal in length. How grateful I am that I had a "fairy godfather," a man I never really knew.

❖

MY FATHER, HARRY HASTINGS, had arrived in Seattle from Colorado about 1908 when he took a job in the Campbell Brothers logging camp in the Woodinville-Redmond area. James Campbell took a shine to Harry and hired him as his personal chauffeur, and my father then lived in their home in Seattle's Capitol Hill neighborhood. When he married my mother, Camille Pugh, in 1923, he went to work for General Petroleum as a truck driver. He remained on that job until he had a heart attack when I was in college.

In 1930, as the Great Depression gripped the country, my family moved from a new, handsome Tudor-style house on a busy street to a modest bungalow on a quiet unpaved street. I now realize how fortunate I was to grow up in this special Fauntleroy community on the peninsula across from downtown known as West Seattle. Three big maple trees in the front yard and a large wisteria at the south end of the front porch added a good deal of charm. My brothers and I grew up with vacant lots next door and across the street, and woods behind the house. Our "playground" allowed our imaginations to soar. Piles of dirt lined the street, left over from sewer installation during the Works Progress Administration era. They remained untouched for months, so we sculpted them into horses, riding single file with each of us on our own individually named horse.

The neighborhood houses, constructed mostly in the 1910s to 1920s, ranged from very modest to formally designed homes of quality construction sited on

Harry Hastings and Camille Pugh on their wedding day in 1923

choice lots with unobstructed views of the Olympic Mountains. Trails pierced through the woods; one ran along a stream full of trout, on down the hill past Seattle's smallest school, Fauntleroy Grade School. Across from the school was the community church with a YMCA center attached.

One of these trails would become my daily route to grade school. In the summer the small, tart wild blackberries played hide-and-seek with us in the woods. They represented a rare source of money, as a three-pound bucket full would fetch twenty-five cents. While my brothers sold their pickings, I usually saved mine for family dining. My mother would create two large pies: one for tonight and one for tomorrow.

During the Depression, there were many workers idled or, like my father, working part-time and sharing the little work there was with other employees. The rewards were more emotional than monetary, as these men could say they did have a job! On his free days, I accompanied my father on walks to visit friends and especially to the swimming pool (the "mudhole," as we called it) in Lincoln Park, filled with tidewater from Puget Sound. In 1941, this location would become the site for the Colman Pool, donated by one of Seattle's earliest pioneer families.

I was the youngest child in the neighborhood. An older girl lived in the house behind ours and a boy next door was about my older brother's age. Up the street was an older boy crippled from polio who was not able to keep up with boys his age, so he played with us. Other older boys had joined the Civilian Conservation Corps (CCC) of single men who worked and lived in forest camps, receiving shelter and food while they built park facilities and developed forest trails and fire lookouts throughout the mountains.

Summertime seemed to be when childhood diseases took their toll. Whether it was measles, whooping cough, chickenpox, mumps, or what have you, we managed it, often playing together despite the pink or blue quarantine signs posted on our front doors.

Molly Alward was my best friend and regular playmate, living three blocks away in a small apartment above her parents' grocery store. It seemed Molly's father had lost his prior business in the crash of 1929 and they leased out their Mount Baker neighborhood house while he pursued a living in the grocery business. They also had a vacation beach house on nearby Vashon Island where we spent many happy days digging steamer clams, looking for scallop shells, swimming when the tide

Jane with her brothers Jim and Art c. 1930

came in over the warm sand, and sleeping on an outdoor porch. One sunny day as we were playing at low tide, we noticed that the ferry from Fauntleroy had missed the dock by a considerable distance to the south and was headed toward us. It stopped abruptly when it hit a sandbar directly in front of the Alwards' house. The few passengers on the ferry were as astonished as we were as the sheriff rowed out in a small boat to arrest the intoxicated captain. The high tide and a tug managed to free the ferry sometime later, undamaged.

During all our daily playtime together over the years, we never really argued, much to our mothers' surprise. We lost track of each other later when World War II sparked many changes in all our lives.

WEEKENDS WERE SPECIAL. Saturdays often started with the family piling into our black Stearns-Knight car. The first stop would be a visit to Father's former employer, Mr. Campbell; at the time, most businessmen worked until noon on Saturdays. We would then head north and west to find a parking place at Pike Place farmers market, where we would spend the rest of the day. Father took charge of the three youngsters while Mother made her usual trek through the arcades. She would decide on her selections of fresh produce but wait to purchase them until late afternoon when prices were slashed before the market closed for Sunday. While she was shopping, we were treated to a huge five-cent milkshake at the creamery across from the market while we watched the workers with huge wooden paddles churning butter or cottage cheese. This was also my introduction to wooden chairs with a writing arm. I would spend many hours sitting in these during my future years of education.

I suspect Mother skipped lunch. We met up with her to visit a store on the lower level where she could purchase staples at better prices than our little local store. The mayonnaise and peanut butter were pumped out of large glass containers into little cardboard cartons, and pickles and olives were fished from barrels of brine. Occasionally, a large chunk of milk chocolate would find its way into our shopping box. Mother would then return to the produce stands to pick up her choices before we drove home.

A special Saturday evening treat was a trip to the neighborhood Granada Theater for a movie—a double feature plus the newsreel and a cartoon. I never found the cartoons as funny as the others did, but I was interested in the newsreels, which told of natural disasters and European politics, mainly the rise of Adolf Hitler and his Nazi Party. I was always intrigued by film clips of the large stadium where the German soldiers appeared to pour over the top row of seats and walk in perfect unison down the seats or steps onto the grass floor at the bottom. I don't remember our family discussing the events of the day, but the spectacle of the goose-stepping soldiers saluting Hitler made a lasting impression that was later deepened when I spent time in Nuremberg after the war.

Sundays were family days with church and Sunday school, and then we would be off to the new Seattle Art Museum that opened in June 1933 in the Capitol Hill neighborhood, where we mounted the historic camels at the entrance. (These camels are now protected indoors at the museum's downtown location.) Sometimes we took a drive along the waterfront on Alaskan Way, where the plank roadbed on pilings made lots of noise, to our delight. Sometimes we were even invited aboard a docked freighter for a tour.

I was fascinated with the little makeshift houses and shacks that made up the "Hooverville" settlement just south of the docks on the tide flats. Their construction materials included anything that could be scavenged and moved from the railroad tracks to the east or the waterfront to the west. Some of the 600-plus men (and a few women) who would otherwise be homeless even planted gardens, and one had a white picket fence enclosure. My favorite was a house made from a large steel tank with a door cut out and windows painted on it, with curtains and window boxes full of colorful flowers all around the tank. I wondered how the builder had decorated the interior. The gossip was that Spencer Tracy and Mickey Rooney were to be featured in a movie made in Seattle's Hooverville. I wondered: Would my favorite tank house be featured? But the rumored filming never happened.

Jane, Art, and Jim at Seattle Art Museum, Volunteer Park

❖

FOURTH OF JULY in the early 1930s was celebrated at my Hastings grandparents' Queen Anne house. From the front porch steps, I could check on the construction progress of the George Washington Memorial Bridge, which was completed in February 1932. Some newspaper headlines had called it "over-building" and a financial waste because the writers believed there would never be enough traffic to warrant the expense. The new bridge and new art museum—two projects that provided construction jobs during lean times—were signs that Seattle was growing into a real city. But I could not possibly know then that bridges would be part of my future design practice.

I still remember the floor plan of the Queen Anne house and the apple-green metal box with a key where the sugar cookies could be found. Access required a chair to crawl onto the counter and then another stretch to reach the top shelf. In the evening we watched the parade of commercial boats with lights and decorations as they came from the west through the Ship Canal on their way to Lake Union and Lake Washington.

Midnight marked the start of the holiday walk-a-thon around Lake Washington, and numerous people competed for the prize money awarded at the end of the next day. A few dollars attracted many participants in those terrible lean years.

In 1933, my grandparents passed away within weeks of one another, and our future Fourth of July celebrations moved to the bank of the Snoqualmie River just east of North Bend. Cousins would come from the other side of the Cascade Mountains to the family gatherings, where we would also celebrate brother Jim's birthday. The last of those picnics was in 1941, just before World War II.

❖

THANKS TO MY BROTHER ART, life was seldom dull. Jim and I could get into mischief, but Art always outdid us. One day, when he was just a little guy, he came running in, yelling: "I didn't set the woods on fire! I didn't set the woods on fire!" Mother didn't even look out the window; she just called to my father to phone the fire department as she knew Arthur had just set the woods on fire.

We subscribed to the *Seattle Star* newspaper, which was known for "telling it like it was." A frequent topic in our house was Dave Beck and the Teamsters Union he was starting. He was trying to force truck drivers like my father into joining his union, and goon squads sometimes beat up drivers. Father worked for General Petroleum, which paid its drivers more than the union scale, so he saw no need to join the union and pay dues. We always worried about Father being attacked, but he never was. The pressure became so great, with so many men beaten, that the company gave in, and the drivers became union members.

In the later 1930s, a new radio became the focus of our household attention. I enjoyed the news, especially FDR's *Fireside Chats* with his reassuring voice. Our favorites included programs like *Fibber McGee and Molly*, and for the kids, *Tom Mix, The Green Hornet,* and *Little Orphan Annie*. Sunday evening was family time with all of us gathered around the radio for *One Man's Family*.

❖

AS CHILDREN with such wonderful opportunities to play and explore, we had no idea of our parents' worries around how to provide for our family. My mother worked seasonally as a milliner, and she took in tailoring. When the older children were attending school, I became the only child left in the neighborhood during the day. The neighbor ladies took care of me when my parents were working at the same time, and they became my close friends. I made daily rounds to check on them. An older couple named Rogers lived across the alley and had a Royal Ann cherry tree in their yard, which I watched with great anticipation for the beautiful fruit each summer. Mrs. Rogers was the first stop on my daily visits, then it was north for a quick stop to see Mrs. Lansbury. And then up to Mrs. Parker in one of the larger houses, on the edge of a hill with a wonderful view of Puget Sound and the Olympic Mountains beyond.

My favorite stop was saved for last: Mrs. Selby. At four years old, I knew every detail of her little house and kitchen, and her stories—plus her candy—were the best! Mrs. S. was the oldest neighbor, her white hair pulled up in a neat and tidy bun. Mrs. S. had to be well into her seventies or eighties, which would have made her birthdate sometime in the 1850s or '60s. I'm sure her stories included tales of coming across the prairie and mountains by covered wagon when she was a child. She told so many tales of early Seattle, rocking in her spindled rocker with the pink gingham pillow in the seat. She would face east into the immaculate kitchen with the wood and coal cooking range glistening from stove polish and the oven door open to warm her knees. I would sit with my back to the east wall with my eyes focused on her beautiful lined face, spellbound by her soft voice until it was time to go home. The visit always finished with her offering my choice from a dish of round pink and white peppermints. It was always the pink one. One day I apparently arrived with my own candy supply, a roll of Necco Wafers. I gather that I had eaten the ones I liked best and was down to what I considered the least desirables. Mrs. S. told my mother that I studied the remaining candies, then took a chocolate one, my least favorite, and said, "I'll just pretend that you are pink." Mrs. S. told my mother, "I hope that she can go through life with that attitude."

When it was finally my turn to start school, I promised Mrs. S. I would still visit each day. I did, but only for a while. My mother told me later that Mrs. S. missed me so much that she cried.

Fauntleroy School – Jane (front row, second from right) with her sixth-grade class

2 | GOING TO SCHOOL

FROM THE FIRST DAY, I loved school. Kindergarten classes were discontinued due to the Depression, and I started first grade at Fauntleroy Grade School at age 5 in the middle of the school year. I later learned that if one more student—me— had not been found, the first-grade class would have been canceled, forcing first-graders to be bused to another school or home-schooled. Buses ran about once an hour, and several transfers were usually required. Few people had automobiles. Even for us, it was a half-mile walk through the woods to school, but I was so happy to be there with the other students. My maternal grandmother, Bessie Belle or "BB," once said I was the sweetest child she knew until I went to school and learned the word "no."

At home, I shared the back bedroom with BB. She had become ill after living with her second husband in Alaska, and my mother was trying to rebuild her health. I remember that every night she would have a glass of brandy before retiring to help her sleep. Our household was a teetotaling one, so brother Art decided this unfamiliar beverage must be sampled. Not willing to commit a crime on his own, he talked his little sister into joining. Our verdict: "Grandma must really be sick if she has to drink that."

BB had another ritual: Each night as she rolled into bed, she said, "The man that invented the bed was the greatest of them all." Over the years, I have thought of her many times as I crawled in between the covers exhausted from a strenuous activity or lengthy travel.

My favorite teacher was Miss Houston, my third-grade teacher who drove a little Austin car. Teaching seemed to be her life. Our classroom windows faced west toward Puget Sound, and the sills were full of jars containing every kind of local wildflower, leaf, weed, or blade of grass. We learned all their names. During extreme low tides the class explored the beach studying sea life—including a baby octopus. We even had class on Saturdays, making field trips to a potter's studio to watch him work magic on his wheel and returning with clay to craft our own works of art.

Other trips included a glass-blowing factory where we observed workers blowing gallon jugs by hand in assembly-line fashion.

I discovered architecture in the fourth grade and told my parents that it was what I would do when I grew up. While Father chuckled, Mother said, "I wouldn't laugh if I were you, Harry." Mother knew her children well! I'm sure my father could not imagine any of his children attending college. He left school after the sixth grade, and my mother dropped out in the eighth grade after the death of her father. Two of my father's sisters worked full time: One was a store buyer and the other owned a millinery shop. As the youngest of five, this aunt was the only one who finished high school. Mother's younger sister completed business college, staying on as the college president's assistant. These three women, all of whom were childless, supported their parents during the 1930s. I knew I would work as well, so best to choose work I liked!

❖

MY PARENTS ALLOWED ME to make my own decisions about my activities, while my brothers required their approval. Looking back, I'm sure I was harder on myself than my parents might have been. I was the only girl in my generation of eight boys, and my aunts were worried I was growing up a tomboy. My mother made it clear I was not to be shown favoritism and was not allowed the smallest gift or anything extra unless my brothers received the same.

My first paying job, starting in the fourth grade, was for a neighbor lady who boarded a teacher and the YMCA director. I helped prepare dinner, serve, and clean up. I ate in the kitchen between my serving duties. Not only was I making money but there was one less mouth to feed at home. On Saturdays, I helped with their laundry and housecleaning.

In the sixth grade, my class had ten students: three girls and seven boys. I was identified as the responsible one, and my duties beyond schoolwork included assisting the nurse who came once a month for a half-day, checking books out of the library, answering the office telephone, ringing the school bells, cashiering in the lunchroom, and acting as substitute teacher in the first grade when a teacher was absent. I thought school was wonderful. The only job I didn't have—considered out of the question—was "safety patrol boy" to assist children crossing the street in front of the building. This honor went to boys only, and two younger tall and lanky twins, Jim and Lou Whittaker, were the most memorable.

I did have play time, and once it got me into trouble. Our school was so small that we had just enough physically able boys to make a complete softball team. This was the one sport that we shared with other grade schools and I'm certain we were the city joke, seldom winning a game. I'd played a good deal of ball with my brothers, so I suggested that if the girls formed a team the boys would have a group to practice against. Mr. Swedine, our sixth-grade teacher and the coach, thought it was a great idea. Our girls team played several good games after school before the fourth-grade teacher, Miss McClaire, discovered us and filed a complaint. My parents were summoned to school to hear about their immoral daughter who was playing softball with the boys. They were not concerned, explaining that I had never had anyone but boys to play with. But that was the end of our mixed "team practice." Mr. Swedine purchased a new softball, had all my team members autograph it and held a little ceremony to present it to me. It was my first award and I have always kept it, wondering what happened to the eight girls who signed it.

❖

AS I'M WRITING THIS MANY DECADES LATER, November 11 is a few days away. When I was a child, this date was special and celebrated each year. On Armistice Day we honored the end of World War I and all subsequent wars. Our Scottish janitor had served as a piper, marching into battle in front of armed soldiers with only a bagpipe as his weapon. He wore his kilt uniform and played the pipes on 11/11 as he marched back and forth in the school hallway. I remember the shredded tartan bag covering the real inner bag—evidence of the many bullets that silenced his pipes during his duty. On that day, we students were to dress in our ethnic costumes as a symbol of world unity. I went home in tears as I was the only child who didn't come from "anywhere." My mother assured me that my roots went back too far, and we didn't know where our ancestors came from, so I would just have to go to school as a little "American girl." The solution was in a trunk in the basement, which produced one of BB's old tea gowns with a wonderful bustle. With a few alterations I, too, had a costume. It was the best in the class.

Years later, I discovered my earliest American roots. The Pugh family (Mother's side), arrived in 1613 with our ancestor John Clay, landing in Jamestown, Virginia, twelve generations ago. So, I guess I do qualify as an "American girl." Next, Evan Oliver from Wales arrived with the William Penn party in 1682. Family members worked their way west through St. Louis, Kansas, and on to Los Angeles. Favorite family legends included tales of the infamous Younger and James brothers and how my ancestors hid Jesse James in their barn.

My father's family is more difficult to trace. I believe "Hastings" may have been a deserter of the British Army from around 1776. We had souvenirs including a heavy small brass cannon used to send messages during the Revolutionary War. The cannon was loaded and fired each July 4, flinging itself a few feet into the air, to us kids' delight. The earliest official record found was my great-grandfather William S. Hastings, born in 1818 in Virginia. He was a farmer in Kansas when he died in 1865 after his wagon was attacked by an American Indian. My grandmother's side arrived from what is now Germany around 1790. They were among early white settlers of the Indiana Territory who farmed along the Wabash River. Around 1904, the Hastings family started west to Colorado, and moved on to Seattle a few years later.

❖

MY BROTHERS FOUGHT CONSTANTLY, but my parents never seemed to argue. My mother always had the last word on what we kids could do and where we could go. The rules were: "If the sport is too dangerous for Jane, it is too dangerous for the boys. They all go, or no one goes." The same rules applied to the movies: "If it is too dirty for Jane, it is too dirty for the boys." I'm sure she thought my presence would keep the boys in check—and why would Mother want one whining kid left at home? This early training helped me later as I pursued my personal goals while so many tried to discourage me. I had learned to play by "boys' rules." Ultimately, that served me well.

During the years at our home at Thirty-Eighth Avenue Southwest and Henderson Street, we siblings really bonded, despite—or maybe because of—the boys' battles. One day Mary Kinzel, a friend from my earliest years, came to play. My brothers were thrilled with a new girl to entertain; they chased each other around the dining table with butcher knives while we girls took refuge on top of the table. Mary screamed and sobbed while I reassured her this was standard behavior and not to worry. Once rescued, Mary told her mother that her older brother Jack was wonderful compared to the awful Hastings boys.

One day I heard my parents having a discussion. Mother raised her voice a bit: "I don't care, Harry. Our daughter is old enough to know that girls' clothes button on the opposite side than boys' clothes." Being the youngest, I had many remodeled clothes that had been altered by my talented mother and grandmother. My mother had purchased fabric to make me a new coat, using money my father thought should have gone to another use. The coat I had been wearing had been my father's, Jim's, then Art's before it came to me. It was good fabric, and many things can be altered, but you can't change the way it buttons. I really didn't understand the fuss; I had become used to buttoning things either way.

Summer meant planning the family vacation—usually a trip to the ocean beach at Copalis. I was required to sit between my brothers in the back seat of our Stearns-Knight to prevent them from fighting, but the fists and jabs flew across me, adding to my black-and-blue spots. Upon arrival our two-wheel trailer was unfolded from its box and the roof supports were set up with cotter pins locking them in place, allowing the canvas covering to float out over the beds that extended on either side of the box and above the ground. Six of us slept comfortably in the expanded trailer box: my parents in one extended bed, grandmother in the other, and me in a sleeping bag on the floor between them. The boys slept under the extensions on Army cots on the ground. Mother and BB would pack the cooking utensils, dishes, and food supplies over to the large community kitchen, an open pavilion with concrete floor, extended roof overhangs, low walls supporting structural posts, and a large wood cookstove that could hold an 8-foot log. Numerous picnic tables were arranged in this rectangular building, with the best tables closest to the stove and on the south side to enjoy sunshine during the day. This structure became our living room for the week or so of camping.

Another family of five had a trailer like ours and always seemed to show up at the beach at the same time. Mr. Dickerson was the president of the Edison Vocational School, which served the Seattle area. The three Dickerson children—two girls and a boy—were about our ages, and we had a great time fishing and eating crab together.

Each morning we youngsters would get up early and race to the beach to search for stubby beer bottles. Each was worth a penny at the grocery store, and fifty pennies would buy a one-hour horseback ride. Competition was keen.

But our daily schedule really revolved around the low tide for crab fishing—the whole reason we came to the beach. We had Dungeness crab for dinner every night and never tired of their succulent flavor. Early on we learned to catch crabs by wading waist deep in large pools left when the tide went out; this is where the crabs would bury themselves in the sand, waiting for the incoming tide. We carried poles like rake handles, with a circular hoop made of chicken wire on the end to scoop up our prey. We were careful to avoid stepping on lumps in the sand—crabs in hiding. Once we found a crab, our hope was that it would clamp on to the wire instead of running so we could flip it onto its back, disabling it, to make sure it was a male and determine that it was at least 6 inches across the back. When all requirements were met it would go into a burlap gunnysack we fastened to our waists and dragged in the water. Each day we cooked our catch in a huge cast iron kettle over an open fire behind the community kitchen. When we packed up for the trip home, our ice drawer under the trailer was full of whole cooked crabs or picked-out meat for canning when we got home.

Sometimes our summer vacation took us to Mount Rainier. I saw the national park rangers as superheroes and took in every story about wildlife and what to do when bears came into the campground at night looking for food. The ground was filled with chipmunks or marmots sunning themselves on warm rocks and treating us to their whistles. White avalanche lilies, Indian paintbrush in reds and oranges, lupines in rich blues, wild larkspur and, best of all, purple gentian carpeted the alpine meadow.

One summer, we went over the Cascade Mountains to see a construction marvel: the Grand Coulee Dam. It had received attention in the press when crews had trouble stabilizing the sliding soil. Finally, a young engineer came up with the idea of freezing the ground, allowing the construction to continue. I was taken with the beauty of the reinforcing steel—like a huge piece of lacework—before the concrete was poured.

Grand Coulee Dam was one of FDR's Pacific Northwest New Deal projects, along with the Tacoma Narrows Bridge, the Lake Washington Floating Bridge, and Yesler Terrace, the first public-housing project requiring racial integration. I recall seeing stacks of fresh lumber on the Yesler site, and I can still almost smell the sweet scent of the wood. I would watch the project develop whenever we went to town. These were the projects putting men to work.

❖

AS WE GREW UP, my parents determined that more space was required, so weekends were spent house-hunting in the communities of Burien and Des Moines. Fortunately, they bought a house just a few blocks away so we could stay in the neighborhood with our friends. But it was a Seattle Box style—"the ugly house," as I called it. I told my parents I would not live in this house, describing its faults in detail from the shape to the terrible paint job. Of course, we did move in, and painting the exterior white seemed to help. The best part was my large corner bedroom on the second floor where I was awakened by the rising sun over the Cascade Mountains. The sound of soft train whistles some distance away announced the start of my day. It was a perfect room, and I selected blue and white wide-striped wallpaper to run horizontally. Wallpapering was a new challenge for my parents and taught us all patience. I loved my "hat box room," perhaps the first project of my design career.

Our new house lacked a garage, an important structure for a retired chauffeur who maintained his own vehicle. An unemployed carpenter who was a family friend was hired to construct a two-car garage with a large playroom upstairs. This was the first real construction project I observed from the ground up. I hung out watching the garage take shape during the school year and over summer break. My brothers were supposed to help carry materials and run errands, but they were never around. I quickly associated each task with the necessary tool and had the proper implement ready for my co-worker when needed. Once the garage was completed, I would have to find an off-site project to supervise.

THE HIGHLIGHT OF SUMMERTIME before school started was always a week at Horsehead Bay Camp. We traveled on the Colman yacht—the *Osprey*—from Fauntleroy through the Tacoma Narrows' whirlpools, where a new suspension bridge was being constructed. From below, the workers spinning the cables appeared to be hanging from a cloud in the sky. The summer of 1940, we steamed under our finished miniature Golden Gate Bridge, which opened that July 1 to fanfare. The span's excessive flexibility earned it the nickname "Galloping Gertie." It was a thrill to drive over Gertie; even on windless days, the car ahead would disappear just like going over a wave. I managed two exciting trips during its short four-month life, before its magnificent dance in a windstorm and collapse into the whirlpools below on November 7, 1940. My '41 *Osprey* voyage was over the sunken steel and concrete remains with forlorn towers near each shore supporting dangling cables. Gertie's final dance was caught on film, and I'm sure every structural engineering student since has viewed it. A decade later I would work at the University of Washington Press on three small books about the design, failure, and new design of the Tacoma Narrows Bridge.

On July 2, 1940, the Interstate 90 Lake Washington Floating Bridge to Mercer Island also opened—a day after Gertie and following eighteen months of construction. People lined up all over the east slope of the hill above the top of the tunnel thinking they would watch its failure when the first car drove across. Everyone knew that concrete does not float and surely the first cars on the bridge would sink it! Both new bridges signaled the end of the Depression, putting men back to work and creating our roads of the future. This floating bridge would also play a part in my own future.

A few other dates stand out, of course. December 7, 1941, was a lovely sunny Sunday when the radio voice announced, "All military personal return to your bases immediately." This was repeated throughout the day. It was not until later that we learned that Hawaii's Pearl Harbor had been bombed. Lives changed overnight. Young men joined the military, and the shipyards and Boeing Airplane Company geared up to twenty-four-hour, seven-day-a-week mass production mode. We lived just over the hill from the Boeing plants along the Duwamish River and were aware that if the Japanese bombed us, they would fly over Puget Sound turning in right overhead. Any fraction of a minute off could mean that our neighborhood, instead of the Boeing plant, would be hit by a bomb. What had happened to the "war to end all wars" that we studied in school?

Within a week the U.S. Army moved into our neighborhood. The vacant lots and some schoolyards became bases for antiaircraft guns, barrage balloons and searchlight groups. December's heavy rain bogged the Army's new tent campsites down in the mud. Neighborhood residents invited soldiers in for dinner on Christmas, trying to lift their morale.

That next March, we had to say goodbye to the two Japanese issei families who farmed the valley floor to our east. We knew they were no threat to our country or us. It was a sad day, and we stayed with them until the Army truck came to transport them to inland internment camps. I was especially sad for the family who had rescued me some years back when I had a bicycle crash at the foot of the hill in front of their house. I remember being dragged from the road just before a car barely missed hitting me. I was taken into their tar paper home where many of the children helped their mother patch up my wounds. The father was called in from the garden, and he loaded my broken bike into his Model-T truck and drove me home. My mother assured the concerned man that I was more scared than hurt, thanking him many times for his family's help. For years they had been good neighbors. We did not want them to leave.

Everyone was working in a war industry. During the summer of '42 our new neighbor, Barbara Austin, was home from boarding school and got both of us jobs at Providence Hospital. I worked from 6 a.m. to 6 p.m. in the hospital kitchen. I had several hours off between mealtimes but never left the hospital, leaving home at 5 a.m. and returning about 7:30 p.m. Sisters Josephine and Geraldine (Josie and Gerry) oversaw my assignments, which included making ice cream, helping in the bakery, and making salads with carrot curls and radish roses. One very hot afternoon I was working near the stove when everything went black. I had fainted, my head landing in a large pan of applesauce. They helped me wash my hair, and there was no applesauce served that evening.

One sunny day I arrived home to see all the Austin family furnishings, clothes, and cooking utensils spread over their lawn, with Barbara crying among them. A priest arrived and tried to console her. She left with him, and I never saw any of the Austin family again. Later, Barbara called to say they were living in a motel, and she would contact me for a get-together, but it never happened. I had heard about foreclosures before; now I would never forget the pain.

The war also introduced us to ration stamps. In some ways we adjusted easily because of our experience working together during the Depression. We had already learned all about rationing and doing without. Paper stamps labeled A, B, C, R, S, and T were used for gasoline, and other books of stamps were issued for sugar, coffee/tea, meat/cheese, butter, and shoes. The shortage of rubber for tires and shoe soles was the biggest problem, and fuel was primarily available for farm equipment and boats. Fortunately, this meant we could continue to go to Horsehead Bay Camp on the *Osprey*, just as we had for years.

The weeklong camping experience was the highlight of our summer. We paid two dollars for the week, but if your family did not have the two dollars—and some families didn't—you could go anyway. The Colman family had long supported youth activities through their YMCA contributions, both in King County and in our little community. How lucky I was that my family was a part of this community with its wonderful opportunities. In 1944 I came home with the "Honor Girl Camper" canoe paddle, the camp's highest honor. After that, I continued to go to the camp as a counselor and as a lifeguard.

❖

ONE WINTER we had a little snowfall—a rare treat—and someone brought out a pair of skis that all of us kids tried out on the hill above the church. Among our group, the Whittaker twins, Jim and Lou, went on to become internationally famous mountain climbers, while most of us just became devoted skiers.

My childhood church was unique for having a woman pastor. Ordained women were rare in the 1930s, and usually they were missionaries in faraway places. Mary McKee was a big woman with a wonderful voice. I believe she had studied drama, and she was very effective in the pulpit. Her sermons were like a university lecture using current events applied to Bible teachings. As this was the church I was raised in, I didn't truly appreciate my Sunday mornings until I visited other churches and found their services boring. One of Mary's sermons included a phrase I've never forgotten: "Some of the finest Christians in the world

Rev. Mary McKee,
Fauntleroy Community
Church

have never crossed the threshold of a church, while others attend church regularly and go out and do unchristian deeds." Perhaps this was my cover for not attending church in my later life.

One of Mary's World War II programs was to invite Black soldiers stationed in our community to the Sunday service, and then church members would take them home for dinner, returning them to the church for the Army truck to pick up. Families were required to invite at least two soldiers so their guests would feel comfortable. Seattle had very few Black residents prior to the war years and none living in our neighborhood, and this program startled much of Seattle society. Our Army was still segregated at the time, so where did Mary find these Black soldiers? Years later I discovered they were members of the Barrage Balloon Battalion; they only had six weeks of training to handle huge balloons that tended to fly away with wind gusts, causing fires or electrical outages.

❖

NEW RULES CAME with attendance at James Madison Junior High School. It seemed the most important rule was to keep boys and girls separated. The boys' stairs were at the north end of the building and the girls' stairs were at the south end, so it was a long walk if you had a class at the north end of the building on one floor and the next class right upstairs above it. For us girls who had been raised around YMCA programs and always played with boys, it took some adjusting. The lunchroom and auditorium were also divided. I joined the Glee Club and Girls Ensemble, and I also sang in the church choir. Art classes were another favorite new subject, especially painting sets for school theater productions.

Cooking and sewing classes came easily as I already had a lot of experience in both. The sewing teacher would send me home with an A+ grade, but Mother and BB would look my work over and say, "Rip it out and do it over." Sewing class was spring semester and because I always finished early, I was taught to clean and oil the sewing machines before they were put away for the summer. I did this every spring, even when I had completed my required home economics classes. I also maintained the machines for the neighbor ladies. One day a man came to the door offering services "cleaning and repairing" our machine. When Mother stated that her child took care of her machine, he said, "So it's your son?" When she said, "No, it's my daughter," he couldn't get off the porch fast enough, muttering, "A girl!"

Miss Wang taught my English class and assigned us to write a paper on what we planned to do in our lives. Of course, I wrote about my goal of becoming an architect. I was asked to report to her after class, and this very concerned teacher counseled me to change my goal, explaining, "I don't want to see you hurt, as they will never let you become an architect." I thanked her, but I was not discouraged and was not going to give up my goal.

❖

DURING THE EARLY PART of the war, the news was seldom encouraging. I later found out that a neighbor woman, who was the secretary for the local head of the Navy, kept her children's bags packed and ready for an evacuation to Eastern Washington. Plans were on file to remove women and children to the east side of the Cascade Mountains. We knew if the Japanese invaded, they would have to either come through the Strait of Juan de Fuca or south of the Olympic Mountains over the Grays Harbor area. Our ocean beaches were now closed to us as the Army took over the campgrounds and vacation cottages for their housing while patrolling the coastline by horseback.

Puget Sound had been planted with numerous mines, so the ferries from Seattle and Fauntleroy had to weave their way through giant mazes en route to their destinations.

Like in our houses, no lights were allowed on over the water, and we could not have beach fires after dark. Brother Jim always had a small sailboat, which we took out after dinner in the summertime. He believed himself a natural sailor who would never need an oar, even when there was no wind. The Coast Guard often saw us out on the water and when we were becalmed and stuck, they towed us back to Fauntleroy. It seemed a foolproof arrangement, until one night, they didn't appear and neither did the wind, leaving us to drift until 3 a.m. We landed on a beach in Des Moines about 20 miles south of Fauntleroy. We sheepishly knocked on a door and asked if we could call our parents. Father came and picked us up, leaving the boat to be rescued later. After that, there was always an oar in the boat.

Seattle neighborhoods were soon all organized under air raid wardens, who were charged with knowing how many people, their ages and genders, lived in each house. The warden also checked to ensure that blackout curtains were in place and no light was leaking out. Our warden was Mr. Ford. He owned the corner Texaco gas station, where I worked after school. His daughter Rosemary was also my good friend.

At school the fire drills had accompanying air raid drills, where we hovered up against the inside structural walls away from the windows, or under desks. These later became earthquake drills, and we found protection under doorways and furniture. We became accustomed to the drills, but one day the alarms went off and this was "real," not practice. As we sat protected against the wall, we were soon playing games to pass the time, but our teacher was in shock. It turned out to be another practice drill, but the school administration hadn't informed any of the staff, and there was much criticism. Could we be bombed? I'm sure we were closer to it than we realized; after all, a Japanese submarine had entered the Columbia River and shelled the Oregon Coast.

Even our residential block had some war excitement. Archie Phelps, a King County commissioner, lived across Thirty-Fifth Avenue Southwest. He was not a very pleasant man and had a large vegetable garden cared for by county employees, paid for by tax dollars. Most irritating was his workday morning routine of starting up his large car, pulling out the hand throttle to leave the engine running while he went back in the house to eat his breakfast. As an official he could use all the gas he wanted while we were all rationed.

One day a special Army group arrived asking us to clear the area while they investigated a reported bomb in the woods south of our house. The "bomb" was carefully removed, and the neighborhood was declared safe. The "bomb" turned out to be Archie's bowling ball. His car had been stolen and the thief tossed out the ball.

❖

MY TENTH-, ELEVENTH- AND TWELFTH-GRADE years were at West Seattle High School, just a few blocks from my junior high school. We had freedom at last, and boys and girls could use any stairway. The girls' playfield had been divided to accommodate an obstacle course for the boys—early training for military service after graduation—and we listened to their grunts and groans while playing soccer.

The first Black students I got to know were new at school, a boy and a girl from two families who came to Seattle to work in the war industries. The girl's family lived in one of the new defense housing projects while the boy's family lived in one of the most desirable West Seattle neighborhoods. They became the stars at school dances, and he was the organizer of the newspaper drive. Another pair of students also stood out: a Russian brother and sister whose father was a sea captain who brought them to the U.S. during the war. They were way ahead of us in math and science, so they took fun classes in shop, art, and music.

After moving to Thirty-Fifth Avenue Southwest, I always had a part-time job. I babysat two neighborhood boys from 3:30 to 10 p.m. each weekday; this included fixing their dinner, bathing them and putting them to bed, plus doing all the dishes. No wonder I didn't fantasize about getting married and having children upon high school graduation! My other jobs included setting type and running the press in the card shop at Sears, Roebuck and Co. to create retail store advertisements; working in the neighborhood grocery store; picking berries and sweet peas in the summer; clerking in the Bon Marche department store bakery and yard goods departments; and my gas station job where I greased cars, packed wheel bearings, and changed and vulcanized tires. I also pumped gas, changed oil, and glued ration stamps onto sheets for the next fuel delivery. But somehow, I always found time for some fun— skiing, swimming, and tennis.

Occasionally, brother Art and his best friend, Jim Brown, would take me fishing. I had to hide in the car until we got past Jim's girlfriend's house because she had been told, "No girls ever on fishing outings." The boys included me as I would climb over the logs, bait my hooks and clean my own trout. I was frequently included in activities that other girls were not because I never tattled on the boys and took my bumps and bruises without complaint.

Many of the boys dropped out of school to join the military, and those who didn't worked part-time at good pay. I recall that my Sears and Roebuck pay was 25.5 cents per hour, then 27.5 and finally it got to 30 cents. Drive-in movie theaters were the "in" destination for a date. We would pool gas siphoned from friends' cars for my brother's friend Dean's big custom Lincoln (with air brakes) for a group outing. The beautiful car had belonged to a movie star. It was the one car I was never allowed to drive.

Don Wallace, Art and Jim

Brother Jim and his best friends—Don Wallace, Dean Dow, and Bob Ebert—finally got their parents to agree that they could drop out of school and enlist in the U.S. Navy. Bob did not go that afternoon with the other three to sign up because he had a date with his girlfriend. However, first thing the next morning he raced down to sign up, so he would be with his buddies. What he didn't know was that all three had been rejected: Don for a punctured ear drum, Dean for flat feet, and Jim for eyeglasses and size 14 feet. Of course, Bob was accepted and was sent off for training in the South. The other three were broken-hearted, but they went to work as mechanics for Pan American Airways. Pan Am had the contract for Navy flights to Alaska. The boys were allowed to join the Navy Reserve when Pan Am requested the appointments.

Jane and Art skiing at Mount Rainier

One of the benefits of Jim's new job was that due to rough flying conditions, the box lunches carried for the passengers often went uneaten, which meant we could have the cold fried chicken for dinner, the only meal our family ate together. All meat was rationed, so this was a real treat. When the Navy acquired its own planes and ended their contract with Pan Am, the boys were in the Navy with a higher rank due to their aircraft experience. Dean went to Whitehorse in the Yukon Territory in Canada, Don to a small island in the South Pacific, and Jim to Alameda, California, with his big feet keeping him stateside.

Jim in his Navy uniform

The war created a few opportunities for girls, too. The drafting teacher was paid to train senior girls for jobs at Boeing and other industries. This opened the boys' shop area, and drafting classes, to girl students. In winter of 1943 I managed to get into an architectural drafting class, the only girl. I became a good friend of Mr. Fred Gorton, the instructor, who saw no reason why I couldn't become an architect. Other than my parents, he was the only person who was encouraging.

The drafting class was after regular school hours, and I became acquainted with the janitor. He was a Native American from a local tribe and his wife was a religious leader. He had her look up "my star" as they believed everyone has a star. He knew all kinds of things about me that weren't in any records. When I expressed interest, he spoke of the future, telling me that President Roosevelt would run for a fourth term, win election and die early in his term. Also, he knew the dates when the war would end in Europe and Japan. And the last prediction was that, when I was in my 90s, we would be in a war again, this time with Asia, and we would lose, ending our reign as a world power. I tucked this away and didn't think too much about it until much later when I realized that he was absolutely on target with the first three predictions and dates. The last prediction seemed like an eternity away to a 15-year-old.

❖

BY THIS TIME, we were making progress in World War II, so the blackout curtains were no longer required, and our little city of Seattle had become a real city. Our "Hoovervilles" and their shacks were long gone. Along the Duwamish Waterway, large dull warehouses for the Port of Embarkation replaced the colorful small gardens, picket fences and fascinating small structures. The wood planks of Alaskan Way were replaced with a concrete slab roadway, and visits to ships at the docks were no longer allowed.

Another teacher besides Mr. Gorton was to have an impact on my life: Miss Belle McKenzie, creative writing instructor. She was tall and lean with red hair tied up in a bun. She probably did more to prepare her students for college than any other teacher. Many written themes were required during the semester, and they would be read in front of the class and discussed. A smaller number would be turned in for grading. The creative part was easy, but putting it down on paper was my failing. Therefore, my work would be returned with a grade of A/E. The "A" was for content and the "E" for punctuation, spelling, and grammar. Despite this, Belle thought I had the potential for becoming a good writer. One day during lunch, I heard voices rising at the teacher's table, and I realized I was the subject of conversation between Belle and Mr. Gorton. He said I would become an architect and she insisted I should be a writer. I'm not sure where the conversation landed, as I was embarrassed and left. I gather they had never really been friendly. Perhaps I should say that this—my life story—is for you, Belle. After all, Mr. Gorton did live to see my licensing as an architect.

The world war was a recurring theme for our papers. Belle often said, "Remember only the ignorant are prejudiced." This is a phrase I have frequently wanted to repeat to some narrow-minded individuals.

It was an active class with students arriving early so they could be close to the lectern to read their work. We all read more papers than required and it was competitive. One day, after reading one of my papers, Belle announced to the class that I would not be graduating with the rest of the class as she could not pass a student who did so poorly in English. A hush came over the room and when the bell rang, Yvonne, the prettiest girl in the class, said, "Don't worry, Jane, I know something will happen to change her mind." I was worried. I wanted to finish high school so I could make enough money during the war to go to college and study architecture.

Well, something did happen. I won first prize in the King County competition for my essay titled "What Young People Think of the Movies." The prize was a $25 War Bond, which I still have. It was $18.25 of 25-cent stamps that I had to glue in a book and turn in. There was a celebration at the end of spring semester, and I had to give a short thank you speech on a microphone. Unfortunately, every word I said bounced off the school building and back to the playfield building, so I'm sure I heard each word a dozen times. I never wanted to use a microphone again.

Like the War Bond, I still have my essay. Here is a short excerpt by Jane Hastings, age 17:

> As a high school student who probably sees more movies on the average than an adult, I am grateful to express my opinion on what kind of movies should be shown. The opinion was gathered from a group of students. … We are tired of watching high school seniors and juniors or even college girls dressed up in dresses and heels. I feel sorry for the people that dress them up this way, that they haven't children of their own or haven't ever seen a seventeen-year-old girl walking down the street.
>
> We want our kids, kids, and not perfect little dolls. Give the girls sweaters and skirts, loafers, saddles or wooden shoes with anklets and a charm bracelet and a couple of silver hair clips. Let their hair hang and come straight instead of gluing it back, curled to perfection. Have a couple of fat girls and some others that aren't especially attractive or have good features. Put some dirty cords on the boys. They are human too. Turn the cuffs up a couple of laps so that they can exhibit their loud striped socks. Make the adults more human. Don't always have the hero come from the poorest family in town and work up to the worlds' best. Don't always make the hero handsome and the villain wicked and ugly.
>
> Movies are the main education in some people's lives; don't discourage them by making them think that they have to be rich and handsome to be a success.

West Seattle High School graduation portrait,
June 1945

I graduated high school in June 1945, and my grand plan to earn my fortune for college came to an end with the end of the war. Boeing's expansion and the shipyards closed almost overnight, even faster than they started up. Seattle was left with a tremendous number of unemployed people, many without job possibilities or funds to return to their former homes. The local housewives who became factory workers at Boeing and the shipyards were expected to return home to their housework, leaving all jobs for returning servicemen. Many women rejected this idea. They found they liked working for a paycheck and having their own funds. One woman bus driver fought the system for years before she won her job back.

College would have to be on hold for a while. I could conserve money by living at home, so my choice had to be the University of Washington. To start architecture school depended on how much I could work and save. I needed to find a job through the holiday season, and then I would have enough money to start at the university part-time in January 1946. I knew I would support myself all the way.

Jane in her cap and gown on the steps to Architecture Hall, June 1952

3 | UNIVERSITY OF WASHINGTON YEARS

IN FALL 1946, at the beginning of my second term at the University of Washington, I waited to meet with Professor Arthur P. Herrman, the chairman of the School of Architecture. He was not in a good mood. I could hear a nice young man in his office saying he would complete his four-year architectural degree in three years. At the time, I did not know that the bachelor of architecture degree was a five-year program that had been shrunk to four years during the war. Because I started at UW while the four-year program was in place, I could have demanded that the shorter program be honored even though the curriculum reverted to the traditional longer program in September 1946. When the young man came out of the chairman's office, Catherine Woodman, the school's secretary, shook her head.

Now it was my turn. The chairman questioned why I wanted to study architecture. Did I know it was not a field for women? Did I realize I would be wasting state money because girls just got married and raised families—thus, not working or using their education? No, I was not discouraged. I did not worry that I was denying a seat for a returning GI who had gone off to war to protect me. Herrman seemed to be enjoying his lecture when I told him I had to leave so I would not be late for work. That was the last straw. He declared there was no way that I could possibly work and complete the program. I explained I would go to school part-time while I worked, and I estimated my education would take seven years. "I'm going to try," I said. When I left his office, Catherine stopped me. "I want to shake your hand," she said. "You are the most logical person who has been through here in some time." Over the next six and a half years, Catherine and I became good friends.

After completing requirements like freshman English and sociology—and the physics and mathematics classes that were more to my liking—I could take Basic Design, a course shared with interior design students in a portable building north of the Architecture School. We had several large classes with seats assigned alphabetically, placing me between Ed Hall and Warren Hill. In this class, we had a great time making space modulators, mobiles, and other abstract creations, which were part of a new instructional system: The ornate details of Beaux-Arts architecture were out, and the clean lines of Bauhaus were in! Those ahead of us envied our new program, but we missed creating the classic Beaux-Arts analytique presentations.

My home base for the years ahead was Physiology Hall—one of the few permanent buildings left from the 1909 Alaska-Yukon-Pacific Exposition—which architecture students shared with medical students. There were 61 of us in the Sociology of American Housing class. The classroom only had 60 seats, and I was the last to arrive each day because I came from the women's gym, so I sat on the windowsill. A week or two went by until one day, one of the older married veterans got up and gave me his seat. I heard a low "boo," and the young man seated next to me said this architecture class was not big enough for the both of us. I said, "That may be, but we'll see." The next quarter he transferred to another major.

Architecture Appreciation, which included a survey of architectural history, was one of our earliest courses and it was the only architecture course open to all students. The large lecture hall could seat some 300 people. Early in the class, I met Gretchen Schneeberger, who became a lifelong friend—all because I had a bathing cap in my briefcase. Gretchen was a senior and I remembered her from high school as a student leader and champion ice skater. I mentioned I was swimming in a water ballet group, and she decided to join. Soon, she was one of the strongest swimmers at our weekly YMCA sessions.

Gretchen also joined me on the ski slopes. The only way I could afford to ski was to get a job in a ski area, and I set my sights on Ben Paris, the restaurant chain that managed facilities at the Milwaukee Ski Bowl at Hyak, on the east side of Snoqualmie Pass. Ben Paris also operated several downtown restaurants catering to men and their sports activities—fishing, pool, and card games—and they were often in basement locations with stairways thick with cigarette smoke and the smell of stale beer.

Each day on my way home from school, I would brace myself to head down the stairs and ask the manager for a job at the ski bowl. Eventually, he relented just so I would stop pestering him. The *Seattle Times* ran a free ski school for students of all ages who traveled to the ski area by train, and my job included selling refreshments on the train, as well as working in the checkroom during arrival and departure. I could ski in between my jobs and also attend the ski school racing class. At the end

Water ballet activity

of the ski school session, we had five races; I ended up with five medals representing second to fifth places. One enduring lesson from the ski slopes: "Take the gates high!" I often remind myself of how important this is—to be prepared and ready—in all facets of life.

I've been very even-tempered my entire life, but I did lose it once on the job at the ski bowl. A high school boy employee had been fondling the female workers, who tried to avoid him. One day he came up behind me during a busy period while I was working at the cash register, deep in concentration, and he started to grope me. I whirled around yelling, "Take your hands off me and never touch me or any of the other girls again!" I got a round of applause from my co-workers and several skiers waiting to check their personal items. The boy, one of my employer's sons, quit.

Apparently, I was the first worker at the ski bowl to balance the cash register at the end of each day, so the next ski season I was promoted to supervisor and could hire my own help. Gretchen and other friends joined, and we had a grand time. I got paid for my weekends, plus free food, lodging, and access to the ski rope tows. One of my architecture classmates was a ski instructor so when we stayed overnight, we did our engineering classwork together.

Unfortunately, the day lodge burned down after my second season, and I was back to paying for my own ski trips.

Jane and Gretchen skiing at Milwaukee Ski Bowl

❖

AT LAST, IN 1947 or early 1948, I had my first art classes. In the sculpture class, we created Roman ears and noses, copies of a collection of plaster castings. In the freehand drawing class, our instructor was Seattle native George Tsutakawa, who was in his first year teaching at UW and working on his master of fine arts at the same time. There were about 200 of us in the Architecture School's freshman class when I began in January 1946, and the class ahead was around the same size, so the university was struggling to find enough space and faculty to handle the influx of returning veterans on the GI Bill. Tsutakawa had been asked to teach part-time to help offset a shortage of instructors. He went on to teach at UW for almost thirty years—and of course enjoyed an illustrious career as an artist and sculptor.

In the '48 spring quarter, I was short of cash, so I dropped out and found employment at Boeing Airplane Company. I asked for any job, such as working in the blueprint room, that might relate to my architecture ambitions. I was told I was too bright and wouldn't be happy to stay in such a job. How could I tell them I wasn't planning to stay? I was worried I would not find a good-paying job, but I did get a call back from Boeing. Because of my college math, they had a job for me working with guided missiles. So, I was off to work reading and plotting telemeter film recording the roll, pitch and yaw from the flights of the test missiles (birds), after their firing at Alamogordo or Tularosa, New Mexico. The GAPA (Ground to Air Pilotless Aircraft) project was Boeing's first step in its space program led by George Stoner, whose division would go on to support the Saturn V moon rocket. I worked with several outstanding engineers, who we called "birdmen" because each had his own "bird" a bit different from the others.

One of our consultants was Dr. Cornelius Lanczos, a former Albert Einstein assistant who was assigned to the GAPA project by the U.S. government. His glasses sat at the end of his nose and he seemed fascinated watching women employees going in and out of the ladies' room. He wore galoshes over his shoes and carried his umbrella every day for the six months of spring and summer that I was there. One day he left his lit pipe in his pocket when he hung up his coat, burning it and the one next to it. After that, we gave his coat a wide berth with all the others pushed to the far end of the rack.

I also made new friends, especially Shirley Baker. She was trained as a dietitian, but she was reading film like me. Shirley was married to another Boeing employee who was an ardent sailor (and knew my sailor brother) and a skier. I had recently taken up water skiing with Gretchen and another member of the water ski club who worked in the same Boeing department, so we spent our lunchtime going through the scrap metal pile behind the building looking for aluminum tee sections to make stabilizers for our water skis.

It was a grand spring and summer with an interesting job and time for water-skiing, camping and play. The highlight was a cruise on a yacht owned by Gretchen's boss, who was a CPA. He was returning from Alaska and a small group of us were invited to meet him at Campbell River to cruise south through the islands and inlets in British Columbia. His 68-foot luxury yacht *Nika* was a dream, and we enjoyed traveling through beautiful Princess Louisa Inlet up the coast from Vancouver, B.C., and dining at the Malibu Lodge with movie stars.

❖

IN THE FALL I returned to school and from then on continued my studies without interruption. I had a job working at Sears, Roebuck and Co. from 6 a.m. until noon, allowing me to get to school for classes held from 1 to 6 p.m. Then, I would study in the library, getting home about midnight. One of the first friends I made at UW was Suzanne Black, the sister of a girl in my high school class. She was also supporting herself and a young son while working toward her math degree. Friday nights we poor students would gather at her house, pooling funds to buy a pound of coffee and play card games. She had a part-time job at the University Press and suggested I apply.

I worked there full-time during the summer, then went part-time when fall quarter started. I worked in the bindery, stitching and covering the course catalogues, some 50,000 of them. One day I was called into the Architecture School office, where Catherine Woodman asked me how much I needed to earn each month to cover living expenses. She had decided I should spend more time in the architecture building, so she gave me two readerships, which meant I graded exams and sketches for Chairman Herrman's classes, including the Architectural Appreciation course with its 300 students.

In spring 1949, another high school friend and I decided we should move near campus and give up our hour-plus bus rides from West Seattle. We found a cozy room near the corner of Northeast Forty-third Avenue and Brooklyn Avenue Northeast that we could rent for $15 per month. It measured 6 feet, 6 inches by 9 feet. We put in a bunk bed, two cardboard closets, a desk and chair. We had a hot plate to make soup, coffee and tea. My roommate, Jaclyn, graduated in June but Shirley Cooke, another high school classmate, was interested in sharing the room for the next year. In fall, Shirley moved in. She was also working her way through school—part-time in the library—while pursuing a medical degree. When we had company, we expanded into the bathroom next door, which we shared with four other renters. It was a nice large room with a free-standing claw-foot tub that provided seating for several people on the edge.

During this period, the campus was in turmoil. The state Legislature's Canwell Committee, led by Eastern Washington Rep. Albert Canwell, had accused eleven of our university professors of being communists, and the university dismissed three of them. The Canwell Committee was a precursor to the national "Red Scare" hearings led by Sen. Joseph McCarthy in the 1950s, which damaged the careers of so many intellectuals, writers, and members of the artistic community. Shirley's Chicago-based family wanted her to return home immediately from this perceived hotbed of communism, and she did leave school for a while to support her family when her father was ill.

In the late 1940s, we were also back to air-raid drills, but this time they were nuclear bomb drills. We were evacuated to the basement of the new administration building, with insufficient air supply for the hundreds squeezed in. For the next drill, we crossed the street off campus to our favorite coffee shop, deciding to meet our maker with a cup in our hand.

IN SPRING 1949, I was in the Sophomore Design Studio, which meant the beginning of all-nighters known as charrettes. I was getting to know my fellow classmates, who all knew of me, of course, because I was the only female. We were given a design problem and assigned a faculty member as a critic, who would drop by our desk once or twice a week offering suggestions. One project was to design a truck terminal on Spokane Street, an area I knew well. My critic was Lionel Pries, known as Spike, who was feared by many students. He did not approve of radios in the studios and had been known to throw them out of the upstairs windows. When he was expected in the studio, an alarm sounded and radios were hidden. His first comment to me about my design was that I should plan to back the trucks out of their loading docks into Spokane Street. I told him this wouldn't work, as Spokane

Street was a very busy main street. When he insisted, I asked if he was familiar with the street. He was not. I told him I was and there was no way a truck could be backed out into Spokane Street. He threw my architectural scale down on my desk and marched out of the room muttering. My classmates planned a wake, thinking I might be expelled. Pries never returned or spoke to me again for the rest of my school years.

The following fall, Shirley returned from Chicago, and we needed to find a new home. Sue Harris, the only girl in the architecture class ahead of mine, wanted to room with us, so we found a two-room basement apartment behind Clark's Restaurant just off Northeast Forty-Fifth Street and Twelfth Avenue Northeast. We were not as close to campus, but it was convenient to stores. A smaller two-room unit was occupied by Jean MacDonald, or "Mac," and the third unit housed an older gentleman who was a dishwasher for the restaurant. We all shared the bathroom, but the dishwasher's hours meant we never saw him. Mac became part of our little family. Knowing my late study habits, one morning about 2 a.m., Mac burst through our door with, "Do you know what? ..." I was annoyed because she had interrupted my thought process as I was solving an engineering problem. I replied, "Yes, you have come to invite us to dinner tomorrow night and you're serving ----." Her face went white and she retreated to her apartment. The next morning, she told me I had said word for word exactly what she was going to say, including the full menu. Later she would often ask what I saw in her "plate glass head" that day.

❖

WHEN SHIRLEY APPLIED to medical school, she was required to have $1,000 in the bank; of course, she had nothing. So, we and other friends collected all the money we had and banked it in a special Shirley account. Then, we dressed her up for her interview; the underwear was hers, but the rest of her outfit was our collective effort. Of course, she was accepted, and the money was returned to us as she had the summer to make her own money for her first year.

This year, we learned we would have a new girl in the Architecture School: a displaced Latvian citizen. Sue and I were called to the school office to hear her sad tale, and we were asked to look after her. We had the impression that she was a hungry orphan arriving with nothing, so we went through our clothes, selecting items we could share, bundling them up for our meeting. The next day, when we met Astra Zarina, we were stunned by this healthy, well-dressed girl—nothing like we had pictured. We took our bundle home and hung our clothes back up. Astra arrived at UW with prior training and university credits from Karlsruhe, Germany. She had also learned fashion illustration while working for a Tacoma newspaper. She was terrific in drawing and graphics and was placed in the Sophomore Design Studio class, the year behind my class, because she was not as strong in the other subject areas.

Our curriculum included a new course, City Planning. We learned terms like "super blocks" and "cul-de-sacs" from the new East Coast-trained faculty member Myer Wolfe, known as Mike. His class was right after lunch, and it was easy to fall asleep when the lights went off for the slides. As the only girl, I couldn't miss class, and I had an arrangement with my seatmate, Jim Noble, to give him the elbow if he nodded off. One day I elbowed Jim and his metal mechanical pencil flipped into the air, landing in the circular glass light fixture above and spinning like a casino roulette ball. The lecture stopped, the lights came on and Mike said, "If Jane can keep her hands off the boys, we will continue."

My bad classroom behavior did not keep Mike and other new educators from carpooling with us to the ski slopes. One Saturday, Mike and I were sharing a T-bar up the mountainside when he fell off and yelled at me, "I'm going to flunk you, Hastings." (I checked my college transcript. I received an A.)

❖

BY THIS TIME, our class had lost so many members that our Junior Design Studio class fit into one big room. Being in all-male classes had never been a problem for me, but one classmate, Willy, could not resist playing jokes on me. I had the feeling other classmates did not approve, but they stayed on the sidelines and were delighted when the tricks backfired. One day, Willy invited me to go with him to the midnight striptease contest at a downtown theater. He was married to a glamorous woman who worked in a high-end store, and I was sure she would not approve of this date. As the date grew closer, he said, "You are not really going, are you?" I assured him I would go. About ten other class members decided to join, and when my friend Jim Noble called his wife, Joan, to say he would be late, she asked if I was going. When he said yes, she said, "Come and pick me up." We two girls, Jim and another friend sat in the middle of the theater while the others ran up to get front-row seats. "Never again," they reported afterward. The strippers were at least forty years older than their pictures advertised and their flesh was tired and sagging. Willy finally gave up on the jokes and teasing.

We developed strong friendships, and the boys who were a year ahead of me loaned me their textbooks, saving me a good deal of money. We also helped each other with projects even though we were in competition. It was the custom for senior class students to draft the most talented members of the sophomore class to work on their drawings. This fraternity-style trick did not sit well with the more mature veterans and soon it was discontinued. However, wives and girlfriends were often in the studio just before projects were due, helping with mundane tasks. I decided to bring my mother in to help with my model for a music camp project. The design of my performance hall had a retractable roof on cables for bad weather days, which my nimble-fingered mother constructed with great skill. The boys cried foul because their helpers didn't have such skills.

On February 14 that year, I came into the studio to find a very large, heart-shaped box of chocolates sitting on my drafting board with a note, "To our Valentine." The class quickly gathered around my desk saying, "Open it! Open it!" I opened the box, grabbed one chocolate, then jumped on my drafting stool and watched as every piece of candy disappeared.

I always suspected a student named Ray Emory was behind that box of chocolates. Ray was a Pearl Harbor survivor who had lost many good friends in the attack. He was older and did not approve of Willy's jokes. I think he took up a collection among our classmates for the chocolates as a quiet way to make up for the harassment I had endured.

❖

IN SPRING 1951 I received a formal invitation to join Tau Sigma Delta, the architectural honor society. It stated that a "tuxedo" was required for the formal installation. These invitations were used across the country and didn't account for the possibility of a woman member, so my talented mother took this as a challenge. She created a long black dress with a beautiful white Venetian lace top with cap sleeves for me.

Installation tradition required initiates to perform a skit. We did a school parody, and I played Catherine Woodman. George Tsutakawa, our faculty initiate, stole the show playing the more senior Professor Victor Steinbrueck, wearing Victor's favorite purple shirt, his beret and gaudy tie. He caught Vic entirely by surprise as Vic did not realize he had been unknowingly lending out his own clothing for several months. After the installation, George always greeted me with a smile as a fraternity "brother."

University of Washington, Architecture School junior class

Another special spring treat: The girls in the Architecture School were invited to have tea at the home of architect Elizabeth Ayers, the university's first woman graduate in the field. It was a Saturday afternoon, and we were not enthusiastic because it meant missing work (and earning much-needed money). Miss Ayers was referred to as "the Colonial Dame" because she designed very traditional houses, and we preferred the contemporary glass box designs. We were won over when Catherine explained that in her many years at the Architecture School, this was the first gesture acknowledging women students.

The Saturday tea date arrived, and I borrowed my family's car—now a Mercury—to take Sue, Astra, Audrey, and Joyce to Miss Ayers' home in West Seattle. The "tea" turned out to be a hearty lunch and a delightful afternoon of stories about the earliest days of the Architecture School. She also wanted to know about our interests and goals. It ended up being an experience we would never forget.

This was also the year the design studios got new lighting. We went from just a few foot-candles of light to real lighting. This is when I discovered I was extremely far-sighted, which had gone unnoticed when I was a child because they only examined children who could not read the blackboard at school. With my first pair of glasses, I was shocked to see that print in books was black, not gray. It jumped off the page, making reading a joy instead of the hard work it had been for so many years.

The university launched an extensive construction program after the war with most of the funds going toward the new Medical, Dental and Nursing School sited on a former golf course just northwest of the Montlake Bridge. Physiology Hall had been shared between the Architecture School and the Medical School for years, and our lower-floor classrooms had a distinct odor from caged research lab animals housed in an adjacent room. Sometimes a dog would get loose and join us in the art room for some attention. We managed to hide some for a few hours of freedom before the lab-coated medical students found them. When the new Medical School was completed, our building was devoted entirely to architecture classes.

The new Medical School building had a nice auditorium, and I was selected to be an usher for a lecture featuring three distinguished guests: landscape architect Lawrence Halprin, architect Richard Neutra, and architect/designer Charles Eames. Halprin was a nice man, Neutra arrived as if trumpets were sounding and a red carpet unfurled ahead of his footsteps, and Eames struck me as a lanky boy filled with wonderment. This was his first trip up the Pacific Coast from California, and he described his discovery of our Washington rainforests: He wanted to stop the car, step outside, and roll in the lush ferns. Eames was my kind of guy.

I also became one of the Dental School regulars; it was close, and I could skip out of the afternoon studio class for dental work when they needed a teaching patient. Root canals were the newest procedure, and the Dental School provided me with three—all for free.

Due to a shortage of funds for maintenance projects, we students were asked to volunteer to help remodel the ceiling of the large auditorium in Architecture Hall for new lighting and acoustical treatment. We worked on Saturdays with a classmate who was employed part-time in the Buildings and Grounds Department. Scaffolding was installed at the lectern and blackboard area and up behind the top row of seats. These and some intermediate framing supported 2-by-12 planks that spanned the space in between, creating a bouncing platform to support us as we cut large circular holes in the suspended plaster ceiling and glued acoustical tiles almost 30 feet above the floor. The best job was up in the ceiling space between the steel trusses at the other end of the saw because the plaster dust fell on the worker below. We had no hard hats or safety gear, but fortunately no one got hurt. No doubt, our assignment would spare embarrassment a few years later when Seattle hosted the 1953 National Convention of the American Institute of Architects (AIA).

One of the Beaux-Arts-era events we faithfully retained was the Beaux-Arts Ball. Two all-school competitions were held for the design of the annual yearbook cover and the mural for the ball. For the mural, the winner enlisted a team to help paint the large centerpiece for this wild costume event, always held off-campus because the university forbid alcohol on its property. (Taverns could not operate within a mile of the campus). I was assigned to oversee decorations for the ball with the theme, "Out of This World." My solution: A sea of spun glass with mannequin body parts protruding, enhanced by a rising mist from containers of dry ice. Murals from the '30s were cherished as works of great art. Earlier balls were legendary for beautiful and daring costumes, including one that was said to have been made of two bottle caps and a Dixie cup.

❖

IN SUMMER 1951, I went back to work at Boeing in the Plant Facilities Department, this time doing architectural work alongside several of my classmates. The large class ahead of mine had graduated, taking most of the available jobs, and many of them went to work for NBBJ, a large architectural firm that had a contract with Boeing to do aircraft cleanup drawings. Boeing had a wonderful policy allowing their staff to go to school, so I continued working part-time through my final year at the university. The work ranged from designing large structures to relining the parking lot to create more parking spaces.

It was a busy summer. My older brother, Jim, whom I had started calling JC, got married in Vancouver, B.C., the home of Norma Heaslip, his bride. We were back and forth across the border frequently with family activities and wedding preparations, and I crossed several times with JC and Norma, who lived and worked in Seattle. Because she was not yet 21, it was illegal for her to travel across the border as a single woman alone with a man.

Soon after fall quarter started, we sent our friend Gretchen flying off to California to marry Sid, a 1950 architecture grad then stationed at Fort Ord. At the time, Gretchen pointed out a "flaw" I learned as part of my architectural education that would emerge when we debated the merits of a design: "You always criticize and never compliment." My answer: "We know what is good; perhaps by a critique we can improve the rest." I try to be more careful now, unless I'm talking with architect friends who understand this approach.

Again, it was time to find housing for my last year of school. Shirley and I would remain together, but Sue was disqualified as she had graduated, and we agreed we would only room with students because others were a bad influence with their playtime. We located a place just south of the railroad tracks (now the Burke-Gilman recreational trail). The apartment came at a good price and had two large rooms plus another bedroom. A shared bathroom at the end of the hall was our only source of water, so we carried buckets up to our kitchen for cooking and dishwashing. We were closer to both the Architecture and the Medical Schools. We resumed our routine of returning to school after dinner—me to the studio on the third floor and Shirley to a first-floor classroom with blackboards. We stayed until the janitor closed our building at 11 p.m. Sometimes we stopped at the Blue Moon Tavern with the boys on the way home.

Shirley knew many of my classmates and enjoyed joining in with the architects on whatever we might be doing. After one Tau Sigma Delta party, I came home at 5 a.m. to change from my party clothes to a bathing suit. Shirley started to get up to join in as usual but when I reported the party was moving to Beaver Lake in Sammamish, she went back to bed. I still remember the disdain on the fishermen's faces that beautiful quiet morning as we came dancing down to the lake for our plunge. Soon they had pulled their rods in and were rowing toward home.

A spring all-school dinner in Architecture Hall enlisted talented students for the entertainment. We few girls were asked to participate, and sophomore Joyce Stevens wrote the following lyrics to the tune of "Life Upon the Wicked Stage," from *Showboat*, the new 1951 movie musical based on a 1927 stage musical. Five or six of us, including a secretary, sang:

> *Life in Architecture School ain't ever what a girl supposes.*
> *She thinks there will be red-blooded men for her, 'til life discloses—*
> *Architecture has no boys or men,*
> *Only pencil-pushers, them.*
> *Life in Architecture School ain't nothing for a girl.*
> *People think the girl to men ratio is really quite terrific.*

Books we'd write about the times we've had, they think would be prolific.
They think we have beers and cheers and smokes—
We don't even hear the dirty jokes:
Life in Architecture School ain't nothing for a girl.

We've been told about how men are pitfalls to our reputations,
But our school is just about the safest place in the nation.
Architects leave us a bit perplex-ed—
Only designs get them interested.
Life in Architecture School ain't nothing for a girl.

❖

ASTRA, WHO WAS NOW in my studio class, had trouble adjusting to the ways of the Architecture School. In European schools, students took exams or turned in projects when they were ready, not on an assigned due date. Sketch problems were required in our last three years of school to teach students to think and respond quickly to a design problem. A small design project was handed out at noon with the finished product due at 10 p.m., and they could be anything: a postage stamp, a piece of furniture, even a uniform for a spaceship. A certain number of sketch points were required to receive our studio grades. Astra often threw hers in the garbage can in disgust and stomped out of the studio, but we retrieved them to turn in so she would meet the requirements. She never became used to these American rules.

In one of my senior quarters, I was assigned Herrman, the Architecture School chair, as my design critic. By this time, I had been his reader for two years, grading all his tests and drawing assignments. He only critiqued one or two students a year and this was the second time he'd been assigned to me. When I asked Catherine what I had done to deserve this "honor," she said I was one of the few students who was not afraid of him.

One day Herrman arrived at my desk and said, "Good afternoon, Miss Harris." I corrected him: "The name is Hastings." He said, "I'm sorry, Peggy." To this I replied, "That was Schroeder" —a student who had graduated three years before. At this point he marched out of the drafting room, not to return. Soon after, Catherine came to my desk and asked me what had happened. Herrman had hastily retreated to his office, sputtering as he asked for the file on "That … that girl in the senior room."

After two years of grading his papers—and being the only girl—he really ought to have known my name!

❖

A MAJOR FINAL-YEAR DESIGN studio assignment was a team project, which included seniors, juniors and sophomores jointly designing a master plan, then individually designing buildings for the program. Team projects had been introduced recently to familiarize us with how architectural offices worked. By the end of the quarter and completion of the project, some students were so bitter toward their teammates they seldom spoke again. For our final team project, my co-leader and I forced a junior to conform to what the rest of the team was doing. He became very angry—until he received his first A grade in design. Then we were friends again.

The final year was also the time for Tau Sigma Delta parties. Jack Crabs and I oversaw the event initiating new honorees and gathering alumni, and we decided to do something special to woo the older, established-architect members to attend. We discovered that the grand old four-mast yacht, the *Phantom*, which had been anchored in the middle of Lake Union since England went to war in 1939, was available for parties. This beautiful mystery ship was as much a city landmark as the 1914 Smith Tower, which was the tallest building west of the Mississippi River until well after World War II. Everyone in Seattle wanted to tour this luxury yacht built for the wealthy Guinness Brewery family, and we had a wonderful turnout of the oldest and most successful architects at the buffet supper on board. Some in our group partied so heartily that we were lucky none fell overboard. It had to be the best Tau Sigma Delta party ever.

Just before graduation the Architecture School announced its awards, including the AIA medal and the Alpha Rho Chi medal for Leadership Service, which I was astonished to receive. Schoolwork was behind us, but we were not quite done: Within a week or so most of us would return to our studio desks to take our Architectural State Board Examination.

4 | POST-GRAD SEATTLE LIFE

A camping trip with friends Arne Bystrom, Dick Yarbrough, Abner (Abby) Baker and Mervane Murray, in background

AFTER SIX AND A HALF YEARS, my university days were finally behind me. I graduated in June 1952 and kept my promise to my mother to go through the commencement ceremony. I was the first member of my family to earn a college degree. Mother was there, and I suppose my father was, too, though I don't remember for sure. About a dozen architecture classmates also rented gowns and joined me, and it was a sunny day for picture-taking on the steps in front of the building that was now named Architecture Hall.

My first purchase after graduation was a brand-new—and finally, comfortable—bed. My next purchase was a very special car I would own for just two years and then forever regret giving up. It belonged to brother Art's best friend, Jim Brown, who had married and had several children. He needed a station wagon and agreed to sell me his 1941 four-door Mercury Phaeton convertible with a 1948 engine, a beautiful bright blue with a white top. He hated to part with his treasure, so he continued to take care of mechanical needs for me. A wonderful arrangement:

a good price and a personal mechanic! Whenever I parked around town, several young boys would be there admiring the car when I returned. They would frown when they saw me, implying that a woman did not deserve such a prize.

Classmate Jack Crabs asked me, "Now what are we going to do?" The first goal had been to get through architecture school. Next, I needed to get my Washington state architectural license, and then my goal was to go to Europe to see all those wonderful buildings and structures we had studied. Photographs are great, but they are no substitute for the physical and emotional experience of sharing the beauty, space, light, and texture of a building.

The Washington State Architectural Examination was scheduled for the week after graduation. It was always held at the university because drafting boards and equipment were still available before they were stored over the summer. We had all taken refresher classes for structural engineering and other topics in anticipation of four full days of exams. At the time, each state wrote its own examination and the requirements for licensing. Some states issued a license based on a university degree, but most required an examination.

Washington was known for having one of the most difficult exams—probably because it was open to anyone who was a U.S. citizen, had twenty dollars, and was twenty-one years old. The state board wrote the exam to ensure applicants were qualified, whether through a degree or other experience. Usually, there were 200 or so applicants, who included recent and former students, new faculty members, contractors, real estate salesmen, and dreamers.

Over four long days we would be tested in five sections, including structural engineering (wood, steel and concrete); mechanical equipment (plumbing, heating, air conditioning and electrical); history and theory; office practice; and design. Structures and design were the sections most feared. Applicants could pass some sections and fail others, and aspiring architects rarely made it all the way through all the exams on the first try. I had an advantage from my experience at Boeing, which introduced me to products and materials I would not have known otherwise. For example, one question asked: What does Grinnell manufacture? I had drawn several sprinkler systems, so this was easy. I believe the design project was a hospital, which tripped up several applicants who didn't know to include the required double-acting doors.

The structures exam was poorly written, and the author had failed to check himself. The problems were not realistic, with bizarre answers that made us second-guess ourselves. The best engineering student, Ray Emory, wrote on his paper, "Whoever wrote this exam should have his professional license removed." I made it all the way through except the structures exam, and I'm not sure anyone passed that section in 1952. I would return the next year to take that section again; our structural engineering instructor couldn't believe I was taking it a second time, as I was one of his top students. In 1953 I would pass and become a licensed architect: Washington State License Number 744.

IN THE MEANTIME, of course, we worked. Jobs in the downtown architectural offices were not available; the classes of 1951 and 1952 were made up mostly of World War II veterans and they were the largest classes the School of Architecture had ever graduated. Instead, Jack and I found jobs at Boeing. We had two choices: work in Plant Facilities doing architectural work or do aircraft cleanup drawings for the largest architectural firm, NBBJ, where Boeing saved money by farming out work.

I had worked the summer of '51 at Boeing and through my last university year part-time. Jack moved to Boeing's space planning group, which paid better. Other classmates remained in Boeing's Plant Facilities architectural division, so it was like an extension of school, but with pay. Steve Dam, Lou Cassetta, Carl Vigna, Morris Jellison, and Anker Molver, as well as former roommate Sue Harris and another woman named Beth (whose last name I do not recall), joined me in the facilities drafting room. There were three of us women in a group of about fifty employees— mostly engineers with about ten architects. Bob Kimbrough was the head of the architects, a great guy who was constantly defending us against the head engineer, Jim House. House thought little of architects and even less of women architects, who he believed should be home barefoot and pregnant. House arranged the drafting room with us three girls in the front row, right behind a row of secretaries in low desks. Beth sized up the situation quickly: Pants were worn only by women working in the factory, and our high stools at the front-row desks offered a great leg show. So Beth installed heavy paper vanity skirts across the front of our desks. Soon after, we were rearranged to work more effectively with others in our group.

The work included many special conditions that most architectural jobs would not involve, providing great learning experiences. One of my assignments was to research women's urinals. Boeing had installed a unit of urinals in one of its downtown office buildings, and I was sent to determine whether it was being used. The fixture was new in the plumbing line, and at first, the janitor had decided the restrooms were mismarked and changed the signs. (With the discovery of a men's urinal in the other restroom, the signs were changed back.) No one in the building knew what the women's urinal was or had ever used it, so the fixture became a slop sink. My amused male co-workers could hardly wait for my report. What a letdown when there was nothing to say—except that it worked fine as a slop sink.

House, the head engineer, liked to give the women unpleasant assignments. I suppose he thought we would quit, but of course we did not. One of my tasks was to accompany an engineer looking for gas leaks under the factory building. We checked out coveralls and gas masks, and I brought an old pair of walking shoes for our adventure down under. Much of the main assembly building was constructed on pilings in the Duwamish Waterway, requiring us to jump from plank to plank. I enjoyed seeing the equipment, pipes, and ducts. Fortunately, neither of us fell in the river full of all sorts of undesirable debris.

The largest project I worked on was a new hangar at the north end of Boeing Field. We did the preliminary drawings in-house, with the structural design and construction drawings sent out to an engineering firm. This would be the first large open-space structure where airplanes, including the finished product, could be moved around and out the door without moving planes still under assembly. We had templates of the new B-52 plane with little bumps in the midsection that we could slide around, ensuring proper clearances. When the prelims went out, we were accused of exposing company secrets—the bumps, or belly wheels (a first)—and our group had a moment of panic. Boeing had given us the templates, and we didn't know what the bumps were.

The structure could easily house three or four planes and was 100 to 120 feet high. Large steel trusses cantilevered over most of the building with columns near the back wall, with the deepest part of the truss measuring 35 feet high, equivalent to about a three-and-a-half-story building. The trusses extended out the back and were tied down to columns anchored to massive footings. Under this space in the back, I designed a three-story office building, which looked like a little hut behind this massive structure. The actual construction was handled by a bridge-building firm during the summer. Sue and I watched much of the construction, especially the work of the connectors (the highest-paid workers) dancing around on the steel truss members high in the air, then sliding down the diagonal members on their knees.

Another job involved the installation of air-conditioning units in the Boeing president's office, which required cutting holes in the roof slab of the administration building. During this time, the worst-kept secret was the day and time of the B-52's maiden flight—all the buzz around the plant. Sue and I had a key to the roof of the administration building, so we decided to take advantage of the prime viewing site. To our surprise, the president and all the ranking officials had the same idea, and the roof was solid with people. If anyone noticed two girls, nothing was said. The following week the holes were cut through the slab; to our horror, the construction was terrible, with steel reinforcing bars floating free of the concrete slab in several places. We were shocked that the roof had not collapsed under the heavy load of B-52 viewers it had never been designed to hold.

❖

JACK HAD DISCOVERED a night class in landscape design offered by Francis Dean of the then-prominent California landscape design firm, Eckbo, Royston & Williams, which had just opened a branch office in the University District. Jack said, "It would be fun to take a class where there are no tests or grades." When we learned the class was full, we contacted Dean, who was thrilled to add us. He had been worried students would simply want plant care information, but knew that between the three of us, we could keep the class on-topic.

Design principles were discussed and each week several students would present their projects, which the class would critique. Our assignment was to design a new yard area. Good friends had just finished building their house—designed by another former student and myself—and they were delighted to give us the plot plan so we could design their garden. When it was our turn to present, Jack arrived early and drew up our project on the blackboard in detail. I did the oral presentation and defended everything we had done—typical from our days in architecture school. Afterward, I asked for comments, questions, and suggestions. The room had never been so quiet. No one spoke, no hand raised. Finally, Dean said, "You certainly don't expect anyone to question any part of your work, with that presentation?" We really had, especially because we had designed the garbage cans to be placed in a sunken space right by the front door for the owners' and the garbage collectors' convenience. We had apparently terrified the class by doing simply what we did all the time as part of our architectural training.

❖

I DON'T RECALL WHY I transferred to Boeing's Plant One, the original factory on the lower Duwamish Waterway, but it was a great place to work. The Plant Facilities team consisted of our team leader, Ted, as well as a mechanical engineer, an electrical engineer, a civil engineer, a structural engineer, and an architect. All types of experimental projects, small and large, happened here. Little metal clips for Bonneville Dam were produced by the thousands; other projects included gas turbine engines for large trucks, a computer about the size of a small building, as well as work with volatile fuels and radioactive materials. Design requirements included projects such as soundproofed rooms and vibration-free footings. Our riverbank site was a real challenge. When new concrete footings were poured, we would first check the tide table, then check the weather report so we could choose the ideal day and time for the pour, hoping the concrete would set before it all popped up and out of the ground. Whenever a large truck crossed the old bridge next to our administration building, our building would shake.

Soon I was on my own, working directly with a crew of carpenters almost my grandfather's age on each project. They always treated me formally and kept their distance. This all changed when they made their first carpentry mistake. They waited for my words, imagining it would require a tear-down and fearing the moment they would have to report it to their supervisor. I looked at the problem and said it would be costly to redo, but maybe we could find another solution. I told them to sit tight until the next day. I designed a detail that would hide the error and look like it was meant to be part of the structure. The crew was thrilled, and from then on, I could do no wrong. They decided to educate me in the construction process, so whenever they were working on something unusual, they held up the job until I was able to observe.

In late spring 1953, Seattle finally hosted the national convention of the American Institute of Architects (AIA) at the Olympic Hotel downtown—a milestone event. Seattle architects and UW students had been preparing for several years. Silk-screened American Indian motif drapes that we had created were hung in the hotel ballroom to welcome our guests. This convention initiated the Investiture tradition of awarding Fellowship certificates (which later became medals) at an evening banquet. We enjoyed perfect weather for a tour of the Simpson Timber

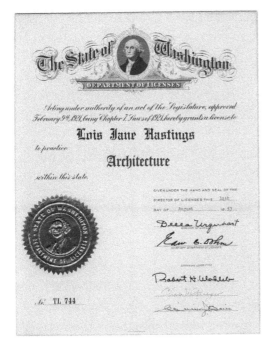

L. Jane Hastings architectural license and official photo [Source: Washington State Department of Architectural Licensing]

Company's Grays Harbor facilities, where we visited their plywood mill, door factory, and acoustical tile plant. A steak lunch at their private park showcased a log-rolling competition and loggers' feats of tree-climbing, and a sunset ferry trip from Bremerton back to Seattle completed the day.

❖

IN SUMMER 1953, I passed the final structures section of the state board exam and was licensed. I believe only nineteen of the 200 applicants were licensed that year, and Anne Detwyler Warren (later Knowles), a 1949 graduate, was the only other woman. Anne and I decided to establish a practice together, working in the evening and on weekends while I was still at Boeing during the week. We rented space on Olive Way from Anker Molver and Bob Marquette in their office under Snooky's Tavern, a longtime pub featuring hot dogs. I accepted two projects: a restaurant remodel and the design of a new residence.

The restaurant project involved merging a new railroad car with an existing older car, expanding Andy's Diner. A new kitchen was to be created between the two train cars. I quickly learned there is little standard about railroad cars, other than their wheelbase. One whole side of the car had to be cut away to open it up, requiring a new steel beam the length of the opening to support the roof. Owner Andy Nagy was acting as his own contractor and one day he called me, livid because the city inspector had red-tagged his job. I was to come immediately! Upon my arrival, I found that they had rejected the steel beam, which was much smaller than the one specified. I asked why he had purchased it. His answer: "This one was cheaper." "Yes," I said. "Steel is sold by the pound." It was an interesting job, but I don't believe I was ever paid for it.

The house, designed for a Boeing engineer, was a straightforward job that was constructed after I went to Europe in 1954. Anne moved to Los Angeles shortly after I left, so neither of us saw the house while it was under construction. Our one-year partnership would end, but we remained friends through letters and visits.

❖

THE LAST YEAR AT BOEING before I left Seattle for Europe, I was the Plant One architect. I used vacation time to spend a week at the University of Washington Dental School, as a patient for state dental board exams. I was there eight hours a day for five days, my mouth stretched out of shape, with countless shots of novocaine. The result: a five-tooth bridge. The cost to me was a bargain $60—$12 per tooth for the material. When I returned to work, my boss, Ted, took one look at my black-and-blue left cheek and said, "Did you have a nice vacation?" My hope was that I would not have to see a dentist again for two years.

Of course, these years between school and travel were not all work. Connie and I, friends from school days, joined two new Boeing friends, Nancy Jansen and Mervane Murray, in sharing an apartment in the University District. Our rules were that each of us cooked one week, did the dishes the next week, and cleaned house the third week. The fourth week was free time. Connie and I, plus Jean, another Boeing friend, had been making plans to bicycle around Europe. We even had reservations to sail on the *Ile de France* in May 1954, but realized that airline tickets from Seattle to New York would cost more than our cabin on the ship. So, we decided to look for jobs abroad while we waited and saved up funds for our travels.

Connie and I had lots of male friends from school years, so our apartment became a gathering place for the unattached. We also often backpacked along the Washington coast or in the mountains on weekends and holidays.

While I was still at Plant Two, an engineer named Roy Veldee was moved next to the architects' section. He had fallen out of Jim House's favor when he refused to work overtime on Saturdays unless there was "real work" to be done. Supervisors loved to pad their own paychecks by calling for overtime. Roy said he would rather go fishing than sit in the office all day doing nothing. He became one of us, deciding architects were more fun than engineers. He had recently married Barbara, a schoolteacher, and they also had an apartment in the University District. Sue lived in the neighborhood—as did Morris Jellison—so we all carpooled together. Barbara would drop us off on her way to school and be waiting just outside the gate when we got off. On Friday nights we would stop at the Red Robin Tavern, a student hangout just south of the University Bridge, for a beer on the way home. One beer often led to two, and soon we would be ordering hamburgers for dinner.

There were skiing trips, too. During the week from December 26 to after New Year's, we traveled to Whitefish, Montana, and its brand-new ski area. I believe there were three or four carloads of us, including my boss, Ted, and his pregnant wife. We occupied most of the rooms at the only lodge, so the few other guests had to join us. The lodge also functioned as the day lodge and served lunch to local skiers. After the tows were shut down and the hills swept by the ski patrol, we headed for the cozy bar until a family-style dinner was served to the eighteen lodge occupants later in the evening. In the morning, we enjoyed a quick breakfast before the lifts opened. Never had we skied in such open spaces or such wonderful snow. We felt like we had the mountain to ourselves.

A Sun Valley ski instructor had been hired at Whitefish to bring in more business, so one day we decided to spring for a group lesson. As I could ski better than the girls in our group, I joined the boys. I did not ski as well as most of them, but I would go for it anyway. All went well until it came time to "jump the bumps." The boys all did it, though not all successfully. I went last and crashed. Something didn't feel quite right, so I took the rest of the session more cautiously. At the end of the day, it was off to the bar. I had no trouble getting there but after warming up and having a beer, I couldn't put any weight on my badly swollen foot. I hobbled to dinner on a pair of crutches and was taken for a ride down the mountain to the local hospital. Going down the hospital corridor, we passed a room where roommate Nancy sported a full-length cast over four spiral fractures in one leg. She hadn't been doing anything dramatic; she was practically standing still when she turned to listen to someone and fell. My X-ray showed no fractures, just torn ligaments, so I was heavily taped and sent back up the mountain. At the lodge, the ski patrol offered me a treatment that would allow me to put some weight on my foot the next day. They packed my foot in snow, then soaked it in hot water, repeating the process over many hours. In the morning, I could indeed put a little weight on the foot.

When it was time to go home, there was no way Nancy could fit in anyone's car. She was five feet, ten inches tall, leggy, and had a big cast with her toe pointed down. She would have to go home on the train. We decided I should accompany her as I would be better off with my leg up, too. Our friends put us on the train before they packed up for the fourteen-hour drive home, and Nancy's parents were called to meet the train in Seattle. The conductor gave us injured girl skiers extra attention, including moving Nancy into the restroom when the train stopped. The door couldn't be shut, so the conductor and I held up a blanket, closing off the end of the car to other passengers while Nancy took care of her needs. Upon arrival in Seattle, we looked out our windows, but Mr. and Mrs. Jansen were nowhere in sight. Finally, I spotted them two cars down watching, horrified, as a stretcher was moved out of a train window. I got their attention and explained that we needed only wheelchairs, to their great relief. I don't believe Nancy ever skied again. However, I was ready to go back at the beginning of the next session, now skilled in the art of taping up.

❖

IT WASN'T ALL SPORTS for our unattached group; we also took in a bit of culture, always in group outings. A new law allowed cocktail lounges, so we no longer needed to bring our own bottle in a brown paper bag to Parker's Ballroom and buy ice and mixers from the waiter. The most popular new lounge was Trader Vic's, with a Polynesian theme, in the Benjamin Franklin Hotel. The house special was a scorpion, a strong concoction of clear liquor served in a bowl with a floating gardenia and a straw for sipping. It came in a variety of sizes, so could be shared by a group, using numerous straws. This was *the* place to go!

The theaters offered readings performed by major movie and stage stars. One of these productions was *John Brown's Body* starring Anne Baxter, Tyrone Power, and Raymond Massey. It was a good show that eight of us attended on a warm summer evening, topped off by a stop at Trader Vic's. We knew they had one table that could seat eight, so we stood on the sidewalk chatting while waiting for the table to be available. As we waited, Raymond Massey, Tyrone Power, and other cast members arrived by cab and joined us on the sidewalk. Soon, a manager herded them into the lobby and, of course, into the bar. Then, the bar manager came out to tell us that our table was not available. He did not approve of catering to celebrities over regular customers, but the manager outranked him, and we would have to split into two tables of four. My table was close to the table of eight and we could easily hear their conversation. I had never been partial to Tyrone Power as he was too pretty, and I couldn't remember any memorable movie roles. But I was fascinated by his conversation. Finally, the table of eight got up to leave, and Power held back to apologize for taking our table. He changed my opinion about one movie star.

❖

I WAS ENJOYING MY JOB, friends, and all our activities, but Europe still beckoned. I needed to experience the buildings of the past, needed to know how they had survived the war. Getting a job in Europe would be ideal. I had word from a former classmate working in Paris: "Come, the U.S. government is hiring." But when I applied, I was told women were not employed in the engineering and architectural departments. The reason given: It would be too dangerous because we would be working with all those men! However, if I was interested in going to Guam or Okinawa, I would be hired. Because they couldn't get anyone to go there, they would take women. I thanked them and said, "To the best of my knowledge there are no cathedrals on Guam or Okinawa, and I am not interested."

So, we went back to the original plan of biking through Europe. However, my friends and I continued to look for possible jobs. Then an announcement on the radio piqued my interest: The U.S. government was hiring recreation directors to work in service clubs for the enlisted military men. As I had practically been raised in a YMCA recreation center, this sounded just fine.

The interview in Seattle was scheduled just before the Christmas holidays, so I applied as I had the basic requirements: twenty-one years old, a U.S. citizen, a university degree, and a good background. The interviewer was concerned that my degree was in architecture, not recreation or sociology: "Don't get your hopes up," she said. "We'll be in touch." Apparently, my personal references sold them and suddenly I learned I could leave in January. I explained I could not leave until late spring because I had other commitments, but each month I received a notice of the monthly departure date and the schedule to take all my required overseas shots. Finally, I reported to Fort Lawton for my shots.

I would leave for Europe in May 1954.

5 | THE ADVENTURE BEGINS

Jane doing a cancan dance with friends abroad the USNS Geiger, May 1954

MAY WAS FINALLY HERE. My footlocker with two years' worth of belongings had been shipped to New York, my papers and passport were in hand, and I had a ticket on a Boeing Stratocruiser. I had been up in small planes before, but this would be my first commercial flight! I planned to arrive several days early to see Tom Fowler, a friend who had moved from Seattle to seek his fortune in the Big Apple. I had never been south of San Francisco or east of Whitefish, Montana; at last, I was on my way to see the world.

We were barely airborne when the pressure unit around the main cabin door of the airplane failed. We covered our ears to protect them from the shrill whistle of the air leakage. Another Stratocruiser had experienced a problem at high altitude with its door, and two seats on that flight had been sucked out over the Caribbean. I was hustled down to the lower-level cocktail lounge, where we were given earplugs and blankets, and it was announced that we would land in Spokane for repairs. I thought, "I'm not even going to get out of the state of Washington on my first big adventure."

The experienced pilot landed the plane so gently that we didn't even feel the wheels meet the tarmac. Repairs were made quickly, and we were back in the air.

I enjoyed the changing landscape from mountains to vast flatlands of farms to tall skinny trees. Then there were the sprawling subdivisions outside Detroit—houses all built from the same stock plans, without a tree, shrub, or even weeds around them. Who would want to live in such houses?

There were refueling stops along the way—I don't recall exactly where—but I remember we arrived in New York at 1:40 p.m. I took a limousine to the Port Authority Bus Terminal ($1.20), the wildest one-hour ride through narrow winding streets, passing cemeteries with tombstones so close together a person could not squeeze between them. Hundreds of TV antennas on the roofs of small apartment houses looked like dead trees after a forest fire.

Tom met me and carried my forty-pound suitcase three blocks to my temporary home, the YWCA. The rate was $2.50 per night! We dropped off my bag and started off to see the sights. First: Grand Central Station, where Tom gave me a map and instructions before returning to work. My next destination was Rockefeller Center, beautiful inside and out. Formal plantings tied it together with colorful blooms and flags of all nations flapping above. I enjoyed the view of St. Patrick's Cathedral before exploring the concourse network—an underground city with wonderful shops and restaurants. The ice arena above was filled with tables and chairs for the summer, and I met my first celebrity: Actor José Ferrer and I nearly collided cutting a corner. We begged each other's pardon.

Next, I went to Georg Jensen's to check the prices on European stainless cutlery, then walked through the old Plaza Hotel—still grand, but a bit out of date. I had my first lesson in jaywalking, a game of cat and mouse with pedestrians scampering between the cars, and in one day, I was as accomplished as an old New Yorker. Tom arrived at 6 p.m. and we went to the top of the RCA Building for the expansive view. When the express elevator went down, it felt like part of me was left at the top. Still on Seattle time and without any sleep, it was hard for me to keep up.

By now, my size 10-1/2, 5A feet felt like size 13C, but we kept going. Next: P.J. Clarke's Saloon, a college hangout with sawdust floors where director Billy Wilder had filmed *The Lost Weekend*. After wiping sawdust off our feet, we went to a little French cafe for an out-of-this-world bowl of French onion soup, a tossed green salad, and boned chicken. Then we caught a cab to see the Broadway show *Kismet* at the Ziegfeld Theatre, the last built by Florenz Ziegfeld Jr. Seeing the interior was worth the price of admission. The show represented over a half-million dollars' investment in costumes and sets, making a Cecil B. DeMille movie production look cheap. I didn't want it to end and still wonder how Tom got tickets to the sellout best musical of the year. What a day!

And it was not over. After the show, we went to an Italian coffeehouse, which had about forty different kinds of coffee and drinks, plus pastries. We chose Roman espresso: thick, black, with lemon rind. Delicious. The snorting, roaring, blatting of the espresso machines was a constant background to our conversation.

At 3 a.m. we had to wake someone to let me into the Y. I dropped into bed hoping to rise for an early start on Thursday—but of course I overslept.

I pressed a skirt and headed to the United Nations building, remembering the film about its construction that I had watched while a student. I hurriedly took pictures along the way to have lunch with Phyllis Hawthorne, a Seattle acquaintance who shared tales of her European travels. When Phyllis went back to work, I returned to the U.N. building, covering it inch by inch. Then I was off to the Empire State Building, with its great views in all directions.

While in the neighborhood, I shopped at the big department stores—Macy's, Gimbels, Saks, B. Altman—in a futile search for a navy-blue bag. I met Tom and his fiancée, Barbara, for a swim in a nice hotel pool, the perfect treatment for my worn-out feet.

Radio City Music Hall was next: $1.50 bought admission to a fabulous show of the NBC Symphony featuring a pipe organ, an adaptation of *Madame Butterfly* with grand sets and scores of outstanding performers, and then the Rockettes in a sensational number. Using black light, they did a routine where one girl was the top section, two other girls were each a leg, and the three together created one complete girl.

The evening's cultural events concluded with a new movie, *Executive Suite*. On to Times Square, where I realized our old *Seattle Times* Building was a small copy, just missing the headlines running around the building in lights. There were mobs of people in the street, a jam session—and a streetside church service with bearded types wearing top hats and carrying American flags. Barbara was tired and went home, but Tom and I continued walking and catching up on what was happening in Seattle before calling it a night.

I was up at 7:30 a.m. to see more sights before reporting to Fort Hamilton. After visiting the newly built Lever House and Grand Central Station, I discovered I had to get to Penn Station for my transportation. I arrived just in time to board a bus filled with women, children, and several dogs. An hourlong ride through lower Manhattan took me through narrow streets and past high-rises, then through Brooklyn to the end of the line.

At check-in, we were assigned rooms, our pictures were taken, and vaccination records checked. Once we were cleared for the day and my suitcase was unpacked, I took the express subway back to the city.

Tom and his roommate, Dennis, had invited me to dinner at their apartment. Dennis was the head of the Speech and Theater Department at New York University and full of entertaining stories. Dinner started with pickled herring in sour cream; included salad, chicken, and broccoli; and ended with a dessert of grapefruit sections in crème de menthe.

After coffee we were off to Greenwich Village, home of artists and bohemians. We walked through Washington Square Park, where people gathered for checkers and chess games through the night. Then we walked by old carriage houses on cobblestone streets that rented for unheard-of sums, while behind them were slums. We went to a wonderful Italian coffeehouse with delicious concoctions and a room full of waitress showgirls waiting for their big break.

Nick's was our next stop, for jazz. People stood at the bar and carried drinks even while dancing—great fun, breaking all the laws from home! The evening was cut short so I could meet others in my new group and return together. At 1 a.m. I was on the subway looking forward to a full night of rest and my feet returning to my regular shoe size.

❖

IT WAS TIME TO START TRAINING for our recreation jobs. Early Saturday, I attended an orientation lecture describing our future work. We were given information about our ship, along with rules and regulations. After baggage tags were handed out, we were set free until 7 a.m. Monday. Of course, I headed back to the city. A new friend, Roberta, and I shopped for uniform blouses and fed nickels into the automat for coffee and snacks. When Roberta claimed she could walk no more, we went to see Cinerama, the newest film medium, which I believe was only available in New York City and Los Angeles at the time. We enjoyed the cinematic rollercoaster ride, water skiing and flying through exotic landscapes. Then, after a nice dinner, we walked even more.

On Sunday I pressed my new uniform and returned to the city to meet Phyllis for a two-and-a-half-hour boat ride around Manhattan Island, offering many new views of the city. After coffee we took in the Museum of Modern Art, where Tom met us. We went on to Central Park, which was packed with interesting people. After a final farewell cup of coffee, I returned to Fort Hamilton to prepare for the start of my European adventure.

I sewed on my arm patches, then repacked my overstuffed suitcase, hoping the hinges would hold. Early Monday, I was on a bus, then a ferry to Staten Island. We were checked off as we walked up the gangplank of the *USNS Geiger* and asked to stay in our rooms until after lunch, when visitors would be allowed aboard.

When the all-ashore announcement came for visitors to disembark, we went to the deck to watch our departure. What a surprise to see Tom waving from the pier! He had said he had to work, so I had no idea he was there. I ran back to my cabin and got my camera for a last farewell shot as the tug pulled us out into the harbor.

In our group of 38 Special Service girls, most were from east of the Mississippi River. Only three of us were from the West Coast; one was from Portland, Oregon, and the other was from Los Angeles. I had never been around so many other women in tight quarters with such varying interests, backgrounds, and accents.

Joyce Stannard, a girl from North Dakota who became a longtime friend, was one of my cabinmates and assured me that our troop ship was much nicer than her previous travel experience. The troops in the hold probably felt differently about their accommodations, but the weather was good, and they had deck time each day.

The staterooms were air-conditioned, and the seas calm like Puget Sound on a good day. My problem was that we had to be back in our staterooms by 11 p.m. and I was never sleepy, so I read and played cards in my bunk.

Some of the draftees on board decided to pool their talents and put on a show with some of their fellow lower-deck residents: Junius Cook, a professional writer; Bill Geleerd, a Broadway director; Morton Meyer, a bass player from the New York Symphony; Jerry Costello, an arranger for Artie Shaw; Ken Kimball, from the *Hormel Girls* show; and Andre Ruedi, a professional ballet dancer. They asked some of the Special Services girls to join their production, *The Private Private*. We had a professional singer and dancer in our group who worked on the production with them, and several of us became "showgirls." Our job was to sing and dance, with the boys writing and organizing the show. It soon grew into a major production requiring all-day rehearsals.

Costuming was a challenge, but we settled on crinoline petticoats over our bathing suits for the dance number. We did our first two performances on Sunday, then three more on Monday. I was never meant for the theater, and I was sure this would be the first and last time I would ever perform the cancan. I was taken aback when Andre, the dancer, asked if I had sung professionally before joining the group. (He never commented on my dancing.) Margaret Farr in our group had five years of opera experience, so she sang with Terry Martin and another GI, Don Jackson, who had a wonderful voice.

Other members in our group had studied art, and some were in journalism and planned to do freelance writing. Several had already been to Europe and saw this as a chance for more travel. Some girls from prominent families hadn't found "that guy" yet and they (or their families) considered themselves above working. I'm sure Special Services looked like volunteer service, much like the Red Cross, and this was an opportunity to get away from home. They were all different in size, shape, personality, and purpose. For some it was pure travel. Some wanted to study. And some wanted to find a man.

With our "Broadway" career behind us, we had an early rise the next day to watch as we picked up the channel pilot who would take us into Bremerhaven. We had a grand view of the White Cliffs of Dover, plus lots of rocks and beacon markers along the way.

After ten days at sea, Germany greeted us with rain, and I felt right at home.

Jane in her summer Service Club uniform on an excursion to Heidelberg

6 | NUREMBERG: GETTING TO WORK

ON MAY 29, 1954, we arrived in Nuremberg for ten days of training before our individual assignments to a Service Club. The weather was warm, and the countryside was beautifully open, free of disruptive billboards. Our temporary home was the Grand Palace Hotel next to the train station (*bahnhof* in German), and the impressive interior spaces contained bathrooms with very tall tubs. My first letter home included the start of my new souvenir collection—toilet paper. I didn't know paper came in so many grades and textures. None of the endless varieties was soft; they ranged from wax paper to starched paper to crepe paper.

The Special Service Clubs' headquarters were in the Palace of Justice, where the famous Nuremberg Nazi trials had taken place. Gen. Partridge headed the organization, which included all military recreation facilities: resorts, movie theaters, gymnasiums, snack bars, the Service Clubs, and most importantly, the post exchange system whose profits funded the whole operation. Our training started with the three-day holiday to mark Memorial Day.

My friend Mary Lou Taylor of Atlanta had a local connection: Lars Thane, a Norwegian businessman based in Nuremberg who knew her father. Lars had a plan to entertain Mary Lou and her friends over the long weekend. We met him and his German movie-actress fiancée for lunch, where we received a quick lesson on European table manners, with instructions to keep our forks in our left hands—quite different from our upbringing. The next morning, Lars picked up four of us for a forty-eight-hour tour of Germany south and west of Nuremberg. It was all a blur. We did check in to hotel rooms but rested very little. We saw Frankfurt, Heidelberg, Munich, and Rothenburg, and then returned to Nuremberg for dinner and dancing at a famous nightclub. By this time, neither Joyce nor I could get our swollen feet into shoes, so we danced in our socks. My German dance partner commented that my friend was not a lady, as she was not wearing shoes. He apparently hadn't noticed that I wasn't either.

Our final stop in the early morning was at the Zeppelin Field stadium, which I remembered from the newsreels of the late 1930s. As a girl, I had been fascinated by the images of Hitler reviewing his troops, who poured down from the top over the bleachers onto the stadium floor. The soldiers seemed to appear out of nowhere, and I had always wondered: Where did they come from? Later, I learned that Hitler had planned to rule the world from this site, a huge, unfinished circular building that was to contain an office for each country. He had selected Nuremberg for his headquarters because it was the only German city that had never fallen to a foreign army. I had no idea I would later spend a good deal of time in this park with its large shallow artificial lake, open lawns, and beautiful gardens.

After our whirlwind tour with Lars, thank heavens we had a day to recuperate before our training started.

❖

OUR FIRST EVENING CLASS included participating in the Merrill Barracks Service Club program. Merrill Barracks was one of the three Special Service Clubs in the Nuremberg/Furth area. It was also the model club where new Special Service girls received part of their training. We were impressed with the facility, the staff, their programs and especially, the director, Gertrude Meriwether, who was Black. The integration of the U.S. Army had just been completed in 1954 and until recently the artillery group the club was attached to had been all Black; now it was about half white.

Our introduction included a game where the girls removed their right shoes and tossed them into a pile. We all wore simple navy-blue pumps. At the signal, the GIs jumped to retrieve a shoe. They then canvassed the room to find the owner, with a prize for the first match. It was a popular game that happened once a month when each new group arrived. We were introduced along with our hometowns, which sparked much conversation, especially when hometowns could be matched. Our group was so impressed with the evening that we worried whether we could ever measure up.

The following weekend we were bused to Berchtesgaden for several days of play. The lovely mountaintop Bavarian village in the southeast corner of Germany, famous as the site of Hitler's Eagle's Nest, was one of the principal recreation areas reserved for vacationing troops. The draft was still in effect, so the Army offered as many amenities as possible. In addition to programs, Service Clubs provided musical instruments and game rooms, and offered craft and photography workshops with local instructors. The mountainous areas of Berchtesgaden and Garmisch-Partenkirchen included ski areas, lakes, fishing, hiking trails, and nightclubs, and the mountains made me feel right at home.

Back at our grand Nuremberg hotel, I tasted my first escargot, and Joyce and I had our first massages. The old walled city was just across the street. After dinner of chicken parmesan in a rich sauce, we explored the pubs, or *gasthaus*, with our favorite being the Mausloch, a hole-in-the-wall down a flight of stairs off a narrow street. The old town within the walls had been devastated in the war and nine years later, it was still in rubble; residents would disappear into the ground, descending to the basements where they lived. Their clotheslines with wash hung to dry stretched across the open areas.

Once our training days were done, we said our farewells as we were sent off to different regional headquarters. We all stayed in Germany, with eight from our group at the Nuremberg headquarters. When asked if anyone was interested in crafts, I raised my hand and said "Hastings!" The response: "No, you were assigned before leaving the States." The group immediately wondered, where would I be going? When we learned it was Merrill Barracks, the group groaned. Why was I going to the model club—the one with impossibly high standards? My friends almost held a wake for me before they left for their smaller-town assignments.

MY NEW LODGING was at 62 Kobergerstrasse, room 424, which was actually the former entrance hall to what had been one large apartment. My room was small, and from my window I could see Nuremberg residents living in some of the worst postwar conditions in the country. The fourth-floor walkup would be good exercise and I had a balcony large enough to step out on and close the door. My first purchase: geraniums for that balcony, which fit into the local culture and soothed my soul. Next, I had to turn my 10-foot-tall hallway into a home. The French doors to the balcony were 7 feet wide with about 30 inches of wall area on either side. The depth of the room was about 10 feet and had sealed doors on both sides that led to the former living spaces—now my neighbors' units. I purchased a bedspread and fabric to make a skirt for my Hollywood bed, pillow covers and a flounce over the 9-foot-tall doors. I took to sewing after work with a kit of a few needles, a jackknife, thread, and six straight pins. I'm sure BB would never have approved, but it began to look like home.

❖

IT WAS MANDATORY that we hire house cleaners because it helped the local economy, and we were not allowed to cook in our rooms, so we ate most meals at the snack bar. But we managed breakfast in Meriwether's large first-floor room, where I was introduced to slivovitz, a strong plum brandy that warms you down to your toes. With heat in short supply, a morning shot did the trick. We took turns, with our raincoats over pajamas, scurrying across the street to the bakery to pick up warm fresh rolls. Meriwether supplied butter, jam, juice, and coffee.

The Merrill Barracks Club was supposed to have a staff of six, including the director. To my knowledge, there were never more than three of us working with Meriwether; she handpicked her team and preferred skills over numbers. I was the first "northern girl" assigned to her, and I was told that I was also the first not to be asked if I minded working with a "colored person," as it was phrased at the time. Of course, it was not an issue and I suspect my letters of recommendation had answered such questions.

I was surprised to learn Meriwether was from Seattle, too. On my first day off, we took a quick road trip together to Passau to see the baroque St. Stephen's Cathedral, which had suffered extensive flooding that summer.

At the end of June, my trunk finally arrived to supplement my lone suitcase that had supplied me since May 1. Due to overtime work at the club, we were practically living in our uniforms. Earned time off allowed for some shopping, including for a car, which would let me make better use of my free time. And I'm sure my family was tired of "send me" letters, but with my water ski and tow rope on their way, I believed I would have everything I needed.

There were a lot of small cars with great mileage available that did not meet the U.S. requirements for import. Many had only three cylinders. I found a little beige Austin A40, available within two weeks for $900, plus $200 for delivery and insurance.

I appreciated that Meriwether's first agenda item at office meetings was to determine which days we wanted off for traveling. After our days off were settled, we would get on to the club business of programs, trips, and classes. The first time I had multiple days off I took the train, third class, to Mannheim where Joyce was stationed. Mary Lou and Gloria also came, and we planned our first three-day trip to Vienna for late July.

For our early travels, we often rode the train, which made it easier to cross the east-west borders in this country divided between the American Zone, the British Zone, and the Russian Zone. Officials came through the train and checked passports, usually just after you had fallen asleep.

Vienna was wonderful, but we had nowhere near enough time to explore all the great buildings and gardens. We toured through the Vienna Woods, which brought back memories of the movie *The Great Waltz,* and walked through the Russian Zone, where we rode on the Ferris wheel from *The Third Man* movie with Orson Welles. Vienna was under the Allies' combined control, and patrolling jeeps often carried soldiers with different uniforms. Each month a different country was in charge, so their soldiers would drive the jeeps. The Russian soldiers were somewhat disappointing: short, seemingly about sixteen years old, and in very drab uniforms. The U.S. was still an "Army of occupation" until summer 1955, ten years after the war. At that point, some of the rules governing our lives would change.

MY ENGLISH CAR had not yet arrived, so I walked and rode the streetcar to work in Nuremberg. I lived across from the walled city, about two blocks from the wall's north gate. Across the dry moat, I could look down at a small cottage known as the "witch's house" from the *Hansel and Gretel* tale. Once through the gate and down a slope, my walking route took me past the house of Albrecht Dürer, one of several well-known artists and writers from Nuremberg's bustling sixteenth century. Further down the hill, I passed the Frauenkirche (1355) with an open square containing a beautiful Gothic fountain and home to an open market of seasonal foods, flowers, and plants, adding welcome color to the devastated gray city. I often stopped to purchase balcony plants and cut flowers for my room. The central walled city was mostly open space interrupted by churches and a few other restored buildings like the town hall and the old hospital that spanned the river. At Christmastime, it became a dazzling glory of pageantry, toys, and ornaments. Once through the center, I walked out the south gate and then rode a streetcar the rest of the way to work.

One day Meriwether said, "It's time for culture." She had purchased two tickets at $9.50 apiece to Richard Wagner's *Lohengrin* in Bayreuth. I fried chicken at the Service Club kitchen and packed up a nice picnic dinner for our outing. It was a lovely warm day when we drove north to the Festival Theatre, and I was impressed with the trumpeters and their long horns up on the roof, calling us in for the opera to start promptly at 4 p.m. In the theater, I was disappointed at first because it was a very uninteresting building inside and out. The seats were hard and I was sure my bottom would fall asleep quickly. But once the music started, I was totally lost in a different world, a magical space with a chorus of a hundred men and eighty-plus women. The voices matched the orchestra beautifully and the first act was over all too soon. If my bottom was suffering, I hadn't noticed. Intermission was also the dinner break and we joined others in spreading a blanket out on the lawn for our picnic. We watched the parade of the audience members—many Germans in formal dress along with a number of GIs. Then, the shock! Unwrapping our chicken dinner, we found nothing but bones. The German kitchen staff had eaten our dinner and carefully rewrapped my package so we wouldn't notice. The music saved the day, but some employees were going to be in trouble. The other bit of excitement was the opera set's swan, which got stuck and then lurched, almost tossing the tenor into the orchestra pit. He hung on to the swan's neck and managed to crawl back up on the stage. We went home very satisfied, if hungry.

❖

IN MY SERVICE CLUB WORK, I had the advantage of years of experience working with men and boys of all ages. My guys learned quickly that they could not intimidate me. On one Sunday afternoon bus tour, the servicemen repeatedly requested bathroom breaks on the way home—each time getting another beer at the stop. So, at the next request, I had the driver pull over to the side of the road and told them all to go relieve themselves. "But there is no place to go," came the chorus as they looked out at an open field. "Fine," I said. "The locals do it, and I promise not to watch." It was a quiet ride the rest of the way home and from then on, our activities went smoothly. The German driver always gave me a big smile when he saw me with the group on later trips.

On one outing to the local ballet, my girlfriends could not believe what we were seeing: It looked like the animal pairs that sailed on Noah's Ark were repopulating

Pinky, the Austin A40 that Jane drove all over Europe

themselves on the stage floor. Of course, when the GIs learned about this, they insisted on a Service Club tour. I wouldn't be surprised if *Abrascus* was the only ballet many of them ever saw. The word was it was so graphic it had been banned in France. Perhaps we saw its only production.

Much of my time was dedicated to the tours we did every Sunday. The GIs who did not have passes were allowed to leave the post with our tours because the Army knew they could call us back to the post quickly if needed. The Cold War was in full swing, and the eastern border of Germany rumbled with constant gunfire, probably more from boredom than threats.

Finally, my little "beige" Austin A40 arrived, and I could start sightseeing in earnest. When I drove up to the Service Club, Meriwether leaned out a window and hollered, "Beige? That's pink if I have ever seen it." From then on, my car was known as "Pinky."

My travels started the next day. I didn't have to start work until 1 p.m., so I took off after an early breakfast and drove as far as I could until I had to turn around to get back in time. I recorded each trip on a map, eventually creating a large

Jane and Nancy Klein

flower pattern. I explored every road out of Nuremberg, taking many photographs of yards, churches, houses, and even hay-drying rakes. Pinky was a jewel, getting about thirty-five to forty miles to the gallon, and gas cost only fifteen cents per gallon at Army stations. By comparison, gas at European stations was almost $1.70 per gallon at the time. (It was easy to understand why the Germans were not fond of us.) Soon, my friend Gloria purchased a blue A40 and Joyce bought a black one, and we had a caravan.

One long training day, our staff was down to two, just Meriwether and me. We were about to get a new arrival for our club. One girl in the training group, Nancy from Cleveland, asked me where I got my hair cut, and then she went and got a "Jane cut." It turned out Nancy was assigned to Merrill Barracks and we became instant friends. From the back we were difficult to tell apart, but I was taller, and Nancy wore glasses all the time, while I wore mine just for reading. It was great fun to do programs together. Nancy got a fancier car, an Opel convertible, and we both had MP boyfriends who we could party with after work.

One day, Lars, the Norwegian businessman/tour guide, called with a dinner invitation. We enjoyed a lovely evening in a small restaurant with violin music as

I reported on the locations of the three other girls from our whirlwind welcoming tour. I assumed his previous romantic engagement was over because several more invitations followed. I realized he was getting too fond of me, so I told him not to. As nice and attractive as he was, I would be returning home eventually to establish my architecture career, and I would not allow any serious relationship while in Europe—with Lars or any other fellow. The head always ruled. Soon I would be transferred out of the Nuremberg area, solving the problem. But I would miss him.

❖

BY THE FIRST OF AUGUST, Pinky had accumulated many miles. Germany is very compact, so it was a quick hop to each historic town with beautiful medieval architecture. Bamberg, Schweinfurt, Würzburg and Kitzingen were each just a quick day's visit. I also discovered a wonderful outdoor Olympic-sized swimming pool in a beautiful park just five minutes away. I could swim each morning before work for just twenty-five cents. Pinky was only one week and two days old, but already had more than a thousand miles on the odometer. As Mother had often said, "Jane hasn't stayed home since she could crawl."

For our first weekend trip to Garmisch, four of us piled into Pinky: Gloria, her friend Jack, my 6-foot-8 MP boyfriend George, and myself—with my water-ski equipment. Unfortunately, it rained, and I couldn't convince the locals to drive the boat, so there was no water skiing. We made it a lazy day with dinner, an ice show and dancing at the Casa Carioca nightclub. Garmisch had been the site for the 1936 Winter Olympic Games, and German engineers had built a tunnel inside the mountain, the Zugspitze, with a cog train that corkscrewed its way up to a lodge at the top, an hourlong ride. I was fascinated by the double doors and how they hinged, providing protection against extreme weather. The Casa Carioca, another engineering wonder of the time, had a dance floor that slid back into the wall to expose an ice arena below. The show was like a small *Ice Follies* with skaters from around the world. It was a fun, relaxing weekend.

One of the benefits of living in Nuremberg came from its role as the headquarters for the Special Service Clubs. We had to be mindful about wearing our hats and gloves—full uniform dress was always required—but our bonus was access to the largest PX (post exchange) in Europe. All items were tried out there first before distribution to smaller stores, and many articles were available only to us. Our PX had a wonderful collection of beautiful fabrics, including Harris Tweeds at $2.95/ yard. Irresistible! More than a dozen color combinations made choosing difficult, but with a Vogue suit pattern selected and material purchased, I had a package to mail home. In Seattle, my seamstresses could create it from a "dodo" or body form, which I made before leaving. With such bargain prices, I had many requests to check the cost of other desirable items.

Of course, my biggest priority was to get in as much travel as possible. In early September, Gloria joined me in driving north from Nuremberg to Bamberg, Coburg and then to Neustadt, the home of the Hummel figurines. We were not allowed to visit the factory, as it was a secret process, and were welcome only in the showroom. We were surprised to learn they manufactured other well-known brands, including Walt Disney figures like Bambi. On another trip, we followed the Rhine River through Bonn, Koblenz, Mainz, Wiesbaden, and on to Mannheim for the night. We were getting good at inexpensive travel; this trip totaled about three dollars per person. We did run out of gas once. Fortunately, Gloria had a full five-gallon can in her trunk, but we discovered we had no way to pour the gas into our tanks. Eventually, we found a Coke bottle, and we transferred gas from can to bottle to tank. For future reference, a five-gallon can holds eighty-plus Coke bottles.

❖

ONE OF MY BLESSINGS was that many people wrote letters to me: my mother, grandmother, two sisters-in-law, my friend Gretchen, her mother Maus, among others. I had a hard time responding to everyone, so all the family mail was addressed to my parents for them to share. New photos of niece Laurie and brand-new niece Debbie, and the rest of the family were often enclosed in returning mail.

Father, of course, was very curious about George. I reported back that he was 21, had completed three years of university work in advertising and then dropped out of school for a break, thinking he was too tall to get drafted. Either the rules had changed, or he misunderstood. He was from Salt Lake City but had lived in the Hawaiian Islands, South America, and all over the U.S.—wherever his engineer father's work took the family. He skied, played tennis and golf, enjoyed music, opera, ballet, books, and was a good dresser, a perfect gentleman, and a great friend. I was sure the MPs loved him because his 6-foot, 8-inch height spoke authority. Whether he could protect himself, I have no idea. He really filled up my car when he got folded into

*A photo of four generations back in Seattle, mailed to Jane in July 1954:
Gerry with Debbie, BB, Camille and Laurie*

it but managed to drive it with his knees almost up to his chest. He was scheduled to get out of the Army on January 15, 1955.

Thanks to Mother, who saved all my correspondence, I can recall some experiences that I'd certainly have forgotten otherwise. One letter from around this time had a paragraph titled "Info for the Men."

"The Germans may make good bread and grow huge flowers but undoubtedly they are the world's worst drivers. American women drivers are dreams compared to any driver here. I understand the French and Italians are carefree and reckless, but these people start getting panicky as soon as they step foot in an auto. They sit tensed up over the steering wheel, use only the horn (continually), full speed ahead, never look at crossroads (someone might be coming), and always drive in the middle of the road regardless of who is coming, unless it is larger than themselves. They also have the largest trucks in the world, I'm sure."

WE RECEIVED THE SAD NEWS that we were losing our wonderful club director, Meriwether, the best in the business. Her talent was perhaps a curse, as she was sent to Service Clubs with challenges, often involving racial issues with career military men who had not accepted the integration of the troops. I had already planned on asking for a transfer when my six months were up, requesting assignment to the Southern Command land of hills and mountains. I wanted to be in real hills, and with Meriwether gone I wouldn't mind leaving Merrill Barracks.

The Nuremberg post had been the Nazis' headquarters during the war, and our Service Club building had been their jail. It still had bars on the windows, which kept most of our supplies and furnishings safe. However, furniture occasionally disappeared, and it did not go out the front door. We learned there was a tunnel connecting our club to the castle across town. Nuremberg had all kinds of incomplete buildings and aircraft runways, and that tunnel must have been something because our best sofa made it through.

My room was christened the "Hastings Hotel" as it was often full of friends. All the Service Club girls who lived in major train transfer areas had the same problem. Those who worked in the smaller towns had to go through the cities, usually coming in after work to catch a train out the next morning.

While still in Nuremberg, we embarked on a French adventure in Gloria's car, from Ulm to Stuttgart and Karlsruhe, then across the border to Strasbourg. With the French, we were back to communicating through arm waving and smiles. I also made a trip northeast of Nuremberg to Selb, a town on the border with then-Czechoslovakia that was home to the factory that made my mother's china. She had slipped a saucer into my footlocker while I was packing. Could I get some teacups to replace a few broken ones? This East German border area had Russian guards and was considered best to avoid. However, a promise is a promise, so it was on to Selb. Mother's pattern was no longer manufactured, so it was just a drive that became more interesting when I read a sign saying, "You are now entering the American Zone." I then realized the road was just over the border. I had been aware of the towers with armed soldiers, thinking they were across the border. As I didn't stop, they did not appear to find me of interest or interfere with my obvious violation.

❖

BECAUSE I COULD BALANCE THE BOOKS, I was promoted to assistant club director. The new title meant more work, not pay, so I was delighted to leave soon after on a trip to Italy. This time, it was just Gloria, George, and me. With Pinky stuffed with supplies, including a funnel for refueling, we set off through Innsbruck, Verona, and Bologna before arriving in Florence. It was a beautiful drive through the mountains, before we happily checked into a nice hotel named Patria. Gloria and I had a room with a wonderful view of Brunelleschi's domed cathedral and the candlelit palace. Our location was perfect, with Pinky resting in the public square. The next morning, we found the streets filled with more Americans and British than Italians. We enjoyed the wonderful architectural sights: the Pitti Palace, the Pazzi Chapel, the cathedral and the beautiful baptistry doors, and the 1345 Ponte Vecchio bridge with the little shops clinging to its sides, fortunately spared during the war. As I was sitting in the cathedral with my head tipped back, studying the interior of the dome, I realized that my far-sightedness was a blessing. I may have lost twenty-two years of potential reading (before glasses), but I could see so many faraway details that others could not.

The colorful Straw Market (*Mercato Nuovo*) reminded me of Seattle's Pike Place Market on Saturday afternoons, with each merchant trying to out-shout the others. When our shopping allowance was spent, it was time to focus on culture. Twenty cents bought a ticket to the Galleria dell'Accademia and Michelangelo's *David*, as well as his other works. With the sunlight streaming through the dome on the approximately seventeen-foot-tall *David*, all the rest were forgotten. The longer I watched, the more alive the marble seemed. The typical tourist usually flitted by then stopped, mouth open and eyes wide, staring for a considerable time without a word. There was a reverence that churches must envy. Florence had so much to offer in its art, music, and food, I knew this would be the first of many visits.

Next was Naples, where we checked into the "Camping Platz" in this "City of Sin." With our tarp up, and our air mattresses and sleeping bags spread out, we went into town for dinner. A waterfront dive with a pizzeria sign was perfect for the three of us grubby travelers, and we could park in front where we could keep an eye on the car. As soon as I stopped, the usual crowd gathered around, waiting for us to alight. When George unfolded himself to climb out of the car, the crowd moved back and we girls fell into place, one on each side, feeling very safe. The place was filled with locals, mostly sailors. We indulged in three large pizzas and six beers as a substitute for water. With the waitress identifying us as "Americanos," we thought, well, there goes our bill. The total—800 lire, service charge included—translated to a little over one dollar.

The next morning, we brewed coffee, packed up and toured Naples. We discovered that every foreign car parked in town had been broken into, and we felt very smug about our camping choice. The terrible road along the waterfront brought us into the real Naples, where carts in garish colors, pulled by beautiful horses with bells and elaborate silver harnesses, created music and a festive atmosphere. The fruit stands were colorful but on closer examination, it was obvious the good fruit was elsewhere. However, grapes were ripe and easily picked for free everywhere, helping to solve our thirst problem.

We arrived in Sorrento just ten minutes late for the last boat to Capri. It had rained every day and now a real storm was rolling in, canceling future Capri runs. We checked into a fabulous hotel that hung off the cliff a good five hundred feet above the sea. Our usual request for a double room and a single room amused the bellhops—especially when we added, "Put all the bags in the large room, as we haven't decided who will be staying with George." They went away giggling, and George took his bag down the hall to his single room. We girls had the bridal suite with a view of Sorrento and Naples, and the deep blue water below. The sky turned black with clouds, and the winds went wild like nothing we had experienced. Most of the hotel was made of tile-floored open terraces that sloped a bit toward the sea. The rainwater ran off the hill behind and over the terrace, and we lifted our feet while eating or lounging. Our bridal suite was flooded, too, with water pouring in from windows and under the door.

The storm subsided by morning, but the threatening black clouds lingered. Capri was still without ferry service, so we packed up the car and headed for Amalfi on the other side of the peninsula. I had never been on such a curvy road, and my passengers became carsick. We pressed on to Pompei and arrived in Rome at 9 p.m., but no hotel rooms were left in the city, so we went back to Lido Roma on the coast. We checked in to a hotel at 3:30 a.m.

The next day we parked Pinky in Rome, and set off on foot, taking in the Trevi Fountain, the Spanish Steps and other attractions I'd seen in recent movies. I telephoned my friend Jack Blount, an Army veteran who had been an instructor at the YMCA back in Seattle. He had met Ivana, a Rome native, while in the service. I had enjoyed following his Italian courtship and marriage. Jack had planned to become a doctor on the GI Bill, but when Ivana was unhappy living in Seattle, they returned to Italy. I found him attending medical school in Rome, and teaching English in his free time. The five of us went to dinner and dancing at an Egyptian-themed nightclub where three different bands played during dinner. The music was followed by a floor show with a toothless striptease artist, and then good dancers (with teeth), a beautiful French girl singer, an American woman singer, and a British male dancer. It was 3:30 a.m. by the time we got to our hotel.

The next day, St. Peter's Basilica was first on the list for Gloria and me. (George opted for a day off.) She and I joined the crowds, and it felt like Grand Central Station but noisier. We checked out the sculptures, mosaics, inlays, carvings, paintings, and the abundant gold leaf. It was all too much—just a huge disappointing tourist attraction, and certainly not a church. Unfortunately, the Sistine Chapel was closed and had to be added to the list for the next trip. We were due at Jack and Ivana's home for lunch, which turned out to be the highlight of our Rome trip. We enjoyed pasta followed by veal scaloppine, several vegetables, tossed salad, and a dessert to die for with whipped cream and different kinds of liqueurs. The lunch courses were accompanied by three kinds of wine. Ivana assured us that the Romans do not consider St. Peter's to be a church and that many, including her parents, had never been inside. After lunch, our sightseeing took us to the Colosseum, the Roman Forum, and out along the Appian Way, the oldest road in Rome dating from long before Christ. The road sort of resembled a tank trap, and Pinky did well considering she was not a horse.

After the touring, we visited Ivana's aunt and uncle's apartment, where they ran a sweater business. Their knitting machines made lightweight sweaters—more like blouses—with nice patterns, faggoting stitching, and a blending of different shades of color and designs. In Seattle, I was sure they would sell in the forty-five to fifty-dollar range, so we were dumbfounded to learn the most expensive sold to the Rome shops for six dollars. We had to have some.

We must have tried on fifteen to twenty different sweaters each, delighting the designers, who had never seen their work on live models. It was an evening of Italian "oohs and ahhs," including great homemade wine and roasted chestnuts. We ordered three or four sweaters apiece and then felt guilty about deserting George, so headed back to the hotel. The wonderful hospitality made this the best day of our trip.

❖

IT WAS A BEAUTIFUL DAY to head north up the coast. We gassed up at a PX for fifteen cents a gallon before arriving in Pisa, where walking around the leaning tower gave me a funny feeling, like vertigo. Next, in Milan, the cathedral was the highlight; it is second in size only to St. Peter's, with some of the finest stained-glass windows in the world. As in so many other cities, there was never enough time to explore.

We continued to Lecco and followed the shores of Lake Como to Chiavenna, the last town before the border, where we stopped to spend our last Italian money on bottles of wine. After crossing the Swiss border, St. Moritz's Camping Platz was our destination for the night. We hadn't realized how high the altitude was and forgot it was now autumn. When the Swiss Army troopers checked us out on horseback with wool bags over the horses' noses, it dawned on us: It was cold! Gloria got in the car, sleeping bag and all, and I was the only one who got any sleep. We had to chip ice off the tarp in the morning.

When I started Pinky up, I thought she had had it. I have never heard such horrible noises. We weren't sure what to expect—an explosion maybe? —and considered perhaps we should start hitchhiking. After a half-hour, the noise wasn't as bad, and we decided to see if we could make it to town. It turned out that the air filter had come off, and when I started the engine, the carburetor was gulping in fifteen- to twenty-degree air.

This was the home stretch, and we said so long to beautiful Switzerland. We drove north with a lunch stop in Landeck, Austria, where we sat outside in gloriously warm sunshine. In Garmisch, Gloria transferred to her own car, while George and I continued home to Nuremberg. I vowed a return trip to Florence as soon as possible.

❖

BACK IN NUREMBERG, I was also back to a difficult club director. My former life had been mostly spent in male-dominated environments, and early on, I had learned how to work with my older brothers and other males. Now I was learning about my own gender. This was the first time I was in an all-women's organization, and there were few others I could relate to, as I was serious about education and career, and I was accustomed to being a team member. Meriwether had been an outstanding administrator, listening to her team, and there was a sense of trust in her crew. However, the new director, whose name I've forgotten, had neither organizational or

communication skills, and she didn't trust anyone. This destroyed our staff camaraderie. We went from the top of the Service Clubs to the bottom. She accused me of
plotting against her—but my plotting was merely focused on maximizing mileage,
time, or gallons of fuel. I was there to do my job and travel. I had already put in for
a transfer, hoping for the mountains and expecting news upon returning from Italy.

The word came: I was going to the Munich District.

❖

BUT BEFORE I COULD REACH the pinnacle of my Service Club career—Oberammergau,
the highest alpine location of all the clubs—I would make a short detour. From
Thanksgiving through mid-January, I was stationed in Gablingen, just outside
Augsburg. I traded a heavy artillery group in the heart of Nuremberg for an infantry
group on an old German airstrip, and the post was so small that mail was addressed
to "Gablingen by Garstoffen by Augsburg." As program director, I reported to Beth,
the club director, and we were the only women living on the post.

My new spacious apartment sprawled across the attic over the Officers Club in
a building full of stairways. The kitchen had neither sink nor stove, just a hot plate.
A wonderful German staff did most of our work and made life in the country a
snap, including cooking our Thanksgiving dinner. With a good supply of dishes,
we could go days before filling the bathtub to wash them—a chore Beth and I did
on our knees.

The winter weather brought a blizzard, closing our road and shutting down all
activities. While doing dishes, I started to laugh. "What is so funny?" Beth asked. I
told her I had been refused a job as an architect because the government said it would
be dangerous working with men. Now, we were trapped with a thousand of them.

❖

TRAVEL FOR AMERICANS had become problematic, and we were restricted from driving on the autobahns after dark due to "autobahn bandits." However, the police
trying to catch the bandits had reportedly shot more people than the bandits had.

Despite the warnings, a group of us decided to take a road trip. Gloria's house-
cleaner, Carmen, was on her way to the States to marry a former serviceman, sailing
from Rotterdam, and we would take her there. Five of us drove north from Ulm in
two cars, stopping in Mannheim where Joyce and Babs joined the caravan heading
on to Cologne and Düsseldorf, known as "little Paris."

Arriving late in Rotterdam, we ended up in what must have been the city's oldest hotel. A steep wooden stairway—more like a ladder without a handrail—took us up to our second-floor room. After a moment of panic, we made it up using both hands to grip the worn treads. Upstairs, the landlady put five of us in one room with two double beds. There was no heat, and a bitter cold wind blew in from the ocean, so three of us tucked into one bed, with me in the middle as the heater. After a breakfast of cheese, cold meats, bread, and the best coffee so far in Europe, we helped Carmen on to her Holland America ship, which we decided was not as nice as the *Geiger*.

Retreating from the stiff winter wind, we went on to the charming city of Delft, where our hotel was warm with normal stairs and hot water; what joy! The next morning, we toured The Hague before retracing our route to Arnheim, stopping to purchase cheese, Dutch gin, and pastries. A local woman asked if we were Americans, then insisted we go to her house for coffee and refreshments. When we arrived, her husband's look said, "She has picked up another group." They told stories about how much the Dutch loved Americans: During the war, retreating Germans had taken all the food, and the Americans arrived with supplies. Then the Marshall Plan aided the rebuilding of their cities. We could do no wrong! Because of the cold, I was wearing my Seattle wooden shoes, which made the locals giggle.

❖

THE GERMAN TOWNS were decked out with holiday decorations everywhere, with Nuremberg the most grandiose. The church square had transformed into a wonderland for the *Kriskinder Market*, the Children's Christmas Market. In Gablingen, with the club and our apartment decorated, we turned our attention to cookies. Beth and I made the rounds of four mess halls, begging for butter, eggs, milk, flour, and sugar. We had a baking party every evening and the troops who didn't want to bake seemed delighted to wash dishes. In our regular programs, the infantrymen were easy to work with and willing to try new games. We had a new girl on staff, Betty, who had always attended girls' schools. She was delighted to sit with the men and listen to their stories each evening, so we decided that should be her job and we would do the rest.

On Christmas Eve, we hosted a crowd for a party that included coffee, hot chocolate, and cookies. We closed late and it was so cold that Beth and I decided to make the rounds to the guard stations on the airstrip with cookies and thermoses of coffee. Pinky was the car of choice for snowy trips, and our midnight run was greeted by a gun raised by a startled GI. Beth hit the floorboard, leaving me as the target. We had not considered our goodwill mission as dangerous! Apologies were exchanged, and the guard called the other outpost to warn them we were coming. We repeated the midnight run on New Year's Eve without incident. Several days into the new year, a GI we had never seen in our club came into our office with a bottle of whiskey. Immediately, I said, "Get it out of here. It is not allowed." He looked hurt and said, "It is for you two. I was on guard duty both Christmas and New Year's Eve and want to thank you." We thanked him and hid the bottle in a desk drawer.

On Christmas evening, friends from Nuremberg (Nancy, Louie, and George) and Ulm (Gloria and Neila) arrived for dinner and an overnight stay. Our party expanded to include three neighbor officers, so our apartment was full. The Officers Club baked a ham and turkey with all the trimmings, and our guests made it a very special dinner. There were a few toys for gifts, prompting the men to compete in boat races in the bathtub and car races down our long hall. It was a very merry and memorable Christmas, my first away from home.

We continued our holiday festivities in Mannheim, where Gloria, Beth and I joined Joyce, Mary Lou, and others for a party. One girl opened a box with a beautiful gown from Paris. When someone said it was probably a copy, the owner, who had just enough to drink to be relaxed, stated, "Oh yes, it's real. Mother has been shopping again. I'm a DuPont." She was Dorothy DuPont Dimmick, and she was soft-spoken, never calling attention to herself. This was our first, if partial, reunion of the Service Club group that first met in New York City in May 1954.

In addition to her MG sports car, Beth had arrived in Gablingen with a Christmas gift from 1953 that had never been delivered. An Army officer friend had carried it from South America as a favor to a young woman who asked him to deliver it to Prince Fugger of Augsburg. He gave it to Beth when she was transferred to the area, saying, "I'm not interested in meeting a bachelor prince. Why don't you take it?" With our troops in the field and nothing to do at the club, Beth decided we should deliver the small package. I had noticed a road off the south side of the autobahn with a sign: "Off-limits to American personnel." Curious, I thought, as this area was in the American Zone. Now we had an excuse to break the rules: This was the road to the Fugger estate.

We arrived in a courtyard with garages/stables to the left and the main entrance directly ahead. It was a large old stone structure that lacked architectural significance but could be called a palace. Upon ringing the bell, we told the maid, "We have a gift for the prince." Her face froze in terror, then she slammed the door, screaming. We stood stunned, unsure of what to do, when a voice called to us in English from a third-story window: "Please, do not go away, I'll be right down." The voice came from an older woman, white-haired and handsome. Soon the door opened, and we were invited in. Our gracious hostess explained: It seems that the word "gift" translated to "poison" in German, and the maid believed we had come to poison the prince.

Our hostess was the bachelor prince's mother; her son was in England for the theater season and her daughter was at a function, leaving her two young sons with their grandmother. Coffee and cookies were served while two servants on ladders lighted hundreds of candles on a beautiful tree that was at least twelve feet tall. The elder Fugger was interested in our backgrounds and travels, lamenting that her life had not allowed such freedom. I had already spent months trying to tell Europeans that the state of Washington was on the opposite side of the U.S. from our nation's capital city, and I had given up explaining the difference. However, when I said where I was from, our hostess asked, "The state or the city of Washington?" I replied, "The state and Seattle." She immediately said, "Oh, it is beautiful with the Olympic Mountains to the west, the Cascades to the east and Puget Sound." I was startled: "You've been there!" She said, "Oh no, my dear, but I do read."

She explained the sign on the road. When the U.S. Army moved into the area during the end of the war, General George Patton took over the Fugger estate as his headquarters. The Fugger family moved into the servants' quarters over the carriage house and stables. Patton's first action was to have his men take a complete inventory of all items in the house, down to the linens. When the inventory was complete, he stated, "Gentlemen, we are guests in a home. When we leave, everything will be just as we found it, and I mean everything, including each piece of china and each napkin." And indeed they were, she said. The Pattons and Fuggers became friends. As a thank you for the care shown, the best of the Fugger art collection was given to the Pattons after the occupation, and our hostess stayed in touch with Mrs. Patton. We were so pleased to hear a good story about war, the victors and the conquered.

The Fugger family had another claim to fame: In the early sixteenth century when the Fuggers were rulers of the Augsburg area and one of the wealthiest families in the world, they bult *Fuggerei,* the world's oldest low-income housing project still in use. Over the centuries, the project has been expanded, upgraded, and today still houses people who pay a pittance for a year's rent.

With the merry holidays behind me, I dreamed of mountain adventures ahead and looked forward to moving day: January 13, 1955.

A 1955 greeting card with a drawing of Jane, Kitty, and Ann by a Service Club artist

7 | O'GAU: MY MOUNTAIN HOME

I **HAD FINALLY ARRIVED** in the mountains, where I felt truly alive.

Oberammergau housing was in an old hotel, now the Officers Club, with rooms for both officers and civilian workers. New housing was under construction across the village next to the Army post, but it was not ready yet, so my first room was a top-floor closet with a small dormer. No doubt this had been a maid's room in the glory days of the Hotel Osterbichl. While sitting on my bed, I could open the window, wash my hands in my basin, get items out of my wardrobe, and cook breakfast on my hot plate.

The word was we would move in about two months. I dreaded leaving because the local ski hill was right behind us, with the lift in our backyard. Recent rains had melted the snow, but I was confident winter weather would return, so I ordered a pair of Erbachers, the best German-made skis. In the meantime, I enjoyed the small stream bubbling below my window and a neighboring church bell chiming every 15 minutes.

The post, my workplace, was on a mountainside across the village, with buildings stepping up the hill parallel to the valley floor. Our Service Club was at the top of the hill in a former stable used by the German mountain troops who had occupied the location during the war. The post was a school with only about sixty residents, including the military staff, instructors, librarians, secretaries, and three Service Club girls. The schools included the MP (Military Police) School and the Intelligence/Language School where student groups rotated through monthly or quarterly and ranged from privates to generals. We also hosted students from other countries and people associated with NATO. The people I met were all brilliant—a contrast to my previous posts where the Service Club girls were usually the most educated. All three of us Service Club girls were new, with no one to show us the ropes. I was second in command, as program director. Jenny was the club director, and Vivienne assisted us.

In between club duties, we made good use of our playtime. On one snowy excursion, I met up with Gloria in Munich, where we darted into open shops to keep from freezing as we walked. Winter boots were in order, so we headed to the cobbler shop. Gloria found a nice pair, but I had to have a pair custom made because German feet seemed to be short and wide, the opposite of mine. The shop owner measured my feet three times before he was convinced that he was correct. He disappeared down a flight of open stairs to the workroom, and soon three heads peeked up from the stairs to have a look at who had such strange feet. Those beautiful boots cost approximately fifteen dollars—one of my very best investments.

After more shopping, we went on to Nuremberg for a farewell party for Louie, who would leave in a few days. George would return home soon, too. Gloria and I planned to travel to England the following week, and Nancy was about to be transferred. We had a grand evening and ended up at a nightclub with a glass dance floor. Soon the lights went dim and out popped a good-sized babe, dressed in only three small flowers, who did a dance routine. What a sendoff for the boys! The next day we shopped at the big PX, where I exchanged some Siamese jewelry, a Christmas gift from George that I would never wear, for a big, beautiful teak salad bowl. I was sure I would never see George again, and every time I used that bowl, I would have pleasant memories.

Gloria drove me home, up the newly plowed mountain road, and spent the night. My mountaintop location drew lots of visitors, so I often slept on an air mattress in the hall and posted a large note warning my British neighbor not to step on me when he came in. My companions were taken with the sparkling Southern belle Gloria, who had whatever it was that turned all men on. After that, I was regularly greeted with "When is Gloria coming?" instead of "Hello!"

At the end of January, Gloria and I headed north to England in her car, the "Blue Goose" or BG, driving through heavy snow on roads covered in ice. Everyone said, "England in January: You are crazy!" We were both fighting the flu, but this was the only time we could go. The BG's trunk was packed with five five-gallon cans of gas, six cans of oil, a Jeep can nozzle, and enough tools to do a major overhaul if needed. The backseat was piled with our two small suitcases, "Herbert" (my big down pillow), blankets, cheese, rolls, cookies, coffee, fruit, nuts, and snacks. We spent our first night in Ostend on the Belgian coast in a typical unheated European hotel room. We shivered through the night, wearing all our clothes to stay warm, before heading to the mail-boat dock in the morning. As soon as we stepped out of the car, a crane picked up the BG and deposited it into the ship's gaping hold. Left standing with just what we had in hand, someone asked if we wanted to go to Dover and routed us to the ticket office. Thank heavens we were on the right dock!

When the sun came out, the sky was a lovely blue and the English Channel smooth as glass. Upon landing, we were inspected and questioned about our financial status. It seems we were to bring lots of money in, but not take any out. We picked up the car and underwent more inspections with high-powered flashlights. We had been misinformed about our auto insurance and they said we needed another policy. Gloria turned on her charm and they let us go with the promise that we would take care of the problem in London. Gloria said to me, "You drive." Driving on the other side of the road was tricky in town, but highways were a snap. I just had to be careful about turning corners and falling into old habits.

London traffic required all four eyes and hands—and an invisible angel on our shoulders giving directions—to find our way to the Douglas House, the only Army hotel in London. The lobby was filled with men waiting for rooms; however, they did put aside one room for servicewomen. After carefully examining our IDs, staff informed us that if no one else showed up by 9:30 p.m., we could have the room. We decided to live dangerously and walked down Bond Street to Piccadilly Circus, lit up like Times Square, taking in the shop windows. We returned at 9:30 p.m. on the dot. We got the room, which wasn't much but looked like heaven to us at the time, even with a shower filled with men's long johns hung up to dry.

Sunday was an unusually warm, sunny day, and we found a free London tour in a glass-roofed bus with a young woman guide who had a great sense of humor. We took lots of pictures at stops like Buckingham Palace and Madame Tussauds wax museum. The next day, we took care of our official business: the car insurance, a new large license plate, and a driver's test for our licenses, which read "hereby licensed to drive Motor Cars & Reversible Tricycles only." We never quite understood what a reversible tricycle was.

I took to walking while Gloria slept in the car, as she was still recovering from the flu. I visited the London Zoo, where I was most interested in the penguin pool, which had won an architectural award. My heart sank when I saw these handsome large penguins living in a mud puddle! How could they have destroyed those beautiful twisting concrete ramps I had long admired in photos? I kept looking and finally found the pool, home to much smaller penguins.

The next day we toured southwest England, taking in Winchester, Salisbury, Bath, Bristol, Cheltenham, Gloucester, Worcester, and then on to Birmingham. Gloria had my architectural history book, which I had shipped over in my footlocker, and she did crash research on each cathedral on the way. Leaving the car parked, we searched for a place to enjoy dinner before catching the midnight train to Edinburgh. It was 10 p.m. and England had locked up for the day. Finally, we found a men's club and asked the desk clerk for help. The sound of women's voices drew all kinds of disgusted attention from the smoking parlor, but we were sent around the corner and down the stairs. I felt like I was back on Seattle's Skid Road. However, we really had to eat something and once inside it was charming, and the food smelled heavenly. The waiters were in tails and our steak dinner was the best food we had in England. On the train we stretched out in our third-class compartment to sleep our way to Edinburgh. Despite the cold, we enjoyed the stores, castles, and cathedral, though I was beginning to think I had cathedraled Gloria to death.

After a quick day and evening in Glasgow—a dirty, busy city without any of Edinburgh's charm—we took a smoky, crowded train back to Birmingham, where we were delighted to see the Blue Goose in the parking lot. Our explorations continued by car through Stratford-upon-Avon, Warwick, Coventry, Northampton, Bedford, and Cambridge, stopping in each town to tour the cathedrals and other major sights. The English cathedrals are all heated, some with potbelly stoves along the side aisles and others with zigzagging ductwork under the stone floor. It was easy to see the layout by where people were sitting. Cambridge was an especially interesting town with universities snuggled together like rowhouses.

Back in London we arrived just a little too late to take in the Sadler's Wells Ballet. Instead, we enjoyed a great night at our last London hotel, soaking in a tub and washing our hair and clothes. Our friendly hotel manager came up with tea and cookies to hear about our adventures, and we put another shilling in the gas heater to keep us all cozy while we shared our stories. It was hard to believe she had never been outside the London area.

The next day, we drove south to Dover for the afternoon ferry—but we missed the boat and killed time visiting the castle and taking in a movie before the night boat to Dunkirk. This time we drove onto the ship, the BG was secured, and we went up to our bunks. When the train came onboard, the rail cars shook the boat like an earthquake. After the rail wheels were chained down, the boat slipped out into the channel, where wind and rain gave us the "briny deep" convulsions. We docked at 3 a.m. and had to drive ashore. Short of sleep, we drove into the countryside and pulled to the side of the road for a bit more shut-eye. At dawn we were awakened by several farmers pressing their faces against the car windows. Startled, we drove off to find a more remote area.

We drove back down through Belgium and spent the day in Brussels where the sun returned, making the beautiful gold-gilt city center glitter. Our search for the famous "little boy fountain" seemed endless. The little fellow is so small that he disappears in the crowd. Driving south toward Luxembourg, we hit another blizzard and found ourselves out in the snow pouring gas into BG's tank and oil under the hood. The next day, our journey wound down with a quick stop in Metz in France before crossing back to Germany and wrapping up our ten-day adventure with a night in Ulm.

❖

MONDAY MORNING, I drove Pinky to "O'gau," as we called Oberammergau. On a mountain road about twenty miles from home, Pinky began making a terrible noise. Was she throwing a rod? I stopped to check the oil, which was full, and I couldn't see what the problem was. There was no place to get help and no traffic, so I held my breath and pressed on, arriving just in time to change my clothes and get to work. The next day Pinky visited the motor pool and then was sent to a shop outside Munich. Each day the story grew sadder, until finally the engine had to be pulled and all the bearings replaced. Apparently, someone put two handfuls of sand in Pinky's gas tank while she was parked in Ulm. It blew my budget for the next several months.

On my next days off, Gloria, our mail clerk and I went skiing in St. Anton, Austria. It is the home of the Arlberg technique—the skiing style of the day—and the crowd included visitors from across Europe, from Sweden to Turkey. Instructors skied by with large classes, yelling at them in German, French, or English. We found a house with thick feather quilts on the beds and breakfast for a dollar a day. The area had wonderful gondolas going from peak to peak, but you had to make reservations well ahead of time to get on one. So, instead we ended up on the chairlift where they bundled you up for your several-mile-long trip to the top. It was so cold that all the fluid in our noses froze; thank heavens for the slivovitz in my fanny pack.

Life back at the Service Club had become very busy; our club director fired our artist, so I was doing the posters and artwork, plus drawing up plans to remodel the club. The director was no jewel, but I grinned and bore it as I did not want to leave my place in paradise. Our new housing adjacent to the post was not ready for our move yet, but we had a problem. Because of the high security, we housed many American civilian employees, such as secretaries and librarians, in jobs usually held by local Germans. Not enough bachelor officers' quarters rooms were built for all of us, so the colonel decided to put us three Service Club girls together in one apartment. Vivienne and I thought it was a bad idea as we all had to work with each other. One day I stopped in to see Colleen, the colonel's secretary living down the hall who disappeared each weekend to go skiing in Austria: "You don't know me, and I don't know you, but if some of us have to live together, you would be my choice for a roommate." Colleen jumped up and ran into the colonel's office, saying, "The problem is solved." She returned and explained that I had saved her from being forced to share an apartment with a woman she had never met.

❖

ONE NICE THING about living in the old hotel was that it was also the Officers Club, which included a good dining room that gave us an opportunity to meet the rest of the staff. About this time, word was out that a general, the air deputy to the NATO Defense College in Paris, had arrived on the post; because most officers wore civilian clothes when not on duty, we played a guessing game to figure out who he was. To our surprise, he turned out to be the younger of the options.

On most Army posts the civilian Service Club girls were viewed as outsiders, if not just general nuisances. So, it was a real pleasure that Colonel Ott, our commanding officer, included us as full members of his small team. The arrival of the "Detachment R" group, and the news that we all would be moving into new quarters, were cause for a grand reception in the Officers Club for all officers and civilian staff, including us three Service Club girls. For us, this was a first! A few days before the party, Vivienne and I took the NATO group on an afternoon tour to King Ludwig's Linderhof Castle. The group included about forty-five foreign officers, most of them generals, ranking from one star to five stars, from our Allied nations. While walking down the path with our busload of delightful men in varying uniforms, our general and his friend caught up to us. He asked, "Young woman, what do you do?" Surprised, I responded, "I'm the program director," to which he said, "No, I mean in real life." I said I was an architect. At this point he turned to his very handsome companion and said, "Five dollars, please." Apparently, my conversation with some of the men in the group had included some architectural terms, which inspired the bet. Air Force Brigadier Gen. Noel Parrish introduced himself and explained that architecture was one of his hobbies. Next, I was to guess the nationality of his companion. I thought his insignia was Turkish, but he did not look like a Turk. Parrish's friend was introduced only as "Fike," and I was correct; he was a Turk. It turned out he was also the man who had purchased all the nylon stockings in the PX as gifts for the women he wooed. Our handsome Turk had quite a reputation!

A day or two later, I received a call at the Service Club from General Parrish, asking me to accompany him to the Casa Carioca nightclub in Garmisch. The NATO group was scheduled for another outing, and didn't this fall under our duties? However, the big night was scheduled on the same night as Colonel Ott's party, and I had already accepted that invitation. When I told the general of my conflict, he replied, "Is it better to please the colonel or the general? I'll speak to the colonel." I assured the general that I would work something out. Also, I was to bring a girlfriend, a date for the Turk, as I was General Parrish's date. The general and the Turk were the only bachelors in this NATO group.

After consulting with my friend Colleen, she recommended I arrive at the colonel's official reception early, go through the receiving line and then join the general. The general agreed and would send his driver to pick me up, along with a girlfriend. Now whom to ask to be the Turk's date? The Turk was the top conversation of the post, and all my women friends would love to be chosen. I did not inform any of them of my task. Finally, I settled on Ellen, a quiet girl who was about to return home. I was sure there had been little excitement in her life during her two years abroad, and she was thrilled.

Ellen joined me at the colonel's party—made more colorful because the Army had just changed their dress uniforms to new models, making them look more like the Marines. The general's car arrived right on schedule, and we were surprised to see that the general had left his party to accompany us. Arriving at the Casa Carioca, the general quickly looked around the dinner tables arranged in a U pattern around the dance floor/ice rink. The three of us sat at a table as far away as possible from the Turk, who was in the opposite corner. The general said, "Watch this, he'll be here in five minutes." The master socializer moved through the tables speaking to

Jane and Ellen with Brig. Gen. Noel Parrish at Casa Carioca

all along the way and arriving right on time. The skating show was delightful, then the dance floor was rolled out over the ice for dancing. Ellen and I, the only women in the group, were very busy. What other American girl has stepped on the toes of a one-star, two-star, three-star, four-star and five-star general—all in one night? Our partners ranged from short, round Italians to a field marshal, the head of England's Air Force, a very large man with heavy eyebrows that cantilevered out like awnings.

The Turk was a wonderfully easy partner on the dance floor. He told me he was called the "bad Turk" but didn't explain. When he learned that I had not been to Turkey, he said he would take me in his own plane. The general—by now just Noel to me—assured him that I was *his* date and would not be going to Turkey. When I mentioned that Fike referred to himself as the "bad Turk," Noel laughed: "Not true. He is known as the Terrible Turk." This had been Fike's nickname ever since he apparently stole Lord Mountbatten's girlfriend away at the Cairo Conference. At that time, Fike had been the head of the Turkish Navy.

What an evening! Up to this point my only dates in Germany had been with Pfc. George and Lars, the Norwegian salesman; now I was dancing with a room full of generals. Finally, Noel and us two girls were dropped off back at the Officers

Club in the Osterbichl Hotel. The colonel's party was still going on with a few die-hards who had too much to drink and were destroying property. My boyish, soft-spoken general friend took one look at the situation and stated firmly, "Gentlemen, I think it is time you go to bed." Immediately, the room cleared, and we said our goodnights. This had to be the most memorable date of my life.

❖

IN THE MIDDLE OF MARCH, Gloria and I took a quick bus tour to Paris. Our German tour guide surprised us when she said Americans were her favorite travelers because we were so easygoing. We saw the Eiffel Tower, the Arc de Triomphe, Notre Dame, the Opera House, La Madeleine, the Louvre, Les Invalides and the Panthéon. We walked until our feet just wouldn't go anymore. We also took in the *Folies Bergère*, which was overpriced, and the girls weren't all that great. However, at the end of the show, a nude male, gold-gilt garden statue came to life and danced. I could not believe anyone could stand so still for so long. The next day we went out to Versailles. I knew I would need several return trips to do Paris justice.

That spring, we were experiencing the warm Italian *foehn* winds, which spike temperatures within minutes. Historical laws protected citizens from any misdeeds sparked by "evil spirits" during the *foehn*. The locals would retreat into their houses, closing their shutters and missing work or school until the evil winds stopped. They still honored this custom. One beautiful sunny morning, I was skiing behind my home in the Osterbichl Hotel on a German holiday, so the hill was crowded. The hum of the rope tow was accompanied by festive folk music broadcast over the slope. Suddenly, a hurricane-force wind of hot air hit me, like someone had opened the door to a furnace. I dropped to my knees, curling up for protection. The wind didn't last long, and I got up to discover I was alone on the slope. The music had stopped, along with the ski tow, and there was not another soul in sight. It was spooky! I skied home, changed my clothes, had lunch, and went to work.

Of course, there was not a German worker on the job; they were all hiding behind their shutters. Yes, I had experienced the *foehn*, the huge barometric pressure change and the "evil spirits." At work we were expecting to have a general inspection, so some housekeeping was in order. With no German staff available, I scrubbed our main room floor and did some other chores. A few days later I noticed a change in the attitudes of our local help. I asked our photo instructor, Gunther, what I had done to upset the German staff. He explained that someone had seen me washing the floor; thus, they said I had lied. What did I lie about? When I first arrived, they had asked me what I did at home. Of course, I told them that I was an architect. Now, they were sure I had lied because educated Germans would never stoop to floor washing.

❖

APRIL MEANT IT WAS TIME to move to our new quarters. I was looking forward to a nice five-room apartment, but I would miss the charm of the old hotel. I would miss seeing the village elders arrive in full Bavarian dress for their curling games on the ice, while at the other end of the lake, younger men cut ice blocks to cool their root cellars through the summer. And I would miss my walks through the village along narrow streets winding between the painted stucco hotels and shops with balconies dripping with red trailing geraniums.

The move was a slow process; I didn't feel well and carrying items up to the third floor wore me out. First, my legs ached, then my teeth hurt, especially the root canals. X-rays showed that my teeth were fine. I followed my Seattle dentist's advice and went to the Army dentist, a charming young man from Georgia. When I mentioned that I had bad teeth, he said, "Oh no, they look fine." But when I opened my mouth, he said, "Oh my goodness, y'all are from the Puget Sound area." He explained that we had the reputation of having the most extensive dental work in the U.S. He could tell that my dentist had graduated from the University of Washington from the bevels on the inlays. I found that fascinating because I recognized the schools that architects had attended from their design styles.

But I was still sick. Soon, my eyes were in trouble and then my stomach. I went to the post doctor, an older German man. He gave me some medicine and that night I broke out in a rash all over my arms and legs. Unfortunately, Vivienne was on a 15-day vacation and our club director, Jenny, was away. I was the only one left, so I had to work. When the rash broke out, I felt better and could at least go up and down the stairs. When Jenny returned, I went to bed. At this point, the German doctor was giving me calcium shots, assuming I was suffering an allergic reaction. He never took my temperature.

My friend Connie arrived from Vienna for a visit; I made it to the train station in Garmisch but I couldn't stand up to greet her. She helped me back to Pinky for our return to O'gau, where I introduced her to Colleen, gave them my car keys, and went back to bed. Connie told Colleen she thought I was dying as she had never seen me in such a state. Colleen asked the colonel if I could be seen by Dr. Major Cavitto, the American doctor based in Garmisch. Fortunately, he was visiting O'gau and came to my bedside. He immediately took my temperature. He considered whether I had polio, but his tentative diagnosis was strep throat. Colleen agreed to take my temperature through the night and if it went up, I was to go by ambulance to the hospital in Munich. But the doctor believed I was past the crisis. Fortunately, my temperature was going down, so I stayed in bed to recover, sleeping 22 of every 24 hours. I lost more than 20 pounds, which I was sure would return.

Months later, I was at a party where someone started to introduce me to Dr. Cavitto. I responded that we had met before. He said, "I pride myself on remembering people," and he was sure he had never met me. When I told him of his nighttime house call in O'gau, he said, "If you are the same person, I didn't realize how sick you were."

❖

GLORIA AND I DROVE to Switzerland for a couple of days, stopping first in Zurich, which reminded me of home because it was full of American cars. The setting was lovely, on a lake filled with small sailboats. Then it was on to Lucerne—even more picturesque—and Liechtenstein, all in wonderful sunny weather and very relaxing.

Word got out that there was an architectural job available in Munich, so I applied. I loved O'gau but working under a second difficult club director sapped enjoyment out of everyday life. Word came from Munich that their budget had been cut and the architectural position was eliminated, but they were impressed with my resume and offered to help me find a position in another area. Major Staley, who oversaw the Service Club at O'gau, had said he would pull strings to get me back in my profession, but I told him, "No way are you going to jeopardize your military career for me."

Staley was tall and slender with a gray crewcut—a wonderful man nicknamed "Major God Damn It" and feared by almost everyone. He came up through the ranks and prefaced all comments with "God damn it." We hit it off right away when he said, "Why are you yelling at me?" and I replied, "Because you are yelling at me!" We were good friends, and his toughness was all bluff. I promised I would not let others know he really was a softie, leaving his reputation intact. He was supporting needy children all over the world. He reminded me of the carpenters at Boeing, an older group of grandfatherly types who had expanded my education in the construction field, and he made me want to get back into architecture—as much for the camaraderie of working with men I respected as actually working on a drafting board.

❖

THE DRAFTED AND ENLISTED men assigned to O'gau were selected carefully; most if not all were college graduates. A number were married, and their wives had followed them to Europe, living on the local economy because no Army housing was provided for them. Many were happy to be with their spouses in Europe where they could travel, and most inconveniences didn't bother them. The biggest challenge was bathing because fuel to heat the water was expensive. Colleen and I had an arrangement with the wives that they could use our apartment while we were at work. Sometimes when we came home, we would find fresh baking left by our floating guests who had used the oven as well as our bathtub.

The students in the language schools were the most interesting, and the guards who sat on the East German border watching for undesirables to cross were masters of Scrabble. There was not a two- or three-letter word in the dictionary they did not know. Normally, their Army duty was quiet, but gunfire was exchanged periodically, most likely out of boredom.

The most common question the GIs asked was, "Where are you from?" When I replied, "Seattle," several said, "I know the nicest twins from Seattle." "Oh," I would say. "You were in mountain training at Camp Hale with Jim and Lou Whittaker." One GI even replied, "How big is Seattle?!" I then explained that we attended grade school together.

One Service Club regular always showed up as soon as any of us came back from a trip. He would ask: Where did you go? What hotels did you stay in? How much did housing and food cost? Tell me all about your recommendations, problems, must-see attractions, and so forth. He was a private first class from New York and he was writing a travel book for servicemen. We were delighted to see his ambition and helped all we could, bragging about our talented author to our director friends from other clubs. A lieutenant agreed to illustrate the book, which was published in O'gau. *A GI's Guidebook to Europe* by Arthur Frommer went on sale in the PX for fifty cents. I'm sure he left the Army with a nice bank account and the beginning of his successful career as the famous author of the series *Europe on Five Dollars a Day*.

❖

GLORIA AND I TOOK the overnight train from Munich to Florence one evening. We slept along the way before arriving in the morning, giving us two full days in Florence. This would be the first of several trips to our favorite Italian city. On later trips, we went shopping instead of touring architectural sites. What fun to shop in the wonderful leather shops, acquiring belts, bags, and lovely pairs of soft gloves. The markets were plentiful and grand, especially the Straw Market, which had anything imaginable made of straw. We practiced our bargaining skills to see just how low the price would go. When we had enough, we walked away, and then the vendors followed us for blocks, carrying their wares and looking like walking haystacks, determined not to lose a sale.

The Mercato Centrale had delicious displays of fruits and vegetables, in contrast to Germany, where the produce was mostly root vegetables and apples. Oh, what wonderful riches for Florence locals! Italians shop each day for their food, and everything is so fresh. The meat and fish markets often displayed their products hanging whole and raw, and completely intact rabbits and chickens hung there—minus fur and feathers, but with beady eyes and shiny toenails intact. Our favorite food was *lasagne verde*, a spinach pasta with white sauce and veal. We looked forward to eating it on every trip south.

❖

ONE EVENING the club had a professional show touring from the States that included six male cartoonists and a former Miss America contestant; while the men sketched their impressions of Europe and did portraits of the servicemen, she played the piano. Unfortunately, the beauty queen became ill and couldn't make it to our "Hilltop Lodge," so we found a GI to play the piano and I was recruited to be their model. One of the portraits of me was by a fellow named Michael Berry, whose comic strip was called "Berry's Babes" and ran in East Coast newspapers. Wow, was I glamorous! The shaggy black hair and my head position were the only recognizable features. I kept my first professional portrait.

In late May, we were off to Spain. We gathered in Ulm where Joyce met up with Gloria, Sue, and me. Two cars would go, Pinky and Genevieve, each with twenty-five gallons of gas, five five-gallon Jeep cans in their trunks, plus oil, tools, and one hundred sixty liters worth of French gas coupons. Most of us brought one small bag, but Sue, a Texan through and through, had two large bags. She had to take them both into hotels every night as she could not remember where she packed her necessary items. She was riding with Joyce, and their back seat was full of bags and a generous supply of fruit and snacks for picnics along the way. Our route took us south through Switzerland, then into France.

One sunny morning, we were enjoying a leisurely breakfast in Montpellier at a sidewalk café, when *bang*! A Frenchman had backed into Pinky, and we feared our trip was over. Most of the noise was from the damage to his car, but Pinky had lost an eye. The man got out of his car, looked at the damage he had done, hopped back in and quickly drove off amidst many shouting Frenchmen. We couldn't converse with anyone, so I decided it was a lost cause. We went back to breakfast and left Pinky with a nude eyeball. After breakfast, we traveled on, stopping to use our French gas coupons before crossing the mountain pass Le Perthus and the border into Spain.

Barcelona was our first real stop. The day after we arrived was a Sunday, the Sabbath, when many locals take a walk in the park, so we started our visit in a delightful park of historic houses and structures that had been relocated in the heart of the city. Many housed craftsmen working the old trades, making crafts like baskets and shoes. There was a food and amusement park area, where we saw a plywood cutout of a life-sized señorita doing the flamenco with her señor strumming the guitar, with their faces as open holes for tourists to fill in for photos. Joyce, who spoke Spanish, decided that we should have a photo for our memory books. She selected three older, very properly dressed businessmen among the locals and asked if they would pose with us. They were delighted, and afterward our new gentlemen friends insisted on taking us to lunch on the waterfront at a charming small restaurant with sawdust on the floor. Our hosts ordered the specialty: baby squid in their own ink sauce, which looked like thickened India ink. My girlfriends refused to try even a taste, so I enjoyed mine and shared theirs with our hosts. I worried: Would I ever get my teeth white again?

We had tickets for the bullfight, so our hosts delivered us to the ring and introduced us to their friend, the chief of police, who promised to introduce us to a real matador after the fight. Our seats were close to the ring, a somewhat dangerous location because items like bottles were tossed from behind us, sometimes falling short of their target. After the bullfight, the chief introduced us to an older, short, scarred, has-been matador—certainly nothing like the posters had promised.

The next day, we went to see the great landmark of Barcelona: architect Salvador Gaudi's Basilica de la Sagrada Familia with its famous towers. We were surprised to find little more than the towers and an empty shell. I decided that one day I would return to see the completed project. (Almost seventy years after my first visit, construction continues.) After our tour, we saw much more Gaudi, including apartment buildings, park walls and benches. We discovered his touches throughout the city.

Traveling south, the lovely coast road to Valencia was lined with orange trees. By this time, we had learned to not lock our cars at night as the locks would be broken and the car thoroughly searched. Each night we moved everything into our hotel rooms with us, except oranges or any canned orange juice that we carried for snacks along the way. We had already lost our soft drinks, cookies, candy, and canned meats meant to supplement the cheese and bread we purchased locally each day for lunch. The next night was in Cartagena, where Gloria and I made the mistake of returning to our room with some evening sweets and placing the leftovers on the table between our twin beds. In the morning we awoke to a black band on the floor about the width of the door. It made a tidy right turn, continuing along between our beds and up onto the bed table—solid black with ants. Horrified, we dressed standing on our beds and were out of the room as fast as possible. A new lesson learned.

Granada was our next important stop further south. Along the way we noted armed Spanish soldiers alongside the road; they seemed to be in the middle of nowhere, and they stopped the locals in their mule-pulled carts loaded with hay or grain. The carts were dumped and thoroughly searched for weapons; then, the farmer reloaded his material, only to likely endure the procedure again further down the road. Spain's civil war had left the country looking more war-torn than the bombed-out areas in Germany.

We arrived in Granada in early afternoon and found there were no rooms available in the Alhambra Hotel, so we went next door to a brand-new hotel, the Los Angeles. This hotel on the hill next to the fortress was only a few stories tall, and our cars were the only ones in the lot. Thank heavens for Joyce; the staff did not speak English, but she had them charmed in minutes. The four of us ended up in a lovely suite—the bridal suite, we later learned. The building was incomplete, and they had opened a portion of it while they raised funds to continue the construction. We left our belongings and were off to see the center city below. Upon our return, other cars were in front of the hotel and a Texan was having heated words with the desk clerk.

Joyce asked for our key in Spanish and we went up the stairs to the second floor, which extended around the perimeter of the building, creating a grand central space open to the large lobby below. The Texan's voice got louder as he yelled at the clerk, saying he had been there earlier when checking in, and had parked right in front. He wanted that spot back. We were almost to our room at the far end when Joyce turned around and yelled back, "Buster, if anyone gets the spot in front of the door we do, as we were here first." The Texan was quieted, the problem was solved, and Joyce became the darling of the hotel staff.

I noted there was still work to be done to the building. Joyce mentioned to the manager that I was an architect, and he insisted on taking me on a tour of the unfinished section. This low-rise hotel actually cascaded down the cliff another ten to twelve stories. The swimming pool and terrace would be at the bottom. The structural work was completed for a very substantial hotel when money allowed. My tour went for several hours, so my friends breathed a sigh of relief when I resurfaced.

The Alhambra fortress was a highlight of Spain. The weather was perfect and a sense of quiet and serenity prevailed through the beautiful gardens. Tourists were few and we felt that we had it all to ourselves. The Court of Lions in the harem section provided a bit of amusement when a woman slipped and sat down blocking the flow of water in the small trough that leads from pool to pool. Arabic architecture uses these features in most major buildings because the sound of a little water running is soothing to the soul, especially in warm climates. Besides flooding the courtyard, this well-dressed woman had a very wet backside. If this was harem life, it was most pleasant. It was hard to leave this handsome Moorish structure.

Back at the hotel the manager had invited us out to an evening of entertainment in what were called the "Gypsy Caves," the Roma community of Sacromonte. They are caves from the exterior, but the interiors look like standard houses with an arched rock ceiling. A performance featured flamenco and other styles of dance, accompanied by food and drink. Would we like our palms read? Joyce immediately said yes because she could understand the palm reader and would not need her fortune translated. She told Joyce some interesting things about herself and said she could see her making a long trip over the ocean soon. Joyce replied, "Of course," because our nationality was obvious, and we would be returning home in about eleven months. No, the trip would be soon, she was told! We had such a wonderful time that we stayed an extra night. Then it was time to move on and the staff insisted on

Jane and Joyce in a "Gypsy Cave"

having a going-away party for us. They said we had been their first customers and were considered very special. After too much food and drink, and in no condition to drive, we left the city and drove just far enough to find some open countryside, where we pulled off the road and all had a good nap. Our Granada friends did not want to let us go. I believe that we were not charged for our evening at the caves. We were the guests of the manager.

❖

WE DROVE ALONG THE COAST through Malaga and on to Gibraltar for a quick visit to see the monkeys on the rock before leaving our cars and boarding the boat for Tangier. I believe we purchased the cheapest tickets, but within a few minutes Joyce had made friends with a senior officer, and we were up in first class. Once off the boat in Tangier, we were surrounded by hotel representatives and cab drivers all pulling us to try and make a deal. Joyce took charge, making them line up and present their best offer. Then, she selected a hotel, and we were on our way. We were in a land of veils and beggars, just like in the movies. The market square was filled with older women, veiled with only their eyes showing, who were determined to sell us their wares. I stepped back to get an overall photo of the market, and as soon as I raised my camera a potato bounced off my head. The veiled ladies were good shots! When they got excited, they sometimes let loose of the veil to yell or throw a rock or their wares. Their faces revealed their age, hard work, and lack of dental care.

Of course, we had to visit the casbah where heiress Barbara Hutton had a house. We hired a car to take us to Spanish Morocco, which required visas we did not have, but Joyce talked to the border guards, and we were in and made our way to Ceuta, a village Joyce wanted to show us from her earlier travels. Then, we were on to the boat for our return trip to Gibraltar. We discovered that, while getting into Spanish

Morocco was not difficult, Joyce had to give an Oscar-worthy performance to talk our way back out. From then on, we would get visas first.

We followed the coastal route, bound for Seville with its wonderful Moorish architecture. There, we found a melding of two cultures, with the cathedral built on the foundations of the old mosque while incorporating parts of it, including the minarets, into the newer structure. I was in awe of the height and volume of the space. Around the large public square, small orange trees by the hundreds outlined open spaces. We were there at the height of the season, so the trees were covered with small orange balls, creating a festive look. Apparently, no one picks the oranges because they are the bitter ones, used to make marmalade. Oh, there was so much to see in so little time!

But we needed to get back on the road and pay attention to our cars, Pinky and Genevieve. With the weather heating up, we decided to check the water level in the car batteries. We stopped at a small village, where we purchased bread for our lunch at the community outdoor clay/stone baking oven and checked under the bonnets (hoods). Yes, the batteries needed water, so Joyce took off in search of distilled water. She eventually found it in a pharmacy. Then, she had to locate another store to purchase a bottle, which she carried back to the pharmacy for the water. Cars were rare in this village and when we raised the bonnets on our English cars, the residents turned out to see what was inside. When the crowd got too large, a policeman arrived to hold the people back while we poured water into something under the hood. One of my favorite travel photos was of Joyce, a fair-sized girl, working under the hood of a small car while under police protection.

Toledo was next, the home of El Greco, one of my favorite artists. We arrived on a religious holiday to find façades covered with large drapes about the size of ample bedspreads. Everyone seemed to be in the streets or hanging out the windows to take in the music and festivities. We visited the cathedral with throngs of locals and were sorry to leave before we even found out what the occasion was.

In Madrid we called on my high school friend and first college roommate, Jacy Lane, who was pregnant with her first child. Her husband, Lyle, was working there on assignment for the U.S. State Department, and he introduced us to the huge, modern city, where we took in the Prado Museum and the cathedral. But we were running out of travel time and needed to get back to work. We drove north to San Sebastian on the Bay of Biscay, and I was happy to be back on a road running along the sea. I'm sure I was the only one who needed a fresh breath of salt air. We left Spain behind and set our sights on returning to Ulm.

❖

BACK IN O'GAU, it was June, but the rains lingered. There was some good news: Jenny had asked for a transfer, and we would soon have a new club director. When a clear day came, Vivienne, photo instructor Gunther, and I climbed the mountain behind the club. In a meadow on top, we made lunch in a herder's hut. These small mountain cabins were never locked and were supplied with food staples. Gunther made us soup and built a fire to dry out our clothes. After a pleasant meal and rest, we cleaned up and left some money for the food and fuel before returning down the mountain.

The village cows would regularly pass through our neighborhood on their way up to the meadows for the day, and their bells served as our alarm clocks. Each morning, a herder collected the cows from the houses, where they typically occupied the lower floor, living indoors protected from the first frost from about early October until April or May, when there is no longer a chance of frost. All the land in the valley was used for raising hay, which farmers harvested several times a season, whenever they had a dry spell between rains. In the early evening the cows would return. Often one of them would have a garland of flowers in her horns, as it was her "Name Day." Instead of birthdays, Bavarians celebrate name days, so all the Bettys or Marys celebrate together. On their way home, each cow would each peel off from the herd in the main road and return to her own house.

Our post was the former home of the German mountain troops and was perched on the side of a mountain that held a lot of history. O'gau has hosted productions of the *Passion Play* since the seventeenth century, and just down the road a bit was the Ettal Monastery, so it was assumed to be a strong religious center. During World War II, O'gau displayed a giant red cross marking a hospital station. It apparently was convincing as it was never bombed. After the war, the Bavarian area became part of the American zone. One day during an inspection a German hand grenade was discovered among a GI's souvenirs. The GI said he'd found it in a cave in the mountain, where there were a lot of grenades. The cave revealed a major tunnel system corkscrewing through the mountain to the valley floor below. The tunnel served as a Messerschmitt aircraft factory, with supplies entering in O'gau and the finished product coming out at the foot of the mountain. When I drove from Munich to Garmisch, the road followed the valley floor except in one section, where it curved over to the foot of the mountain and then through a tunnel. This seemed strange, as did the three large patches on the mountainside inside the tunnel. The patches were actually sealed doors where the finished planes came out when it was safe to take off. The highways were also designed as runways for the aircraft. I was always amazed at the tunneling that took place during the Nazi years.

❖

LIVING IN A RESORT brought a constant stream of friends to stay in my mountain nest, and our apartment was a magnet for entertaining locals, too. Before Nancy Klein returned home, she came for a farewell visit to play and swim. She claimed that the only home-cooked meal she enjoyed during her year in Europe was at our apartment. Another visitor was my friend Estelle Radin, who I had seen frequently during my Nuremberg days. She was stationed in Bamberg, and we decided we would take the train together to Copenhagen later in the summer. In the meantime, our new club director, Kitty Fouty, had arrived and seemed very promising. These rainy July days meant no water skiing—just farewell parties for departing students, staff, and other personnel.

In August, Estelle and I traveled to Copenhagen. The evening we arrived, we signed up to stay in a private home for $1.40 per night for two, including breakfast. We could walk to the city center, so we started at Tivoli, the fabulous 135-year-old amusement park. The entrance fee of twenty-five cents gave us access to twenty-five restaurants, a stage, a concert shell, and a concert hall. The wonderful music seemed to be everywhere in the beautiful two-square-block park of gardens illuminated by colored lights. At midnight a tremendous fireworks display closed the park until the next day. We took a tour up to North Zealand and the Kronborg Castle, better known as the Elsinore of Shakespeare's *Hamlet*. It wasn't very ornate and was one of the nicest castles I had visited to date.

We also saw a good deal of the coastline—and of course, the *Little Mermaid*, who was smaller than expected. Finally, it was time to shop, which we did enthusiastically, purchasing stainless-steel flatware for myself and a friend in Seattle. The food was great, and the ice cream was the richest I have ever tasted. The flaky pastries oozed with butter—heavenly. Of course, we were encouraged to drink lots of beer, because the state-owned brewery profits all went to support the arts. One of the most memorable sights: beautiful, well-dressed women smoking great big, fat cigars. We returned home with sunburns after experiencing the warmest weather since arriving in Europe.

Colleen's mother came to visit from Scotland, so Colleen gave up her master bedroom and moved into my room. Mother Jean was delightful with her strong accent, and I was glad she was spending time with her daughter. When we had moved into our apartment, I had been sick and dragging, and Colleen had just lost her Austrian boyfriend, whom she had planned to marry. The couple had intended to emigrate to Canada, but he had died of a heart attack while hiking. Mother and daughter had never spent much time together because Collen had attended girls boarding schools in England while her parents lived abroad, up until World War II. Each morning during this visit, Colleen was up early making tea, which she served to her mother in bed.

Because Colleen did not have a car, the three of us made several short trips together. The first was to Salzburg for the Mozart Festival. We were fortunate to have an "in" and stayed in an old hunting lodge on Wolfgangsee Lake. We had a wonderful evening enjoying *The Magic Flute* with contemporary sets that probably would have made Mozart cringe. The music and costumes were outstanding, and the unique opera house used an old cliff of catacombs as the back of the stage, allowing the performers to suddenly pop out of the wall—perfect for this opera. Colleen and I could not resist an early-morning dip in the lake, where the water temperature was chilled by melting ice.

Our next outing with Mother Jean took us to Venice, where Connie joined us for a few days. We found a hotel just off St. Mark's Square, convenient for sightseeing, but not for sleeping as the tenors performed all night walking the adjacent streets. The public square is full of people and pigeons and is so large that six to eight bands can play at the same time and not interfere with each other. What a wonderful, lively, peaceful place to spend twenty-four hours. Where else could a person forget that cars even exist? They are all parked in a large garage at the edge of the city, where water transportation takes over. We took a balmy nighttime gondola ride through the canals, never needing a sweater. When the clock sounded the hour to feed the pigeons, the sky turned almost black as thousands of birds gathered in the square for their seeds. We took in all the "architectural musts," including St. Mark's Cathedral and several others that architectural students are required to sketch for their classwork.

❖

IN MID-SEPTEMBER the fields around O'gau were filled with lavender and pink autumn crocuses. The first snowstorm was followed by a return to lovely fall weather, but the cows would soon be locked up inside for the long, cold winter months. I finally did get in some water skiing, and when we crossed the German/Austrian border, the border guard was upset that I only had one ski on top of my car. He was sure I had lost the other one somewhere along the way. Water skiing was still very new in the area and skiing on just one ski seemed to irritate egos, especially those of men.

The Service Club in Garmisch was closed, so we were busy accounting for supplies and property. Summer 1955 was the tenth anniversary of the American occupation of Germany, and the U.S. was returning property to the Germans, except for Nazi Party facilities. We were now subject to local laws, and we had been warned about potential conflicts. For example, the Americans had always enforced speed limits in populated areas, but the Germans drove at full speed, riding your bumper and cutting in front of you for no reason other than to show off, especially to our woman drivers. Few German women drove. Driving was a matter of male honor!

❖

THAT OCTOBER, my friend Connie and I headed to France for an eleven-day tour with our *Sir Banister Fletcher* architectural guide in hand to be sure our facts were right. Our first night was in Mannheim with Joyce, then on to Verdun, where we spent a night with Pat, a friend from Nuremberg. We were treated to dinner, a dance and all-night conversation catching up with news of our friends. The next day we toured the Verdun battlefields on our way to Rheims to see the cathedral before continuing to Paris, where we could enjoy another free night at an apartment owned by the family of Alain, one of our French officers at O'gau. Alain was from French Morocco, where his mother was the head of the museum, and one of his younger sisters, Barbarina, was in Paris studying at the Louvre. She didn't speak English, but Alain had told her we were coming. We arrived after dark, and when she opened the door, fortunately she looked like her brother. "Barbarina?" I asked. "Jane?" she replied. And that was all we could understand of each other. She was a lovely host, making coffee and leaving fresh rolls from the bakery along with a key before she went to the Louvre in the morning.

After sightseeing in Paris, we drove north to Amiens and its cathedral, and then to Rouen, where we had a good sleep in a plush hotel. We rose early to go to Mont

Saint-Michel, the famous monastery on the island. Because of the narrow roads, more like passageways, cars are out of the question. We left Pinky in the lot below the entrance while we climbed the hill to the small monastery, which was well-sited for protection.

Next, we drove south to see the many chateaus of the Loire Valley. Then we found our way to the most handsome Gothic cathedral of all: Chartres Cathedral. It felt like we could spend days looking up at the beautiful stained-glass windows, and it was a joy to sit there, staring up into the vaulted ceiling with the sun streaming in.

Back at the Paris apartment for a three-night stay, Barbarina greeted us with several English-speaking friends from the Louvre. They brought food and we had a grand evening of conversation, chattering and questions. We organized our plans to see all the Parisian monuments such as the Opera House, Notre Dame Cathedral, and the Arc de Triomphe, in the most efficient manner. Philippe, our other French officer assigned to O'gau, was home visiting his parents, so he invited us to go sight-seeing and picked us up in the family Citroën. I was familiar with these French cars, but I had never seen one with the engine hood much longer than the cab section and a gold plate with the family crest and name on the door. It was impressive! We took in the Invalides, a beautiful building that houses Napoleon's tomb, the Pan-théon, and numerous other sites. Then we wondered, shouldn't we go to the Eiffel Tower? I assured our host that he need not take up his valuable time with us, and we could go on our own. Then Philippe confessed that he had never been up the tower and wouldn't we please take him along? The three of us rode the elevators as far as possible and then walked up the stairs to the top level.

The following day, Barbarina took us shopping in a neighborhood outside the touristed area where the prices were better. On the way back, we were told there was a shortcut back via "the no-good street." This sounded like a good idea, so off we went, with the three of us walking up the middle of the street. It was a long block or so with no traffic, and we had hardly started when the prostitutes came out of their houses of business on both sides of the street, yelling and hissing at us. We simply walked faster, realizing we had experienced a part of Paris that most people miss.

Finally, we heard from some of those whom we had left messages for at the em-bassy, and we had an invitation from Noel, my general friend. We enjoyed lunch in a nice dining room, but we were constantly interrupted by women who came over to speak to Noel. He had told me the reason he had never married was he did not want to subject a woman he loved to a military life. Of course, he was perhaps the best catch in Europe and every single woman in government service or an elected position looked him up when in Paris. Were we, the two new girls in town, a threat? He apologized, saying he should have taken us to a place with fewer Americans. We agreed to get together on his next trip to O'gau. However, I did not return to Paris, nor he to O'gau, before I returned to Seattle.

One day years later, I was reading a book about the "Red Tails," the Tuskegee Airmen, and was surprised to see the book included General Parrish's name and his great admiration of the 99th Fighter Squadron, the Black pilots group. This inspired me to research the man who was my most interesting date ever. As the Tuskegee Airmen's commander, Noel had fought—with the support of Eleanor Roosevelt—for their right to fly. I knew he was born, raised, and educated in the South, and joined the Army in 1930 because he was hungry and could not find a job. But he had not told me much about his military life. He was a man of true integrity who believed Black people could fly as well as whites, and their war performance helped lay the groundwork for President Harry Truman's desegregation of the U.S. military in 1948 and later the civil rights movement. The most prestigious award of the association of Tuskegee Airmen was named the Brigadier General Noel F. Parrish Award in his honor. Noel retired from the military in 1964, married and became a college professor. He died in 1987 and rests at Arlington National Cemetery, and his papers are housed in the National Archives.

❖

IT WAS TIME TO SAY thanks and goodbye to Barbarina and move on to Fontainebleau and Belfort. Nearby in Ronchamp, we visited Le Corbusier's new small masterpiece chapel perched on top of a hill with magnificent views in all directions. It was almost finished, and work continued with several monks whitewashing the exterior surface. We were early surprise guests and photographed both the exterior and the unique interior plan, which provided worship spaces for individuals and small groups, as well as the larger main space. Under the sloping hat brim of a roof was a door accessing a balcony pulpit to serve an outside mass or gathering. Other than the chickens running about and a couple of monks, we had this architectural icon all to ourselves.

The holiday season was drawing close, and more people were leaving the post, so parties were in order. Alain, our French interpreter officer and an anthropologist, was being sent to the African front because of his fluency in Arabic, as well as

French, German, English, and Spanish. His parting words were, "I'm not a soldier, I'm a lover." I have no idea what happened to him.

I spent Thanksgiving with Connie and a few friends, and looked forward to the possibility that skiing could start any day. We seemed to be stuck in a cycle of snow, rain, snow, rain. Would I ever have a chance to wear my new Bogner stretch pants, the hottest new item on the slopes? When I purchased them, I insisted that they not be skin-tight even though German women wore theirs tight. This amused the shopkeeper, a former Olympic skier, who referred to me as "the American with the baggy pants."

Colleen and I procured a good-sized tree, which we decorated with real candles. Of course, they were against the rules, but Colleen insisted that she always had candles and they were so beautiful. Christmas preparations also had me shopping for family and friends back home; so many packages had to be sent! Then I packed up many of the things I had collected in a footlocker, which my friend Gertrude Meriwether would take back to Seattle. I had turned down a promotion to club director and was eager to return to my real career—architecture—before UW graduation when there would be more competition for jobs. It would be very expensive to get my belongings home.

The traditional Christmas Eve parade started at the edge of town, with choirboys in robes singing while carrying lighted candles on long sticks enclosed in paper stars that rotated from the candle heat. They walked behind the horse-drawn, wedge-shaped wooden snowplow, and people came out of their houses to follow on their way to church. The sky had cleared after too many snowy days, the moon and stars were out, and the village was the perfect Christmas card scene. I would never enjoy another Christmas Eve as magical as 1955.

Finally, everyone packed into the church chest-to-chest; with all the swinging incense pots, we could hardly breathe, even though from the waist down it was bitter cold. The cold from the icy stone floor gradually cooled our feet, then crept up our legs. After the service and back in our warm home, we received a telephone call inviting us to a cocktail party at one of the officers' residences. We explained that we had some enlisted men with us, so protocol was forgotten for the evening, and we all went to the party.

Christmas dinner in our apartment was a big success; the 24 original invited participants expanded to include another dozen or so who showed up at our door from Garmisch, plates and flatware in hand. In addition to the turkey, ham, and trimmings prepared by the wives' group, we had the extra treat of homemade candy and cookies sent from Seattle. We topped it off by singing carols and lighting the tree candles, a first for most present and a vision never to be forgotten.

Finally, the snow came down seriously, too seriously. Some of the roads were closed and we—the Service Club at the top of the hill—would be the last to be plowed out. After days of assuming the plows would arrive soon, I gave up and decided to have a program for the troops that included a snowball fight. The South and the North would go back to war, with the two teams decked out in identifying banners. Once hit, you would be carried in by stretcher to the Service Club for a hospital treatment of hot chocolate and cookies. Eventually one team would win, and all would be enjoying the refreshments in the Club. The boys were excited about the program, borrowing gloves and extra clothing for our grand evening under floodlights. We used a small balcony as a referee station to oversee the activity in the parking lot. We were well stocked with food, and everything looked promising with a clear night forecast. I arrived for my one o'clock shift at the Club to find that after a week, they had plowed our roads and my snow was gone! Distraught, I headed for Major Staley's office to plead for my snow back. Shaking his head, he phoned the motor pool, instructing them to truck snow back up the mountain to the Club parking lot. They, of course, thought he was kidding. The program was a huge success, but the motor pool boys never let me forget it.

❖

OUR NEW CLUB DIRECTOR, Kitty, had received a puppy as a Christmas present, but two days later went ice skating and broke her kneecap. So, I took on mothering an eight-week-old puppy, mopping up, feeding, and petting. I'm sure he didn't think I was a good substitute for his own mother. It was the end of the year, so all kinds of reports were due, and I did that work plus covering the Club without Kitty and with a puppy in a box going back and forth. Word came from headquarters that I was being promoted to club director and would be stationed in France—prompting me to reveal my plans to quit right after the Olympic Games and return home to my real career. As my time was short, they left me in O'gau and I started planning to attend the Winter Olympics in Cortina, Italy.

I had made reservations and paid for Olympic housing and tickets through proper Italian channels, so it seemed all was in order, and this was to be Pinky's last

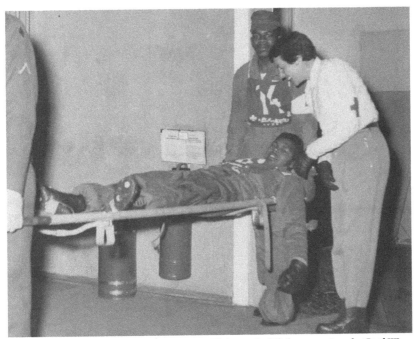

Jane attending to a participant in a Service Club snowball fight reenacting the Civil War

major trip. I had decided that there was too much red tape to take my beloved car home, so I had promised my friend Peggy I would sell Pinky to her. Just as we were ready to leave, word came that my paid reservation in Cortina had been canceled and I would receive a refund after the Games. Thank heavens for a car, as now we would have to stay outside of the immediate area. Fortunately, we found a place with a French girl who needed a ride into Cortina. Her payment for the ride was to charm the Italian guard at the town entrance to let us in, because the parking area was a long distance from the activities. She was very good, getting us in each day, but then spent the rest of each day playing hide-and-seek from the guard she had promised favors to.

Cortina had a big problem: no snow. That year in much of Europe, the snow was so sparse that it was like skiing on grass, and I even had grass stains on my new stretch pants. All you need to do is plan to host the Winter Olympics, and it will be the first time in 100 years that you do not see snow. The Italian Army was busy filling train cars full of snow and hauling it into Cortina. The main street through town had a snow-packed sidewalk down the middle of the street so skiers could be filmed sliding through the village. The races were moved way up into the mountains, so anyone holding tickets for the viewing stands had wasted their money.

My skiing friend, Janet Burr, was supposed to be on the U.S. team, but she was injured. However, another former skiing friend, Dottie Sorter, was on the team. She invited us to the hotel where the Americans were housed. She had a television so we could watch what was happening way up on the mountainside. It was great fun sharing some time with our athletes. Toward the end of the Games, the snow came and with it the real winter set in. We went from too little to too much snow, and in Austria, avalanches destroyed two villages. This was the weather we would drive home through.

Outside the Innsbruck Valley, there was a major hill that was a thrill to drive even in the best weather. At the top, a huge billboard with skull and crossbones warned drivers in all languages of extreme danger and cautioned us to use the lowest gear. This was the hill we had to go up! The foot of the hill was full of cars that could not make it. Pinky, being light, had always been good on snow and somehow just stayed on top of it. So up we went. We took it slow and steady, inching our way to the top. We could hardly believe it.

Back in O'gau I still had vacation time, which I had planned to spend on the French Riviera. However, the Riviera was buried in a foot of snow and the hotels had no heating systems, so I retreated to Garmisch to spend my last days skiing before heading north to start my journey home. With most of my things packed or sent stateside, February 20, 1956, was my date to leave for Norway and Sweden before boarding the *Stockholm*, an icebreaker bound for the U.S. While in Cortina I had met a Swedish newspaper reporter; when I told him I was going home on the *Stockholm*, he gasped, "Oh no, it is the worst roller afloat." "Great!" I thought.

The current weather report in Sweden: 41 degrees below zero.

❖

IT WAS TIME TO SAY GOODBYE to Oberammergau and begin traveling home. I wondered if I would ever return to this charming Bavarian village that would always hold so many special memories. On February 20, I caught an evening train from Munich to Mannheim, where I spent the night with Joyce. We ate her fresh-baked gingerbread while we reminisced about our 22 months together. My last German dinner was with Joyce at the Red Ox Inn in Heidelberg before boarding the train for Hamburg and then another for Copenhagen. At Grossenbrode, the train went onto the ferry for a ride that took twice as long as scheduled because they were blasting the ice to make a channel. While in Copenhagen, I ran into a student from Munich who I recognized, so we enjoyed a fish dinner on the waterfront together. Traveling alone turned out to not be lonely!

The next train ride, crossing to Stockholm, required more blasting of the ice. Stockholm turned out to be somewhat warmer than expected—maybe only 30 degrees below zero—but the locals seemed downright frosty and unfriendly. That evening, I found a new American movie playing, *Interrupted Melody* with Eleanor Parker and Glenn Ford, and I decided that they would be friendly, even if the film was dubbed in Swedish. It was in English, and I enjoyed it so much that I watched it twice. Afterward, looking across the sea toward Finland, I could see small fires all over the frozen channel where skaters were camping out while skating between the two countries.

My last stop was Oslo, where I enjoyed some window shopping. Norway was still suffering after the war and there was little money to spend, but my fellow window shoppers seemed happy and outgoing. Norway also had the wonderful smell of saltwater that I had been missing. I stayed at the Hotel Viking used by athletes for the 1952 Winter Games, where the room was tiny, but the location was great. I took the city tour, but I was running out of time. I would be sailing out of Göteborg, Sweden, on March 1. Norway was another addition to my "must visit again" list.

Once in Göteborg, in the steamship's office window I saw a model of the *Stockholm* with fins coming out of each side of the hull. The "worst roller afloat" now had stabilizers to control the roll. I felt better, as I knew this was going to be a challenging crossing. The ice was too thick for the ship to make a planned stop at Copenhagen, so those departing passengers had been sent by train to board in Göteborg. I had the top bunk in a cabin near the stern, where the bunks went crosswise of the ship. Most bunks run bow to stern, so this must have been the bargain cabin, but as it worked out, this was a blessing. From Göteborg to Bremerhaven, our progress was slow as we cut our way through the ice with more reverse action than noticeable forward motion. I had a cabin to myself, so I assumed that my roommate would board in Bremerhaven and be German.

Our day in Bremerhaven was a special day, March 3—my birthday—and friends from O'gau, club director Kitty Fouty and 1st Lt. Jim Delevett, had braved the elements and driven north to see me off. While in O'gau, I had dated Jim while

Kitty was dating a captain, and the four of us often went out together. Jim and Kitty had always loved to dance together, and the captain and I had often said they should be dating each other.

They brought me a bottle of Champagne and a bouquet of daffodils, which had frozen on their short walk to the ship. I thought I would never see Jim or Kitty again, so it was an emotional goodbye. I told Jim—as I had many times in the past—that I was not interested in marriage. Home and my architectural career came first.

After we had all returned to the U.S., Jim and Kitty reunited and married. I visited them in their Florida home in 1993, Both of them passed a few years later.

❖

WE ARRIVED IN NEW YORK CITY on March 12, 1956, during a blizzard, late at night, several days behind schedule. And I arrived with an expired passport. I knew when I left Europe that I had about two days of grace if we arrived on schedule, so I got off with a mere scolding. All transportation connections had to be rearranged, but within a few days, I began working my way across the country, stopping to see friends along the way. I knew once I was home that it would be a long time before I could afford to travel again. The sale of Pinky gave me enough funds for traveling west and a trip to Mexico with Mervane Murray, a friend from my Boeing days.

I started my U.S. journey with Southern belle Gloria Perkins in Atlanta. We slipped right back into our travel routine, trying to see everything in the shortest amount of time. Atlanta was a city of Colonial and Georgian-style residences, and a detour took us past a house that belonged to an architect and resembled an early version of the contractor-built houses constructed in Seattle suburbs after World War II. The folks in Georgia thought it was "way out," but it struck me as a common Pacific Northwest suburban style.

We visited Stone Mountain and saw a lot of red clay as Gloria and Mary Lou Taylor, also from Atlanta, gave a running narration on the wonders of Georgia. Along the way, they tried to break my habits of shaking hands with everyone and eating with my left hand. While shopping, I noticed the stores were filled with new gadgets in bright colors like yellow and turquoise—even the floor mops and dustpans. It looked like the Easter bunny had taken over. The department stores were full of beautiful women dressed in the latest fashions, and I felt like a peasant just off the farm. In Europe, no matter how we dressed, we had always been more fashion-forward than local women. As Mary Lou said, "In Europe you could be in your oldest clothes and still be the best-dressed woman on the street, while at home you felt like a peasant in your best clothes."

Gloria and I drove to Savannah so I could meet her parents. The azaleas were in bloom all along the way, as well as the dogwood trees. The Perkinses were delightful, but the real highlight, other than Savannah itself, was that we were there on St. Patrick's Day. The street was painted green and there was an unending parade of partiers, all African Americans, in full costume and marching with numerous bands.

On my final evening, Gloria and Mary Lou hosted a dinner for me at the famous Aunt Fannie's Shack. What a feast! We enjoyed great quantities of a thick soup, corn muffins, tossed salad, fried chicken, corn pudding, baked squash, turnip greens, rice and gravy, biscuits, coffee, and pecan pie. The next day, I was on my way to the airport at 7 a.m.

❖

MARY LOU WORKED FOR DELTA AIRLINES, and she had arranged all my plane tickets to the West Coast. The next stop was Lexington, Kentucky, for a short visit with my friend Alice from Boeing. Alice's husband, Dick, was away on business, so we girls toured about and went to a famous restaurant where I tried Smithfield ham. I think it is something you appreciate more if you grow up with it, but I felt my introduction to Southern food was complete, now that I had tried black-eyed peas, grits, hush puppies, and the ham. Lexington was beautiful and we toured one of the horse farms it is famous for. A special treat was a visit to Ashland, the estate owned by the nineteenth-century statesman Henry Clay; his sister was one of my great-great-great-grandmothers.

Cleveland was my next stop, to catch up with a Service Club friend, Nancy Klein. I arrived late and that first night, we stayed up until 4 a.m. looking at photo albums and talking. The next day, we went out with two of Nancy's friends who had also been stationed in Germany. At a German restaurant with Bavarian-costumed servers, the four of us ate and drank beer and sang German songs, feeling almost like we were back in Europe. We did not get home until 5 a.m. Late Sunday afternoon Nancy and a friend drove me through a blizzard down to Kent to the home of Vivienne Bruce, another friend from our crowd.

Monday morning Vivienne and her husband went off to work and school, so I covered the town and Kent State campus on foot. Later in the day, a group of us drove to check out the newer pieces of architecture in the Akron area. The residents thought their architecture was great, but those of us with West Coast standards wouldn't even put the buildings in the modern architecture period. I also had a fine time cooking while Viv was working, and I also sewed on some curtains in progress, which made me feel useful after all the pampering from my friends' mothers.

❖

I WAS FINALLY BACK on the West Coast. In Los Angeles, I called home to assure my parents that I was getting closer and that I was safely tucked in at Anne and Louis Warren's house. When I had left Seattle almost two years earlier, Anne was still working on some of our after-hours architectural projects. Anne's husband was an entertainer, so while I was in Europe, they had moved to LA for better job opportunities.

A few days after I arrived, my friend Estelle Radin, another former Service Club girl, joined Anne and me for shopping and a tour of the UCLA campus—Estelle's alma mater—as well as some luxurious houses. The next day, we visited the lovely Wayfarers Chapel designed by Lloyd Wright in Rancho Palos Verdes. That night, Estelle and I stayed up late going over slides, photos, and stories of our days in Europe.

LA offered the opportunity to catch up with more friends, including my college roommate Shirley Cooke ("Cookie"), who was at Los Angeles General Hospital doing her medical internship. She joined me and Mervane Murray for dinner the night before Mervane and I drove south to Mexico.

❖

MERVANE AND I HAD PLANNED our trip via mail while I was still in Europe. As we started out, we drove past newly opened Disneyland, which we rejected due to the high entrance price of $2.50. We drove on through orange groves to Palm Springs, a fabulous place. By now, it was really hot and Palm Springs had the most expensive motels anywhere, at $25 per night. We retreated to the outskirts where we found a good deal at a motel managed by an old friend of Mervane's.

On April 8, we crossed from California into Arizona, planning to return on April 19 and be back to Seattle by April 28. The day we crossed the Mexican border at Nogales, we were among throngs of travelers. We were supposed to purchase our tourist cards and auto insurance there, but the border station waved us through because most travelers only cross for the day. This sort-of-a-free-city concept—with no border checks or questions—was new to us. We thought there would be another station after Nogales, and we were right, but they didn't do paperwork, so back we went through the tourist-mad city to demand that they look at our papers. After an hour and a half of white toothy smiles and flirting, we were able to get our required stamps and luggage stickers.

The roads south were better than I expected, as were the drivers—a treat after my European experiences. The cattle and other animals were all fenced out, instead of in, which really rattled Mervane. I was doing all the driving, and I assured her that I was used to animals on the road: The cows and horses usually move slowly, while the pigs and goats are the frisky ones that dart out at any time.

It took multiple attempts over our first two days—and driving more than one hundred thirty-five miles—to find a clean and beautiful motel, finally, in Culiacan. The problem: It was fully booked. As it was getting late, the nice manager couldn't turn away a couple of young women, so he called a friend and arranged for us to stay in her home. It was very dark as we followed a boy on a bike into the city center. The road suddenly dropped down and it felt like I was driving over a dry riverbed (which turned out to be correct). Then we drove up into a part of the town with only a few streetlights. We stopped in front of what looked like old barn doors. The boy rang a bell, and a pleasant older woman came to welcome us. We found ourselves in a lovely tiled space that wrapped around a beautiful central courtyard garden filled with fragrant roses. It was late, so we were shown to our very comfortable bedroom, which had a bathroom shower entirely open to the sky.

The next morning, we got a better look at our hosts' home when we were served breakfast at the edge of the garden. The entire house was a walled-in garden with only the sleeping rooms and baths having any privacy. The only means of closing off the living spaces from the garden and weather were light curtains dropping from the ceiling. It was one of the oldest houses in town and faced onto the village square. This lovely large block park was surrounded by the cathedral on one side, official buildings, a school, and several similar houses. I noticed a table with reading material, which included an American architectural magazine. I commented on the magazine and our hostess said her son was a structural engineer who also practiced architecture and she was sure he would like to meet me. Our accommodations were so comfortable, we decided to stay another night.

Late in the afternoon our hosts' engineer son knocked on our door. We were not the only guests in the house; apparently a Los Angeles fruit buyer was a regular guest and a friend of the landlords' son. The two men decided to entertain us for the evening. The engineer's uncle owned the best ice cream parlor in town, so we started with healthy portions of ice cream and then went sightseeing. The engineer was proud to show his work, which included the governor's house up on top of a hill. As we approached the house, we were confronted by heavily armed guards; at the front door seven guards were stationed. The governor wasn't even in town, but we learned later that the former governor had been shot, which explained the security.

The next day, we headed to Mazatlán, promising to come back and stay again on our way north. In Mazatlán, we booked ourselves into the only multistory (three floors) hotel, on the waterfront at the center of the harbor. After parking the car, we walked through the city and surrounding area with a nice woman guide. Just out of town, there was a delightful collection of large rocks in the ocean; someone with a real design sense had built bridges, stairs and platforms connecting them. It was a wonderful place to enjoy the crashing waves and the refreshing ocean spray.

Mervane and I discovered fresh shrimp, one of their major industries, which we enjoyed at every meal, including breakfast. This was a great place, so we decided, why continue to Mexico City? It was an easy decision: less driving, more beach time, and more shrimp. We had air mattresses, which were great for sunbathing while bobbing along on small waves. We used them in a lovely cove close to the hotel, which had a lifeguarded beach. One day as we floated, not paying attention to the tide, I was surprised when the lifeguard swam out to grab the corner of my air mattress and drag me closer to shore. I gather I was headed for an ocean voyage. Too soon, time ran out and we had to head for home.

❖

AS PROMISED, Culiacan was our first stop as we traveled north. We were back in our lovely room when our gentlemen friends called to say we had a date. It was Carnival—festival time in the town—so off we went to dinner, shows, and a cockfight. It didn't take long for Merv and me to realize we were being used. Our engineer friend was the most eligible bachelor in town, and he was flaunting us in front of the young local women who would give almost anything for a date with him. It got to the point that we became a bit worried for our safety. We were glad when we finally returned to our room. The next morning, we were back on the road, but by way of the railroad station, where we met our fruit buyer for a watermelon to enjoy on our trip north. He selected one that was too ripe to ship, and it was probably the most delicious melon I ever ate.

The sun followed us up across the Arizona border, and as we neared Phoenix, I decided we should look for Taliesin West, Frank Lloyd Wright's winter home and studio. As I turned off the highway, Merv asked where I was going as she did not see any signs. I assured her there was one, just a red square on a little board. Arriving at the school we were greeted by a student reporting that they were closed, packing up for their return to Spring Green, Wisconsin, and Taliesin East. He let us prowl around with a warning to look out for snakes. The frayed canvas roofs did not look as if they would make it through another season.

The Grand Canyon was our next destination. The drive was easy but once we started going up into the mountains the temperature plummeted. By the time we arrived in our shorts, sleeveless tops, and sandals, we were in several inches of snow.

In Las Vegas, we were fascinated by the hotels, where rooms were rented for ten hours instead of twenty-four. The night shift was cheaper as most serious gamblers were up all night and slept in the daytime. A nighttime room was fine with us, and we went off to the gaming halls. We selected a casino where Johnny Ray was performing. The shows were all free; plus, when you were gambling, they offered free drinks. Johnny was from Portland and went to high school with my friend Jean MacDonald, who was a pianist, as well as now-movie star Jane Powell. The three of them entertained servicemen during the war. I believe we had budgeted five dollars each for our evening at the slots; this kept us busy for hours. A quick night of sleep and we were off to Bakersfield. Then, we made it to San Mateo to stay with Grandma Bessie Belle, Aunt Lois and Uncle Clarence.

From San Mateo we headed for San Francisco, where we both got haircuts, and Merv got a permanent. Hopefully, our families back home would recognize us. While waiting for Merv, I walked around downtown and checked out every piece of fabric in The City of Paris store. I had to rest my feet awhile before taking in a flower show at Union Square.

After a couple of days in the City by the Bay—and a couple of very full years away—we were finally going home.

Early in Jane's long history of volunteer involvement she was an AIA judge for a 1959 Parade of Homes contest to select a woman delegate to the National Housing Conference. Pictured with her: E. B. Vaughters, Robert McBreen, and Mrs. J. Kirk Douglass.

8 | BUILDING A CAREER IN SEATTLE

I **WAS HOME AT LAST,** although it felt like I was still on a bit of a tour, showing slides to friends and family all over town. I tailored the shows to my audiences, knowing many wanted to see only landmark buildings and familiar sights—and my mother said she learned something new each time. My favorite shows were those I did for colleagues, featuring recent modern structures or more unusual designs.

My father believed I had come home to stay, so he was disappointed to learn I had found a little apartment in Seattle's Capitol Hill neighborhood to share with Mervane. I didn't tell him I had promised my mother I would not live with them again; she was ready for their "alone time." Mervane and I moved into an old house on North Broadway that had several levels with small apartments tumbling down the hill. Our unit was next to one rented by Lou Cassetta, a former classmate and Boeing employee, and our upstairs neighbors included three more architects: Al Bumgardner, Dan Streissguth, and Dale Benedict, who shared a large apartment. The owners lived on the street level and the floor above it, and our full house was a lively place.

It was June 1956—time to find a job. Of about 150 local architecture firms, only five had ever hired women, who were often assigned to interior design work. Catherine Woodman, who was still at the UW Architecture School, recommended contacting Bob McDaniel, another former student who was looking for help. Bob operated a one-man office in the Orpheum Theatre building, doing residential work for private clients as well as contractors. He was married with several young children, and we got along just fine. I could handle all phases of the firm's projects, and it seemed like a great place to start before opening my own practice.

One day Bob answered the phone, picked up a booklet and started quoting liquor prices from the state-run liquor store. I didn't understand until Bob told me his office phone number was once the liquor store number. When a drunk was on the phone, it was easier to answer the question than explain the problem. I soon realized Bob was very familiar with the liquor store and had his own problem; when one of his buddies showed up for lunch, he was often gone until late afternoon. I was sure Catherine was aware of the situation and thought I might be able to help.

Despite the challenges, I really enjoyed working with Bob. For one job, we went out to measure an old building that contained several small apartments, which we were going to remodel. The tenants all worked, and the owner had contacted them about our scheduled visit. We rapped on each door first to make sure the apartment was empty before entering, and all went well until we entered a basement unit, startling a couple in bed. The woman, stark naked, leapt up and fled. We backed out the door, but the tenant, covering his lower section with a towel, followed us insisting that we come back and finish our job. He wanted his apartment measured. The door was the only way out, so we wondered, where had the naked lady disappeared to?

I was assigned to open all the doors while Bob looked the other way, then I would give the OK and we resumed measuring. The tension grew with each closet door, but the lady was not to be found. Upon our departure, we decided the only possible place she could be was under the bed on the cold concrete floor. We had covered every other corner or hiding space. If she was paid to be there, I hoped she was paid well!

❖

SOON AFTER RETURNING TO SEATTLE, I bought a car. It was the only one I ever owned that had no personality, but the price was right, and I needed wheels. Of course, auto insurance was required. One day, a man knocked on the boys' apartment door upstairs and asked for "Mr. Hastings." Dan responded that it was "Miss Hastings," but the visitor insisted, "No." He was looking for a mister and an architect! "Yes," replied Dan, "*She* is an architect." The man left.

I learned later that Safeco Insurance, the largest firm in the city, had refused to insure my car because I was over 25 and never married, thus a bad risk! I had owned a car in Seattle before living in Europe, then drove for almost two years in Europe, and I never had a claim. But my record was meaningless. I was considered unstable; thus, no insurance. Friends could not believe this, but my sister-in-law who worked for an insurance company assured me this was the normal policy. So, my insurance policy was listed under L.J. Hastings; occupation, architect.

❖

BOB'S LONG LUNCHES had become more frequent, and soon he was short on funds for my paychecks. I needed to find another job, so I walked up Stewart Street, a block to the west, where an office building housed several architecture and engineering (A&E) firms.

Leo A. Daly was a large A&E firm with a home office in Omaha and several branch offices. When I applied, I was sent to a vice president's office to meet with an older man temporarily assigned to the Seattle office to help with hiring. He seemed delighted to see me, explaining that they didn't have any professional women in the firm, and he thought it was time they changed the policy. I was hired because he knew I would make the grade, but it was clear that if I didn't work out, I would be the first and last woman they would ever employ. The Seattle office had almost one hundred employees and the only other woman was Norma, a draftsperson in the mechanical engineering area who became a good friend. After several months, another young woman architect was hired, so I knew I passed the test.

Many projects were in other cities, including a new building for the Leo A. Daly headquarters in Omaha. Those of us working on it thought the style was too trendy, but we were just doing the drafting and thought maybe we didn't understand Midwestern taste.

A co-worker, T.G. Connelly, had followed his Iowa classmates west for the job. T.G. was good-looking, talented and had a winning personality. He also had a girlfriend, Katherine, in Arkansas, who he was serious about. So when girls pursued him, I came to his rescue. I didn't know Katherine, but I saw how uncomfortable he was with the attention. Finally, T.G. went back to Arkansas and returned with his bride.

One day the vice president summoned me: "Will you go to San Francisco for ten days to help out in our office there?" I could leave the next day, and T.G. and Bruce Mecklenberg (also married) were the other two on the team. Neither of them had been to San Francisco, so they were thrilled that I could be their guide. There was one problem: The San Francisco office manager had requested "the three best architects, but no women." I was told to go anyway and remember that I worked for the Seattle office; they were the ones who paid me. I should do my job and ignore the office manager.

The three of us stayed at the Stewart Hotel in the heart of the city, an easy walk to the San Francisco office on Maiden Lane. The office was upstairs from the

famous Iron Horse Bar, where we quickly became regulars. Our project was to produce the working drawings for a Catholic girls' boarding school in Ottumwa, Iowa.

My desk was in a corner with walls in front of me and to my right. The manager
never spoke to me. When he made his rounds, he cut across the corner and did not
stop at my desk. However, I knew he was checking up on me; when I came back
from lunch, the tools on my desk often were moved. The rest of the crew, men from
the local office and branch offices in Omaha and St. Louis, were amused and kept
a close watch.

Most evenings, we worked late and took a short dinner break before returning
to our drafting boards. Then, we stopped down at the Iron Horse for a goodnight
drink before walking back to our hotel. If we didn't show up by midnight, the bartender would come upstairs to check on us. As this was T.G.'s and Bruce's first visit
to San Francisco, I also scheduled places to eat or see in the evenings, no matter how
late. Our stay was extended from ten days to three weeks, and when I suggested a
night off from sightseeing, my teammates were relieved.

When our project was finally completed, we planned a farewell lunch at the
Iron Horse. Of course, we had a charrette—an all-night work session—the night
before, so there were a lot of bloodshot eyes and five o'clock shadows. That day, I
was the last to arrive at the bar. *Life* magazine had just published a big spread showing where "swinging singles" met in the major U.S. cities, and the Iron Horse was
"the" place in San Francisco. A librarian convention was also in full swing, and as
I entered the bar, I was surprised to see a crowd of beautifully dressed women, all
wearing hats, having lunch. I had to cross the center of the bar to a private corner,
where eighteen men stood up to greet me. I was wearing a linen skirt, blouse, and
loafers—I was certainly no one special—but all eyes followed me. My co-workers
could not resist playing along. I'm sure to this day the librarians thought they had
seen a celebrity, but who?

Back upstairs after lunch, we gathered our belongings and lined up for goodbye
handshakes before we all returned to our respective branch offices. I put out my
hand, just like the guys. The manager shook it and said, "The next time I need help,
I'm sending for you!" These were his only words to me during those three weeks.

❖

BY THIS TIME, I had moved into a delightful one-bedroom cottage that had originally
been a houseboat—a real find in the choice Madison Park neighborhood. It was

on land between a house on the street and another on pilings in Lake Washington. There was a nice small yard behind it and a front lawn leading to the lakeshore. A large porch across the front, as well as one in the back, marked its former role. T.G. and Katherine found a little rental house across the street. In early Seattle the area had been an amusement park and racetrack reached by the Madison Street streetcar line running from downtown to a Lake Washington dock, where ferries ran to Kirkland on the east side of the lake. The neighborhood retained a vacation village image and attracted young artists, dancers, and singles. And while neither Katherine nor I had enough dishes to have a real dinner party, we could easily tote borrowed items across the street. It was a wonderful arrangement, and we became very close friends.

I had been dating fellow architect Dan Streissguth since returning to Seattle, but one day I received a call from Nels Johnson, a high school friend home on vacation from his job in Africa. I was perhaps the only single woman he knew, so each evening he took me to a fine restaurant, the theater, or both. He could sleep in late, but I had to work and looked forward to the occasional evening off when he would get together with his fraternity brothers instead. I had never been courted so lavishly.

Nels was a vice president for Texaco Oil, covering West Africa. The company was building a new house for him in Liberia—really, a marble palace—and I enjoyed advising him on interior finishes and furniture. He returned to his work, but soon afterward one of his parents fell ill and he was back in Seattle. When I saw him next, I commented on the large diamond ring he wore, as this was not usually seen on a man. It was for me, he said—my engagement ring. He could take it out of the country as jewelry but transporting an unset stone was a problem. I was stunned and quickly explained I did not have that kind of feeling for him. Then, he confessed that he had met a Canadian girl on the ship coming home and thought he would contact her. I certainly approved. Pauline looked lovely wearing the diamond in her wedding ring when I met her, and the three of us remained friends until Nels' passing.

❖

MABLE, THE DIRECTOR'S SECRETARY at the Daly firm, became a close friend. She was a Nebraska native who lived in a women's housing facility operated by Goodwill, and she delighted in learning about her new home in the Pacific Northwest.

She dated Herb Buller, a draftsman in the electrical engineering section of the firm. He was a New Englander whose love of the mountains had brought him west. He was climbing something every weekend until he became ill. In the hospital, he learned he was highly allergic to gluten. After that, he was soon back climbing mountains, carrying jars of baby food in his pack. After Mable and Herb married, she learned to bake gluten-free breads and create all kinds of special meals. Meat, potatoes, rice, and corn were staples, as well as veggies and fruits. I stood up with them at their wedding and was godmother to their son, John.

One day Mable came into the drafting room upset and asking for help. Her boss, Mr. Lockwood, dictated letters for her to type, and of course, his letters contained construction vocabulary she didn't know. She always did her best on a rough draft, but he laughed at her spelling errors. She politely suggested that he spell out construction terms, but he replied, "Oh Mab, this is the only fun I have all day." She was determined not to bite, so came for help. "He wants me to type lizards in his letter," she claimed. I asked what the problem word was. "Salamanders," she said. "I'm not typing any lizards for Mr. L. to laugh at."

"Mable, the job is in Alaska, right?" I asked. "Yes," she said. I told her to type it; a "salamander" is a smudge pot. Word was out that we were on the short list for a new Alaska gas pipeline project. I was to be one of the staff members issued a miner's lamp and proper clothing for the trip north, but the 1957 trip was postponed and that pipeline was never built.

❖

ALMOST EVERY WEEKEND, rain or shine, a group of us went backpacking, picnicking, or hiking. If the weather looked promising, we went west to the Olympic Mountains or ocean. Otherwise, we drove over the Cascade Mountains to the drier eastern side of the state. Usually there were two to three carloads of us, and we traveled family-style with several individuals or groups assigned to fix meals. I always seemed to be assigned a dinner, and over the years I developed a system to minimize fuss and waste on the trail. I prepped at home, marinating chunks of beef fillet in red wine, as well as cleaning mushrooms, cherry tomatoes, and green peppers for grilled kebabs. One pan was for minute rice, and another was for our vegetable—often onion sautéed in butter with sliced summer squash. I brought a fruit salad with honey-lime dressing and added a banana right before serving. My garbage consisted of a butter wrapper and rice box, both burnable, along with the banana peel. When it became available, we enjoyed wine from a box; thus, no bottles had to be carried out.

Eight of us—three women and five men—planned out a weeklong hike over Cascade Pass, but by the day of departure, our hiking group had dwindled to Dan, Dale, and me. The other five decided they would camp with us the following weekend at our destination, Lake Chelan, and bring us home. At the last minute, Al Bumgardner's young employee, Al Dreyer, asked to join. I added another ration, not knowing how much food a young man required. Joyce Stannard, my friend from Germany days who was working at Fort Lewis, agreed to drop us off at the trailhead and take my car back to Seattle.

The day we started out on one of Washington's most scenic trails, we saw nothing but our own feet. Under dense clouds, we carefully hiked step by step. At the summit, where we planned to camp for the night and have our last real meal (steak and trimmings), there was no wood to build a fire. We dug up roots and gathered anything that might burn, while heavy rain clouds surrounded us. We made camp and reassured ourselves the weather would improve.

We had brought a bottle of scotch "just in case of snake bites," but as we became wetter, we decided snakes were unlikely, and the bottle came out. We had just poured ourselves a drink when two men came up the trail from the east side. Instinctively, we hid our drinks and reassured our visitors that it was just a short distance back to the parking lot and (we assumed) their cozy car. If we'd had a car there, we would have turned back.

We settled into our sleeping bags under tiny tents and hoped for a restful night. But we were up with the first light and soaking wet. When I suggested breakfast, the three miserable men barked, "Not till the sun comes out!" We packed up and started down the steep Pacific Crest Trail. After several hours of slow descent, the sun popped out. I was in the lead and stopped at a small stream that tumbled across the trail. They were annoyed, but I reminded them they had agreed to breakfast as soon as the sun was out. We stood on the trail, two on each side of the stream, preparing breakfast. My companions relaxed a bit once they had some food, and I decided we might make it through the week without mutiny. I had learned early in childhood that the best way to deal with men was to make sure they were fed. With spirits improved, we continued down the mountain on the most challenging part of our trip.

We had to cross a large rock/boulder slide area, inching our way over huge, jagged stones with our backpacks shifting and throwing us off balance. We finally made it to a flat area where our exhausted group decided to make camp for the night. Al grew up in Eastern Washington and had done a lot of camping in the area, so he picked our site to provide protection from the wind and easy access to water. While he was scouting, I laid my sleeping bag out over the hot rocks and spread out all my belongings, including my underwear. The boys followed suit. Amazingly, everything dried, including our sleeping bags, thanks to the hot Eastern Washington sun. Things were bound to improve.

Our second night, we managed to sleep, and peace and cooperation returned. The next morning, I awoke with my muscles aching and my raw heels on fire. My extremely thin feet and skinnier heels (shoe size 10½, 5A with an 8A heel) had always been a problem, so I had moleskin and had bandaged them for years. However, I had failed to properly prepare and the only ointment available was margarine. The ache in my muscles eased once I started walking, but I was stuck with the excruciating heel pain. The boys made me walk last so they didn't have to watch me limp.

Each night after Al selected the site, we had a design competition for our shelter. I don't recall that we had a dominant winner, but we created some interesting structures. Al and I had fishing gear, so we supplemented our dinners with trout while Dan and Dale picked berries, which I added to gelatin mixes for dessert. We could not fill Al up, so we were constantly praying for good fishing.

I had camped most of my life, so I had no fear of the woods, and I knew to make noise to not startle a bear. The only weapon we had was my large jackknife for cleaning fish. One peaceful evening as we were enjoying our bonfire after dinner, we heard a loud crashing sound coming through the woods. We looked at each other: What would we do? Then a large mule stepped out of the forest. He seemed happy to see us but quickly realized we had no food for him, so he ambled on. Other mules dropped by later, too. Apparently, workers on nearby trails were using the mules to haul in supplies. Once unloaded, the mules were turned loose to find their way back to their home pasture until their services were needed again.

Near the end of our trip, we approached the village of Stehekin at the north end of Lake Chelan and passed women carrying rifles. They explained the bears were so bad that they had to walk their children to school. The mothers were stunned that we had been out in the woods for a week and carried no rifles. We had never given it a thought.

We arrived in the village the day before we were to meet up with our friends, so we took the opportunity to have a bath in the lake. It was *cold* water, right off the snowfield, so the best strategy was to take a quick dip, get out and lather up, then dart back in to wash off. I wasn't sure I would ever get soap out of my hair. When some women campers saw my heels, they insisted on patching me up. The *Lady of the Lake*, the Lake Chelan boat that carried mail and groceries, arrived carrying campers from the south end of the lake and our friends to meet us. For our last night, others did the cooking, but we missed the absolute quiet of the trail.

Over the years, our group enjoyed many more hiking and camping trips, but this one was the longest.

❖

FORMER ROOMMATE SHIRLEY COOKE returned to Seattle following her medical internship in Los Angeles, at first moving into the complex on North Broadway, where she joined the artsy social group. After breaking her leg skiing, she moved closer to Children's Orthopedic Hospital, where she was doing her pediatric residency. Despite her heavy plaster cast, she helped me paint my Madison Park cottage, sliding about on the floor.

One day she told me she had a good job offer in Chicago and was considering returning home to her family. But she also told me she was in love with architect Ralph Anderson, my former classmate and a good friend. She felt he was in love with her, too, but would not acknowledge it. He had recently received national publicity for his design of a Mercer Island house with soaring cantilever decks, and he was considered the leading bachelor architect. I knew Shirley really did not want to leave Seattle, so I decided to call Ralph and tell him about her plans. If he didn't care, she would never know about my action. He asked me how he could reach her. That evening she called to say they were getting married and asked me to stand up with her.

On a beautiful Sunday morning I hosted a brunch to celebrate their nuptials with their closest friends and a seemingly endless supply of Champagne. We made a game out of our many bottles, seeing who could shoot the Champagne corks the furthest off the front porch toward the lake. The party and laughter went on until

Party for newlyweds Ralph and Shirley Anderson. Top row, from left: Chris and Evert Sodergren, T.G. Connelly, and Anker Molver. Middle row: Ralph's client, Dan Streissguth, Shirley and Ralph Anderson, Arlene Molver, and Jane Miller. Seated in front: Dale Benedict, Jane, Bob Marquette, and Jack Miller.

late afternoon, and neighbors on both sides took note of the festivities. They had barely said hi to me before this; the next day, I had greetings all around. Were they waiting for the next party?

❖

I BECAME ACTIVE in the all-volunteer American Institute of Architects (AIA), chairing the "Home of the Month" committee, which was a joint program between the *Seattle Times* and the Seattle Chapter. Each month the newspaper would feature an AIA architect's new residential project, which was then open to the public on a Sunday afternoon. At the end of the year a jury selected a winning entry; the homeowner was awarded a $500 prize and the architect was given a sculpture or artwork. The newspaper selected a young promising artist and commissioned a piece of their work. The award dinner was one of the biggest AIA events of the year with twelve architects and their clients and contractors all gathered for the announcement of the "Home of the Year." This program was the envy of other AIA Chapters nationally and continued for fifty years, from 1954 until 2004.

The Seattle Chapter was responsible for the 1958 conference for the Northwest & Pacific AIA Region (Montana, Idaho, Oregon, Washington, Alaska, Hawaii, and Guam). Al Bumgardner, Dave Anderson, and I were in charge, and we decided we would not solicit sponsors, so our budget was very tight. Because our region surrounds British Columbia, we decided to boost attendance by holding it across the border and inviting the Canadians. Harrison Hot Springs, B.C., was chosen as the location; next, we needed a special program. Louis Kahn was a new rising architect from Pennsylvania who had never been to the Pacific Northwest, and he agreed to come without a fee if we covered his travel expenses. Architectural students from all the regional schools showed up, and our members turned out in record numbers. The conference was a smashing success with young people staying up all night in deep discussions with Kahn about his work and design philosophy.

❖

AFTER OUR RETURN from the San Francisco project, work at Leo A. Daly slowed down and many of the 100 employees were laid off. Lead engineers of Structures, Electrical, Mechanical and Civil divisions remained along with some architects who could perform all the drafting disciplines. I spent much of my time cleaning out files while T.G. left and joined some of his classmates at The Richardson Associates (TRA).

On July 30, 1958, I received a phone call from prominent Seattle architect Jim Chiarelli, inviting me to lunch. This might have been routine with men, but not with a woman. I was delighted to attend and surprised when he offered me a job in his firm with better pay and more interesting work. I was hired to be job captain for the University of Washington's new Burke Museum and the remodeling project transforming Seattle's old Civic Auditorium into the Opera House. I supervised two graduate architects. This was a wonderful opportunity to start a new career chapter—but it lasted only about six months because both projects were put on hold.

The Civic Auditorium remodel was delayed when attorney Alfred Schweppe sued the city because the referendum providing funds had specified a "new" Opera House. However, the approved public funds were not enough to purchase property and construct a new building. Plus, Seattle's Century 21 Exposition (World's Fair) was in the planning stages, and the auditorium was one of the main structures

AIA Home of the Year Jury (Jim Chiarelli, Burr Richards, John Detlie, Jane, Harrison J. Overturf, Bob Durham). [Seattle Times Co., 1958]

on the exposition site. Upgrading the building would allow it to be ready for the World's Fair opening date in 1962.

In the case of the new Burke Museum, the committee approval was withdrawn at the insistence of architect and UW graduate Minoru Yamasaki, even though he missed the meeting. The decision forced the project to be relocated; instead of adjoining the Henry Gallery and nearby performance halls, the Burke Museum was built in a then-isolated northwest corner of campus. As constructed, it was not the building that was originally designed, a true loss to the beautiful campus. All this due to one man's enormous ego!

By the end of 1958, I had passed another examination—Site Planning—and was awarded my National Council of Architectural Registration Boards (NCARB) Certificate #3504, which allowed me to practice in other states. At the start of 1959, with several jobs of my own, it was time to launch my own architectural practice.

My experience included work in small and large firms, and I had gained expertise with large structures, industrial buildings, office buildings, a milk-processing plant, a museum, an opera house, and a sewage treatment plant. But I hadn't designed a residence since before going to Germany. I enjoyed working with homeowners, designing to their special needs. This personal relationship is more satisfying than working with a business where low costs are the highest priority.

We had been rightly informed during our university years that architecture is not the road to wealth. A prominent architect said, "You do it because you have to."

Happiness is loving what you are doing, and I have never considered changing course.

Century 21 Seattle World's Fair, 1962: Jane and Victor Steinbrueck at the AIA Booth, which he designed and she managed. [Seattle Times Co., 1962]

9 | BEGINNING MY PRACTICE

I N 1958, I MOVED into a little duplex owned by former classmate Earl Powell. Earl built the concrete block box structure with Miles Metsker back in 1950 when we were all still students. It was located at the end of Ravenna Avenue where the street dead-ended just north of the Forty-fifth Street Viaduct. Undeveloped University of Washington property was adjacent to the south, making the duplex a true hideaway in the woods; trees in front hid old railroad tracks, and a hillside of blackberry bushes behind buffered an apartment house. The tri-level building featured concrete floors with hot water heating coils and a slate finish. Both units had fireplaces, and a carport provided cover for two cars as well as storage for firewood and tools. Upon his 1951 graduation, Earl married, and the honeymooners moved into the upper unit's two levels, renting out the lowest level. Architectural students had always rented that lower unit, and parties were common at the end of the road. When I rented the upper unit and Marilyn Mattocks moved downstairs, she was the first resident who was not an architect.

In my apartment, a shoji screen between living areas provided privacy, and the bathroom had the only interior door. The first floor of my unit was big enough for my single bed and a drafting board, so I was in business. However, working at home by myself had disadvantages; it was too easy to cook and answer friends' calls during work hours—not a professional atmosphere!

Early in 1959, I went to work part-time at Tucker and Shields, formerly Tucker, Shields and Terry. I had applied to the firm years earlier but was not offered a job then. I'm sure part of the issue was that they were bachelors and lived in the office; a woman employee did not fit the image they wanted to project. But by 1959, they had other living arrangements and had hired my former roommate, Sue, who had worked out well. I was taking some graduate courses, but I decided I could also work part-time for them. This got me out of the house regularly but allowed me to do my own work at home, too.

I had several of my own "jobs," as I called the design projects, including a new house for Roy and Barbara Veldee, friends from my Boeing days who now had a baby girl. I looked at several properties with them, weighing the pluses and minuses of each site. Many families were moving to the suburbs where land was cheaper, and I explained that sewers, roads, sidewalks, and schools would follow, along with new taxes. We selected a lot on Mercer Island on a ridge with a lake view, and they were a joy to work with. Their new home featured vertical-grain Douglas fir paneling in the living/dining room, highlighting the beauty of our Northwest wood. I remember catching the electric company just in time to prevent them

Ralph and Ruth Leistikow Residence,
Issaquah, Washington, interior

from installing the unsightly meter next to the front door. One of my early lessons.

Another job was for two new houses at the end of an old coal-mining road outside Issaquah. The Leistikow brothers, Boeing engineers who were originally from Nebraska, had purchased five acres with a stand of timber. How these trees had avoided the loggers' saws was a mystery, and it was a beautiful, remote piece of land. The brothers, LaVern and Ralph, divided it into two parcels with a shared well, and they and their talented wives did their own construction. LaVern and Lorna built first, with both couples working together. The women split shakes from cedar blocks and installed them on the roof. Much of the lumber was cut at a work site near their Mercer Island apartment and hauled to the construction site, where they worked on the project in the evenings. Even the exacting rafter's birdmouth joints were cut off-site, with contractor friends hooting, "They will never fit!" Of course, they fit. These were true engineers working with a borrowed transit; everything was plumb, level, and precise. I spent several Saturdays working with them. When we were done each day, we walked through the woods, and I introduced the family to native plants. We became lifelong friends.

The design for Ralph and Ruth Leistikow's house required much more finish craftsmanship. A large garage/workshop structure was built first, making it easier to do more work on-site. I learned many lessons—including to pour the concrete floor slab early in the morning to avoid troweling all night.

The fireplaces in both houses were of river rock from Denny Creek. A special Forest Service permit allowed us to gather the stones under the guidance of Ken Harms, an artist and sculptor who helped construct both fireplaces. Ken also became part of the family.

❖

SPRING BROUGHT a new remodeling job from another former Boeing co-worker. I'm sure he did not remember me, but I had never forgotten him—physically large and intellectually off the scale. By this time, George Stoner was the head of the Boeing space program.

The original Stoner Residence had an extensive yard. It was a Mercer Island house originally built when residents would arrive by boat, so the front door faced the lake. Later, bridges and roads connected the island to Seattle and Bellevue, and the entrance from the road was through the kitchen. Boeing frequently used the large Stoner property to entertain business associates, so the house needed a new entry, a remodeled kitchen, and a substantial deck addition. While measuring the structure, I found a problem: a void in the middle of the lower floor. It turned out to be the former owners' secret air raid shelter built shortly after World War II.

It was an honor to work with the Stoner family, including their four bright children, who joined all our meetings. Peter, the oldest son, later became a noted architect. The contractor was hired by the Stoners, but he was told to work directly only with me. If something was wrong, George would call, asking if I had been by the house that day. My reply was usually, "No, but I'm planning on visiting tomorrow." Then George would tell me to be sure to look at the issue. He never discussed the job with the contractor because that was my job. He claimed he didn't know anything about architecture. Ha! What a brilliant man. He was lost much too soon, from cancer in 1971.

I have often said, only partly in jest, that architects probably know more about their clients than psychiatrists do about their patients; psychiatrists must depend on what their clients tell them—but we get to look in their closets. We witness the best family relationships, as well as troubled ones that require creative building solutions. The Stoner family was close to perfect.

❖

IN JULY 1959, I purchased a Barbara James painting, "The Melons," after promising my friend Jack Miller first rights if I ever wanted to sell it. That same month, Estelle Radin, my friend from Service Club days, arrived from Los Angeles for a visit in her new Austin Healey sports car. The top was down and Seattle was sunny, so we enjoyed sightseeing al fresco. We drove to Canada by way of the Olympic Peninsula, catching a ferry to Victoria and then another to Vancouver, B.C. Just before docking, there was an announcement over the loudspeaker: It was raining in Vancouver and the driver of the California car might want to put the top up. We tried—and the deck hands tried—but it would not budge. Estelle had purchased the car with the top down and had never had it up. We docked in the heart of Vancouver, and I drove while Estelle held an umbrella over us in pouring rain. I knew where the auto shops were, and we made our way across town with residents laughing and pointing all the way. "I'm sure glad they don't know I'm a local," I told Estelle.

Fall brought a remodeling job that started with a call and a plea: "Please don't hang up. I need help." Mrs. McCroskey had phoned several other architects about her utility room, and they couldn't be bothered, but I wanted to meet her. She had four preschool children, a husband who traveled—and a utility room that was in the basement while the bedrooms were on the second floor. There was one bedroom on the main floor next to the kitchen, and I transformed it into a grand utility space plus a new playroom with a deck out to the sunny back yard. It really worked. Years later I saw her at a football game. When I couldn't place her, she said, "I'm the woman with the most beautiful utility room in the city."

❖

I HAD NEVER FORGOTTEN my student days and the tea at architect Elizabeth Ayers home. Just before the Christmas holiday break, I invited the women architecture students from UW to tea. There were probably four or five. Garney Moe, a WSU architecture grad a few years older than me, and Betty Austin, the UW architectural librarian, also attended. We enjoyed the afternoon, and after that, I hosted students for several years—until there were too many women to fit into my small house.

Kinkade House, Vashon Island. The house earned Jane's first AIA Home of the Month Award in March 1962.

On December 15, I secured a new project, a residence on Vashon Island for the Kinkade family. Duane Kinkade had started out studying architecture before becoming a math major, and he remembered me. They had contacted well-known Seattle architect Paul Kirk, but he was not taking any residential jobs under $25,000. I was flattered to be their second choice. The site had a beautiful east-facing view, including Mount Baker to the north and Mount Rainier to the south. I designed the house as a long rectangle, with French doors in all rooms opening to the view. The floor construction, a slab on grade, was finished with a terrazzo treatment containing hot air ducts to create a wonderful warm surface. The framing was a Kirk-style post and beam with a flat roof.

This was my first house design where I liberated the sink. When the plumber told me it could not be done, I assured him I would find another plumber who could do it. I thought: How can they have sinks located in islands within interior spaces in commercial construction, and I can't do this? In 1960, I designed the Kinkades' sink in a counter with nothing but open space around it and views of the Cascade Mountain range to enjoy in the distance. You do not have to have a wall in front of your sink!

This was my first job where the subcontractors challenged me. The general contractor gave in to them, which made me the bad guy. I'm sure none of them had worked with a woman before, and it was like walking a tightrope to get them to change their ways without losing them. Only the mason walked off the job after I refused to accept his crooked fireplace flue. I thought for a moment I was going to be the recipient of the brick he had in his hand, but he finally put it down and left.

In early 1960, I also took a job designing a house for Bill Howell, a Boeing bachelor at Lake Tapps. Bill said he wanted space—a big lot and a big house. There was plenty of room for the house, a tennis court and more. When the foundation forms were in place, Bill commented on how large they were. I thought, he has no idea about the actual size. Usually, at this point in a project, the client calls to say there is an error, thinking that the formwork is too small. Understanding scale can be so elusive.

By the time the Howell house plans were completed and the building permit issued, I had finished several other jobs. I preferred to get bids from at least three contractors, because often the contractor who won the bid was too busy to actually do the job. One firm I really wanted to work with never seemed to be available. One day one of the firm partners told Al Bumgardner, an architect friend of mine, that they really wanted to take one of my jobs but were afraid to work with a woman. Al howled with laughter and told them I'd do half their work for them. They took my next job and tested me by reporting that they couldn't get this or that material. Of course, I always got it for them. They ultimately did many of my jobs and we got along beautifully.

When it was time to bid the Howell job, my favorite contractors could not do it because Lake Tapps was too far away. Partner Cliff Hjelm, who had Nordic roots, had an idea. The little town of Buckley was the logical place to locate potential contractors, and he took a day off to accompany me to interview firms there. Many of these small contractors were Scandinavians, and he reassured them I was knowledgeable and helpful. It worked and I found two nice men who insisted on calling me "Miss Haustings."

I designed the Howell house with a massive brick fireplace wall in the center of the living area that was designed to carry heating ducts to the second floor. I laid out the brick pattern with the firebox bricks laid flat instead of on edge, which made it more fireproof. However, the building inspector couldn't understand this and demanded the 35-foot-tall, 4-foot-by-10-foot masonry structure be removed and rebuilt. I couldn't believe it, and went to the Pierce County Building Department,

Fashion Group classes (with Fred Bassetti). [Seattle Times Co., 1963]

plans in hand. The director said it was the most complete set of drawings he had seen, and that the inspector would be removed from the job. The director would personally sign off on the project; he knew the contractor's work, which was good enough. The contractor was thrilled, thanking me for my "magic."

❖

THE FASHION GROUP, a national professional women's organization I joined in 1956, offered a career course for young women and older women who wanted to enter or return to the workforce. FG members worked in design fields, and the group included modeling school owners, fashion illustrators, media personnel, department store buyers, furniture and textile designers, toy designers, a landscape architect, and me. Member Charlotte Pritchard had one of the most fascinating careers, designing the interiors of Boeing airplanes for luminaries like President John F. Kennedy and other world leaders, including African kings who demanded luxurious, colorful materials. Charlotte told the women in the course: "There is only one job like this and I'm not ready to give it up. However, you never know where your career may take you." When the interior design firm she worked for had been first hired by Boeing, she was not thrilled with her assignment, thinking she would be working on office spaces. As it turned out, her job was one in a million.

In April 1960, I attended my second of what would be many AIA National Conventions. This one was in San Francisco, which also gave me the opportunity to visit Mervane, who had moved to the city, and see my grandmother BB and Aunt Lois.

By this time, I had moved my office out of my bedroom and into the University District, where I shared space with former schoolmates Mike Soldano and Anker Molver and their employees. Comparing jobs one day, we had a contest over who had the smallest contract. I won with "front porch stairs"—a project for the beloved UW professor Giovanni Costigan.

One day Mike and I began reminiscing about childhood vacations on the Washington Coast. We were both interested in purchasing vacation property, and I found an ad in the paper for oceanfront lots on the Long Beach Peninsula in the far southwest corner of the state. Mike's wife, Alex, packed a lunch and the three of us set off for the coast on a Saturday in late June. The site was at the end of the oceanfront road—with a roadbed of crushed oyster shells—just north of the historical town of Ocean Park. Twelve 100-foot parcels (replatted from the original four 25-foot lots) were available for $2,500 each, or $25 per oceanfront foot. We could not pass up this opportunity and purchased the two most northerly lots.

Monday morning the office talk was all about our wonderful discovery. Within a few days the other ten lots were purchased, sight unseen, by nine architects and a doctor friend. One day we would have our own little vacation community on sand dunes covered with wild strawberries and colorful succulents. I did not have $2,500 and banks did not loan money to women to buy land, so I borrowed the money from my friend Gretchen's mother, repaying her twenty-five dollars a month. For years we laughed about our big land purchase.

Salisbury Stable (former Morris Graves property), Woodway Park, Washington

❖

I WAS BUSY the rest of the year with six new remodeling jobs, plus my part-time work at Tucker and Shields. One job was a stable on a ten-acre plot formerly owned by the famous Northwest artist Morris Graves. While I researched the horses' housing requirements, I also reviewed the unique design of the concrete-block house that Graves had built in the late 1940s from drawings by Tucker, Shields and Terry. It resembled an Egyptian temple, and Graves christened it "Careladen." The planned stable, a focal point seen from the kitchen and dining areas, would be a part of this special picture. I designed the stable as a smaller concrete block with a clipped gable roof over the hay loft—and a small apartment for the family's children to play over the two stalls and tack room. It was a delightful little structure that gave the horses a garden view from the arched windows of their stalls. Years later, it became a section of a large home.

In 1961, I made my first appearance on KING TV's morning show with Beth Leonard. I also realized I needed to pare down my part-time activities, which added up to several full-time jobs. I dropped my graduate classes and decided to leave Tucker and Shields, even though I enjoyed my co-workers and the projects, which had ranged from a ski lodge to several residential projects. My time at the firm also coincided with a milestone for the city: Construction had begun on the new Interstate 5 freeway, and the houses across the street from the Tucker and Shields office were torn down. The fellows I worked with spent lunch breaks throwing rocks through the windows before the bulldozer came. As my grandmother said, "Men are only boys with long legs." For my part, I rescued two newel posts from a porch and later turned them into garden lights.

❖

MARCH 1961 brought unexpected heartbreak. One morning, the phone rang so early that I picked it up asking, "What is wrong?" My mother told me the news was in the morning paper: My brother Art's small boat had been found off Admiralty Head, and he and his fishing buddy had likely drowned. Brother JC and I joined others searching Whidbey Island beaches for the rest of the day, hoping to find something. Later, we went to the Coast Guard station to claim the boat and gear that was found. I was deeply impressed by the kindness of the young guardsmen. In the Coast Guard's downtown office, we received the full details of their search and the ongoing efforts to notify the commercial ships in the area.

When we were kids, I had always been closest to Art. Like me, he was into sports, and we skied together. I was the only girl the boys would take fishing, and I was always treated just like another guy. Art was the brightest of the Hastings siblings; for him, school was too easy. He also had a beautiful singing voice that he rarely shared with the rest of us. Even with all these talents, he was often unhappy. I remember lecturing him as a kid that if he worked half as hard at being happy as he did at being unhappy, he would be the world's happiest person. But at our last Christmas Eve family gathering all together in 1960, I remember he was in such a wonderful, joyful mood. Everyone there commented about his smiles and laughter.

❖

THE NEXT MONTH, the AIA Convention was in Philadelphia, and I had been planning for months to attend. I hoped to meet Joyce there and then travel together to see some sights, along with friends from Service Club days. My parents urged me to go, and the memorial service for Art was put off until June.

When I arrived at the Philadelphia railway station, I heard, "Yoo-hoo, Miss Hastings!" It was UW Architecture School Chair Arthur Herrman. Ten years earlier, he didn't know my name, but now he remembered me. We enjoyed the convention—especially the party in the museum, where an older architect told Joyce she was the most beautiful woman in the room. After the convention we traveled to West Point, N.Y., and then to Washington, D.C., where we split up to see different friends. Joyce and I planned to meet up in New Orleans to finish our trip together.

But in New Orleans, we missed connections and I found myself alone. After checking into the hotel, I went out into the steamy city and found a bar and grill that looked like a cool place for lunch. It was busy and being a single I decided to sit at the counter. Soon, a gentleman sat beside me. He asked if I was a nurse. When I wondered aloud why he thought so, he said it was because I wore such a sensible watch. He was a British doctor working for a pharmaceutical company and visiting Tulane University Medical School. I said I was an architect, that this was my first time in New Orleans, and that I was meeting a friend who had yet to arrive. He told me to get busy sightseeing but not to go out in the evening alone. He invited me to join him for dinner, along with a widow friend and her daughter who he was entertaining, if my friend did not show. I decided, "Why not?" and enjoyed a delightful evening with his lady friend and her 17-year-old daughter. We did the town until late, when my new friend, Dr. Pepper, dropped me off at my hotel.

He invited me to Sunday brunch the next morning at a doctor friend's home. Dr. Pepper was determined to show me as much local architecture as possible, and we arrived about 9:30 a.m. at a grand old mansion in need of a lot of maintenance. The first-floor ceilings were fourteen feet tall, and the walls were covered with portraits of the ancestors—huge paintings full of holes and tears. The house had been in the family for generations, but the current owner did not have the resources to restore it.

When I arrived, I was given a Sazerac, a drink of whiskey, sugar, and bitters over a little ice. I don't remember snacks, but there must have been some as the drinks kept flowing until we left to drive across Lake Pontchartrain to a seafood restaurant. We finally ate at 4 p.m., then drove back to a small house on the waterfront. The party expanded to about twenty people; beer was the house drink accompanied by peanuts and hot dogs. At 3 a.m. I excused myself, thanked Dr. Pepper and took a cab to my hotel, as I was flying to Dallas later that day to meet up with Joyce. I thought I had staying power, but I was no match for the New Orleans folks.

❖

MY BROTHER ART'S early June memorial service was followed several weeks later by a family gathering at Snoqualmie Falls Lodge. The loss was especially difficult for my father and oldest brother, JC. The Hastings brothers' homes were separated by only a few blocks, and JC took over teaching Art's widow, Gerry, to drive. He sold Art's boat and put the family finances in order. He was also substitute dad for Debbie and Randy, who was too young to remember his father.

Happier news that year brought an invitation to the Matrix Table Dinner honoring Washington Women of Achievement. I had previously attended in 1952 as the outstanding UW woman senior student in architecture. (Of course, I was the only woman architecture student!)

And in November 1961, I went on my first date with UW School of Architecture Professor Norman Johnston. I don't remember exactly what we did, but he probably took me to the opera or the symphony or a movie. He was a nice guy—among several nice guys I knew and dated at the time. I was focused on my career and certainly wasn't thinking that one day, many years later, Norm and I would marry.

❖

THE NEXT YEAR, 1962, was an important one for Seattle as we mounted our second world's fair, the Century 21 Exposition. Planning had been underway for years. I remember an earlier planning meeting when all the large local architectural firms were vying for the plum expo building projects. It was a warm summer morning at the Olympic Hotel, Seattle's finest, and the firms' leaders met over breakfast to discuss the upcoming commissions. I was the only woman in the room, most likely because I was a Seattle AIA Chapter board member, but I was not a contender for any projects. Both of our famous Pauls—Thiry and Kirk—were there, as well as NBBJ partners, TRA partners, John Graham Jr., and Fred Bassetti. Due to the heat, a portable fan was placed in the room; after some conversation, it was decided to turn off the noisy thing during the meeting. One after another, these great architects got up to turn off the fan, but no switch did the trick. Finally, our middle-aged waitress with a Swedish accent arrived to refill the coffee and someone asked her if she knew how to turn the fan off. "Ah sure," she said, and pulled the cord socket out of the outlet. Not one word was said as these talented, big-name designers went on with their meeting.

Century 21 became a big part of my daily life for six months starting on May 23 with the opening of the Seattle AIA Chapter's booth. Al Bumgardner was the chapter president, and he talked me into managing the AIA booth designed by

UW architecture professor Victor Steinbrueck. I scheduled four volunteers a day to work with two architecture students, who received scholarship money to serve as our core staff. Al and I selected Don Curry and Carolyn Dueter from several applicants. Don had a ready smile and I'm sure he was the most beautifully groomed student in the university's history; his shoes were professionally polished every day. Carolyn was working on her second university degree, and she had a stutter that tended to show up when she was nervous, so Al was initially reluctant to hire her. But I pointed out that she was more mature, loyal, and responsible. I told Al I had to have her. Of course, she became our mainstay, frequently covering for Don when he didn't show up.

My four daily volunteers typically included two architects' wives working during the day hours and two architects working the evenings. The booth promoting local architecture was required to be open daily from 10 a.m. to 10 p.m. We frequently changed the exhibit boards within the booth, and we always had fresh flowers provided by the Ballard Blossom Shop. I had a fair pass, so I would also accompany friends to the fair. For those six months, I was there almost every day.

To fit the Century 21 theme, exhibits presented the future as imagined by manufacturers, trade organizations, scientists, and dreamers. The House of Tomorrow was popular with new gadgetry as well as unusual building materials. One day, I must revisit it in the Expo records to see how many of the ideas actually came to be. The huge Gothic-inspired arches of the U.S. Science Exhibit designed by Minoru Yamasaki were surrounded by exhibits that took visitors into outer space and allowed them to play with all kinds of physics experiments. There was also a huge screen with fifty-some images designed by Charles Eames, the famed architect, industrial and furniture designer. It had one of the longest lines—in competition with the Belgian waffle booth.

The old Civic Auditorium had been remodeled and transformed into the Opera House, the project that I was briefly involved with in 1958. The Armory became the "Food Circus" with two floors of restaurants and shops. The outer track of Memorial Stadium was converted into a waterway for water-skiing shows. The other major building was the Washington State Exhibit Pavilion designed by Paul Thiry. It originally housed the Bubbleator, a huge plastic spherical elevator, but after the fair it was destined to become a major concert venue and sports arena.

Like its Seattle predecessor, the 1909 Alaska-Yukon-Pacific Expo, Century 21 finished in the black and did not lose money. It left good buildings for future civic and cultural use, just as the 1909 fair left us the framework of the University of Washington campus.

❖

THAT MARCH, my Kinkade Residence project on Vashon Island was featured as the *Seattle Times* "Home of the Month." I had chaired the AIA committee for several years, but this was my first house to be published and opened for a Sunday afternoon tour. The open houses took place just before completing the finishing touches like painting and carpeting to protect surfaces from damage by the hundreds of viewers walking through. Mrs. Kinkade reported that her mother cried when she first saw the house with its flat roof; in her home state of Kansas, only chicken coops had flat roofs. Once inside, she decided the house was nice after all when she saw its marble terrazzo floors and French doors leading to the striking Cascade Mountain views from the patio.

At the end of the summer, my first architectural business partner, Anne, returned to Seattle and joined me on a trip to San Juan Island, where we were the guests of Hans and Elaine Jorgensen at their beach cabin in a beautiful private cove with the bluest water. It was tucked into the woods without any neighbors, and we enjoyed nights sleeping on platforms out in the woods. Elaine had become one of my closest friends after we met in the Fashion Group. She was a weaver and textile designer but also worked with her photographer husband, Hans, setting up displays he photographed for publications. Every organization I joined over the years brought me at least one new lifelong friend.

❖

I HAD MADE MY TV DEBUT in 1961. Now I started my time on the speaking circuit by addressing the "Electrical Women's Roundtable." These women represented appliance companies, manufacturers, home economists, and writers, and the businesswomen always dressed in suits, high heels, hats, gloves, and jewelry. One woman looked very familiar and teased me as I could not place her. Finally, she volunteered that she was Doris Brown. I immediately said, "Of course, Doris! I didn't recognize you with your clothes on." The room went quiet. I had to start my presentation explaining that Doris and I had belonged to the same water-ski club, and I had never seen her in anything but a two-piece bathing suit. Thank heavens, it was a meeting of all women.

Several days after the roundtable, I was working in my office when I felt an anxious need to go home. After resisting for about ten minutes, I knew I had to go check, or I would never get anything done. Pulling into the carport, I saw that the windows to Marilyn's apartment were black. I approached the door and could immediately feel heat. I ran up the half-flight of garden stairs to my door. My poodle, Missy, came shooting out as I opened it. Because my entry level was a slab on grade, I knew I was safe as I called the fire department. I started to give detailed directions because the house was hard to find, but the dispatcher said he knew where it was and hung up. He could see the smoke from the fire station. I caught Missy and put her in my car, then went back inside and grabbed my clothes and bedding as smoke filled the house. Two fire trucks came up our little dirt lane.

I called Marilyn at work to give her the bad news. Her unit was destroyed, with her belongings a total loss. We wondered, what could have started the fire? The floors and walls were all concrete with only a bookcase wall in the living area that backed up to a closet. Whatever the cause, Marilyn was left with nothing but the clothes on her back, which on this warm September day was one of her oldest summer dresses. Marilyn's father was an executive for Safeco Insurance and had assured his daughter that paying for insurance was stupid because our little concrete house couldn't burn. I, on the other hand, had a renters' policy that cost about $15 for three years. I was well into my third year when the fire occurred, and the policy covered cleaning costs.

My only loss was some fringe on a rug where the fire had started to move up the wall from below. The firemen assured me that if I had called ten minutes later, my place would also have been destroyed. Through my life, I have had several psychic experiences and I do follow them. They have served me well.

It must have been a slow news day because we hit the TV news big time. I called my parents to assure them I was fine. The fire was so hot that even the toilet and basin were charred black, but the fireplace damper had been open, saving the windows from being blown out. Friends showed up with gifts and spare clothing, and one male friend arrived with some beautiful underwear. Someone brought a bottle of scotch; however, Marilyn had discovered that her bottle of scotch had survived—but the fire had blown the cork and perhaps we should drink it before it spoiled! She had planned to go to her parents' house but drank enough that she knew they would not approve. I decided to put up with the smoke smell and stay put because the news might encourage people to pilfer the house. So, I cooked what was in the refrigerator—a smoky dinner, including Marilyn's first eggplant—and Marilyn decided to stay with me for the night. She had been complaining about her old clothes, but now she could start over. She decided to wear her good clothes to work in the future.

Her first night's stay turned into many months. Too many. Marilyn had her routines and was not flexible, so I had to adjust to her daily patterns. I made up my mind to move out, and I started looking into buying a house. Why pay rent when I could invest in property? Even after the lower apartment was repaired and she moved out of mine, I kept up my search. But could I find anything I could afford?

❖

THE WORD GOT OUT that if an organization wanted a free speaker, I was it. In 1963, I participated in an Easter Seals panel and presented at the Edgewater Hotel, as well as at historic preservation meetings and a Fashion Group event at Seattle Center.

I was active in the Stevens Pass Penguin Ski Club and agreed to prepare plans to improve the club's kitchen. Our ski cabin could sleep close to one hundred people but seldom housed more than fifty at a time. Club members included doctors, lawyers, insurance agents, building contractors, and electrical, heating, and plumbing contractors—as well as engineers and architects. We managed our affairs without any outside help, and summer work parties were almost as much fun as winter skiing weekends.

I was also enjoying my regular dates with Norm—as well as Dan Streissguth and Donald Hanberg. That year marked the first time Norm asked me to marry him. I didn't say no. I just said I wasn't ready to get married yet. He was a very patient guy.

❖

A BIG FIRST IN MY ARCHITECTURE PRACTICE was hiring an employee: In 1963, Carolyn, my AIA World's Fair booth scholarship student, started working for me part-time. She was finishing school and had married Jonn Geise, a sculptor who had also volunteered at the booth while working for an architectural firm, where he made models. I moved out of the office space I shared with Anker and Mike, and down the hall into my new office. I had a view of University Way and the University

Book Store across the street. The building on the northwest corner of University Way and Northeast Forty-Third Street had been an apartment house during the 1909 World's Fair. The upper floor was converted to office spaces but retained wide corridors with skylights, making it bright and cheerful. It was filled with architects' offices, artist spaces and a ballet studio.

I was gaining a reputation for residential remodeling projects—partly because most architects only wanted to do new work. Gertrude Meriwether, my Service Club director and friend from Nuremberg, contacted me about designing a fourplex. It was fun getting together, but the project did not advance. That was the last time I saw her before she moved to the southwest part of the state.

ONE LATE NOVEMBER DAY I looked out of my office window to see a young man sitting on the curb sobbing. What could possibly be wrong? I turned on my radio to hear the news that President Kennedy had been shot and was on his way to a Dallas hospital. Time just stopped. I told my architect friends in the building, and for the rest of the day, the radio news and sad music consumed our attention. That weekend, I had plans to attend a brunch out in the country, and we watched President Kennedy's funeral on TV while we tried to eat our wonderful meal.

The end of the year brought Al Bumgardner's annual office holiday party and a bit of much-needed cheer for our group of longtime friends. Al's December party eventually became so famous that local organizations like the opera and symphony were careful to schedule their fundraisers around it or they wouldn't have a good turnout.

In early 1964, Dr. Pepper, my English friend from New Orleans, called me as he was returning from Asia and changing planes in Seattle. He could not remember my name, so he called the AIA office and described me, so the manager gave him my number. The AIA office was all abuzz about this English gentleman and his wonderful voice, and I was required to tell the story of my two wild days in New Orleans.

❖

OUR SEATTLE AIA CHAPTER was the envy of architects around the country for the "Home of the Month" program. At the end of the year each month's architect submitted a 30-inch-by-40-inch presentation board with a rendering and floor plans of their winning project, and from these the "Home of the Year" was selected. Although the boards remained the property of the architects, the AIA had requests to exhibit them in bank lobbies, department stores and other public spaces—where, of course, they brought us future jobs. Over my many years in the AIA, I hauled and mounted these boards all around the city.

In early 1965, Victor Steinbrueck and his wife, Marjorie Nelson, hosted a party for former classmate Astra Zarina at their historic house on Franklin Avenue, which reminded me of a ferry with its large rounded front porch. Astra was back in the city after working in Minoru Yamasaki's office in Detroit and living in Rome. Many school friends reunited to hear of her adventures.

I was hired for an interesting new job: an addition and major remodeling of a small beach house on Perkins Lane, one of Seattle's most notorious landslide areas. The clients were the Karrows—a skiing friend's brother and his wife. Like many houses on the lane, the house sloped toward the Puget Sound waterfront. When Carolyn and I measured the house, she said she felt like she was going to slide off the edge. She had climbed Mount Rainier several times and was never as nervous on the mountain as she was during that measuring job. This strange little job became an important project later in my career.

Two days later Shirley Anderson and I were on our way to Hawaii to visit my friend Joyce (formerly Stannard) and her new husband, David Park, who was stationed in the islands. Shirley's husband, Ralph, seemed a bit stunned at the airport, their two little boys holding his hands as he said goodbye. He had promised Shirley a vacation several times, but it never happened, so one day she called me, saying I should phone Joyce and she would get our airline tickets. Joyce said we should stay at Maui's famous Sheraton Hotel, built on a cliff out over the beach. Of course, it was impossible to get a room, but Joyce somehow got us a confirmed reservation.

When we arrived, the desk manager was dumbfounded as they had been solidly booked for months. We agreed to stay next door at a new hotel for one night; then they could give us a room. The other hotel was fine, and Shirley wondered why we didn't just stay—but I said it was a "must" for me to stay at the Sheraton. Once there, we were treated like royalty. The staff was sure our reservation must have come through someone very important, and we received an enormous fruit basket with the largest Red Delicious apple I have ever seen. The beach sand washed out every day, as Hawaiian natives had warned it would, so bulldozers worked all night pushing it back in place. After our high living, we spent time at the Parks' home, telling them about our adventure.

❖

THAT YEAR, THE NORTH SEATTLE GROUP of the Soroptimists service group wooed me into their organization, introducing me to a new group of businesswomen, including a lumber yard financial manager and mortuary owner. Two Soroptimist women—Irene Peden, an electrical engineer on the University of Washington faculty, and Judge Carolyn Dimmick—became long-term friends.

March 30, 1965, was a day I would never forget. I was working on the remodel of an old house on the east side of Lake Washington in the Clyde Hill neighborhood, and we discovered a building permit had been issued to build a house just north of our project and forty-five feet forward from the required setback—blocking my clients' view of the lake. I had considered all possible legal setbacks and potential view blockages when I did the design; therefore, my clients decided to sue. The other party could not produce a set of drawings, but they had a building permit, no variance and were going to start construction. Relocating the house in the required front yard did nothing to improve their views.

My client, a Boeing man with a Ph.D. in mathematics, asked me to be an expert witness for their case. Their attorney, Steve Watson, instructed me to only answer "yes" and "no," if possible, and to never offer any information. This was my first courtroom experience.

A pretrial hearing included only people directly involved in the case, with no spectators or jury. Watson was a large, good-looking young man—no doubt a former college athlete. The other attorney was a short, stocky California fellow named John Erlichman, a nephew of a much-respected older Seattle attorney, Ben Erlichman. John Erlichman specialized in a practice of breaking land use laws and local covenants. When I was sworn in, he immediately questioned my right to be a witness. The judge's response was, "Counselor, she has the same credentials in her field as you do in yours." That should have been a clue that the judge was not fond of him.

Erlichman yelled at me over my "yes" and "no" answers, and he swore at me as I looked around to find the audience who he was trying to impress. The judge stopped the proceedings and took the attorneys into his chamber. He told Erlichman to "knock it off," but he only came back angrier. He threw a large map in my lap; the five-sided piece of property in question was about the size of my thumbnail and he demanded that I identify the front yard. It took a little thought, but I pointed to it. My client was called next, and he said, "She is absolutely correct." The little Bantam rooster of an attorney got madder, swearing in my face until the judge said, "This is ridiculous. I excuse the witness."

Afterward, I was told that I had blown his ego because he could usually break witnesses, but he could not get me to contradict myself. Watson was so impressed he said he wanted to use me again as an expert witness. I said, "No, thanks." I never wanted to cross the threshold of a courtroom again. I wish I could say that was the last I ever saw of Erlichman, but at least, I never faced him in court again.

❖

BY 1965, THE WOMEN'S MOVEMENT was taking hold, and I was invited to speak at several more university programs. The field of architecture was becoming more welcoming to women. In 1963, the Seattle Chapter of the AIA had 618 members; 10 were women. In 1965, there were 1,107 member architects and still only 17 women. But great change was on the way.

The year of 1966 was a banner one for me professionally with new residences to design, expanding well beyond remodeling projects. And I hired my fourth student intern. The intern after Carolyn was the delightful Harlan Dunn from Eastern Washington; he refused wages, just wanting the experience. Next came Rod Knipper, and years later, Knipper and Dunn returned to their Eastern Washington roots to form a successful partnership. Rick Sundberg was my fourth student worker, starting in 1966. He later became a partner with Jim Olson and a celebrated Seattle architect.

At the same time, there was unrest in the University District: The Berkeley Free Speech Movement had arrived, and the corner of Northeast Forty-Third Street and Fifteenth Avenue Northeast became known as "Hippie Hill." Young people littered the lawn during the day and moved into the business district at night, breaking windows and blocking The Ave—precursors to the much larger antiwar and civil rights protests in the late 1960s. The police dispersed the vandals with tear gas, which my early 1900 timber office building soaked up like a sponge. I carried my current work home each night as I feared a fire could destroy everything. The tear gas affected my throat more than my eyes, and each time it was used, it took several days to air out the office before it was habitable again.

Thanks to my male colleagues' referrals, I was also providing counsel to young women considering architecture as a career. I could no longer go quietly about my business unnoticed. Women were on the move into the professional world. I was asked to serve on the University YWCA Board of Directors, where I met other talented and concerned directors. I had to smile at the request. Throughout my life, I had always been part of the YMCA.

Sketched portrait of Jane at the AIA Convention in Denver, 1966

10 | THE FREMONT HOUSE

I **STILL WANTED TO PURCHASE** my own home. In March 1966, I received a call from an agent who had located a house for $9,000! My first question: "Is it habitable?" Yes, people were living in it. This I had to see, so I went to the Fremont neighborhood to tour the 1891 Victorian Gothic two-story house. I could not pass up such a bargain, and I made a deposit contingent on my older brother JC's examination and approval. I had promised my mother I would consult him before making any major purchases, as he felt responsible for his younger, unmarried sister.

My brother arrived for the inspection and the agent almost fainted when JC jumped up and down on the floor with his size 14 feet and 230-pound frame. All was solid and the house passed the test. What was I going to do with a seven-room, two-bathroom house that had never been remodeled except for the plumbing, which came in from the backyard? The budget price was based solely on the 25-by-120-foot lot, which was zoned for apartments and worth $10,000; it would have cost about $1,000 to knock the house down and clear the lot.

The house's frame rested on floor beams set on posts secured to brick pads, and the siding and windows were rot-resistant Western red cedar. The clearance from the bottom of the floor joists to the dry soil below created a very shallow crawl space. The floors were clear Douglas fir boards directly on top of joists with no subfloor, which allowed air from the crawl space to circulate up to the first floor, where the boards contracted during cold months. We found no rot in this well-ventilated house. The first floor had 10-foot ceilings and double-hung, cedar-framed windows with sills eighteen inches above the floor and heads at about eight feet. The windows were covered with plastic lace printed curtains hanging well short of the window-sills, reminding me of little boys whose legs have outgrown their pajama bottoms.

Heat was provided by a gas stove in the living room, which vented into a brick flue that looked like a fireplace chimney outside but had never had a fire box. The kitchen's 18-inch-wide gas cookstove was the only other heat source. The electrical

The Fremont House, the historic 1891 Victorian home that Jane purchased and renovated

service was two fifteen-amp fuses, which provided a light in each room. The back room held a laundry sink, a washing machine, and a gas clothes dryer. A large wood and coal bin had once held fuel for the original stoves, and a trapdoor in the laundry room floor revealed the former well, which was filled in with soil.

I was the third owner of the house, which had originally served as a doctor's office and family home. The living room had been the reception area, and double doors led to the parlor/examination room. A large back closet was the lab and supply room. Perhaps recovering patients were put to bed upstairs.

When the house was first built, the kitchen was in a single-story wing attached to the back. When indoor plumbing was installed, a second floor was added over the kitchen, providing a generous bathroom and large closet for the west bedroom. The east bedroom lost some space to create a hallway to the bathroom. The addition was skillfully constructed, and the exterior gave only the tiniest clue that it was not part of the original building.

The house came with furniture, mostly beds and chest of drawers, reflecting its other former use as a boarding house. The second owner, a commercial fisherman and his wife, acquired it shortly after 1900. He was out to sea when she saw the for-sale sign and made the deposit of a streetcar token to hold the house until her husband returned. Over the years they took in boarders—likely bachelor fishermen—as they had no children. After the wife died, a housekeeper/cook was

Missy

hired to care for the gentlemen. When the owner and the last boarder died, the house was put on the market by the inheritor, a middle-aged woman who made a business of assisting elderly people without families. She was happy to sell me the house on contract—a bonus as I was very aware that banks did not loan money to self-employed unmarried women. I wanted a challenging project and I certainly had one now.

April 9 was moving day. I filled up my Volvo wagon and unloaded it at 916 North Thirty-Sixth, over and over again. Finally, I was down to the last load and a quivering poodle in her dog bed, wondering what was happening. Missy was so relieved when I picked up her bed and said, "Come on, we're leaving." Marilyn thought I had lost my mind and assured me I could return and have my apartment back, even though she was looking forward to moving into it. "I can't leave you here in this cold place that smells like old people," she said. She couldn't understand what I saw in this historic gem. My, what a good time I was going to have making it mine! This first house helped turn me into a preservationist.

❖

SPRING ALSO BROUGHT several new design projects, which helped fund the work on the house but reduced the amount of time I could spend there. Herb Buller, a former co-worker from Leo A. Daly, was the first worker who came to my rescue, taking on the wiring of my house. The few existing wires ran through old pipes that had powered the original gas lights, and a new electrical panel had to be installed before any power tools could be used. Herb was my angel, working on weekends and refusing pay for his services. I was godmother to his son John, making us family.

Once I had electrical power, it was vital to get a heat source before winter. The former lab area became the space for the new gas furnace, which served new ducts running between the floor joists in the crawl space. Heating the main floor was easy, but to reach the second-floor bedrooms and bathroom, the ducts ran on the inside of the walls between the windows. Eventually, I would build and insulate a wall around the ducts, which set the tall windows in recesses.

Insulating the floor became a weekend project for JC, my parents, and me. My brother and I wriggled on our backs through the crawl space, while Father fed the insulation from the roll to us through a small trapdoor. One of us held the insulation up above our face and the other stapled it to the joist. It was a long, dirty, miserable job, and both of us got the giggles several times, making Father exclaim, "What is going on?!"

❖

AROUND THIS TIME, architect Paul Kirk called to ask for my help with a visiting group of young Japanese women who were interested in architecture. Touring them about the city was a nice break from the remodeling work at home. I would soon become involved mentoring and working with many women around the world.

Then, on October 1, my longtime friend Gretchen moved in with me. Her husband had told her to pack up and go home, so she drove her VW with suitcases of clothes across the country from North Carolina. After years of supporting him while he did graduate work in the States and abroad, she was devastated by his rejection. She returned to Boeing, working in the accounting department. Unfortunately, I was the one who had introduced her to her architect husband, but I never felt they were a good match. She had so much to offer a deserving spouse.

To add some cheer to our fall, we planned an old-fashioned Halloween costume party with games, including bobbing for apples in washtubs that came with the house. The new, exposed heating ducts were covered with orange and black crepe paper, and a huge pumpkin with a happy face greeted our guests on the front porch. On the back side of the pumpkin, the carving was a sad face bidding farewell to guests leaving the party. It was to be the prize for the best costume, but during the party it was stolen from the front porch. The gathering was a chance for friends to welcome Gretchen home and see my new house. I was determined to save and restore my little Victorian jewel, which had a different design carved into each of the gable bargeboards.

My aunts and uncle took a special interest in "Jane's project" because the house was from the same period as their childhood. Uncle Walt refinished the round oak kitchen table into a fine piece of furniture, and I was given a beautiful blue and white quilt that my great-grandmother made for her first granddaughter, my Aunt Ruby. For over seventy years this quilt had been carefully stored, never in actual use.

My new house brought our family closer together at an important time. Just a few months later, on the morning of December 6, my father had a heart attack while shaving. Medic One arrived in minutes, but he was dead before arriving at the hospital. Father had gone to join his second-born, Arthur.

My family would still celebrate Christmas, now in a new place. With the 10-foot ceilings in my living room we could have a Noble fir, and its wonderfully spaced strong branches meant I could use my candles. I had talked so much about the beautiful candle-lit trees in Germany; now my family could enjoy the special event. JC helped me decorate the tree, which included about three dozen snap-on adjustable candle holders. Behind the red candles were strings of small clear lights used during most of the season. On Christmas Eve the candles were lit with all the guests seated quietly—except for my brother and me. We stood beside the tree with candle snuffers and fire extinguishers. My three nieces and young nephew were in awe while the candles burned, the only light in the darkened room. After the candles were snuffed out, our attention turned to the gifts under the tree. The children could hardly wait until the next year, to see the candles lit again.

❖

A SNOWSTORM BLEW IN at the start of 1967, making me eager to tackle a hole in the living room flue and install a cast iron firebox and decorative front developed to fix the lack of a damper. I have always felt that every Seattle house needs a fireplace.

The economy was finally improving, bringing in many interesting new design and major remodeling projects. Two projects were in the Magnolia neighborhood: the Karrow beach house remodel and a new residence for the Quam family. Curt and Marlyn Karrow's house on Perkins Lane could be expanded by adding floors, but only after leveling the existing structure and strapping the fireplace and flue to the house. The new upper floor with tall ceilings became the entry hall and stairs, still well below street level. The new section had a living room with a vertical opening to the dining room below and a master bedroom with a small balcony. In addition to the dining room, the former main level included a kitchen and a guest room,

Karrow House, Seattle, Washington. [Photo: Robert (Bob) Nixon]

as well as a large deck facing the water, supported by an existing retaining wall. The little boxlike structure was finished with horizontal siding grooved to make it appear larger than it was.

This project made me realize how much power one person can wield. We were almost finished when I received a frantic call from Marlyn Karrow telling me about a Metro King County project planned for just north of their property. There was an underground pumping station for the sewer system at the western edge of the shoreline, and Metro intended to build a road for vehicle access. This steep hillside is called the land of "floating monuments" because the survey markers along the beachfront are all off and about five feet to the north. But Metro chose not to honor this history; they told my clients that they would build a 15-foot retaining wall

Quam House, Seattle, Washington. [Photo: Robert (Bob) Nixon]

within inches of the north wall of the Karrows' house, blocking all windows and ventilation. I remembered that architect friend Al Bumgardner was a member of the Design Commission that reviewed and approved all public work, so I called Al and asked if he had seen this project. He hadn't. Metro work was typically underground, and the agency never submitted projects for review. Metro had skirted the law!

One call from the Karrows' attorney, and work stopped. All Metro projects were halted for three days. The man who had terrified Marlyn returned and politely asked her to approve a fence design—and he asked for the house stain color so they could match it.

My favorite compliment about the Karrows' project came from an architect couple who had looked at the house when it was on the market and considered it hopeless. "When we saw what you did with it," they said, "it just makes us sick that we didn't buy it." Later, the Karrow Residence would receive a good deal of press coverage.

When we started work on the Quam family's new townhouse, we discovered that we could extend the city street, which stopped just short of the back of their property. This added value to a difficult site and allowed their cars to be parked at the back of the main level while protecting a coveted water view at the front. Again, we expanded vertically, with the sleeping level below, the formal living room above, and a large roof deck taking advantage of the views out to the water and into a native garden area next door.

❖

MY AIA WORK that year also brought me a great new friend, architect Bob Nixon. Photography was his hobby, and he had a lab in his home. Our early "Home of the Month" 30-inch-by-40-inch display boards had been adorned with renderings and floor plans, but new rules allowed photographs to replace the hand-drawn renderings. Bob volunteered to photograph my projects and printed them just for the cost of materials. What a blessing. This gave me professional boards for eight of my ten "Home of the Month" projects, as well as quality boards to enter in competitions. Over the years, we enjoyed many weekends photographing projects and laying out boards together. Bob later sponsored me for my AIA Fellowship, filling my portfolio with his photos. He was a generous friend who played a major role in the development of my career.

Early on, I started making models of my new house projects after the preliminary design phase. Clients related to the three-dimensional models more readily than to lines on a flat sheet of paper, and a model allowed the architect to study all sides of both house and site. I often let a client keep the model until the house was completed, and then it would be returned to my collection and displayed in my office.

With the passing of my father, my mother had time to spare, so I asked if she would like to make models for the office. She was delighted to apply her skills to a new medium. My mother and grandmother were both talented seamstresses, and I had been perhaps the best-dressed poor kid in the city. Later in life, they still made me beautiful designer clothes. But when my mother completed her first house model, we both studied it for a while. I said, "I can't understand how you can sew so straight and glue so crooked." She looked at me a minute, then burst out laughing: "I really deserved that." From my earliest school days, my sewing projects always stood inspection by both mother and grandmother. They usually said, "That's nice. Now rip it out and do it over." I cannot count the number of times I heard, "I can't understand how you can draw so straight and sew so crooked." It was a wonderful mother/daughter relationship—and all my mother's future models were top quality.

❖

THAT SPRING BROUGHT the grand Matrix Table, with Seattle's leading businesswomen gathering in their finery to celebrate the new Women of Achievement honorees. The annual event was a rare treat to enjoy time with so many other professional women, including former roommates who had also become leaders: Dr. Shirley Anderson; Jean MacDonald, manager of Boeing's technical library; and architect Sue Alden. A few weeks later, we gathered again at the 1967 Interprofessional Women's Dinner, the first year that women architects were invited to join the women lawyers and doctors.

Soon after, I was in New York City for the AIA National Convention. I stayed in a new Hilton Hotel that promoted its ice makers—one in every room. However, many of the ice makers did not work and a few, like mine, would not stop working. Fortunately, they were located over the toilets, so the overflow fell into the bowl. The word got out that I had ice, so I was constantly answering the door to friends with ice buckets in hand.

Our own Bob Durham of Seattle ran for national AIA President, so a team of us made the rounds to promote our candidate, who eventually won against a heavily financed Texan. I quickly realized politics were not my calling. After the conference, several of us continued north to Montreal, which had just wrapped up its World's Fair, to see the exciting new structures before we headed home.

❖

OVER THE YEARS, former friends and colleagues often resurfaced. Mary McKee Chester, the wonderful Fauntleroy Church pastor from my youth, now lived in the University District with a caregiver. Mary would call to say she was coming to The Ave for some ice cream, and I would drop work to meet her.

Another surprising connection to my past came one beautiful summer afternoon when my brother JC talked me into joining him at the celebration of a ship transfer, which he was attending as part of his civilian job for the Navy. A new ship would be transferred to the Turkish Navy, and my brother needed a date because his wife was out of town. Besides, "The Turks throw a good party," he said. A band piped off an American crew, and a Turkish crew was piped on. Then the guests retired to a lavish reception. When JC introduced me to the Turkish naval representative from Washington, D.C., I remembered my Oberammergau evening with "the Terrible Turk," who was the head of the Turkish Navy at the time. So, I asked if he knew Fike. The man laughed, and said, "Now, it's Jim's sister asking!" He had just told someone that this was the first party where some woman had not asked him about this man. He had never met Fike, but said he was a legend and had been forced out of his position. Fike was now a successful businessman. I said, "I'm sure he is!"

❖

SUDDENLY, A LOT of small remodeling jobs arrived in the office. The economy was improving, and the construction industry was surging. However, my family needed attention, too. After taking care of arrangements when my father passed, my mother went to San Mateo to spend time with my grandmother, who was in her mid-nineties, and her sister, my Aunt Lois, who was recovering from a stroke. While my mother was there, I had to call with the news that she was losing a grandchild. Thirteen-year-old Debbie, Art's daughter, had been diagnosed with cancer of the adrenal glands and was expected to live only a few months.

Mother needed to come home, and we would make other living arrangements for BB and Lois. While JC and his wife, Norma, looked for a Seattle apartment for the two Californians, I packed two pairs of dirty jeans and caught a plane to San Francisco in mid-October to pack up and sell their house. When I arrived in San Mateo, my mother and I sent BB and Lois to Seattle with one suitcase each, while we closed out their lives in California.

My mother had lived in San Francisco when she was a young woman, so I decided we needed a two-day vacation. I booked us into the St. Francis Hotel and purchased opera tickets to *Tristan and Isolde*. In addition to enjoying some fine dining, we visited the shop where she had worked as a milliner, which was now a men's

Rice Summer House, Useless Bay, Whidbey Island, Washington, 1968. This was the second house that Jane designed on Useless Bay. Another Home of the Month Award winner, it featured a multipurpose carport that provided a covered play area for the Rice children during inclement weather. [Photo: Robert (Bob) Nixon]

clothing store, and the employees took us through the back rooms where she had worked. On the plane home she said, "You have shown me more of San Francisco than I had seen in all the years I lived there."

MORE NEW WORK was coming in, including a beach house on Whidbey Island that would become one of my favorite jobs. However, I spent much of my time at Seattle Children's Hospital with Debbie as I was the only family member who lived close by. Gerry, her widowed mother, worked and had six-year-old Randy to care for, which made hospital visits difficult. One day when we were in the hematology department's waiting room, a little blind girl bumped into Debbie's gurney, making Debbie groan. The girl's mother, who drove from Bellingham almost daily for her daughter's treatments, told her, "That is Debbie, and she does not feel well today." The child responded, "I'll read to her," and reached for a scrapbook of greeting cards with comforting messages. With the book upside down, she turned the pages while she made up positive sayings. There was not a dry eye among the adults in the room full of terminal children who would not see another year.

This was the second difficult holiday season in a row. Doctors told us to celebrate Christmas early, but we decided that was too much for the other young family members; it would be admitting that we had given up, and Debbie was determined to live to see the lighted candles on my Christmas tree.

When Christmas Eve arrived, my brother, who had been a substitute father since Art's disappearance, planned to bring Debbie on a stretcher in the back of his station wagon. But Debbie, who was at home for her last few days, said it was too much to come. Gerry would not leave her daughter, so only Randy arrived carrying small gifts for each of us: Christmas tree ornaments that Debbie had made while in the hospital. The tree lighting took place after dinner with the three young ones, my brother, sister-in-law, and mother, but the absence of Debbie and her mother cast long shadows over the evening's cheer.

Debbie made it into the new year. Her funeral featuring her Rainbow Girl group was very difficult for her family and friends. Young girls are not supposed to die.

❖

THE FASHION GROUP'S fundraising fashion show, luncheon and cocktail party landed on Valentine's Day 1968. Carroll Righter, a popular astrologer who did horoscopes for Hollywood celebrities, agreed to be our guest speaker. Beth Leonard, the KING TV "Lady of Charm," and I were selected to entertain him while he was in town. Richter decided to make his visit a mini-vacation, arriving early and staying longer, keeping the two of us busy. His farewell dinner was at the Golden Lion, the upscale restaurant in the Olympic Hotel. Would our guest do our horoscopes, as he had hinted? Beth was born in July under the Cancer sign, but he did not use the term due to its negative image. Instead, he told her she was a "moon child." That was all he said before turning to me, a Pisces. He thought about this for a while and then said, "Without a doubt you are the most un-Pisces Pisces I have ever met." There was no horoscope.

I was so busy with my growing practice that I decided to resign from the Soroptomist Club and the University YWCA Board. However, I continued with the Fashion Group and, of course, the AIA, where I helped create a pilot architectural drafting program to launch at four community colleges around the country. My work with the national AIA would continue for many years.

In April the Quam Residence was awarded the "Home of the Month." In June, I attended the AIA National Convention in Portland, which started in Oregon and continued in Honolulu. My mother and my teenage niece Laurie joined me for the Hawaii segment. After the meeting, we traveled to the Big Island and Maui for swimming, tennis, and sightseeing—a much-needed break. It was a great trip for the three generations to share.

I was also enjoying a rich social life with three bachelors, who all cooked and had their unique talents. Daniel Streissguth was an architect, UW faculty member, and backpacker. He loved his home and was happiest working in his garden. His mother once told me he belonged to a former era. I agreed with her and could picture him as the lord of a grand European estate. Donald Hanberg was a forester, sailor, camper, and hiker. He was always prepared with tools and materials for the next task. Like me, he was starting his own business, so we shared common concerns. He was content sitting on the beach just watching the breakers. Norman Johnston was an architect, artist, author, traveler, and UW faculty member. He was a man of action, and I had to run to keep up. He loved music and history and was happiest reading a good book while listening to an opera record.

I often saw all three wonderful men in the same week. I also enjoyed camping and skiing trips, dinner parties, shows, movies and theater with many other friends—a rich and active life.

THAT YEAR, GRANDMOTHER BESSIE BELLE fell and broke her right arm. BB was a regular at the hospital, undergoing surgeries on her stomach and intestines. Each time she was admitted we were told she probably would not make it. But then she would bounce back. When she broke her arm, she had an infection that would not heal, and they amputated her arm at the shoulder. This would be it, they said; she couldn't survive such a surgery. I thought they would know better. She wasn't ready to give up. However, Richard Nixon was running for president, and he was at the top of her all-time list of undesirables. I told my mother that if Nixon won, Grandma would likely check out. But so far, she had surprised us.

As the holiday season approached, my social life quieted down. Norm went to Turkey to teach for a year on a Fulbright scholarship. Dan came by in early November to tell me he was marrying his next-door neighbor, Anne, in December, and

Don went East to work. Our family was busy with BB and her physical therapy as she learned to be left-handed. However, the annual caroling party, the third in my Fremont house, brightened up the season.

At the start of 1969, BB went back to the hospital just before the "Home of the Month" annual banquet at Seattle's Rainier Club, where the Quam Residence was honored as the "Home of the Year." My prize was a beautiful American Indian blanket box constructed and painted by a promising young artist, Duane Pasco.

Soon after, BB passed away—the night before Nixon's inauguration. I knew she was not going to stick around to see him become president.

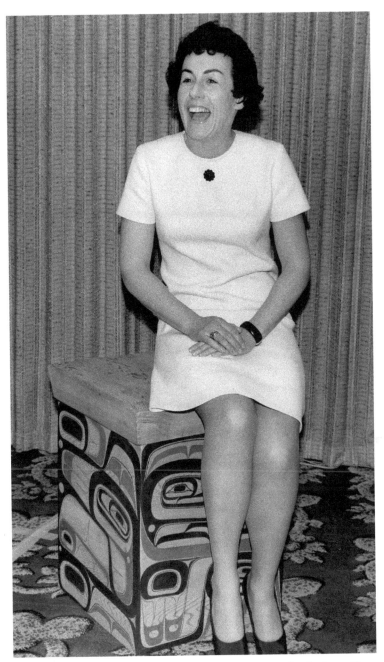

*Jane with the Blanket Box (created by Duane Pasco), the prize for the Quam House,
which was selected AIA Home of the Year for 1968*

11 | AN INTERNATIONAL ARCHITECT

Jane with Princess Grace at UIFA Congress held in Monaco, 1969

I N LATE FEBRUARY 1969, my jolly nisei mailman arrived in my office announcing, "A letter from Paree! A letter from Paree!" What could he be talking about? The envelope was indeed from Paris, and it was an invitation from Her Royal Highness Princess Grace to the International Congress of Women Architects—what a surprise! The next day I told the mailman that Princess Grace had invited me to Monaco, which gave him the giggles. After that, each day he would come into the office saying, "Princess Grace," and giggle. This continued for weeks.

I called Jean Young, another woman architect: Had she received an invitation? No, she replied, but she thought we should both go. Of course, I wanted to return to Europe, but I had not seriously considered it until that moment. We made plans for a whirlwind trip the following June. We would start in Paris, go to Sweden to meet Jean's relatives, then work our way south, taking night trains until we reached Oberammergau for a quick visit with my old German friends. I wrote Norm in Turkey to see if we could drop in on him after leaving Monaco, but he had already made plans to return home. We would have to wait to get together again in Seattle.

Starting out, I had not realized that my profession would open so many doors to me. Architecture is a very respected profession, and for some people, it is almost mysterious. Architects are often welcomed into special places, typically not opened to the public, because we fully appreciate and respect the structure, the design, and the history.

❖

BEFORE PARIS, I traveled to Miami that spring to put the final touches on the proposed AIA/Community College Architectural Technician Training program. The meeting included representatives from the program's four trial cities. I was the only woman in the group, which I was used to, but others were not. One man asked, "What's that secretary doing in the room?"

The comment reminded me of my earliest correspondence with our national AIA headquarters ten years earlier: I had received mail addressed to Louis James Hastings, AIA. My request for a correction didn't receive the courtesy of a response, so I addressed my return letter "Dear Roberta and Dear Williametta." Problem solved.

❖

IN JUNE, JEAN AND I WERE OFF to Europe. I left my office in the care of Audrey Morgan, who had been a few years behind me at UW. I had several projects "on the boards" but the gathering in Monte Carlo was more than I could resist. This was also Jean's first trip abroad and I was determined to show her as much as possible in our limited time. We squeezed in one night in Oberammergau, which hadn't changed much at all.

The 1969 Congress was the second held by the UIFA (International Union of Women Architects), and it included several hundred participants—mostly Western Europeans but also some architects from Communist countries who presented papers, which was required for them to attend. Central and South America were also represented, along with Asia and Africa. Four American women registered: In addition to Jean and me, there was another Jean from California who had also graduated from the University of Washington. The fourth American was a Californian who left after she met Princess Grace and did not attend any meetings. The other participants decided that all American women had the same name and they called us all "Jean." Princess Grace was even more beautiful than in photographs and was absolutely charming, spending extra time talking about "home" with us.

We were asked to bring exhibits or other material to present. I brought a copy of the Seattle AIA Chapter film *ABC (Action Better City)*, produced while Fred Bassetti was chapter president. The film showed several small groups of architects studying parts of our city and making proposals for improvements; it was shown at public meetings to enlighten elected officials and the public about ways to improve the built environment.

After showing the film, Jean and I took questions from the audience, who were moved by this concept of offering suggestions to our civic leaders. The then-Communist Hungarians proposed a resolution to follow this American example to educate the public and their government leaders.

A delegation of Japanese women had been unable to attend; one of them was a UIFA vice president, and she asked that an American delegate be selected to replace her. Because I was the most visible member, UIFA President Solange Herbez de la Tour appointed me vice president to represent both the USA and Japan. There was no election of officers, and this became another lesson learned: Democracy is our American system but is often not practiced elsewhere.

❖

WE MADE WONDERFUL FRIENDSHIPS at the Congress, and someone was always available to translate information into English. The final banquet featured regional cuisine in a traditional folk restaurant located on the yacht harbor where the main road ran between the restaurant and the water's edge. Many attendees wore their finest national costumes, looking very colorful and flamboyant. The bowls of bouillabaisse had whole baby crabs and whole fish heads peering up at us with penetrating eyes. That was too much for our group, so dinner became bread—and much too much wine. The Western style of jeans and cowboy boots was popular, and the group asked us Americans to teach them to square dance. We explained this was not possible—we didn't have a caller, after all—but the pressure was still on. Then Indira, a delegate from India, said, "Well, let's do the Virginia Reel." The last time any of us had done the reel was in childhood, but it was easy, so we moved out into the street and danced. Cars stopped and passengers got out to join us. Soon people came up from their yachts and joined in the singing and dancing. We must have looked like an all-woman United Nations meeting gone wild with saris and other elegant outfits floating in the summer breeze.

We spent our last evening in Monaco enjoying the ballet in the Opera House where we all behaved like proper ladies. When I greeted a gentleman with "Good evening," he studied me and said, "I don't believe I know you." I assured him we had not been formally introduced but we had danced together for the better part of an hour the night before. The look on his face said, "You were one of those?!"

AFTER LEAVING our new international friends, Jean and I went to Italy and my favorite city, Florence. Then we stayed with former classmate Astra Zarina in the heart of Rome. Astra had won the coveted Rome Prize, and she had made Italy her home. She set up her apartment as a school with drafting boards in every corner for students visiting from Seattle. Over the years her "Rome Program" became a major part of the University of Washington curriculum in the College of Architecture and Urban Planning, and eventually other departments would share UW facilities established near Campo de Fiori. Astra's apartment was near the Pantheon, and I had several opportunities to step inside the temple and admire how subtle shifts in the light streaming in from the oculus changed the mood. It became my favorite building in Rome.

Back home, I discovered that we had no applicants to lead the new architectural drafting program we were launching at Seattle Community College. The agreement required that the instructor be a licensed architect. But the economy was booming, architecture jobs were plentiful, and many young architects were starting their own practices. I assured the college that if we could not find someone, I would cover the first year until a permanent instructor could be hired. I was determined that after two years of hard work, planning, and organization, this program would launch. It would not end in failure.

12 | A TRUE PARTNERSHIP WITH NORM

Jane hiking in the snow with Norm (far left, on his first camping trip), Morris Jellison and Marilyn Mattox, far right, July 1969

NORMAN WAS HOME FROM TURKEY and ready to take up camping and hiking. Once he discovered how well we ate on our trips, he was a convert, and fall 1969 was busy. In addition to our backpacking trips, I had two jobs: running my office and teaching community college courses for the launch of the architectural drafting program. And with family needs hopefully behind me, I finally said "Yes." I was ready to marry Norm.

He was a man of many wonderful qualities—especially patience—and he had been in love with me for years. He had proposed the first time back in 1963.

My aunts and father had never understood why I did not get married right after finishing high school or college, like most of my friends. When they asked, I simply said, "I'm still looking for a foot massager," like my father. But Mother had never asked. She knew my career came first, then travel. She never questioned my decisions, even in childhood.

Jane and Norm on their wedding day, November 22, 1969

I had established my architectural practice, lived and traveled in Europe, and seen the historic buildings we studied in school. Plus, I owned one hundred feet of Pacific Ocean beach where the music of the surf was available 24/7. I had dreamed of these things, and I had achieved them. Now I was ready for marriage. My mother was thrilled to have a new son-in-law join our family, which had recently lost members in four generations. We set our wedding date for late November, and I knew this holiday season would be a happy one.

It was fun to plan our wedding; I shopped in Canada for dress fabric, met with Peggy Goldberg to print our unusual invitations, and worked with Ruth Pennington to design my ring. During an all-day, all-girls party at the Anderson house, we made hundreds of hors d'oeuvres to store in the freezer.

On Saturday, November 22, 1969, Norman and I married in the Plymouth Church chapel, forty-six years after my parents had been married in the first Plymouth Church building on that same site. I had fulfilled my promise to my mother that if I married, she would be at the wedding. Our families and a small group of close friends attended the ceremony, which was followed by a large reception at the Richard White Art Gallery in Pioneer Square. This was the beginning of the transformation of the old "Skid Road" into a vibrant area of shops and offices, and some of the neighborhood's residents pressed their noses against the windows, checking out our festivities.

Jane with her brother Jim on her wedding day

Our honeymoon was short, just two nights at the Iron Springs Resort on the Washington coast, before returning home to prepare for Thanksgiving. Norman wanted our first holiday dinner to include his extended family, whom he had celebrated the holiday with for many years. The Johnston and Hastings clans numbered almost thirty diners. We rented a long table and chairs and managed to seat everyone in the dining room at the Fremont house. A football game on TV and a broken water main in the street out front kept the men and younger members entertained while the food was prepared. The next day, Norm said, "I'm glad we did it. Let us never do it again." And we didn't.

The annual caroling party and Christmas dinner with our candle-lit tree provided a festive end to 1969, a very good year.

❖

WE FOUND MARRIED LIFE EASIER than either of us had imagined, quickly falling into a routine that gave us time to continue our normal activities. We had been concerned about this, because we had both stayed single until we were forty and fifty years old. Even as a child, I knew I would always work, just like all the women in my family, and I decided I would not marry just for love and financial security. It had to be more—mutual interests and values, plus a best friend for life. Indeed, I had married a real winner! And when Norman took over our household accounts, I discovered what a jewel he really was. He gave me a check, my allowance to spend just as I wished. I had never had an allowance before. Since I was ten years old, I had always had jobs and paid for my own necessities like bus tokens. My first allowance, at the age of forty-one, almost brought me to tears.

Norm kept surprising me. On our first married Valentine's Day, he gave me a genuine teddy bear, remembering I had never had a real teddy bear. (Of course, I did have a small zoo of stuffed animals crafted by my mother and BB from the remnants of aprons and dresses.) And there was his delightful sense of humor, always so on target, which he shared only with his dearest friends. I especially loved his ability to laugh at himself when he did something stupid—a truly special quality.

JANUARY 1970 MEANT that in addition to my practice, I was back to school, in my second term of teaching. Teaching had always been at the bottom of my list of aspirations, next to nursing. In 1953, when I was asked to consider an architectural teaching position at the University of Kansas, I was mortified. It's true I had always been an organizer—from starting the sixth-grade softball team to getting this new community college program up and running. Organizing something did not mean I wanted to lead it, but I was committed to leading and teaching the drafting program through the end of the school year. I started thinking about ways to share this responsibility with other architects.

I enjoyed working with my students in that first class; some were recent high school grads, while others were returning veterans. It was a challenging academic year with protests and disruptions across college campuses nationwide, and in one alarming moment, a Black student was almost dragged out of my classroom when a group stormed in, demanding he join them at a demonstration. He left, assuring me he would be all right. The next day he was back with a note from his mother apologizing for the disturbance. Demonstrations were not new to me; my architectural office in the University District had been so saturated with tear gas that I took work files home.

NORM AND I CHOSE to live in my 1891 Fremont house because of its spacious seven rooms and two bathrooms. Norm moved in his Eames chair, Evert Sodergren console cabinet, art collection, books, and clothes, and we welcomed our first guest: Professor Dogan Kuban from Turkey, a friend of Norm's from their recent Fulbright year.

I also welcomed the arrival of summer, when I could focus on one job—my practice— and then our long-awaited real honeymoon. Our trip started with the AIA Convention in Boston, which then reconvened in London. Afterward, we traveled through the British Isles by car. Over a month away from phones, school, and business demands—what a joy! We had time to talk and make plans for his house, my house, and our future house. His house in Seattle's Montlake neighborhood would serve as my office until we were ready to move.

During our travels through England, Scotland, Wales, and Ireland, we planned to take turns driving, but Norm found it difficult staying on the left side of the road after turns; on one turn he ran into someone's yard to miss a truck. So I became the official driver with Norm as navigator, driving through beautiful countryside and villages, and visiting grand gardens on our way north.

The Irish roads made me wish we could tour in the upper deck of a London bus. The hedges and greenery were so dense it was like driving through a green chute and we wondered what was hidden behind them all. Finally reaching Ireland's west coast, we were delighted to see the sea and charming little villages. Housewives sat along the roads, knitting sweaters to sell to tourists. This was just what I wanted, so we stopped to check the prices. When I got out of the car the elderly woman looked up and said, "Lassie, you have come home!" This little girl from nowhere, at last, had roots proved by my very dark hair, blue eyes, and pink skin. The price was reduced substantially for a lassie who had returned. Norman was impressed, so he said he was also Irish and would like a sweater. There was no way she was going to let a Scotchman fool her. There were no bargains—and no purchase—for Norm.

Dublin needed an economic lift and a good cleaning. Begging appeared to be one of the major jobs for women, who beseeched us with babies in their arms. Around one corner we stumbled onto their headquarters, where they had put their baby dolls down on a break while comparing their successes of the day. There was not a real baby in the lot.

❖

BACK IN SEATTLE we hosted the Satow family, friends from Oberammergau who had moved to California, and that summer we began a tradition of spending a weekend each year with two Oregon couples who were Norm's longtime friends. Over the years, we discovered hidden pockets in both of our states, and Norm was a real camper at last.

The community college school year started that fall, and this time I had teaching help from several colleagues, who led courses related to their interests and talents. The program was expanding under a new administrator who let me delegate as I wished. No architect wanted to teach full-time, but they all enjoyed contributing a few hours a week over a quarter each year. The students were fortunate to have their unique expertise; I remained on staff, teaching less while doing more administrative work.

That fall, we hosted a dinner party with two other couples whose wives had become good friends of mine. I have always included people from all corners of life at my gatherings, trusting that they would get along and enjoy each other. What fun discovering that Judge Carolyn went to high school with Bill, Geri's husband, and that Norm went to Olympia High School with Cyrus, Carolyn's husband. Cy was the school jock and Norm the nerd, so they had never known each other. The dinner went on into the wee hours, and we all complained the next day that our stomach muscles were sore from laughing.

Around the same time, one of my students invited me to a tea in honor of Dame Joan Sutherland, who was performing in a Seattle Opera production. Norman, the true opera buff, never got over the fact that he missed meeting this wonderful soprano. And the Fashion Group stayed busy, with some of us even modeling at the Frederick & Nelson department store. To think, at one time my figure was a size to be asked to model.

Before the holidays, I had my first appointment with Dr. James Lane, Jr., a rheumatology specialist who was recommended for my arthritis. My medical records were under "Lois Johnston," but as we talked, he said: "I know who you really are. You are Jane Hastings and I have your phone number on my desk to call about remodeling our kitchen." It was the beginning of a long, special relationship.

❖

AT THE START OF 1971, I followed Norm's suggestion and attended the UW Faculty Wives meeting to sign up for an activity. I'm sure he never considered that the activity might be skiing. I did not teach on Tuesday or Thursday, so I rationalized that I could ski on Thursdays and spend Saturdays in the office. This was another group of active women whom I enjoyed as much on the bus rides as on the ski slopes.

We were shopping for a house, which meant finding a home that fell within Norm's walking radius to the university and so far, we had been unsuccessful. So, when we were asked if we would consider building a new home on a good lot coming onto the market, we were intrigued. The lot, a former formal garden for a charming house in the Laurelhurst neighborhood, was within the walking circle. Following the agent's instructions, we climbed over a brick wall and through a space in the yew hedge into what had been a rose garden. To the east was a 3-foot-high rockery with a large unkempt lawn bordered by fruit and decorative trees; this had been serving as the local teenagers' beer-drinking hangout. The yard to the original house was 8 to 10 feet above another rockery and that house had no views into the old garden below. Because of the site's narrow wedge shape—approximately 20 feet across the west view frontage and 60 feet across the back—most people did not consider it a buildable lot. We looked around for about ten minutes before crawling out to call and say, "Sold!"

❖

I RECEIVED A SURPRISE PHONE CALL from Shirley Cartozian, a former student, asking if she could forward my name to an organization looking for a woman architect to participate in an international program. The American Women for International Understanding (AWIU) was arranging a trip to Israel, Egypt, and the Soviet Union to meet with their counterparts in professional fields and service organizations. Norman was not thrilled because the program was just for women and he couldn't go along. Fortunately, soon after, he was invited to join a small group of urban planners who spent a month touring German cities.

Norman arrived home from his tour on April 15, and I left on the 20th for my month abroad. I joined thirty-seven women, who included a doctor, nurse, lawyer, judge, engineer, school administrator, dancer/movie star, social worker, psychologist, newspaper editor, artist, musician, student, a presidential appointee in the U.S. Labor Department, a director of a blood bank, members of art museums, opera and symphony boards, and others. We represented a variety of religions, economic levels, political views, and races, and our group's ages ranged from twenty to sixty-eight years old.

In Washington, D.C., we attended a whirlwind of State Department briefings, embassy parties, and a White House reception with First Lady Pat Nixon. She was a pleasant surprise—warm, charming, and well-briefed about each of us. We wore identification badges that noted where we were from, and I was surprised by the attention I received at the Soviet Embassy, until I realized that they were connecting me with Washington's Senator Henry "Scoop" Jackson, who they worried would be the next U.S. president.

Our trip started in Israel, which smelled of oil even before we landed. There was no time for rest; we were meeting with important leaders immediately and having a difficult time keeping our eyes open. We toured Tel Aviv, where our guides proudly showed off the university. Each building had been donated by Jewish donors from abroad, many from California. We visited historical sites and spent time in Jerusalem before visiting a kibbutz for an overnight visit. Bus delays made us late for the Friday dinner, the only one the parents ate with their children, and they were not happy about waiting. The mothers in our group struggled to understand the kibbutz system of raising children separate from parents, and to our group, communal living did not seem appealing.

Leanne, our student member, was given two tickets to a symphony concert with Leonard Bernstein conducting, and I had the privilege of accompanying her. Returning late from an outing, we had to attend in our travel cottons and sandals. We reassured ourselves that no one would know us, but friends at the concert found us right away.

To get into Egypt, we had to spend the night in Cyprus, where our passports were stamped. Israeli officials had put their stamps on a separate piece of paper, which we could remove from our passport. With no official indication of our time in Israel, we would be allowed to enter Egypt—all part of the political game of the time.

Upon our arrival in Cairo, the porters insisted on carrying our luggage, which was not put on the bus with us. Were they going through our things for security reasons? We checked into the hotel with only our purses. Soon, it was time for our grand reception, and we all had to attend in our grubbiest travel apparel. Well, all of us except one: Our newspaper editor could not resist taking a bath and washing out her traveling clothes, so she had to remain in her room wrapped in towels while we dined with our elegant hostesses. The truck with our bags arrived later that night. Another lesson: Never wash your clothes unless you have other clothing in hand.

While in Cairo, I became friends with Marge Champion, the famous Hollywood and Broadway dancer in our group, because we shared the same early morning swimming routine. Our group's adventures in Egypt included a trip up the Nile to Luxor and the Valley of the Kings, site of the famous temples and tombs. It was only April but very hot. At the Temple of Ammon, where construction was started by Queen Hatshepsut, I was the only one who got off the bus in the 120-degree heat. I had promised Norm I would take a photo of a petrified orange tree stump from 1550 B.C., one of many remaining from trees that once lined the entrance avenue. Norm had seen these on an earlier visit—but only as dimples in the soil from the hilltop above. Needing to show scale, I found a cigarette butt for my historic slide, which would later reside in the UW collection.

In early May, we flew to Moscow, where we landed in snow and acquired an entourage who accompanied us throughout the remainder of our visit. We were told they were reporters and photographers filming a documentary, and every time we moved to a different city, they were there to greet us. We knew they went through our belongings when we were out of our hotel rooms, and some in our group reported missing rolls of exposed film. I decided to carry my film in my purse.

We had been told we could take photographs of everything except bridges and airports, so Leanne and I did not understand the problem when we were stopped by the KGB. We had found the only building of contemporary design, just off Red Square, and we were taking photos. A young Russian woman translated that the KGB wanted our film. A crowd gathered as the officers requested our passports, which of course were at the hotel, so they settled for our film. Leanne opened her camera and handed them hers, but they did not take it. They just wanted to make sure it was exposed, ruining the images. So, I simply opened the back of my camera, exposing only the most recent shots and saving most of the film. By the time we were allowed to leave, our circle of onlookers had grown to about twenty people. Leanne was a liberal student, and the Soviet Union had been her dream trip; now she was shaken and wanted to return home. But the only way out was through a medical or family emergency, so she would have to stick it out. When we returned to the U.S., we were informed of records in Washington, D.C., saying we had been detained by the KGB. No doubt someone in our Moscow audience had reported the incident.

Over two weeks, our travels also took us to Tbilisi, Yalta, and Leningrad, before returning to Moscow, where the snow was gone, and bulbs were about to bloom. In Tbilisi, Georgia, we discovered the men liked to pinch women's bottoms. In Yalta, we visited beautiful vacation cottages; Soviets were all equal, but some were more "equal" than others and had several homes. In Leningrad, the people did not seem as afraid of the KGB as in the other cities. Everyone there was interested in cars and had the cash to buy them but had to wait until vehicles were available. The home-buyers purchased apartments while the buildings were still under construction and then finished them to their own designs. Through most of our trip, we attended prearranged meetings with officials, so it was a real treat to meet fellow professionals one-on-one in Leningrad and hear their stories of life in the Soviet Union.

Other Soviet memories included the two little dishes of caviar—one black and one red—served at each meal. Also, we learned to always finish our meat, or hide it, because anything left on the plate would come back in the soup the next day, often revealing teeth marks because it was too tough to chew.

The day we started home, we spent almost all day at the airport. Several in our group had been singled out for a thorough search of belongings and bodies. After several hours everyone had returned but a woman named Marcy. We had boarded our Pan Am plane when she finally rejoined us. She had been subjected to a com-plete body search—everything but a pelvic exam, she said. Marcy had the face and figure of a movie star, so we decided her inspectors thought she could not possibly be real and were looking for silicone or some foreign material. She had a wonder-ful sense of humor, saying it wasn't all bad because in scouring her purse, they had found an old paper with a phone number that had been lost for over a year. We were the only passengers on the large plane and followed the pilot's instructions to huddle in the middle until airborne. When we made our first stop, in Copenhagen, our entire group burst into laughter, releasing our pent-up tensions. We had not realized how stressed we were from being constantly monitored.

My biggest takeaway from that Cold War-era trip was that governments are out of touch with their people. The Israelis we met were not that friendly; they mostly wanted to ask why the United States was not giving more financial aid. Egyptians were not supposed to like us, but they were charming and helpful. The Soviets would run if you asked them a question, afraid of their own police. Locals engaged with us only in Leningrad, where they were further from Moscow and more accus-tomed to Western visitors.

❖

WHEN I ARRIVED HOME, Norman surprised me with an enthusiastic welcome and the announcement that I had won a national design award for the remodel of the Kar-row Residence. The award was presented at the AIA Convention in Detroit, which

I could not attend, so my friend Al Bumgardner accepted it for me. This newest award put me on the design jury circuit, first for the Southwest Washington AIA Honor Awards in Tacoma in September and then for the "Home of the Year" jury in December. I was also invited to write for the *AIA Journal;* my article on remodeling appeared in the December 1971 issue.

The new year of 1972 started with the Fashion Group Career Day conference, followed by a panel at The Evergreen State College entitled "Women in Professions." Our group included a lawyer, doctor, judge, several other professionals, and me, and we gathered in a beautiful auditori-

Norm's welcome home card for Jane

um on the newly completed campus. The academic on the panel had recently been featured on the cover of a national newsmagazine for a story about how she walked away from her husband and children to start a new life. This was early in the women's movement and our large audience was full of grubby students in muddy boots who climbed over the brand-new seats, making me cringe. I was the only woman in the room wearing a skirt rather than pants. After the session, Norman and I were invited to a student-prepared dinner, but Norm took one look at the group and said he would take me out. He was afraid to eat anything they had prepared.

Spring also brought new office help. Carolyn and Jonn Geise had separated, and she had returned to Seattle from the East Coast. She started working for me part-time while she debated between returning to architecture or continuing her new career path in advertising. At the same time, I moved my office out of Norm's Montlake house, which we wanted to sell, and into shared space with Arne Bystrom across from REI in Seattle's Capitol Hill neighborhood, which was closer to the community college. I was busy with the office and teaching, so Norm started cooking three nights a week while I stayed at the office late working on plans for our new Laurelhurst house.

Around this time, R. Buckminster Fuller, famed architect of the geodesic dome, was invited to give a lecture series at UW. Norman picked him up at the residence of his cousin, Richard Fuller, founder of the Seattle Art Museum, and delivered him to the UW sports pavilion, where a capacity crowd waited. Bucky, as he is affectionately known, held the audience spellbound.

Afterward, I climbed into the back seat of the car with Bucky in front, and told Norm, "Head for the Baskin-Robbins ice cream store." Bucky always had raspberry sherbet and tea after a lecture. With the sherbet in hand, we headed home to the Fremont house to make tea. Our tea party lasted past 2 a.m. as Bucky shared stories from his life and adventures. Norm and I wished we had invited a group of students to join us, but we had no clue what a special evening was in store. An architectural giant, all to ourselves; it was a memorable night we would cherish.

❖

ON ONE SUNNY AFTERNOON I received a call that I was needed on the Balcom job—now! Two painters were waiting for a decision on a paint color. The job, a summer house, was in Thorp, on the east side of the Cascade Mountains and several hours away by car. A company plane would pick me up at the Bellevue Airfield in thirty minutes. "Fine," I replied and wrote down the number of the aircraft.

I waited on a bench beside the tarmac while men worked on their personal small planes until all eyes looked up to watch a new twelve-passenger jet circle and land. Yep, those were my numbers! Soon, we were on our way, flying over the Cedar River Watershed, Seattle's water source, to the Ellensburg Airfield. Arriving on site, I quickly selected the paint color and the painters went to work. Then the Balcoms and I settled in to discuss the project over a glass of wine. Yes, architecture has some very good days.

❖

THE AIA REGIONAL CONFERENCE was set for Anchorage, eight years after the terrible 1964 earthquake forced it to be rescheduled. Norm and I wanted to attend—both to support our colleagues up north and to study the recovery and post-earthquake designs and development. The third reason: This was the 30th anniversary of when Norm first went to Alaska while serving in the U.S. Army during World War II. We

Stevens Residence, Tacoma, 1972. Constructed adjacent to a wild area of Dash Point State Park and on a tight budget, the innovative design utilized free used telephone poles as exposed structural members. [Photo: Robert (Bob) Nixon]

were trying to save money for the new Laurelhurst house, so we agreed to make the trip but not purchase anything. This was especially difficult for Norm, who liked to find art everywhere he went and add it to his collection.

After the conference in Anchorage, we traveled north on the slowest train ever to see Mount McKinley (better known as Denali to an Alaska resident). The ride to Fairbanks was a wonderful way to watch the scenery and wildlife as the moose found the tracks an easy trail. On their own time, they eventually moved off the tracks for the snorting engine and posed for the cameras. The inland community of Fairbanks, Alaska's second largest city, experiences extreme seasonal temperature changes, and nearly 24-hour summer daylight produces amazing vegetables and flowers. The huge bugs were equally amazing, so we were glad to be there in late August after the height of summer.

Of course, we had to visit the stores featuring Native Alaskan goods and art. Norman found a Nunivak Island mask featuring an owl and otter that had won a design award. He was in agony, because he could really see it fitting perfectly into the collection he had started thirty years earlier. Remembering our "no purchases" promise, he left the shop to wait for me outside. I could see him pacing back and forth on the sidewalk, so I asked the saleslady for her card and went out to join him.

We traveled on to Nome, where Norm had been stationed during the war, for a sentimental trip through neighborhoods that had changed little since he was last there. Dogsleds had been replaced by rusting snowmobiles, and the older buildings had been dragged out of town and left on the tundra, where they were gradually sinking into the permafrost. Old mining dredges remained here and there over the landscape, resting in the spots where they had last been used. I'm sure Nome was much prettier under a blanket of snow. From Nome, we traveled to the Arctic Circle and the town of Kotzebue, where we enjoyed an Eskimo blanket-tossing competition and saw Native Alaskan craftspeople at work.

Back in Anchorage before heading home, we were still checking out the shops with their native handcrafts, but with each mask we saw after Fairbanks, Norm would say, "It's good but can't compare to the owl and otter." I decided I had to risk my marriage and renege on our promise. I found a postcard and wrote a note to the saleslady in Fairbanks asking her to hold the mask until I could contact her from Seattle.

❖

AFTER ONLY SIX DAYS HOME, I was again on a plane, this time to Romania, for the third Congress of the UIFA. I met up with several other participants at the airport in Beirut, Lebanon, to catch the flight to Bucharest. Lebanon was one of the most war-torn countries in the world, and we received a harsh education in airport security. Before we boarded, we were each taken individually into a curtained cubicle and frisked to a level they could have found a hidden pill. The process was a shock to all of us.

This UIFA Congress attracted more attendees from the U.S., mostly from California. The women's movement was gaining momentum and three young, well-financed East Coast students decided to make the Congress their platform. They did not register to participate but drove in from Western Europe with a car loaded with media equipment, setting up headquarters in a nearby hotel. They invited international members of the Congress to come for interviews, which conflicted with our published program agenda. Solange d'Herbez de la Tour, UIFA president, came to me and said, "They are yours, do something to stop the interference." Fortunately, we had enough members to tell the interlopers to either join us or leave. We did not want them to use the Congress for their cause.

Following the meetings, we bused north to the wonderful collection of painted churches unique to the region of Moldavia, dating from the fifteenth century. We visited Voroneț Monastery, constructed in 1488 and one of the best-known Romanian medieval monuments. The frescoes covering the exterior walls give the monastery its exquisite colors, and the interiors are equally rich with every surface another piece of art. Certainly, these small structures are world jewels.

We also toured some of the small villages. They are just a few kilometers apart, but each village had its own architectural style and character. At the mouth of the Danube River, we were treated to rowboat rides through the delta, where we collected a type of water chestnuts for yummy munching. Finally, we went swimming in the Black Sea, where the resorts were favorites of the Italians.

On my way home, I stopped in England for an overnight stay in architect Heather Lomax's historic Lambs House. The stone floor was worn from hundreds of years of constant traffic. The bed was as cold as the stone floors, but my thoughtful host had placed three hot packs in between the sheets, giving me a cozy night of sleep.

Writing this about fifty years later, I realize how often I was away and traveling. But Norm was on the road just as frequently as I was; he served on several committees and often traveled for many days at a time. We both believed in being team players, supporting each other and our interests.

❖

ONE DAY WHILE REVIEWING my family background, I found an old family photo of a very interesting St. Louis residence, the home of Charles Cicero Rainwater. I recalled a story about my grandfather, Sam Pugh, visiting his Uncle Charles when he was a boy. His uncle told him it was time for him to meet the president. I'm assuming that Sam was about ten years old, so it must have been President Rutherford B. Hayes. Architecturally, the house was unusual, so I shared the photo with Norm, who immediately replied, "I know the house. It is on Benton Place, one of the historic private streets in St. Louis." He found a sketch of the house he had made while writing his dissertation for his doctorate on early urban planner Harland Bartholomew. Truly, it is a small world!

Late in the year I became more active in the UW Faculty Wives group, giving lectures and running tours. Carolyn and I also decided to teach an evening college class on designing your own kitchen. We had developed a standard document for our remodeling clients with instructions explaining how to measure their own houses. Some clients were enthusiastic and did a good job, while others were complete failures. This was an educational tool that helped us in the office, so we brought the document into the evening class full of adults who had a wonderful time with it.

A woman named Patti was our top student, a true star. After her redesign, she also enrolled in a cabinet-making class. She was a woman of unbelievable energy, and she invited Norm and me to dinner to see the finished project. The delicious dinner featured homemade bread from flour she milled herself and fresh tomatoes from her summer garden that she had stored for winter use. She had an important full-time job, ran miles on her lunch hour, and devoted weekends to teaching skiing and mountaineering. Her teacher husband sat relaxed the whole evening. On our drive home, Norm said, "How does he stand it? I thought you had energy. I couldn't handle her."

The holidays of 1972 were once again marked by sadness. Aunt Lois had caught her dress on fire and suffered severe burns. The fireman who took her to the hospital took me to coffee and said, "They will try and save her, but they shouldn't." After eight days, with the help of Dr. Shirley Cooke Anderson, we asked to have her removed from life support, and said our goodbyes.

13 | THE HASTINGS GROUP

The Hastings Group 1975 Christmas card: Norm Millar, Phyllis Harris, Carolyn Geise, Jane, and Kate Hills Krafft

THE NEW YEAR MEANT A NEW OFFICE. In early 1973, Carolyn and I began renovating an old storefront on Olive Way in Seattle's Capitol Hill neighborhood, breaking out our hammers and saws, and practicing our carpentry skills. One day, a contractor friend checked on our progress. He took one look at our spackling and rolled up his sleeves. With mighty sweeps of his muscular arm, he wielded the trowel to give the walls a professional finish. Our skills obviously lay in demolition and design, not finish work.

What fun to be on the bustling street level and to have space to accommodate several employees, including a secretary. Carolyn brought in some of her own projects, so we formed a partnership—The Hastings Group—and went to work.

We also had the Interprofessional Women's Dinner on our plate. Each year a different professional group organized the May event; the architects' group was the smallest by far, and this was our year. We enjoyed getting acquainted with other professional women, so Carolyn, Lois Wardell and I invited veterinarians and church ministers to join the event.

UW ran several programs for women who were returning to school, and I was constantly being asked to take part. The 1970s were the decade of women in the workforce, and I began to think life was better before we were "discovered." I could get so much more work done when I stayed in the office. I also served on several city committees that evaluated the response of women-owned businesses to legislated set-asides for minority and women-owned business.

At UW, we elder women architects agreed to meet with recent graduates, including some already working in professional offices. The potluck dinners at Lou Daly's home included a group of about fifteen young women who had bought into the hype and believed they were being discriminated against. We listened to their sad stories about how they were underpaid and not given proper recognition. I remembered my tea parties for the small group of women architecture students in the late 1950s and early '60s. My advice was still the same:

- Never accept "no" for an answer; there is always a way.
- Do not butt your head against a brick wall. Use your problem-solving skills and creativity to find a different path.
- Even if you're not accepted, stay positive.

Those earlier tea-party conversations had stayed focused on future goals—how to apply for a job and find firms that employed women. But this dinner-party group just wanted to complain. Hadn't they received the same warning I had: that architecture was not a financially rewarding profession? I knew they were being compensated the same as the men; in one firm, they actually earned more.

After too many complaint-filled dinner parties, I decided to devote my time elsewhere. An AIA study confirmed that more women than men left the profession; some left architecture for related fields where they could earn more—such as the business side of construction—while others left the industry altogether. The AIA reasoned that those women who left found the lack of promotions and potential legal liabilities in the profession were not worth the financial rewards.

WE HAD OUR OWN CONSTRUCTION PROJECT well under way at our Laurelhurst house, and my mother often joined me to check out the site. She had always wanted to build a house; now she could do it without solving the problems or paying the bills. It was an ideal arrangement, she said.

Years earlier when my father was alive, my parents had purchased a vacant lot near brother JC's house to build their retirement home. I knew they did not have the financial resources to build, but I designed a house for them anyway. I dragged the process out, hoping they would face reality on their own. But eventually Mother pinned me down and I had to explain that she was too old to build a house. Even if she had all the funds required, which she did not, making decisions about fixtures, colors, finishes, etc., would be too much at their age. My father had already suffered a heart attack, and neither was physically able to paint or do the landscaping. When I said this, my mother cried. I was devastated at hurting her. Later, she apologized for her tears and said I was right, but I have never gotten over the fact that my honesty killed her dreams.

❖

NORMAN STARTED THE TRADITION of surprising me each November with a getaway on the weekend before our anniversary. Every year, he secretly researched new romantic locations, and my only clue to our destination was his instruction to pack either my dancing shoes or hiking boots. We discovered wonderful hidden gems together.

In early 1974, one of Seattle's wettest winters finally dried out enough that the contractor could work full time on our Laurelhurst house. As the framing grew upward to three floors above the basement, I anticipated calls from the neighbors. Before we started building, we showed them the plans and a model of the house. Their response: "Why don't you build a little bungalow as there are just the two of you?" We explained that the shape of the lot and setback requirements meant we had to go up, and the square footage wasn't any greater than their houses. The only homeowners who lost some of their view actually liked our plan because we shielded them from the main street below.

Now that I was a well-established architect, I had no trouble getting good contractors to take my jobs. For our house, I selected Hjalmar Froyland, who I thought of as a Norwegian elf. He was small in stature but muscular and agile. Eric the Swede—probably the finest finish carpenter in the area—was his best man. We had worked well together on other projects, so I knew I was in good hands. Of course, we were behind schedule, and Norm and I had to move in before everything was

Laurelhurst House, aerial view, and floor plans from BUILDING & REMODELING magazine January/February 1980

finished. So, for a while we shared our home with workers like Eric, who arrived about 5:30 a.m. after dropping his wife off at her job. He drank coffee and read the newspaper until starting work at 7:30. He drove a Volvo with squeaky brakes that announced his arrival coming down the hill to our house. The neighborhood was delighted when Eric's work was finished.

I had a new requirement for our house: It had to be burglar-proof. Break-ins were a bigger problem in this affluent neighborhood than in Fremont, and my

Laurelhurst House exterior with garden [Photo: Mary Randlett]

solutions included double-keyed cylinders on all ground floor doors and wire glass in the two-story greenhouse, which was part of the kitchen. We did not have any break-ins, and I dearly loved the wall of glass that allowed me to enjoy my indoor/outdoor garden, even though the greenery was always demanding my attention to weed and trim.

Norman gave me other problems to solve. He wanted a high entry space and stairway to hang a contemporary Swedish chandelier with dropped glass crystals that had been in storage because it was too large for his Montlake house. He also required a study/library and a special place for his custom 7-foot-long music cabinet designed by Evert Sodergren with a mosaic tile top Norm had created. We both wanted wall space for artwork and plenty of natural light. The 10-foot living room ceiling with a light well into the center of the house met these requirements.

Norman always said he was my worst possible client: He complained about the costs, and he didn't pay the architect. He decided we would build from out-of-pocket money, along with proceeds from the sale of our two homes, so we would not need a mortgage. He reasoned that if something happened to him, I could support myself if I didn't have house payments. We both remembered people in our childhoods who lost their homes. Our investment broker called us "un-American" because we had no debts.

My new kitchen was the highlight of our house. From my control center—the kitchen island and sink—I looked over Union Bay, with the campus beyond. I had my garden flowing from inside to outside at my feet. What a place to cook!

❖

THAT YEAR, I LET MY FRIENDS Paul H. Kirk and Jack Morse talk me into running for president of the Seattle AIA Chapter. Our membership stood at about one thousand six hundred and still had very few women, with only two of us active. Paul and Jack said it was time for a woman to serve as president: "You are the only one who can do it." I protested that the boys were not ready for a woman. "They really are, but just don't know it," Paul and Jack replied. I insisted that a viable male candidate had to be on the ballot, too. I refused their first two suggestions because they were not strong enough, but when Dave Hewitt agreed to run against me, I said fine. I won the election, and Dave was gracious about his loss. The secretary commented that members she had never met had voted. No doubt, those were my former university classmates.

In winter 1975, I taught a studio class at the UW School of Architecture, taking a leave of absence from Seattle Central Community College (renamed when the community college campus expanded to North Seattle). Because of pressure from the women's movement, UW was bringing in more female professionals to teach. They hired two women during summer school and one during each of the other three quarters, giving them a total of five women instructors for their records.

Jane with students learning to build snow houses at Alpental

The studio was a mixed group, including some students who arrived straight from high school, some who were changing majors, and several who were returning older students. The best part was they all really wanted to be there. I assigned projects from my office, which gave them experience with actual site visits. When I asked if they would like to construct something, they gave a resounding "Yes!"

The design problem involved free material: They would build a snow house. Architect friends who taught snow-house construction to Boy Scouts and mountaineers were guest lecturers in the studio. Those who wanted to build met on a Saturday morning and carpooled for the 45-minute drive to the Alpental ski area. A client couple owned a ski cabin I had designed, and they offered this as our headquarters for meal preparations and bathroom facilities. The students were expected to sleep in their snow structures. One student asked if we could get local news media to cover their adventure; yes, I had a TV friend who might be interested.

That Saturday turned out to be beautiful and sunny, and the TV crew arrived while all the students were hard at work creating their individual sleeping units.

Everyone had a wonderful time, and the TV crew left just in time to get their footage on the evening news. The class gathered for dinner, which I fixed with the help of the cabin owners, who joined us to be part of the fun. The class then returned to their snow houses with their sleeping bags for the night. Soon we heard them coming back in one by one, until all but one gave up their survival houses for the comfort of the cabin. It was a perfect weekend, even though they missed getting to see themselves on TV.

Two members of my class later became employees of my office, where we helped them get into graduate school. Janelle Forgette went to Washington University and Norm Millar to University of Pennsylvania, and both had promising futures. Several of my SCCC students went on to the University of Washington and also worked in the office. Kate Hills (later, Krafft) with her gold curls, hazel eyes, and perfect complexion sat at her front-window drafting board, where her welcoming smile greeted everyone as they came in the door. The office was in a convenient location, but we dealt with the usual street problems related to drugs and alcohol. One day, a policeman came in, asking if she had seen anyone strange that morning. Kate looked up with her usual smile and said, "Officer, everyone is strange around here but us." He was investigating a murder that had happened across the street, but he couldn't resist a smile.

❖

THAT YEAR, MY DUTIES as AIA Seattle Chapter president took me to Tucson for the national grassroots meeting; to Big Sky, Montana, and Portland for regional meetings; and to Atlanta for the national convention. My mother accompanied me to Atlanta, where she had the chance to meet friends from my Germany days, along with their mothers. My busy work life provided lively topics for my keynote speech for the Architectural Secretary Association; I called the talk "See Jane Run."

Other AIA duties required serving on the Council of Design Professionals and the Washington State Council. But there were perks of the job, too, such as the invitation to join the mayor and other dignitaries on the maiden flight of a new route for a regional airline serving Seattle and Victoria, B.C. The beautiful flight over the San Juan Islands was followed by a lavish buffet dinner before we flew back to Seattle, where I was invited to sit in the cockpit during the landing at Seattle-Tacoma International Airport. I often thought back to that unique perspective when I arrived home from other trips.

Blomberg   Hastings   Sales   Feinstein

San Francisco design jury with Dianne Feinstein

After classes were over in June, Norm and I took a trip to New York City, and in a twist, it was just for fun. After enjoying museums and other sights, we drove a rental car north to Troy to visit one of Norm's Army buddies and his Finnish wife. Like Norm, Bob Anderson was a professor, and they had a grand time talking about their Army adventures in Nome and the changes we observed there in 1972. I was surprised how much I enjoyed upstate New York with its beautiful old farms and historic houses.

In Buffalo, we toured Frank Lloyd Wright designs and other treasures, and of course, we saw Niagara Falls, a must for all brides. We had been married six years, but somehow this visit made it official.

In mid-July I boarded a morning flight for a day in San Francisco to serve as the out-of-state judge for an interior design awards program. I joined three impressive local women: Betty Blomberg, an interior designer; Enid Sales, a planner; and Dianne Feinstein, then a candidate for San Francisco mayor. After our jury duty was completed, we participated in a panel discussion on women's issues in male-dominated professions. I remember Dianne being an outstanding public speaker.

❖

DURING THIS BUSY TIME, I was also a member of the regional General Services Administration (GSA) committee to select architects for government projects. Our region covered Montana, Idaho, Oregon, Washington, and Alaska, and the committee included a representative from each state. Because I was local, I was the lone representative at many meetings; afterward I would contact the other four members to discuss what went on and get their feedback. The experience reassured me that I was happy doing private rather than public work.

The biggest GSA decision at the time involved the National Oceanic and Atmospheric Administration project at the former Sand Point Naval Air Station in Seattle. Our committee named five firms to the short list, and the final selection was made in Washington, D.C.

One firm that I insisted on including was John Graham Jr.'s, which had already completed the preliminary study in partnership with a local African American architect, Ben McAdoo Jr. However, the other four firms were very strong, so we all thought Graham probably would not get the job. I was stunned when I learned that the Graham firm wrote to one of our senators requesting that I be removed from the committee, claiming I was prejudiced against them. The GSA team was happy to report that I was the only regional-committee member who had advocated to add the Graham firm on the short list. Of course, the final decision was made back East. The job went to another firm.

Now that women had been "discovered" and given more roles to exercise their skills and training, it was suddenly important to have one on every agency committee. The problem: There were just not enough female architects to cover all the requests. Paul Kirk got me on a former mayor's committee addressing architectural barriers for those with disabilities, and it took me years to get out of those meetings. Once on a committee, it was impossible to get off.

❖

AS THE SCHOOL YEAR ENDED, Norm and I prepared for a big change. We both had sabbaticals and could be in Europe from July 1976 to July '77. Norm would be doing research for his first book, *Cities in the Round,* while I would be taking photos for my architecture history course. We were barely settled in our new Laurelhurst house, but Norm felt the sooner we went the better—especially because my 80-year-old mother planned to join us overseas in spring 1977.

But before we left, I had a national design opportunity: *Family Circle* magazine had contacted The Hastings Group to develop a special house plan— "the house designed and built by women with everything women want." Carolyn and I flew to Cleveland to meet with a large prefabrication construction company, but their typical houses were larger and more expensive than our design, so we decided to work with a local builder.

We incorporated our signature kitchen features into the design—including under-cabinet lighting, a freestanding island workspace and cabinets that opened into both the kitchen and dining areas—and the plans were set before Norm and I departed in July. Carolyn would complete the job while I was away.

Two of my early clients, LaVern and Lorna Leistikow, agreed to move into our Laurelhurst home for the year. Their grown son would stay in their house in the Issaquah woods while they tried out city living—taking over our lifestyle, complete with the cat, Despina, and our opera and symphony tickets. Lorna also took this opportunity to finish her university degree while keeping our house and garden in order.

It was time for a new grand adventure. Norm and I were ready.

FAMILY CIRCLE/SEPTEMBER 20, 1977

ALL PHOTOS BY VINCENT LISANTI

The average price of a new house today is $55,000.* Ours is about $48,000.*
And it's loaded with extras you probably thought didn't exist anymore.

THE HOUSE THAT WOMEN BUILT

The price alone could sell you on this house, but that's only part of its appeal. The thing that's really extraordinary is its total practicality. This house was designed by women, for women, with the needs of women in mind; flip through the following pages to see what that means. Everything about this house makes sense: The floor plans are spacious and functional; the woody tones go well with all types of furniture; the clean lines are timeless; the built-ins are super-serviceable, as well as good-looking. The 1,700 square feet of space contains a living/dining/kitchen area that runs the width of the house, plus a separate entranceway, powder room and utility room downstairs; and, upstairs, a large main bedroom, smaller second bedroom and bath. There's also lots of closet space. Why so cheap? Wise choice of material and careful planning of detail kept the cost down. The old-fashioned sash windows, saltbox overhang and modern rear deck would look just as great in the suburbs as on the West Coast or in the New England countryside. Produced in collaboration with the American Plywood Association, the house was built by the Creative Homes and Development Corporation, with furnishings by JCPenney. Plans are available through a coupon on page 111. They include complete directions for the house, kitchen and deck. By ROBERT L. ANDERSON and ELIZABETH GAYNOR

* Prices include land: U.S. Commerce Dept., April 1977

≫→

FAMILY CIRCLE 9/20/77 **83**

Family Circle House, a page from the magazine article [Courtesy Dotdash Meredith, Family Circle, 1977]

14 | OUR SABBATICAL YEAR ABROAD

Jane and Norm aboard the Stefan Batory sailing from Montreal to Bremerhaven, Germany, July 1976

WE SAILED FROM MONTREAL on a Polish cruise ship, the *Stefan Batory*, a former Holland America ocean liner. The Polish Ocean Line was a good price, and we could take footlockers at no extra charge. Our fellow passengers were mostly Fulbright students or others on sabbaticals, and we enjoyed the relaxed crossing. During the evenings we played silly games with the Polish crew and joined them in laughing at their bad jokes. The scent of French onion soup always seemed to be in the air, from breakfast to bedtime. Perhaps it was the crew's standard fare.

Our first port of call was Southampton, followed by Rotterdam and finally, Bremerhaven. My longtime friend Joyce met us and drove us south to Unter-türkheim, a village outside Stuttgart that would be our home for the year. This was my second arrival in Bremerhaven; Joyce and I had disembarked here in 1954 for our Service Club jobs. Joyce was now a military wife living with her family in Zweibrücken on the French border, not far from our new home. How wonderful to have good friends close by. In Europe, so many destinations are relatively easy to reach, especially for those with cars.

Untertürkheim is home to the Mercedes-Benz automobile company, and its financial success had turned this wealthy community into one of the least architecturally interesting places in Germany. Charming timber and stucco houses and shops had been modernized, covering over the details of the traditional regional design. The town's biggest draw was a beautiful park with a racetrack where Mercedes tested cars. Entering Stuttgart, we drove across a bridge above the track, often hearing a loud "swoosh" as a new model vehicle flew by below, showing its stuff.

Joyce deposited us at the home of our friends, Wolfgang and Ruth Henning, who lived on the outskirts of the village across from a meticulously maintained cemetery where family members tended their loved ones' plots on Sunday afternoons. The Henning house was a large three-story structure designed by Wolfgang, an architect from Berlin. Land stays in the family, so this property belonged to Ruth's family, and Wolfgang married into it. Behind the locked garden gate, the home's entrance opened into a reception hall where stairs led to two upper floors, each occupied by a large family apartment. Ruth's sister and her family lived on the second floor, and the Hennings and their three daughters lived on the top floor. The two families seldom spoke to each other, and their children did not play together. They were related but separated by social status because Ruth had a professional spouse, and her sister married a shopkeeper. These class rules were considered very important.

The entry level contained an office where Wolfgang sometimes worked, and a small apartment where we lived for several weeks before moving down the hill into the village. Our actual home-away-from-home for a year was a larger apartment in a building with four other apartments. It was owned by Wolfgang, who had it furnished for our arrival. The kitchen had a new East German range, a small refrigerator, two chairs, and a small table with wood slats—more attractive than functional. The living room was a respectable size, but the adjacent bedroom was small, and the tiny bathroom would have fit comfortably in a train car. A few dishes, glasses, flatware, cooking utensils and linens saw us through until our footlocker arrived with additional supplies.

While still at the Henning residence, where vineyards crept down the hills next to the yard, Norm and I hosted our first guest. Janelle was a former student of mine who had just completed her studies at the UW Rome architectural program. She stayed on our sofa for two nights, to the disapproval of our landlord. We learned that Wolfgang, who was also an architecture professor, had two personalities. When he was teaching in Seattle, he seemed totally American, even hosting student parties at his apartment. I had often told Norman he was not like the typical Germans I had worked with in the 1950s. Now, we were seeing another side to Wolfgang. Status was important, and Wolfgang expected that class differences be respected. This reminded me of my experience in Oberammergau; by scrubbing the floor, I lost the respect of the German employees. They were sure I had lied about being an architect because no professional would scrub a floor! We would have to adjust to local protocols.

An important early order of business was to pick up our new Swedish Saab car in Frankfurt. I had ordered it in Seattle and would bring it home after our year abroad. Before I agreed to buy the car, I asked the auto dealer in Seattle to park the same model in our Laurelhurst garage to make sure it would fit.

❖

OUR NEW HOME IN THE VILLAGE CORE was just two short blocks from the bakery, grocery store and laundry. Our new neighbors had all lived in the building for many years, and the only resident who spoke English was Renata, the daughter of the couple who lived on the top floor. Norman had studied German for a year before our trip and people could understand him, but when they answered, he had no idea what they were saying. I could translate a bit because the Swabish dialect was similar to Bavarian, considered just a notch up in status from the lowest form of the language. To our relief, we found that most young people spoke English. However, the person I most wanted to speak English with, the grocery store manager, insisted he did not.

We quickly fell into a daily routine. Norm was up first, and he went down to the bakery for fresh warm rolls while I made coffee. During breakfast, Norm would propose our adventure for the day, and then we often set out with a picnic lunch.

When our footlocker arrived at the rail station, Renata's retired father wanted to go with us to help with the retrieval—and to ride in our new car. We were the only residents of our building who had a car. So far, Renata's family had been the only neighbors to communicate with us with anything more than a nod. I'm sure most of our neighbors thought we were far above them on the social scale because we were educated and foreigners. We would find a way to address this issue.

❖

OUR SABBATICAL COINCIDED with the hundredth anniversary of the Bayreuth Festival, and Norman had been trying for a year to get tickets to attend *The Ring* cycle. He was a Wagner connoisseur who had never missed a Seattle Opera production of *The Ring*, so this would be the pinnacle of his music experience. No tickets were available in the U.S., so Wolfgang had pursued them through his German channels. Still, no luck. Norman was still determined to visit Bayreuth, even if we just drove up to spend a day or two to enjoy the ambiance. Because I had attended an opera there in 1954 and described its wonderful acoustics, Norman was even more determined to go. And Bayreuth was only a few hours' drive to the northeast.

When we arrived, we decided to see if a hotel room could possibly be available, and to our surprise, we were soon checked in. Norman asked the young man showing us to our room if he happened to know of any tickets we could buy. It turned out his mother had one for the following day that she could not use—what amazing luck! Norman insisted that we needed two, but I said we would take the one because this was so important to him. The young man even sold it to us at face value. Relishing our good fortune, we freshened up and returned to the lobby, where we were seated for dinner at a large table with several others. Our table neighbors included an older man, his grandson, and a middle-aged woman, all speaking French. I had no idea what they were talking about, but I assumed opera.

As they finished, the woman turned to us and asked us in English where we were from. When we said Seattle, her face brightened and she immediately engaged us in conversation. Norman told our sad tale of no tickets, how we had miraculously found one, and my insistence that he go without me. We could not travel so far and not both get in, she said. She handled all the festival tickets, so I was to show up at the ticket office the next day and she would find a place for me. My, did we sleep well that night after all our good fortune! When we arrived at the festival hall the next day, I noted how much work had been done to improve the garden grounds since 1954, including the addition of a dining hall. No need to bring your own picnic lunch. Norman entered the hall and we agreed to meet at the first intermission and order our dinner for the second intermission. When I appeared at the ticket office as scheduled, our new friend reported sadly that she couldn't find even standing room for me. I thanked her and assured her I would be fine enjoying the gardens while the performance was on. I remembered that the exterior wall of the hall had several large doors that opened to display sets and costumes from other operas, so I started my walk around the building.

About three-quarters of the way around I came to a small garden next to a door in the wall; music was piped out and several young people with librettos in hand were following every note. I had discovered the performers' garden where they could take a break, returning to the stage when required. When the door opened, the young people gathered about, getting the singers' signatures on their librettos. I had a great seat in the garden and did not miss a note. During intermission I gleefully reported my good luck to Norm, insisting that he keep his seat; I would stay in the garden and meet him for dinner. After dinner the sun was setting and the evening air was cooler, so I told Norm I would take the car back to the hotel and he could walk back the short distance after the final act. As we were parting, our new friend popped out of the crowd looking for me. She had secured a seat for the final act. Luck was still with us! I settled into my seat several rows in front of and almost directly in line with Norm's for the last act of *Götterdämmerung*. I was astonished by the contemporary French production; later I discovered the opera world was, too. When the final curtain closed, foot stamping and cheering exploded for the performers, and then thundering booing took over for the production. After forty-five minutes of this cycle of cheers and boos, with no indication that it would ever end, Norm and I left for the hotel.

❖

THAT SEPTEMBER WE SET OFF on the longest adventure of our sabbatical year. We boarded a train for Travemünde, north of Lübeck, to catch the ferry—really a ship—to Helsinki, where we would meet architects from home at the Pacific Northwest Regional AIA Convention. I had helped plan this meeting for years, and I looked forward to seeing friends, especially my business partner, Carolyn, and to hear updates from home.

The ship's main salon featured a beautiful ceramic tile mural that covered the whole wall; we discovered it was the work of an artist from the Arabia Studio, the producers of fine tableware. We had already planned to visit this famous design center, a Helsinki highlight. We settled into our cabin for a good night's rest before meeting the Seattle group, who had already arrived.

We had been away only a few months, but what a pleasure to be back with an English-speaking crowd. We toured architectural treasures, old and new, in this land of design where even the smallest objects were treated with the greatest respect. I wondered: What was it about this Northern European country that brought out the beauty of proportion, scale, texture, and color into their designs for everyday living? Perhaps this came from the large number of architects and artists, many of whom were women.

Carolyn had a surprise for me: the new *Sunset* book featuring kitchen designs, including our Laurelhurst house. I had no idea it had been published. She also caught me up on the progress of the *Family Circle* "House Women Built" project, which she had under control. After saying our goodbyes to those returning to Seattle on the charter flight, Norm and I joined others on the train to Leningrad. Before leaving, we mailed home our newest art purchase: a tile piece by Rut Bryk, the artist who created the ship's mural.

❖

THE FIVE YEARS since I had last traveled to the Soviet Union had brought great changes. Local television now carried information about the world beyond the USSR borders, and the government had lost the tight control of its citizens. People were no longer afraid, and they wanted to talk to strangers from abroad. We photographed palaces and gardens, and visited museums, including one that featured a small exhibit of early Alaska Native artifacts, which I remembered hearing about during my university days. Then we went south to Novgorod, a charming town largely rebuilt after the Nazi destruction. There we learned about a special park with old houses, farm buildings and shops a short boat ride down the river. This was my chance to learn how the local carpentry differed from the styles developed in the West.

It was a lovely, warm afternoon for a cruise through the countryside to the park landing. After we examined the historic buildings, the air began to cool, and it was time to get back to town. We waited and waited for the boat, which we eventually realized was not going to return. Norm tried his German, French, and English with the few remaining bus drivers, hoping to seek passage for us and two Swedish women who were also stranded. The last bus, carrying a tour group of blue-collar Russians, finally came to our rescue. The passengers insisted we take their seats while they sat on the floor. We were the first Westerners they had met, and they were interested in everything about us. Thanking them kindly for their assistance, I couldn't help but feel a bit guilty about the wonderfully free life I had been privileged to live.

The highlight of our visit to Moscow was the opera, a production of Rimsky-Korsakov's *Sadko*. The sea tale of Novgorod featured ships sailing past each other high above the stage, just below the proscenium arch. The hero dived off the boat, lowering himself to the bottom of the sea, never missing a musical note on the way down. "The Song of India" is only one of the beautiful solo arias of the opera, but I'm sure the production costs keep it out of most opera houses. I still visualize this production whenever I hear the song.

In Kiev (now Kyiv), the cultural highlight was the ballet. Supposedly, the Kiev Ballet was the second company of the USSR, but the performance we saw was disappointing. The best part of the evening came when I ran into our next-door neighbor from Seattle in the ladies' room. "Sally, I thought you were home looking after Despina!" I said, referring to our cat. I had no idea she was planning to travel, and she said it was a spur-of-the-moment trip. We wrapped up our time in the Soviet Empire visiting Tbilisi, Georgia, and its historic monuments, and then turned south to the Middle East.

❖

WE HAD TRIED ALL KNOWN AVENUES to get a visa to Iraq but had failed. We had hoped to spend a week there before going to the UIFA Congress in Iran. We would not get to visit the valley of the Tigris and Euphrates, or the remains of the hanging gardens, important historical sites for Norm's research. What made us, two architects, so undesirable?

Our planned week became a single day spent in the international airport lounge waiting for a flight to Tehran. Upon landing in Baghdad, we walked across the tarmac to a small building surrounded by sandbags that we had to step over on our way to the door. To our right was a clear path to a more promising entrance with a sign saying "Boeing Engineers." How I wished I still had one of my old Boeing badges! Our lounge was packed with families accompanied by children of all ages, apparently heading to Mecca. The women, clothed in black and veiled, could be distinguished by the varying quality of their clothing fabric and shoes. They made themselves at home on the floor, where they nursed babies, cooked meals on a little stove, and served food to their families.

No announcements were made, and we saw no boards with notices or schedules, but now and then a group of people mysteriously lined up for boarding. We wondered: How did they know when to board? Every hour or so the routine repeated. Two couples waited for a Paris flight, and I noticed beautiful dresses under the women's burqas and their lovely manicured hands with brightly polished nails. I was surprised to see one woman had a gold cigarette holder and was smoking under her veil. I was sure once she was in the air the black wrappings would be discarded and a very modern woman would emerge. Finally, our long day ended, and we boarded our flight to Iran. Perhaps we had seen enough of Iraq.

❖

TEHRAN WOULD BE OUR BASE for about a month. We had a week before the UIFA Congress started, and we were ready for a bit of rest. Our hotel in the center of the city was an easy stroll from wonderful shops filled with far too many treasures. At the largest antique shop in Tehran, the owner surprised us when he immediately recognized Norm and said he would like to buy back the large eight-pointed tile Norm had purchased there in 1968. We knew it was an outstanding piece; this confirmed it.

While walking in the park, we met some of the locals, who asked for our help learning English, which would help them get better jobs. They were careful not to be seen with us in the hotel or business districts. The Shah was still in power, but tension was already in the air and armed guards rode in the vehicles taking European workers out to the oil rigs. Everyone in Tehran dressed in Western clothing, and the university students wore jeans and T-shirts, although we saw them only at the campus entrance because we were not allowed to go onto the grounds.

After our restful week, we joined the UIFA group, which included about a dozen Japanese women, plus one husband who did most of the English translation. The Danes, Germans, French, and Nigerians from the 1972 Congress were in attendance, as well as a Spanish woman, more women from the U.S. and several men.

Our group was divided into two buses—English or French-speaking—for a trip north to Ramsar on the Caspian Sea, and our English-speaking bus included the

Japanese group and Nigerian women. The tour guide gave a running commentary about how many people had been killed in accidents on each bend on the steep mountain road, which had no guardrails. The Nigerian women, who had never seen such peaks, sat on the floor between the seats, heads buried in their hands, sobbing that they would never see their children again, while the Japanese group remained quiet and composed. The Iranian guide and driver, who clearly resented their assignment chauffeuring a group of women, seemed to relish the distress caused by their horrifying tales.

Our meeting site was at a former casino/hotel with gardens and a lovely distant view of the sea. The rooms were on the second floor with a wide staircase that deposited us in a small lobby; our room was in the left wing, and the right wing was closed off for our host, the Empress of Iran, Farah Pahlavi. An armed guard was posted at the outer door of her wing. Once, Norm and I startled the dozing guard, who greeted us with a machine gun pointed at our heads. After that, we made a good deal of noise going up the stairs. This beautiful, frail woman seemed to be a prisoner in her own country.

The seaside was not to be missed, so four of us rose early and took a cab to the shore to swim. The breakers, salt air, and beautiful seashells provided a great start to the day before the UIFA sessions on all types of subjects, many completely off-topic and ignoring the Congress's themes.

After the sessions ended, we went back to Tehran for the Shah's birthday party. Our visa information had been cleared months earlier, allowing us admittance to this grand spectacle. At the celebration, Norman and I sat on concrete benches in a large stadium, where marchers paraded in—and then suddenly started assembling cars. In a matter of minutes, the cars were ready to drive away, with the marchers/assemblers hanging on doors and fenders as they exited the arena. It was a show straight out of postwar Soviet propaganda films. The Shah and his family seemed to enjoy the huge display from their private glass box high up in the stadium.

The day's biggest excitement came while we were walking back to our hotel. Cars leaving the celebration raced by us, driving on the sidewalks as well as the road. We held onto the building facades, wishing we could be like Spider-Man. The traffic was so bad that the police refused to go into the streets to direct it, afraid for their own lives.

❖

WITH THE FORMALITIES BEHIND US, we set off to tour some of the highlights of Iran. We boarded our two different buses and drove south to the grand mosques of Isfahan and the historic cities of Shiraz and ancient Persepolis. A German and a French architect joined our side trip by taxi to visit the 226 AD remains of Gur, part of Norm's research on circular planned cities. Gur's ruins consisted of lumps, bumps, and the remains of the fire tower, but Norm appreciated seeing one of the earliest examples of a circular city as he gathered material for his upcoming book. Gur also gave us a bit of quiet time and a nice break away from the larger group.

On our way to Persepolis, we purchased delicious fresh dates along the roadside and drove past Bedouin camps, where a flag on top of one tent identified the school. Persepolis was a highlight of the trip. In 1971, Iran had put on a spectacular celebration marking the 2,500th anniversary of the Persian Empire at Persepolis, and we all remembered the extravaganza from television broadcasts and newspapers. Some of the tents and events remained. The light show theater's canvas seats had mostly rotted, so we chose our seats carefully, but the light show itself was still functioning well and we were treated to the highlights of 2,500 years of history.

Finally, it was time to return to Germany, where we looked forward to our own bed and food. We were ready to stay closer to home until after the holidays.

❖

WE SPENT THANKSGIVING 1976 with Joyce, David and their six young ones in Zweibrücken, where I enjoyed having a larger kitchen to make the pies. That holiday Friday, the ten of us piled into the Parks' station wagon for a day trip to Luxembourg. At the border, we discovered that we were one passport short. The six children had all remembered theirs, but Norm had forgotten his. Fortunately, the guard took the stack of passports, took one look at our overloaded vehicle, and gave them back, waving us on. This was arguably my fault. Norm had lost his passport once while we were in Iran, prompting several hours of panicked searching. I finally found it—in his raincoat's inner pocket, where he had hidden it a bit too well. After that, I carried it for the rest of the trip. We decided that I should take care of our passports for the remainder of our travels.

The Parks sent us home after Thanksgiving with popcorn and cranberries to string for our Christmas decorations, and we got busy crafting a few ornaments for our tree. I even figured out how to bake cookies in an oven that had no separate controls for the upper and lower heat elements: I made sure it was hot enough, then turned the elements off when I put the cookies in, hoping for the best. I got pretty good at it.

We decided to invite our apartment neighbors in for a holiday party, even though our landlord, Wolfgang, assured us that they would not accept because they never socialized with each other. But they did accept, and we all kept Renata busy translating over cookies and punch for hours. Wolfgang later reported that he drove by and was stunned to hear laughter, the first ever coming from this building.

Jane and Norm with their Christmas tree, Untertürkheim, Germany

❖

IN JANUARY, WE JOINED THE PARKS for a tour of Spain, a first for the men and a return visit for Joyce and me. Our fellow bus passengers included about a dozen Brits, several Germans and French, a few tourists from other countries, and us four Americans. Our tour guide was Dutch and gave his talk in French, German and English, rotating among the languages. We started out on the Costa del Sol. After our first dinner at the hotel, we decided that the food there was not for us. The boys and I walked the beach checking out the restaurants, both formal establishments and casual cafes that didn't look like much but were packed to capacity.

The next day, Joyce led the way to one of the local cafes for lunch. She immediately charmed them with her Spanish and asked for the house specialty. The food was wonderful, and they told us to come back the next day for more treats prepared just for us. On one day when they were closed, the staff coordinated with another small diner, which also took great care of us. We didn't want to leave!

On this trip, we traveled back to my favorite place, Granada, where we enjoyed the recent preservation work on the Alhambra. We also toured the Great Mosque in Cordova and the Giralda in Seville—wonderful Moorish spaces I appreciated revisiting. Ronda, in the hills inland from Malaga, was our most delightful new discovery. This little town on the crest of a rock ledge was the cradle of bullfighting and is a must for anyone traveling to Spain.

Our group ferried across the Strait of Gibraltar to Morocco, where we visited the Kasbah of Marrakesh, which looked straight out of a Humphrey Bogart movie. On one of the first days there, when we were leaving a restaurant after lunch, a group of beggars accosted one of our French members, who was a Black man. We quickly retreated inside and were sent out a back door, where they bused us away. Another day, our bus got stuck with many other vehicles on a highway that had turned to a sea of mud. A mass of young men and boys were up to their knees in the gooey mess, trying to push the vehicles out. After several hours, we resigned ourselves to spending the night on the bus, and then somehow, magically, we made it back to solid ground. The story was that the highway contractor had run off with the money and deserted the job.

❖

NORM AND I DECIDED to focus on Egypt in February. We had both been there before, but not together. We were not allowed to enter Egypt as independent travelers, so we signed up for an American Express tour, which meant that fifty-three Germans accompanied us on our adventure. With our own guidebooks in hand, we told the tour guide that English translation was not necessary; we just needed to know our hotel room number, and the times for dinner and departure. Of course, the guide wanted to practice her English, which irritated many of our companions.

Norm found a young Egyptian policeman who agreed to take him to see one of the ancient circular city sites he was interested in. It required some rough traveling and I would not be allowed to go, so I decided to join the Germans on a day trip to the Suez Canal and Red Sea. Upon our arrival at the sea, they immediately changed into their bathing suits and danced out into the water. Seeing that I had not brought my suit, they asked why I had come along. They had not come to see the locks; they just wanted to say they had been in the waters of the Red Sea. I was learning this was a fascination for many Europeans. They took pride in comparing how many seas, or famous waters, they had been in. I don't recall any of them actually swimming. I suggested that it would have been nice if they had told me beforehand about this important plunge as I would have brought my swimsuit. Sharing information was not one of their priorities.

After Cairo and Luxor, we traveled to Aswan and closer to our top goal of seeing the temples of Abu Simbel. We crossed the Nile, at the first cataract, in the *Canada*, a small Felucca sailboat. We could have waded across most of the river, but we got caught on a rock, and our pole man fell overboard, frightening our fellow passengers, who were already terrified by the rough waters. The visit to the Nubian village and ruins were lost on the rest of the group; all they could think about was they would have to cross the river again to get back.

Several groups from England, France, Spain, United States, and other countries were staying in our hotel, all of us waiting for flights to Abu Simbel. Something had gone awry, and our group did not have a confirmed flight to our destination. Each day others came and went while we and our German travel companions waited in disappointment. Some of them became downright angry. The Germans decided to sue the tour company, but we insisted we could not participate in a lawsuit. How that turned out is still a mystery. For us, Abu Simbel would just have to wait until our next trip to Egypt.

❖

BACK IN GERMANY, we had the chance to attend outstanding local opera productions and the world-famous Stuttgart Ballet performances, and the Amerika Haus library provided choice reading material for leisure hours between travels. In March, we traveled to France, where Norm had several research projects and we both wanted to do some architectural photography. We enjoyed the food, people, and buildings we discovered in little towns that tourists often miss and still found time to see famous chateaus and leave our footprints in the paths of the world's pleasure gardens.

In April, we headed south to Italy and Sicily, on our way to Greece. It was a blessing to have our own car to travel when and where we wished. Our route south took us through Freiburg where Norm decided we should splurge and stay in the heart of the city in a hotel on the Münsterplatz next to the cathedral. We had a wonderful afternoon walk taking in the city before settling into our deluxe accommodations—for a sleepless night with church bells ringing every 15 minutes at a volume that shook the windows. Another lesson learned: Pay attention to a hotel's location.

We traveled through Milan and Pisa and down the west coast to Naples, where we boarded a ferry to Palermo, Sicily. We had both seen much of Italy before, but this was our first time seeing it together, and now we were both in new territory. Again, we often found ourselves in small towns where tourists did not tend to tread. What a pleasant surprise to discover so many small Greek temples, which we strolled through without anyone else around. If Greek temples are your thing, Sicily is a must!

At the most easterly point at Messina, we boarded a ferry for the short crossing back to the mainland of Italy. We followed the coastline north before cutting across to Brindisi for our ferry trip to Greece. We were traveling at the height of the orange harvest, and the traffic was full of trucks laden with oranges on their way to juice factories. Each curve of the road was adorned by beautiful orange balls that had managed to escape the trucks. We stopped to rescue a few and they were the most delicious oranges we had ever eaten. What a memorable feast. We bought a bag of oranges to share with our family and friends, who we were meeting in Athens.

Upon our arrival in Greece, we discovered it was a holiday and everyone was leaving just as we were trying to go into the city. The exiting traffic occupied three of the four highway lanes, which was not a problem until we came to a bridge that narrowed to three lanes. It was a game of bluff—or stupidity—as I moved into my legal lane, which the other drivers ignored. It took all my courage and drawing on my European driving skills gained in the 1950s. When we arrived in Athens on May 1, we exhaled in relief.

Shortly after noon we made it to the hotel where Mother and Laurie, now 24, were staying. We had a joyful reunion after our ten months apart. Ted and Dorothy, Norm's brother and sister-in-law, who were also from Seattle, joined us for our family dinner.

May 2 found four Johnstons, two Hastings, and Wolfgang and Ruth Henning all aboard the *Stella Solaris* for our long-planned cruise of the Greek islands. We arrived early in the morning in Crete. After a quick tour of the sights, we sailed on to Santorini, where we were tendered ashore for a donkey ride up the hill. Mother skipped this adventure, saving her energy for our visit to Rhodes the following morning. After docking there, a bus took us to Lindos, where Mother climbed all the way to the Acropolis, with a bit of help from Laurie and me. She said the view was worth every step.

After touring Ephesus and Kuşadasi with an especially good guide, it was time for the ship's masquerade party. Laurie won first prize for originality for the lighthouse costume we fashioned out of a shower curtain and a flashlight. On Friday, May 6, we visited Istanbul, a city packed full of churches, mosques, palaces, art, jewels, frescoes, rugs, rugs, and more rugs. The following morning on our own we

Stella Solaris cruise through the Greek Islands. Front: Laurie, Camille, Jane, and Norm. Back row: Wolfgang and Ruth Henning, Dorothy and Ted Johnston.

went to the Golden Horn—a special moment for my mother, who said she had never dreamed she would visit this place she remembered studying back in her Ohio grade school.

A Sunday morning visit to Delos revealed swaths of wildflowers blooming among the ruins dating back to the fourth and fifth centuries B.C. The island's only inhabitants were the museum keeper and the men handling the small boats arriving from the cruise ships.

Our last stop was Mykonos, where Laurie and I took our final swim in the Aegean Sea. Summer was officially still a month away, but the hillsides were already brown and dry. After docking in Athens, we spent several days taking in the important sights. We said farewell to half of our group, and then Mother, Laurie, Norm, and I continued by car, visiting Delphi, the Corinth Canal, and Olympia on our way to Patra, where we boarded the ferry for our long crossing back to Brindisi, Italy.

❖

NORTHWEST OF BRINDISI, we drove through the Trulli District—an area I had wanted to visit for years. The little Trulli towns of stone beehive huts, houses and buildings are a unique architectural treat dating to the eighteenth century. From here, we traveled to Rome by way of Bari and the coast. We drove through mountains where the villages seemed to cling to the slopes and visited Tivoli's beautiful Villa d'Este water gardens. Like it or not, the Hastings women would see gardens!

In Rome, Norm and I were guests of Tony Heywood, Astra Zarina's husband, while she was in Seattle. Mother and Laurie stayed next door in a convent run by Swedish nuns, across the street from the Palazzo Farnese, and the girls took in the tourist sights while Norm and I went on architecture tours with Tony. Tony was a perfect host, cooking dinners and taking us to the opera. One day the sky turned very yellow, with rain falling as yellow mud. It was sand from the Sahara Desert, and umbrellas, cars, and buildings were all covered in it. Tony assured us that this only happened occasionally; for us, one experience was enough.

Next, we went to Florence by way of Orvieto, the town on a pedestal. I was thrilled to be back in my favorite Italian city for food, shopping, and culture, and playing tour guide for the girls. Back on the coast, Laurie and I enjoyed the surf and sand at Rimini on our way to Urbino, where we enjoyed dinner with one of Norm's longtime friends.

In Venice, we found ourselves in a major rainstorm, so Laurie and I went umbrella shopping. Each shop produced a new color or interesting pattern, and we returned to the hotel with seven or eight umbrellas. The price was right and the colors fantastic—and they would be great in rainy Seattle. Once we had seen all the major sights and it was time to move on from Venice, the sun came out, lighting up the poppy-covered fields along our way to Palmanova. This was the perfect example for Norm's book about planned circular cities, so it of course required a stop.

We drove across the Yugoslavian border and down the beautiful Dalmatian coast, where we finally found an old castle-type hotel at Novi Vinodolski in Croatia. Our rooms were so large, we felt we could get lost in them. It must have been grand living in its day.

The next day we reached the famous Plitvice Lakes National Park, where we were bused into a land of fantastic rock formations, waterfalls, lakes, streams, walkways on steppingstones, and bridges made of twigs that wound around, up and down, and occasionally dead-ended at marvelous viewpoints. Mother was delighted that she had crossed them, but happy to be on solid ground after clutching onto us through much of the passage.

We had one night in Ljubljana, and Norm and I knew that we must return one day to discover the rest of the southern coast. After a morning walk around the city and purchasing some travel snacks, we left for Austria. Soon we were in the mountains with rainstorms and tunnels that obscured the region's beauty. We settled for the night in Werfen in a quaint seventeenth century hotel, complete with a balcony to enjoy the craggy glacier-covered peaks all around. One peak even had a castle on the very top.

In Salzburg we had a wet but fast tour of the highlights, including the catacombs. Then we were on to Berchtesgaden, Germany, and a trip up to the Eagle's Nest, which was bathed in sunshine. The view was wonderful, and Mother had reached her highest peak.

The next day we went back across the border into Austria for an afternoon in Innsbruck and up the mountain to Seefeld, where I used to ski. Our travels took us through more of my old haunts, including Garmisch and Oberammergau, my former home in the mountains of Bavaria. My good friends, the Schwaigers, booked comfortable rooms for us in a neighbor's house, where a familiar sound turned out to be a lamb enjoying the hospitality of the warm kitchen. After a tour of the Passion Playhouse, I took the girls on a shopping trip to my favorite stores. Overcast skies prevented us from taking a ride up the cable car, so we moved on to the big city, Munich.

One stop along the way made a lasting, somber impression: Dachau, where so many Jews were put to death. The site would remain a memorial to them forever. We saw German schoolchildren come out in tears. I remembered that in the 1950s, many Germans wanted to close and destroy the site, but the agreement at the end of the U.S. occupation stipulated that Dachau could never be closed to the public. Certainly, this was the right decision.

The last stop on our way home was Augsburg, bringing back many special memories for me from my first Christmas away from home in 1954. We made a quick revisit to Fuggerei, the world's first low-income housing project that was founded in 1519 and still operating. Norm was delighted to view this bit of history, which was maintained in beautiful condition.

❖

AFTER TWO MONTHS ON THE ROAD, we were back home in Untertürkheim at #17 Otztalerstr. When we stopped at the store for dinner provisions, the young manager immediately noticed Laurie and rushed over, starting a conversation in beautiful English. This was the same guy who had insisted he spoke no English when we arrived eleven months before. Oh, what a pretty face can accomplish! We were happy to be back in our own beds and to show Laurie a few of our local sights before putting her on the train north for her nonstop flight back to Seattle.

Now down to three people, we fit better into our small apartment and could concentrate on showing my mother the parks, gardens, opera house, and other sights of Stuttgart. We still had so much to share with Mother, including Regensburg and Nuremberg, where we visited my 1954 apartment and workplace, as well as the Romantic Road villages and Schwabisch Hall.

Norm still had more circular cities to visit, and he gave a lecture at a university in Bonn, which had been arranged by a former student. Afterward, we traveled south to the Castle Park at Schwetzingen and on to Karlsruhe for touring and dinner with more former UW students before returning to Stuttgart.

❖

STUTTGART WAS HOLDING the German garden show for 1977, which we took in before our next short trip south to Lake Constance for a visit with some former clients of mine. It was wonderful to see Ernst and Elizabeth Florey and their two girls in their new home. They had been lured back to their European roots to help set up a new university—a very impressive undertaking in a country that did not scrimp on higher education. University students received free tuition, as well as living allowances. What a contrast to our own university experiences.

Leaving our friends, we continued on for a sample of Switzerland, visiting Zurich, Lucerne, and Zug, and traveling through the countryside before returning to Stuttgart to host our neighbors at a farewell dinner. After the success of our holiday party, we had promised to do an American-style hamburger feed before we departed. We picked a big bunch of pink, blue, white, and red wildflowers on our way back to adorn our dinner table. The building residents gathered for burgers, potato salad, chips, pickles, and olives, with much conversation and laughter—until our landlord and friend Wolfgang arrived. We had invited him because his wife was in Spain, and once again, we had goofed by not honoring the local class system. As

Gertrude, Bola, and Jane in Copenhagen

outsiders, we could socialize with our neighbors, but this did not carry over to our friend, and the party went flat.

❖

WE FINISHED PACKING and shipped off our footlockers. Then the three of us said farewell to Stuttgart, driving north with limited baggage. We would leave our car in Sweden for its cruise to Seattle. On our way, we had many circular cities for Norm to visit and photograph in Germany, France, Belgium, Netherlands, Denmark, Sweden, and Norway for his book, *Cities in the Round*, which would be published in 1983. Somehow, we squeezed in all of Norman's cities, castles, gardens, and museums. A wonderful smell of salt air greeted us as we arrived at the coast. We didn't realize how much we had missed it. Soon it would become part of our lives again.

A special treat near the end of our journey was staying with an architect friend, Gertrude Galster, in her two hundred-plus-year-old thatched roof cottage in Lyngby, just outside of Copenhagen. Gertrude had restored the cottage, and she encouraged and helped others in the little town to restore others. The cottage had a low ceiling, so Gertrude designed a solution, creating steps from the entry down into a lowered floor, providing for sufficient headroom. The traditional building structure was preserved: half-timbered wood framing with stucco wall finishes and earth filling between the wood members, which provides fire control. Gertrude had a surprise for us—another guest, Bola, a Nigerian architect friend. Bola had a project in Sweden and was on her way home. We all had a great time catching up, as well as enjoying an evening at the Tivoli Gardens.

The ferry to Malmo, Sweden, led to our car's last European adventure, driving up the coast to Göteborg, where it was shipped to Seattle. The three of us boarded a train for Oslo, where we would then fly home. The Viking Hotel, built for athlete housing during the 1952 Winter Olympics, was across the street from the train station—both convenient and nostalgic, as I had stayed there on my way home twenty years earlier. I forgot how tiny the rooms were; when we found they charged per person, not per room, we each took a room, trotting up and down the hall as needed.

At the airport, Norman took Mother and boarded the plane while I spent our last European funds in the duty-free shop. As I arrived at the gate, I heard angry voices; the airline had overbooked and was not allowing some ticketed individuals to board. When I reached the airline agent, I pulled out our three passports, explaining that my mother and husband were already aboard the direct flight to Seattle without passports. I worried they might be sent back when they landed. The problem was solved by removing someone who was already on board, allowing me to take their place and join my family.

We were ready to be home.

15 | BACK HOME AND BACK TO WORK

Architects Elaine Day LaTourelle, Carolyn Geise, Jane, and Lottie Eskilsson.
In 1980, they formed Architecta, a joint venture in pursuit of larger government projects.

AFTER A YEAR AWAY, it was time to catch up with old friends and new business. My first call was to Floyd Shiosaki, who was putting together the class list for the twenty-fifth reunion of our UW School of Architecture class. In the works since before our sabbatical, the party drew a big turnout from the alumni of 1951 and 1952, the two largest classes to graduate in architecture.

I returned just in time to judge the Red Cedar Shingle Bureau national awards. My longtime friend, Al Bumgardner, was also on the jury, and he caught me up on the local news. I knew my business partner, Carolyn Geise, had undergone facial surgery while I was away, and in a recent photo, she looked great—even glamorous. Al mentioned there were other changes, too, and when I got back to the office, I understood what he meant. The stutter Carolyn had struggled with was almost gone, and she glowed with confidence. When I left for our sabbatical year, she had

Twenty-fifth class reunion, UW Architecture Class of 1952

worried that she couldn't run the office without me. I had reassured her and while I was away, she discovered that indeed she could. It was wonderful to see a new, self-assured Carolyn.

One of the things I appreciated about Carolyn was how she embraced cutting-edge trends in architecture, fashion—really, everything. She was our source for what was hot. When I returned from Europe, she was eager to explore the opportunities available in new federal and state mandates for set-asides for minority- and women-owned businesses on government projects. She also proposed a name change for our firm to give her more recognition. I agreed that of course she deserved to be better-known, but a new name wouldn't solve the problem. I would still be the elder and more established member of the firm. So, I suggested we separate our business. We had plenty of work to share, and this would allow her to move to a downtown location, put her name on the door, and go for the set-asides. She quickly agreed. We divided most of our clients' projects according to which of us was working closely with each site, and we invited the remaining clients—as well as our employees—to choose between our two practices. Our colleagues were shocked. Carolyn and I were still the best of friends and had no money problems or quarrels; we simply wanted to operate different types of practices. It worked and Carolyn blossomed in her new firm.

Oh, and Carolyn took all the bachelor clients, as I had a spouse. That tactic worked out well: She married one of them a few months later.

❖

IN 1977, OUR OFFICE LEARNED that the N. Johnston Residence won both an Honor Award from the AIA Seattle Chapter and an Environmental Award from the Seattle-King County Board of Realtors. Of course, this was *our* house in the Laurelhurst neighborhood, with my perfect kitchen and its two-story greenhouse offering views of my indoor-outdoor gardens, Union Bay, and the campus beyond. The kitchen was my control center and where I spent most of my time when I was home. It also received much local and national media attention and was even featured in a Japanese publication showcasing kitchens from around the world.

After a flurry of speaking engagements around the country in spring and summer, July found me in Kodiak, Alaska, to design a new residence for the Hollands, a crab fisherman's family. Many Alaska residents subscribed to the Sunday *Seattle Times* and used the "Home of the Month" feature as a resource when selecting architects for their homes.

❖

AT THE BEGINNING OF 1979, I looked forward to a year of international engagements and adventures. We hosted our friend Dogan Kuban from Istanbul, and soon after took off on a two-week trip to India and Nepal. As a child I had seen the movie *Lost Horizon*, and I remembered its story of Shangri-La, the land where people never aged. At last, I landed in a beautiful tropical valley tucked among snow-covered mountains. This was a peaceful land from another era, still without cars and moving at its own slower pace.

This was also Seattle's year to host the UIFA Congress, drawing architects from all over the world. During our sabbatical year in Europe, I met President Solange d'Herbez de la Tour several times in Paris to plan the event, while my UIFA colleague Jean Young worked on plans from Seattle. Jean was the secretary general of UIFA, and I was a vice president representing the Americas and Japan. Upon my return, it became clear that Jean was taking complete charge of the event. I prefer a

Solange, Fola, and Bola in Seattle for the UIFA Congress, 1979

team approach, but I realized my input was not welcome so I stepped back, hoping that her system would work out.

When Jean refused to share any information with me, especially about the funding, I became concerned and consulted a legal adviser about whether I could be held financially responsible for her commitments. The answer was, as an officer of the organization, probably yes. I could not risk her unpaid bills, so I made the difficult decision to resign.

I knew many of my international friends did not understand, but I stayed on the sidelines while the planning turmoil continued. The Congress took place in Seattle as planned—the first in the U.S.—and apparently it was a success. I did not attend, but we hosted fourteen friends from faraway places to dinner at our home.

Unfortunately, Jean took on personal debt to produce the event, and over many years, she asked our mutual international friends for money to help pay it off. It still makes me sad that her ego did not allow her to work with others who could have helped resolve the problems.

Continuing the year's international theme, I hosted a group of Soviet women touring Seattle and attended a luncheon with American Women for International Understanding (AWIU) members and guests. Later in the year I traveled with the

AWIU to Japan and Korea. One of the members was married to a publisher of automotive magazines, which inspired the Japanese car manufacturers to compete over who could entertain us most lavishly. I cherished those memories with each subsequent visit to Japan.

In Korea, Western tourists—and especially American women—were still rare, and security was high. Hotel windows were shuttered, barring views of the adjacent government buildings. Minimal electricity meant hotel corridors were so dark that a flashlight or match was required to find the keyhole to your door. Seoul streets were crowded with businessmen and workers, all rushing on their way somewhere.

A bus trip south to the old tombs took us through the countryside, where the trees on the hillsides were in perfect lines, every direction you looked. This tree-planting effort began in earnest in the 1950s and continued each April on Arbor Day to restore forests destroyed during Japanese colonization and the Korean War. The regimented pattern was designed to make it hard for any future soldiers to hide among the trees.

In addition to the prominent Seoul women who entertained our group, we met other women at a U.S. Embassy gathering, including Julia Lee, an American architect and wife of the crown prince. The two had met when they were students at an Ivy League college. The prince, who had no role in government, was living with his mistress in Japan, so when Julia was in Korea, she shared the old palace with her mother-in-law. Three of us were invited to Sunday brunch with them at the palace, a low-rise medium-sized structure that was not ostentatious at all. I loved the old building with its wonderfully detailed wooden connections and joints, but I'm sure it was a cold, drafty place to live.

Each of my trips must be remembered with a souvenir, and in Korea I selected a pair of decorated wooden ducks that are a traditional part of Korean wedding ceremonies. The male duck has a string tying his bill together, defining his role in the marriage.

On my way home, I routed my flights through Anchorage and Kodiak so I could check on the construction of the Holland House. My nephew Jay Johnston and his friend Bruce were building it and most of the construction materials, including cabinets, were shipped in containers from Seattle. I had designed the house for maximum use of the framing members and minimum waste, so the framing had to be almost perfect, or the finished cabinets and fixtures would not fit. The boys were doing a masterful job. But I discovered a large bathtub had arrived onsite—a replacement for a flawed fixture—and the replacement was the wrong model and a foot too long. When I told the supply company, they said they would order the correct tub and get it on a boat to Alaska. It would be in Kodiak in about a month. "No," I said. "Put it on an airplane." They looked at me like I was crazy. "Do you know how much these things weigh?" they asked. "I don't care," I said. "I think it's cheaper for you to put that thing on an airplane than it is to pull my contractors out of Kodiak, bring them back to Seattle, and then ship them back when the tub arrives." The next thing I knew, I got a call saying a tub had arrived on an airplane in Kodiak, and one question: "How did you do it?"

❖

THAT FALL AND WINTER, I served on the National AIA Honors Award jury, working to narrow down the projects to be considered for the final award. In January, I met up with the associate and student members of the jury to visit four buildings in Wisconsin and Indiana. (I volunteered to take the northernmost projects so I could wear my silver fox hat, which was much too warm for Seattle.) The students wanted to go along to see the Michael Graves house on our list.

One of the projects, the New Harmony Atheneum in Indiana by architect Richard Meier, was so famous that it was on the cover of the next issue of the AIA magazine. It did not win, prompting much turmoil among the editorial staff who had banked on it taking the top honor. This type of jury duty was not easy; voices were raised, and some on our team pushed for design quality while the opposite camp lobbied for their favorite headliner architects. I stood with the designers. In the end, design substance prevailed over big names and personalities, and I'm sure the losing teammates never wanted to work with us again.

❖

WITH SO MUCH WORK and travel planned for 1980, I decided to resign from my part-time teaching job at Seattle Central Community College. Plus, the program had changed directions and was not working as we'd originally intended. Students ranged from college grads who wanted to get into the graduate program at the university to recent high school graduates to former inmates who had never even made it to high school. As instructors, this forced us to aim somewhere in the middle, a frustrating catch-22.

I do have some good memories of students who went on to further schooling and fine careers. I especially remember five or six deaf students who arrived with a sign-language interpreter; her hands and face were riveting as she worked. Their drafting skills were good, but it was a challenge to help them understand the process and vocabulary. My heart also went out to the Nigerian boys assigned to the program whose faces were covered in tribal scars. Their English was fine, but visual concepts were difficult for them, and they could not understand that stairways are aligned from floor level to floor level on the construction drawings. I remember talking with them about the games they played as children, which helped me understand how different our experiences were.

❖

BECAUSE I WAS WORKING on several projects in Alaska, I decided I should be licensed there. I needed to pass a Cold Regions Engineering Course, which was offered over several intense weekends at the university. Students flew in from all over the country on Friday night, returning home on Sunday night, and we were amazed how much we learned in this compacted time frame. I enjoyed solving the problems of permafrost, ice crystals, and freshwater issues.

Spring break coincided with an architectural tour to China and the Philippines. Tourism was still new in China and there were few accommodations. Norm and I were fortunate to stay in a new hotel near Tiananmen Square in the center of Beijing and centrally located for walking.

The snows had just melted, so we were among the first of the season to travel to the Great Wall. One bus transported interior designers, the second the architects, and we had the wall mostly to ourselves. After our brownbag lunch, Norm wandered about and stepped on a manhole cover, which suddenly flipped up and tossed him on his face. His thick eyeglasses left a deep gash above his right eye but missed the larger blood vessels. The doctor spouse of one of the designers patched him up and said he should go to the hospital for stitches. Our local guide, Mr. Lee, wanted to rush the group back but I reassured him that Norm would be terribly unhappy if he missed the tombs and other sites.

Back at the hotel, we were put in a large government car that raced out—and hit a bicyclist—on our way to a nearby hospital that treated foreigners. The hospital building looked just like the English had left it in the 1930s, with perhaps an extra coat of paint. I was allowed to stay and take photographs in the emergency room while two nurses cleaned up Norm's wound. A tall handsome young doctor arrived, insisting, "No English." As he prepared to start stitching, I told Norm, "I can see all the way into your head, and there is nothing there." Dr. "No English" roared with laughter.

An hour and a half in the emergency room, with two nurses, one doctor, and a bottle of pain pills resulted in a bill of $12. We chose to walk back to the hotel rather than ride with the government driver, deciding that was safest for us and the city.

One day Mr. Lee seemed upset. We were not receiving any U.S. news, so I asked him if anything was wrong. He said "Mount Helen" was going to "run over" the U.S. capital. I told him not to worry: Mount St. Helens was not anywhere near our national capital; in fact it was located in a forest in our own home state of Washington. He seemed relieved, and Mount St. Helens waited until mid-May when we were home for her big moment.

Our trip wrapped up in the Philippines, and our visit coincided with peak mango season. This was gastronomy heaven, and we indulged in mangos in every way and at every meal. Our time there was short, but we met many wonderful people who looked after us.

❖

BECAUSE OF THE OPPORTUNITY to pursue federal set-asides for women-owned businesses, four of us with individual practices—Carolyn Geise, Elaine Day LaTourelle, Lottie Eskilsson, and myself—created a joint venture firm we called Architecta to pursue larger government projects. The city of Seattle was accepting submittals to design a new jail, so I recruited two nationally known women architects to add to our team credentials. We worked in the evenings and weekends putting our proposal together, having a grand time on our "girls nights." The selection committee told us the quality of our submittal blew them away, but we were not selected. I knew we would never be awarded such a high-profile project, but Carolyn was an eternal optimist. After that effort, we stopped pursuing public projects together, but still enjoyed our camaraderie.

In between trips and the joint-venture exploration, I still managed to find time for my practice's demanding projects. One local job involved remodeling a mansion owned by the Andrews family and designed by prominent New York architect Charles Platt during the 1920s in The Highlands, an exclusive residential area along Puget Sound north of Seattle. Although they had six fireplaces, Mrs. Andrews wanted one more. The project also included converting the former servants' living room into a large family room and updating the kitchen. The couple had each come to their marriage with four or five children and all but the youngest were in private boarding schools around the country, so the house needed to accommodate around a dozen people during vacations.

The project involved expanding the terrace, which sent us on a search across the U.S. and Canada for bricks to match the existing historic masonry—a tremendous challenge because bricks were no longer fired as hard as the originals. Our last resort was to try and sell the city of Seattle's engineers on the idea that if we could dig up some old streets that contained matching bricks under the current paving, my client would be happy to pay for replacing the damaged streets—even make them better. Money was not a problem! The city engineers looked at us like we were crazy and rejected the proposed street improvements. So Mr. Andrews had to settle for bricks that were not quite a perfect match.

In 1980, Cincinnati hosted the AIA Convention, and this year my mother traveled with Norm and me to watch me receive my AIA Fellowship Medal. She also designed a beautiful new formal dress matching the garnet ribbon on the medal for me to wear to the Convocation Dinner, adding her special visual touch to this big moment in my career.

Norm and I looked forward to September and our cruise from New York to England on the *Queen Elizabeth 2*. This was supposed to be the ship's last season, but cruise ship travel was just starting to become a major industry and the *QE2* was saved from the scrapyard. She had a facelift and served many more years on the high seas.

However, the *QE2* was still quite threadbare for our journey. We disembarked in Southampton, England, for an overnight stay, then reboarded and traveled on to France, where we rented a car to tour the coastal sites. In Paris we stayed with my friend and UIFA colleague Solange, who wined and dined us as if we were royalty. One evening, we enjoyed a candlelit dinner cruise on the Seine, where locals lined the banks, mooning us.

Using our Eurorail passes we wandered through France, Austria, and Switzerland to Italy, where Norm stayed to teach for the fall quarter in the UW Rome Program while I returned to our home and work. This was the first year in our marriage that we were apart on our wedding anniversary and Norm's early December birthday. I left money behind in Rome with Astra Zarina and her husband, Tony, with instructions to throw a big Italian party on his big day. The reviews came back that the party was a big success.

❖

NOW THAT MY TEACHING CAREER was behind me, I felt I could really be productive in the office. And because architectural preservation was becoming ever more important in the industry and my practice, I accepted an appointment to the Seattle Landmarks Preservation Board. Norman was enthusiastic about this volunteer work because he was writing articles for the *Seattle Times* about architectural issues across the Pacific Northwest. Our board meetings were open to the public, and many passionate people came to support or oppose the landmark designation for the historic building nominations we reviewed. One particularly dissatisfied individual dumped garbage in the doorway of my office. I thought, "Why?!" but decided that public officials must learn to shrug off such incidents.

At the end of January, I was back in Washington, D.C., for the AIA School Awards Jury—a more pleasant experience than the Honor Awards Jury. It was also simpler because we worked only with the presentation material and photos and made no onsite visits. On February 2, Norm and I departed D.C. on a Northwest flight out of Dulles International Airport. We expected an easy flight home, but shortly after takeoff, an explosion in the right engine caused the lights to go out and the plane to roll over onto its wounded right wing. Norm grabbed my arm saying, "This is it," thinking at least we would go together. "No, it is not," I said. "I'm psychic and we would not be on this plane if there was a problem."

The plane righted itself, lights came on and the co-pilot's voice reassured us that as soon as they could dump fuel we would return to Dulles. An experienced flight attendant prepared us for a crash landing, and we were soon on the ground without further problems. As we deplaned, a young man in front of us turned and said, "Thank you." He had two infants at home and all he could think about was his wife raising them alone, so he was reassured by my comment about being psychic.

As we prepared to leave the aircraft, one elderly lady stayed tucked into her seat. When the attendant asked her to leave, she said, "I'm OK, honey. I'll just sit here while they fix it." She had to be convinced that this plane wouldn't fly for many days before she finally got up to join us. No doubt this lady experienced a lot during her life.

❖

EARLY THAT YEAR, I received a letter from the Marquis Who's Who publishing company saying they were including me in the *Who's Who in the World 1982-1983* edition. My reaction was "Why me?" Women were seldom included in the group of approximately one hundred twenty to one hundred forty honorees. I was sure the only explanation was that four women, including me, had been inducted into the national AIA Fellowship the prior year. Years later, I discovered I was the only new woman Fellow included in the publication, so the mystery remains.

Norm was in the middle of a long-term project working with the National Council of Architectural Registration Boards (NCARB) to standardize and computerize an examination for all fifty states plus Canada. This would simplify the licensing process for the architecture industry, which had become a more national and international profession—especially for larger firms.

That year my office also enjoyed working on the design of three homes that were among twenty designs produced by seven Pacific Northwest firms and marketed nationally. The high-quality energy-efficient designs included solar-energy features and were packaged along with all the building/finishing materials, instructions for being your own general contractor, and financing arrangements. Each of these "Windfield Homes" was handsomely presented in an 8- by 12-inch booklet. It was an innovative concept to contribute to, but I've often wondered how many of these homes were ever built.

16 | THE BUSTLE OF THE NATIONAL AIA

Group portrait of AIA Board of Directors at AIA Headquarters, Washington D.C., 1982

IN AUGUST 1981, the organizer in me decided it was time to take on a stronger role in the national AIA. I was annoyed by the chaotic planning that led up to our Northwest regional meeting at White Pass Ski Area in the Cascade Mountains, and I resolved to run for the open regional director position on the national AIA Board of Directors. Our Northwest region had two directors to represent Montana, Idaho, Oregon, Washington, Alaska, Hawaii, and Guam, and while the outgoing director was a nice guy, he was too busy to assist the local chapters, which deserved more attention. Norman was not excited about my decision, but I stood firm.

At this time, Michael Graves was probably the best-known architect in the country. He was in Portland finishing up the City Hall project and agreed to be our keynote speaker at White Pass, which helped us draw a crowd. I picked him up at his Seattle hotel on a sunny day, and as I drove my sports car through the winding roads into the mountains, I could tell he was terrified looking down at the steep canyons below the guardrail. If we hadn't been tucked into bucket seats, I think he would have jumped into my lap. But when we arrived at the meeting, he charmed the group, just as we had hoped.

An architect from Hawaii was also on the ballot, but I won easily with support from the Seattle crowd. I did not immediately realize the immense impact this election would have on my life through the following decades. And despite his early skepticism, Norman became my most important—and enthusiastic—partner during my AIA Board service. I'm sure he was glad I did not let him talk me out of it.

❖

SOON AFTER THE MEETING, my mother and I were on a train to Los Angeles. I was going to a meeting of the American Women for International Understanding, but this trip was special because it was Mother's first visit back to

Jane on the Cunningham Hall job site

her birthplace in eighty years. We had heard about Amtrak's fine dining and frills, but the railroad was losing money and all those niceties were eliminated a week before our trip. However, our time together on the journey gave me a chance to record her early history and learn more about our family. My friend Colleen picked us up in Santa Barbara, and we spent several days at her home in Ojai before going to Los Angeles. While I attended the AWIU meeting and then returned home to work, Mother visited cousins and saw it all, including Disneyland.

That year, I was working on my first University of Washington project, restoring the Alaska-Yukon-Pacific Exposition Woman's Building, one of the few structures remaining from 1909. I was familiar with the building from my student days because it was across the road from Architecture Hall. It had many uses over the years: In the late 1940s, it served as Navy ROTC space. For a while, it provided extra studio space for the Architecture School, and volcano scientists worked there after Mount St. Helens' eruption. UW had planned to replace the building with a modern structure, but the campus women's group discovered its history and worked to save it from demolition.

I had restored my 1891 Fremont house, so there were few surprises in the AYP building. It had no foundation walls, square nails, decorative brackets that were not structural, and wonderful straight-grained timber members. The second floor was piled almost to the ceiling with stored papers and records weighing much more than the original designers could have imagined. I'm sure it was the old-growth lumber that saved the floor from collapsing, and I shuddered thinking about the staff and students who had worked for years in the building unaware of the risk. I fought the university to retain the historic features, including a boarded-up fireplace we uncovered and restored. We also preserved the wood window sashes, and the gallery space and lecture room became among the most popular meeting rooms on campus with wainscoting and windows that opened for fresh air.

I was used to working with skilled carpenters, but for this public project, the university selected the contractor. Unfortunately, this was the firm's first building project after a background in road construction. They hired a carpenter to run the job—a good approach if an effort was made to find a skilled one, but we quickly realized that the nice young carpenter they chose was still in training. So, I found myself teaching again. His hardest lesson: learning how to correctly lay out the stairs. The hardest part for me was signing off on the job, even though I was not satisfied. Welcome to public work!

At its dedication, the restored building was named Imogen Cunningham Hall in honor of the renowned photographer who was one of the most famous UW women graduates. I had acquired a nice architectural rendering created by architect Elizabeth Ayer, the first woman to graduate from the School of Architecture, and I gave it to the new Women's Information Center, where it was displayed in the director's office. The building eventually housed the offices for the UW Women's Studies Program.

❖

IN 1982, MY FIRST FULL YEAR on the AIA Board, Norm and I settled into a cadence of regular cross-country travel and meetings that would be the rhythm of our lives for many years. In mid-January, I was back in Washington, D.C., for an AIA grassroots meeting, which included a visit to the Beaux-Arts-style Cannon Office Building to meet the lawmakers from Washington state.

The end of the month brought a new job remodeling one of Paul Thiry's early modest houses in Seattle's Madrona neighborhood. The house was a small jewel, and I appreciated how he made the most out of limited space and resources. All it required was some updating. I asked Paul for the original floor plans, but he had thrown them away. I said, "Paul, please do not throw any of your work away. Give it to the UW Libraries Special Collections and you can claim a tax deduction." Those last two words caught his attention.

Around this time, I was surprised to get a call from a woman who wanted to feature our Laurelhurst house's kitchen in a Japanese publication. I'm still not sure how she found me. The finished publication was about two hundred glossy pages, featuring kitchens of all types from around the world—commercial and residential, even airplane galleys—with our kitchen as the main feature. The beautiful layouts showed all the tools, equipment, utensils, and gadgets. I was just sorry I could not read Japanese.

In early February, I was back in D.C. for an AIA Design Committee meeting. When I returned home, we were out for dinner almost every night at friends' or colleagues' homes. One evening, we hosted architect Elizabeth Wright Ingram, Frank Lloyd Wright's granddaughter, after she spoke at the university. She was working with students at a campsite in the Southwest desert where they were studying conservation, preservation, and society's effects on the environment. Right after that, I was off to D.C. again for the AIA Secretary Advisory Committee.

I was already spending so much time in airports that I decided to invest in a membership to the Northwest Airlines Club. A lifetime membership was about a hundred dollars—maybe less—and certainly the best investment I ever made. My membership was honored by many airlines and served me well through all of my later travels.

❖

IN BETWEEN AIA MEETINGS, around Norm's UW spring break, we looked for opportunities to travel internationally. In March 1982, we left on a long-planned tour of South America with friends.

We started in Quito, Ecuador, where we met a local architect. He had a large collection of pre-Columbian artifacts, making his home the highlight of the trip. He had an agreement with the farmers to buy whatever items they unearthed, and his goal was to keep them in the country until a museum was established to permanently house them. I hope he succeeded.

A page from the Japanese publication featuring the Laurelhurst House kitchen

Peru was next. After a stop in Lima, we flew to Cusco, where we shopped while acclimating to the altitude. Then we were off to Machu Picchu, the primary destination of our trip. We rode a train along switchbacks to the 13,000-foot elevation level, then transferred to a bus for more switchbacks to the top. There, we were surprised to find a lodge with a dining facility and about eighteen rooms. We had been told to expect rough accommodations, but we did not need our flashlights and camping supplies after all.

The buses returned down the mountain, taking people back to the train and city, and our little group curled up by the fireplace for cocktails. We were just outside the gate to the ruins, and we had the area all to ourselves. Norm and I were out early the next morning with only the alpacas, llamas, and wildflowers for company. We had hours of solitude before the train returned with a new crowd, and it could not have been more idyllic. On our way back to Cusco, I fell in love with the panpipe music that one of the guides played—the perfect accompaniment to a beautiful trip.

Our next stop was Bolivia. Like many countries, Bolivia had its share of political unrest and at the time there was a curfew, leaving the evening streets unnervingly empty except for a paper rustling about or a dog trotting along. Early the next morning we left La Paz, the Bolivian capital built in the caldera of a former volcano, to travel to Lake Titicaca, where we explored islands that were home to straw and wood buildings along with Inca ruins.

In Asunción, Paraguay, my first college roommate, Jacy Fuller Lane, met us. Jacy's husband, Lyle, was the U.S. ambassador, and Norm and I stayed with her at the U.S. Embassy while the rest of our group went to a hotel. Unfortunately, Lyle's mother had just passed away, and he was in Seattle to take care of arrangements, leaving Jacy to entertain our group of architects. The official party at the embassy included local architects, and they in turn invited us Americans to a barbecue. This turned out to be a nerve-racking evening in a large garden where every other chair was occupied by an automatic handgun. I'm sure we all took mental notes about where to take cover if the shooting started. German was the primary language spoken at this party, and I suspected most of our hosts were former Nazis. Weaponry notwithstanding, the food was incredible: Spits over a fire roasted a lamb, a calf, and a pig, all dressed in wonderful sauces. It was a party to remember, but we were all relieved to make it back to our lodgings unscathed.

Next, Rio. The manager at our beachfront hotel insisted on locking up our passports, jewelry, and money, and he warned us to avoid the beach after dark. Norm had arranged for a guide named Rick, who took our group to a museum and the Ministry of Education, which was designed by Modernist architect Oscar Niemeyer, and then out of town to Roberto Burle Marx's home and gardens. Rio was better known for its crime than its architecture, and friends were later shocked that we went off with a total stranger on such an adventure. We were lucky Rick was an honest guide.

The next morning, Rachel—a friend and fellow architect—took our group through the new government building where she worked. On our walk from our transit stop to the building, the men in our group were surrounded by prostitutes offering their services, and it was entertaining watching the guys fend them off. Our visit was topped with a visit to the Christ the Redeemer statue. What a view of Rio and its surroundings!

We had one day in the capital, Brasília, which was a ghost town without its workers on the Sunday we visited. From there, we traveled to the delightful old city of Salvador, where our hotel was a former convent. Our rooms had been the nuns' cells, and the narrow slits of windows looked out on the central courtyard, where an expanded well created a reflection pool and served as a small swimming pool. The beautiful restoration project was full of wonderful artwork and charm.

In the little town of Ouro Preto, we watched Easter parades and marching bands wind through car-free streets from the church at the lower end of town to a church at the top of the hill. As we returned to a Niemeyer-designed hotel for our last night in Brazil, the band played "The Stars and Stripes Forever." Yes, it was time to go home.

❖

BACK IN THE OFFICE there was much to catch up on with my staff, who included Paul Wanzer, a Washington State University grad, and Patty Holland of Kodiak, who kept our work humming along while I was off playing. I had hired Paul during a prior summer *Ring* cycle opera season and told Norm that I had hired "Siegfried," with his masses of blond curls and bright blue eyes. (I did not ask for a vocal audition.)

At the end of April, I flew to Pullman to give a talk at Washington State University. The women's movement was very active, and WSU had invited women representing careers in the construction industry to share their stories. In my introduction, I mentioned that the most frequent question I had been asked over the years was, "Why did you choose architecture?" At last, I had an answer! I had recently read about a study that tried to determine whether there was a difference between male and female brains in infants. The conclusion was yes. The part that I remembered was that male babies responded to visual cues and female babies responded to audio. So, I said, I must have a male brain in a female body because I am totally visual. Suddenly, a young woman with steel-rimmed glasses lunged from her front-row chair, screaming, "That's not true!"

I learned later that she was a Danish exchange student; she was very involved in the women's movement and did not understand my humor. Of course, the rest of my talk is long forgotten.

In May, the meetings picked up again: Energy Seminar, Seattle Landmarks Preservation Board Retreat, AIA in Tacoma and Yakima, Historic Resources Committee, AIA Senior Council, and a four-day Housing Committee Meeting in Monterey, California, where I had extra time with friend and architect Joyce Stevens in her hometown.

After two days at home, Norm and I flew to Hawaii for the three-day AIA Board meeting in Kona before the weeklong AIA National Convention in Honolulu, where Norman was awarded his AIA Fellowship Medal on the beautiful Oahu beach. Now our household had two Fellows! After the convention, we went to Ralph and Shirley Anderson's beach house on Kauai. It was designed by Vladimir (Val) Ossipoff and situated on its own point with a private swimming lagoon. No question, it was architecturally the finest house on the island at the time. A few months later, it was destroyed in the November 1982 hurricane.

The year was half-over, but there was no break from the rhythm of meetings and travel. The AIA Design Committee and Secretary Advisory meetings in D.C. were followed by the regional AIA meeting in Alaska, which was followed by an AIA Board meeting in Vancouver, B.C. There were chapter meetings in Spokane, Montana, and Idaho, and I juried the honor awards. I flew to Los Angeles for another AWIU meeting, which led to another AIA Design Committee meeting, and then to a New York weekend to see some shows with friends, before D.C. again for another secretary advisory meeting.

Norm and Jane, both AIA Fellows, at AIA meeting in Honolulu

Just ten days later, in early December, Norm and I were both back in D.C. for the annual AIA Board meeting, where new board members and officers assumed their positions. The finale of these meetings always included a lovely formal dinner in a beautiful historic space. For Norm, this would be the first of many of his December birthdays we celebrated in Washington, D.C.—usually at Old Ebbitt Grill, the capital's oldest saloon.

Through my many years of travel, I learned how to get a lot of work done during flights to the East Coast. I also became a master packer, filling my suitcase in about 15 minutes. In between airports and architectural projects, I still managed to squeeze in July 4 berry-picking parties, camping trips, and our anniversary celebration weekends. Each November, Norm thoughtfully chose a surprise destination, and gave me only one clue: the instruction to pack shoes for either hiking or dancing. And we ended every year celebrating the holidays with our friends and family in Seattle.

This was just the first year that moved to this rhythm. Many, many more would follow.

❖

IN MY OWN PRACTICE, I had never pursued the set-asides for women-owned businesses, but several firms begged me to partner with them because my participation made them more likely to win large public projects. So, I joined the TRA firm for a few projects at Seattle-Tacoma International Airport and improving state buildings in Olympia. Longtime friend Vic Gray needed my help to work on the new I-90 floating bridge approach connecting the pontoons to the earthwork, so THG (The Hastings Group) served as the design adviser for the shape of the piers and other structural elements. Engineers had a higher pay scale than architects, so we made more money as consultants. After this project, we partnered for about ten years with another engineering firm working on the Mercer Island tunnel lid. As a child, I had been so fascinated watching the construction of the Aurora Bridge; fifty-plus years later, I was in the bridge design business.

The next bridge project was the most fun. The Flaming Geyser State Park Bridge in a beautiful valley along the Green River at the entrance to the park required a four-person team: Vic Gray was the structural engineer, Rich Haag was the landscape architect, George Tsutakawa was the artist/sculptor, and I was the architect. We started the project by picnicking in the park with our spouses, then we walked the riverbank, tramped through the unmowed meadow grass, and tossed out our wild ideas. Vic finally brought us back to reality, reminding us we had to sell the design to the King County Board of Commissioners. We settled down and designed a structure with pylons on both sides of the river. George then wrapped the pylons in stainless-steel abstract totem pole designs honoring former Native American river dwellers. The county board loved the design, and the drawings went in the drawer to await funding.

Youell Vacation Home, Harstine Island, Washington. The second house designed by Jane on Harstine Island, it featured a unique fireplace and was used as a getaway home by the family, who were Laurelhurst neighbors

❖

IN MARCH 1983, the national AIA Board meeting came to Seattle. I told Norman that because I was the local host, he would need to plan an event for the spouses. In the past, this was often a tea party or fashion show. "No way," he said, retiring to our study. He emerged hours later with a plan. The event would be an all-day tour of Seattle, starting with a shopping trip to Pike Place Market. Then, a UW campus tour would be followed by lunch at the Faculty Club. In the afternoon, the group would tour Seattle's Olmsted-designed parks and the Ballard Locks with its fish ladders. The day was planned from breakfast to dinner with the assistance of some faculty wives. It was such a huge success that all the AIA men, who had been in meetings all day, were jealous.

AIA Board members stayed in the Westin Hotel's modern circular towers, and the president hosted a party in the penthouse on a windy evening. I was impressed with the amount of sway as the tower danced in the wind; it was like being on a houseboat. As the locals, Norm and I were invited to join the president's party for dinner at Seattle's hottest new restaurant. I was amused when the cab dropped us off at Settabella's across the street from THG's office. Over time, we had watched the incredible transformation of old Snooky's Tavern, closed due to two murders, into this popular, expensive Italian restaurant, where the owner's red Ferrari was frequently parked out front.

Norm's Seattle tour became an AIA legend. Every committee that met in the area requested an encore performance, and Norm had a new role planning all spousal outings wherever the AIA meetings took place. He was in his element—the history professor holding class for an adoring group of women who learned more about what their husbands had studied in school. In the beginning, he had not been keen on my decision to run for the AIA directorship. Now, he anticipated each meeting with delight.

❖

BACK AT THE OFFICE I had several repeat clients. The Karrows, whose remodeling job brought me my first national honor, were planning a new home on flat ground. Their hillside house with all its stairs had become too much for their worn-out skiers' knees, so a single-level model was underway on my drafting board. Also, the Legges, who had remodeled their city house twice, decided to retire to their summer home. We replaced the old vacation cottage with a three-story structure that included a rental unit on the lowest floor and great beach views throughout.

Later that summer, Mother, Norman, and I returned to my roots to attend the Seattle landmark designation hearing for the Fauntleroy Church. Afterward, we took a ferry across Puget Sound for a picnic and a quest to find a piece of long-lost family property.

During the 1909 Alaska-Yukon-Pacific Exposition, two of my aunts had purchased a lot in Manchester, near Port Orchard, for $150, sight unseen. My father later bought Aunt Hazel's half to save peace in the family, and it was a family joke during my childhood because Aunt Ruby and Father were co-owners of a piece of land—but they had no idea where it was. The taxes were about forty cents per year. When my father passed away in 1966, Aunt Ruby said she was tired of the taxes, which had grown to about five dollars per year. She told my mother that if she gave her half to me, Ruby would give me the other half. It cost ten dollars to change the deed. Thus, three years before I was married, I was a woman of property. I owned my 1891 Fremont house, the ocean lot I bought in 1960, and the mystery lot my aunts purchased in 1909.

Norm had researched the location, so after our picnic we went looking for it. We were about to give up when I decided to try one more undeveloped road.

Jane with the travel group in the Soviet Union, 1983

A paved road veered off to the left—and it was our road! Six relatively new houses were on one side with five others and a vacant lot, mine, on the other. Under fir trees, Norm and I picked delicious little wild blackberries—enough for a pie. A family mystery was solved! Eventually, the sale of this lot would supplement our retirement fund.

❖

AUGUST WAS MY INTERNATIONAL MONTH, starting with a meeting in Longbranch, Washington, at Riptide, the summer home of AWIU board member Mary Ripley. From the group, I gathered messages to take to Moscow later that month. Then, I hosted a group of Australian architects through the People to People International organization. After Seattle, they traveled across the country, and I connected them with AIA Board members in Chicago, Boston, and Washington, D.C. In Seattle, we took them to our homes for dinner, but I explained that when they were on the East Coast their hosts would be more formal. I was sure there would be no dinners in private homes, and they should not take any coolness personally. In later years, when I met the Australians at professional gatherings, they often thanked me for explaining the differences between East and West Coast architects.

The Soviet Women's Committee had invited three AWIU members to be their guests for a ten-day visit: Lee Kimche, a museum administrator from D.C.; Bernice Hemphill, a blood bank manager from San Francisco; and me. In Moscow, our three hotel rooms were spread out with several rooms separating us. Were we suspected of being up to something?

This was my third trip to the USSR, and I was curious what new adventure our hosts had planned for us after our meetings. It turned out to be a visit to Moldova—a first for the three of us. The capital, Chișinau, was a small city where a seven-story building was a skyscraper. We were surprised when Bernice mentioned that she was from San Francisco, and our hosts said it was the same size as their capital. Moldova was one of the USSR bread-basket states, and it seemed to be predominantly agriculture land. Rows of small apple trees were trained on wire fences so the fruit could eventually be picked by machines. Fields of flowers and vineyards covered the land. A winery trip ended in the tasting room, which was decorated to the hilt with artificial cobwebs and stones to make it look hundreds of years old. It made me think of Halloween.

One evening, we were hosted in a private home for dinner. The house was brand new, as were the furnishings, with tags still attached so they could be returned to the store the following day. The residents proudly toured us through the house, showing off its amenities—the kitchen with its beautiful sink, the bath with a tub and lavatory, and even the closets. Over dinner, we got acquainted with the extended family, who told stories about their lives and the terrible war they had suffered through. (However, we noted they were not old enough to have experienced World War II.) Then, they asked us about ourselves. One of our members, Lee, had Russian heritage, which our hosts enjoyed learning about. I talked about Seattle and my teen years during World War II, when I worried that Japanese bombers would fly over our house on their way to the Boeing plant. Then, Bernice described living in Hawaii when Pearl Harbor was attacked. Her Navy husband was on his ship and she was at home. Because she had a science background, she ran to the hospital offering her help, not knowing whether her husband was alive or dead. By the time we finished talking, the mood at the table had completely changed. They had never met anyone like us.

When it was time to catch our flight back to Moscow, we were late, so the driver drove right out onto the tarmac and blocked the plane. We were laden with fresh fruit and beautiful flowers—all in glamorous Lee's arms—to take to friends in Moscow. Others on the plane assumed Lee must be someone famous, but who could she be?

Back in Moscow that Sunday, Bernice asked our guide if she could attend Catholic services. After a search, they found a church, so Lee and I took a walk around the block during the service, stopping in a store with just a few items on the shelves. We returned to find our guide in a panic. She thought she had lost us. She did not let us out of her sight again until we each made our flights the following day.

My flight was to Frankfurt, where I transferred to a New York-bound plane. Nothing was on schedule because Soviet planes did not depart until they were full, and in Frankfurt, I got the last available seat on the flight home. Of course, I had to crawl over the man seated on the aisle, weighted down with my last-minute gifts. My neighbor asked, "Are you just coming from the Soviet Union?" When I said yes, he said, "Then you probably don't know about the plane incident." He told me the Soviets had shot down a Korean passenger plane—news that provided the real reason why we had been so protected. I asked him what else was in the news. His answer hit closer to home: Washington Sen. Henry Jackson had died! This was a real loss; he was such a nice person when we visited with him. I said to myself, "Please no more news."

❖

EARLY DECEMBER 1983 brought the annual AIA Board meeting and changing of officers, along with the selection of an AIA Gold Medal recipient. Shortly after I joined the board, I had received a letter from a former member saying, "You have a Gold Medalist in your backyard." The letter urged me to ensure that British Columbia architect Arthur Erickson was recognized. I knew I was not going to make this happen by myself, so I contacted Samuel "Pete" Anderson, the board member from Richmond, Virginia, and an Erickson admirer. We teamed up on a Gold Medal presentation. Pete covered Arthur's books, and I explained the value of his built work. When we finished, the response was: "Who is he? But he is not an American!" The Gold Medal is an international honor, but that fact was lost on this group. I concluded that most of the board members were the business partners while the more knowledgeable designers were happy to be at home doing real work. There would be no Gold Medal awarded in 1984, and we would have to resubmit our nomination.

This was the beginning of my third—and last—year as an AIA Board director. I had been saving up my travel funds to make a six-day sweep visiting chapters in Guam, Hawaii, and Alaska. I was the first director to visit Guam in many years and arrived in time for the governor's annual affair honoring architects, engineers, and construction industry representatives. I was given the seat of honor next to the governor. In my talk, I mentioned that I had actually been offered a job there thirty years earlier but rejected it so I could go to Europe and see the historic Western architecture there. I apologized because I realized that Guam did have a rich architectural history with many monuments, including some dating from Magellan's 1521 visit. I was treated like royalty by local architects, who showed me around the whole island.

From Guam, I took a short trip to Narita, Japan, where I met with my former employee Neil Warren, who was working in Tokyo. We had about four hours to tour and catch up on news from both sides of the Pacific. Guam had been hot, but Japan was suffering from a very cold spell with a good deal of snow. We went to a lovely snowy park that evening, but our visit was cut short when we were chased by a flock of starving swans.

The Honolulu leg brought me the relief of warm weather and shorter meetings because the Hawaii chapter members made it to the mainland more frequently than their Guam and Alaska colleagues. When I arrived in Anchorage, the airport crew immediately snatched my Japanese fruit—what I referred to as an apple-pear (and now known as an Asian pear), which was not yet available in American markets—insisting they were full of bugs. I said perhaps I should not be allowed in either as I was full of the fruit with the bugs. I assumed they enjoyed eating the apple-pears later.

Back home, I had another "Home of the Month" to celebrate. I had originally designed the Reed Residence in West Seattle for Norm's brother and sister-in-law, but a dispute with a difficult neighbor ruined their desire to live in the area, so the lot and plans were sold to the Reeds. It was for the best. The vertical house on a small, very steep lot required young knees to truly enjoy its magnificent view of the city.

❖

THE HIGHLIGHT OF THE 1984 AIA CONVENTION in Phoenix was a formal dinner at Taliesin West, hosted by Frank Lloyd Wright's widow. This was my second visit to the school and studio. In 1956, the roofs had been canvas and the school was very active, with only architects finding their way up the road. That road was still gravel and a challenge for our high heels and long dresses. We gathered at the main center and awaited the arrival of our frail hostess, who settled into a canvas campaign chair lined with a polar bear pelt. The rotted-out canvas roofs had been replaced with plastic, and Taliesin had expanded into new buildings. The student-prepared dinner resembled Kentucky Fried Chicken with instant mashed potatoes and canned peas and carrots. Tourists paid $100 for this experience, which included music composed by Wright and performed by the students. Some people knew how to make architecture pay.

Then, Norm and I were off to Europe to lead our first University of Washington tour. Most of the group had attended a series of evening lectures by Norm before the trip, and as we visited French chateaus and gardens, Norm gave the lectures and I solved the problems when plans went awry. After a few weeks, the group returned home, and we continued on for a few more weeks, visiting German friends on our way north to beautiful Copenhagen.

When we returned, I did not put my passport away. Norm and I were soon off to Quebec for our joint AIA Board meeting with the Canadian architectural board—an excellent chance for Norm to practice his high school French. After one late meeting, I returned to the hotel surprised to find him in bed with the lights on. He had fallen and his face was a mess with black eyes and bruises blooming into more color every hour. I was boarding a flight to Berlin for a UIFA Congress the next day, so Norm had to return home alone. What kind of irresponsible mate did he have?

By the time I arrived home from Berlin, Norm was mostly healed. That fall, I had a good stretch in the office and started focusing on a new task: teaming up with Linda Banks to plan a UIFA Congress in Washington, D.C., for 1988. UIFA members were delighted that an upcoming meeting would be held on the East Coast.

At that December's AIA Board meeting, I received a beautiful gift from my teammates: a Christian Dior navy-blue scarf with "AIA 1984" embroidered on it. Norm tried to convince me that it was a man's scarf and I should relinquish it to him, but my answer was always a firm "no."

Pete and I again gave our Gold Medal Award presentation in support of Arthur Erickson, but we still did not have the votes. One of our most popular and talented recent board members was nominated and he was a sure winner. This was my last year as a director, so I would have to find someone to carry on my mission for an Erickson Gold Medal.

❖

AFTER YEARS IN CONSTANT MOTION, 1985 was a time to be at home for a while. My brother Jim was losing his battle with cancer, and it was important to be there for our mother and his family. His memorial service was February 10 in the Fauntleroy Church where we were raised. Don Wallace, Jim's closest friend who I called my third brother, came up from California to sit with Mother and me while Norm was away in D.C. The "new" church, as we thought of it, was all glass on the east façade, looking into the woods sprinkled with rhododendrons and seasonal color. Outside the window, we could see Jim's dinghy with its sail waving in the light breeze. He was always the happiest in a sailboat out on the water. Mother looked at me and said, "Don't you dare go anywhere. You're all I have left." It did seem unfair: She had lost her father as a little girl, her second son in his early thirties, her husband, a granddaughter at thirteen years old, her mother, a sister, and now her firstborn at the age of sixty.

❖

JUNE FOUND US IN ONE of our favorite cities, San Francisco, for the AIA Convention. This was a big year for Norm and me: Our nominee, Masako Hayashi from Japan, would become an Honorary Fellow. Masako was Japan's "first lady of architecture" with an international reputation for her outstanding work. We had first met her and her architect husband, Shoji, at the UIFA

Shoji and Masako Hayashi, both Honorary FAIA

Congress in Tehran. During that same congress, Yuki Kawashina and I had become wonderful friends over a package of nasturtium seeds, and she and her husband, Genshi, were also in San Francisco, their first U.S. visit. We had a wonderful time partying with the Japanese visitors at the Palace of Fine Arts.

I still had unfinished business with the AIA Board: our Gold Medal candidate from B.C. Needing a strong person to carry this forward, I contacted William

Jane with Arthur Erickson and his AIA Gold Medal

Muchow from Denver, a former chancellor of the College of Fellows, a current board member and active on the National Council of Architectural Registration Boards (NCARB). He was respected and admired, and I wondered if he could fit one more project into his schedule. He said he would consider my request, so I forwarded him the nomination information. A month or so later he called to say he would do it. I later learned he had traveled to British Columbia on his own time to personally view Arthur's work and was impressed. In December, he got the votes. Arthur Erickson would receive the Gold Medal at the 1986 convention in San Antonio.

❖

IN OCTOBER IT WAS A GOOD TIME to pack our bags again, this time for Thailand. Mother was nicely settled into her new apartment in a retirement home. My brother and I had disagreed about this before his death, but now I rested easier knowing she had continuing care. This was a real vacation just for Norm and me with no responsibilities, and Thailand was warm, colorful and relaxing with many opportunities to take photos and find gifts to bring home.

We were also excited that our group could arrange a five-day trip into Burma (now Myanmar), a destination that we weren't sure we would see because of its volatile politics. Following our guidebook instructions, we each purchased a bottle of Johnnie Walker Red Label Scotch and a carton of 555 cigarettes to sneak into the country. These items were said to be the best monetary system, and sure enough, the border guards bid on our illegal packages. Norman sold out, but I waited until we got to the hotel in Rangoon, where the price was almost double. Our dealing gave us all the funds we needed for our stay and shopping.

The city infrastructure was in desperate need of help. The once-grand Rangoon Hotel was large and hollow with huge cockroaches skittering across the floor. When the bathwater ran out as mud, I settled for a sponge bath. But Mandalay and the stupas of Pagan were more than worth any inconvenience or tension caused by the ever-present gun-carrying military guards.

As we wrapped up our year in D.C. with the AIA Board meeting and Norm's birthday, we learned I wasn't done with the constant AIA director meetings, after all. I was asked to fill out the term of a director who had to resign. Norm was delighted; he would be rejoining the spouses' group, and the women were equally thrilled to have him back.

❖

MY THG OFFICE had a new project designing a model bathroom for display at the upcoming National Association of Home Builders Convention and the AIA Convention. This was a Kohler Plumbing Fixtures commission featuring their products. Everyone in the office was invited to come up with a design, then we took a vote to choose one of the designs to develop.

In June 1986, Norm and I were in Texas, first at Marble Falls for the AIA Board meeting and then lovely San Antonio for the convention—a special moment because Solange d'Herbez de la Tour, UIFA president, received her honorary Fellowship and Canadian architect Arthur Erickson was finally awarded his Gold Medal. I had nominated both talented architects for their honors and was proud to see them recognized. Unfortunately, I missed Erickson's acceptance speech and was surprised and humbled to learn later he had personally thanked me.

Back home, it was time for our annual summertime influx of houseguests from around the country and the gathering of six of us friends born in the spring and summer of 1928. Our birth year was the "Year of the Dragon," so we called ourselves the "Dragon Ladies." Our group started celebrating together during our university days and eventually grew to include several younger members. We also attended Norm's fiftieth high school reunion in Olympia, where I met his old school friends and former teachers.

The October AIA Board meeting was in Pittsburgh, my first visit to the city. Local architect and fellow board member Syl Damianos engineered the meeting highlight: a formal dinner party at Frank Lloyd Wright's famous Fallingwater, about an hour southwest of the city. The afternoon of the event, I saw the public member of the board, the Rev. Dr. Robert Schuller of the Crystal Cathedral in Los Angeles, leaving the meeting. I asked if he was not joining us for the evening, and he did not know what I was talking about. I had not supported his nomination to the board because I could not believe it would fit within his schedule. However, he was a celebrity of the moment, as was his Philip Johnson-designed glass church, and he was voted in. He only attended our meetings when they took place near major metropolitan areas, and he was on his way that afternoon to New York to meet with the publisher of his new book. As I had suspected, the board was about what we could offer him, not what he could do to contribute. I try not to judge people, but when I do and they prove me right, I feel better.

As at Taliesin West, our evening at Fallingwater found us carefully making our way in high heels and formal dresses down a gravel road. At the bend where the structure came into view, we exclaimed in unison, "It is not white!" We were told that this was what the architects always said because of course, when Fallingwater was first photographed, film was black and white, not color. Although Fallingwater is cream in color, it did not disappoint.

Normally, food is not allowed in this docent-protected monument, but we were served dinner—with napkins constantly appearing from nowhere to slide under any plate or glass before they could rest. We were even allowed on the slippery rocks at the water's edge to enjoy the best of the photo views. We carefully picked our way back up the road in the pitch dark that evening.

IN 1987, I WAS INTERVIEWED by a graduate student for her master's thesis on women architects. I was pressed to come up with answers to the "why" questions that I had never thought about much. Why architecture? This was the most difficult question, and I never really had the answer until 1994 when I discovered a book, *The Secret Language of Birthdays*. Each day of the year had a personal profile based on psychology, history, numerology, tarot, and astrology. March 3, my birthdate, is "The Day of Design." I realized I had never known anyone with the same birthday until I joined the national AIA Board, where I meet two other members who shared it: Tom Teasdale and Ted Pappas. I guess we just didn't have a choice! It was true that I was fascinated by the building process from the time I was a young child. It was something I simply had to do.

The book also gave me some insight into why I was a natural organizer—and thought of as a teacher—from my youngest days. I remember being shocked when I was offered a university teaching position in Kansas a year after I graduated. I wanted to travel, not to teach! Now, I realized that my teaching career truly started when I opened my office. An architect is always teaching: teaching clients about possibilities they had never considered, teaching employees how the office is organized, helping staff and contractors hone their construction skills. I smiled remembering that I started teaching at the Seattle Community College only because I wanted to save the program I had spent years developing. Yes, I guess teaching was always there as part of my organization talents, even though I had never really thought about it.

In thinking back over my career, I realized that I had never thought of myself as competitive. Certainly, winning is nice, especially for a team, but I didn't have the same ego as many of my fellow architects. I competed mostly with myself, striving to do each job better than the last. I usually did well in sports, though. For me, they were mental games, as well as physical, and the more competitive types often lost control in their aggressiveness to win.

But that was enough self-analysis for me.

❖

SPRING BROUGHT US VISITS from friends across the country. Genshi and Yuki Kawashina stopped for a short visit on their way home to Japan after spending a year in the U.S. We could not believe what an effect one year had made on Genshi, who had been a very formal professor the last time we saw him at the start of his year teaching at the University of Michigan. Now, he walked off his California flight in jeans, cowboy hat and boots, wearing a jeans jacket covered with patches from all the places they visited while driving across the U.S. A small, choice space remained on his jacket to add three more patches for the University of Washington, Seattle, and Washington state. We had three wonderful days together seeing the peak bloom of the UW campus cherry trees and winning their hearts. With hugs and tears, we put them on their plane home. As faculty members, they had given up their ranking positions in Japan to spend the year abroad. Now, they had to work their way back up to their former academic status.

That summer, I spoke at the Pacific Rim Forum: The Architect's Meeting Point in Hong Kong. Joseph Esherick, FAIA, of San Francisco and I had been invited to represent the West Coast. Joe focused on his specialty, high-rise design and the urban scene, while I talked about vacation houses and the environmental scene. Many new buildings had been constructed in Hong Kong since my last visit seven years earlier. At the end of the meeting, a New Zealand architect asked if I had become an architect because I lived in the most beautiful place in the world. I had not thought about that, but after seeing much of the world I realized I had been raised in paradise. New Zealand is much like the Pacific Northwest, so the question surprised me. And yes, my slides were very good!

My friend Colleen Bard had decided to join me on the trip if I agreed to go with her to Singapore to find her birth records. This was my first visit to Singapore. Much of the old city was intact, but they were starting to destroy its charming architectural history. Colleen's father had been a British diplomat stationed in Singapore when she was born, and church records from her baptism were easily found, to my Scottish friend's delight.

❖

THAT YEAR, AT OUR FAMILY'S ANNUAL JULY 4 PARTY, we celebrated at the Wallaces' beach house in Gig Harbor—but the festivities were cut short when I squatted down for a group photo and lost my balance, falling through the rope railing to the rocky beach eight feet below. At high tide the water would have been at least three feet deep, but unfortunately it was low tide. I remember telling the medics that I thought my left arm was broken. The next thing I knew, I was in a Tacoma hospital room surrounded by hospital staff.

I was in the surgery unit because they were sure my spleen had been ruptured. That was not the case, but I had suffered many broken ribs along the left side of my spine, a compressed vertebra, separated shoulder, and I had a hole in my head. After four days in the hospital, I was released. At Dr. Lane's office on our way home, he explained I would lose up to an inch in height. When I started muttering about taking up my hems, I realized from the sober faces around me how terrible I must have looked and sounded. Norman became my nurse while I spent most of my hours in bed on the main floor of our house. During the night I would ring a cowbell for him to come and pull me up for a bathroom visit. The neighbors were wonderful, bringing in food for us.

Less than two weeks later, I was back in the office. I was grateful to be back on my feet as we realized the fall could have left me a paraplegic. Seven days after that, I made my public debut at a celebration of Al Bumgardner's life. My wonderful friend and mentor had slipped away while I was recuperating, and the architectural community had suffered a true loss.

*Backpacking with friends at Deer Park in the Olympics: Marilyn Mattocks, Jane Gerhardt,
Jim Egbert, Jane, Norm, and Al Bumgardner*

After the accident, I took my days at a more leisurely pace, and enjoyed celebrating my mother's ninetieth birthday. Her three grandchildren, two widowed daughters-in-law, and I were her only remaining family.

That September, Norman and I were scheduled to escort a University of Washington tour to Germany and Austria featuring the Romantic Road. The doctor approved my travel if I promised not to pick up anything weighing more than five pounds. Others would have to carry all my things—a great arrangement! Surgery to repair my left shoulder was delayed until the following spring while the rest of my body healed. I was really looking forward to this trip returning to my mountain home of Oberammergau and the other charming old German villages. I was certainly in good hands with our group, which included the former dean of the UW Medical School, a pharmacist, an ophthalmologist, and a registered nurse.

All went smoothly until we arrived in Salzburg, where we had reservations at a central city hotel. We had been preempted by a University of Pennsylvania group and our lodging was moved to another hotel far out in the countryside. But Norman had planned this experience around the central city experience. I called the Swiss travel broker and said that if the lodging situation were not remedied, the university would never use him again. (I believe the word "Washington" helped.)

Soon we were packing up our belongings and returning to a five-star hotel, even better than the four-star hotel we had originally booked. Our new accommodations included a beautiful garden with a concert that was free for us, and some in the Penn group even paid to share in our enjoyment.

Back home I signed up for an evening palmistry class at the UW Experimental College—a fun project to take my mind off my slowly healing back. The first two-hour session started with our twenty-five students enthusiastically inking up our hands to make handprints. These became our textbooks. A few weeks later, we were down to seven regulars trying to read each other's palms.

At the final session, the instructor told me I had the best-balanced hand he had ever seen. He explained that my positive traits matched my negative ones. I learned a good deal about reading character from the palm and I added this to my observations when interviewing potential employees. I admit I considered birth signs and handwriting, too, when possible. The office is a team, and no amount of talent can take precedence over the importance of teamwork.

❖

THE 1988 UIFA CONGRESS was coming up, and much work remained to fulfill my 1984 promise to help plan it. My major coup was lining up the new, beautiful award-winning Intelsat Headquarters Building in Washington, D.C., for our general sessions. It offered the latest technology and would make it easy to deal with the many language requirements, plus it had wonderful soft seats for our long meetings. Linda Banks, my colleague from Boston, worked on the program while I arranged the site and fundraising. (It was the host group's responsibility to raise the money to put on the event.) The AIA agreed to provide a $10,000 loan as seed money while I signed up friends and prominent architects to contact building supply businesses with international clients. Of course, Weyerhaeuser was in my territory, but I dreaded contacting them. The director of their foundation was known to shun funding requests, but I mailed her my proposal. A few days later I received a letter asking why Weyerhaeuser would want to be associated with supporting an event that was bound to fail. She gave several reasons—we started too late, we didn't have a prominent international keynote speaker—and her criticism really got my dander up. I replied that I was truly sorry they chose to be left out. The Congress would go off on schedule and be as successful as ever, and if I had listened to people like her, I would not be in the career position that I was today. I felt much better. A week later, I received a check, but no note, from Weyerhaeuser.

❖

THE YEAR OF 1988 BEGAN WITH TERRIBLE NEWS: The *Washington Post* reported that Intelsat management had been charged with corruption, and they were now re-organized under new leadership. Intelsat was my greatest accomplishment for our UIFA Congress; they were granting the use of their facilities at no charge. I was on the phone immediately to explain the promise of support for our nonprofit interna-tional organization, which could not make alternate arrangements at this late date. Silence was the response and it seemed to last forever. Finally, they reviewed the records and agreed to honor the commitment. What a relief.

I was pulled between these UIFA preparations and pressing family needs at home. Mother was in the hospital, and Aunt Cleo passed away. But from February on, I was working constantly on the UIFA Congress, arranging for translators and preparing Congress materials to mail out to members across the U.S. and abroad.

At an AIA International Relations Committee meeting in Washington, D.C., I firmed up final location details for the UIFA Congress. The AIA would host a party with local women architects helping with tours, including the White House. Networking and teamwork made our plans come together.

I took a break in March to mark the sixtieth birthdays of the Dragon Ladies. We spent a week at the Andersons' beautiful new house on Kauai, which replaced the one destroyed by the 1982 hurricane. We did it all: food, nightlife, and touring the island. From a helicopter, we saw circular rainbows in Waimea Canyon. But the new house was the best part. It was situated on its own point jutting into the Pacific, with a swimming pool of lava rock within a garden of ferns—private enough for skinny dipping. I enjoyed this respite, knowing that when I returned home, I faced shoulder surgery.

After the birthday trip, the procedure successfully fixed a protruding bone issue. Among the costs: My arm was now shorter.

❖

IN JUNE 1988, the AIA Convention in New York convened with the investiture of the new Fellows on Sunday afternoon at the Cathedral of St. John the Divine. Both organs were at full volume in the memorable ceremony—the scene Norman wished he could have presided over when he was chairman of the Fellows Jury. I think he actually enjoyed it more as a relaxed spectator.

The next day brought a tremendous honor. Late in 1987, Anna Halpin, who was one of only two women to have served as AIA Vice President, had asked me for my resume. What I didn't know was she had decided to break up the old boys' club that determined how the College of Fellows selected their new board member each year. The COF Board was made up of the chancellor, vice chancellor, secretary and bursar, and a new bursar or secretary was elected each year to serve a two-year term, before moving up to vice chancellor. From the beginning of the COF, board members always picked a friend to join them. Anna decided the process for these prestigious positions should be democratic. She reached out to the chancellor to discuss creating an open nominating system, and he agreed. Anna then nominated me, and I learned I was to be elected in 1988. At this time, there were just a few women Fellows among the large group of men.

The COF business meeting was held in New York City's University Club, the imposing Italian Renaissance palazzo on Fifth Avenue designed by McKim, Mead & White— and the place where the College of Fellows was formed in 1952. When the time came to announce the bursar nomination, my name was announced, and the room went silent. Then, the applause began, recognizing the election. A good friend later told me that when the room was asked if there were additional nominations from the floor, the fellow next to him started to stand but he stomped on his foot. I knew he was joking, but I do believe a small shock wave passed over the room. Along with offering congratulations, colleagues asked, "How did you do it?" Of course, the answer was, I didn't. Others had nominated me, and I was as stunned as everyone else. Just like my presidency of the Seattle AIA chapter in 1975—when others talked me into running—my colleagues deserved the credit.

Anna Halpin of New York City and Sarah Harkness of Boston, both former AIA Vice Presidents, also had left a couple of cracks in the COF glass ceiling for me to squeeze through to become the first women architect to hold a top AIA office. In 1992, I would become chancellor, with Susan Maxman following as AIA President in 1993. Yes, it was well past time for the men to get used to women being in the room.

That 1988 New York convention had one more surprise in store: Lars, my Norwegian friend and tour guide from Nuremberg, was in the city on convention-related business. He managed to find my hotel phone number among the sixteen thousand-plus attendees. Norm and I met him the following day, and he said, "I just knew you would be here!" We caught up on the many happenings over the thirty-three years since we'd last seen each other. I have always enjoyed my many opportunities to reconnect and share stories with friends from years past.

❖

EARLY SUMMER IN SEATTLE brought us Bettina, daughter of our good German friends, the Hennings, who was now a medical student. She had a two-month grant to study at the Fred Hutchinson Cancer Research Center. We were determined to show her the wonders of the Pacific Northwest, and every weekend we drove to beautiful sights like Mount Rainier, the Olympic Peninsula, British Columbia, and the Cascade Mountains.

In late September I was in Washington, D.C., for the long-awaited UIFA Congress. Professor Milka Bliznakov arrived from Virginia Tech University with a group of her women architecture students and said, "Put them to work." What a bonus this group proved to be. I had heard of Milka and the project she launched in 1985, *The International Archive of Women in Architecture*. She was from Bulgaria with an ever-present smile that could warm the coldest day—and she had the fortitude of the heaviest-duty Mack truck. She knew how to get things done!

The Congress moved along smoothly, from our wonderful space at Intelsat to our welcoming reception at the AIA National Headquarters building. Our group even enjoyed a private tour of the White House. One of our D.C. friends had arranged the tour through her connection with a White House guard, and with the presidential family away, our group could sit in any chair, play the piano and peek in all the corners. Such freedom was unheard-of in other countries, and while I didn't join the tour, it was clear it made quite an impression! I knew President Solange d'Herbez de la Tour was disappointed that we didn't have a government official welcoming us, as was typical in Europe, but I didn't even try to sell a women's group to Nancy Reagan. I thought the informal White House tour more than compensated.

At the December AIA Board meeting, I presented a report on our successful UIFA Congress and presented a check, a repayment of the $10,000 the AIA had loaned us to plan the event. The board asked, "What is the money for?" Apparently, they had already written off the amount as a donation and there was never an expectation that it would be returned. They said that had never happened before.

From my perspective, I had only asked for a loan, and so I repaid my loan. The board decided the money would go to the AIA Foundation, and I wondered, am I the only fiscally responsible architect?

❖

IN EARLY MAY 1989 I lost my mother at age ninety-two, rather young for the women in our family. She was the last of my immediate family, and as Norm said, now I was an orphan. But I still had two wonderful, widowed sisters-in-law, two nieces and a nephew. Mother's late afternoon funeral service was followed by a buffet dinner at sister-in-law Norma's house, a lovely place where old friends could reminisce and comfort each other. My mother had been an important part of so many special moments throughout my life—and dressed me beautifully for many of them—and she would be missed.

In early June, I was inducted into the Hall of Fame at West Seattle High School. But that honor was overshadowed by the terrible news of Beijing's Tiananmen Square student protest and massacre. All tours to China were immediately canceled, including one we had planned. Certainly, I could use the time in the office, but I grieved for the reason.

Now that I was sixty, I was starting to think about future retirement and how to navigate it. A young architect who had worked for NBBJ was now working out of his home and was interested in renting some of my space. He was talented and highly recommended. Perhaps he would be interested in taking over the office one day. I am sure everyone dreams that others will take over their work, but my staff at the time wasn't interested. I would need to find another solution.

❖

OUR 1989 TRAVELS included five days in Boston as part of the 1992 AIA Convention planning team. That would be the year I would become chancellor of the College of Fellows. I really wanted the investiture to take place in H.H. Richardson's beautiful 1877 Trinity Church in the heart of the city. History is important in Boston and it's not easy for outsiders to gain access to cherished landmarks. We had to make the case to Trinity about how important this once-in-a-lifetime event is. Finally, Trinity agreed, but we were not allowed to hold a reception or offer food service. I had something very special to look forward to over the next few years.

Later that fall, we went to Merida, Mexico, on the Yucatán peninsula for an AIA international relations meeting. Afterward, Norm and I rented a VW bug with our Atlanta friends, John and MaryAnn Busby, to travel to Uxmal and see the Mayan ruins. I drove with John serving as my co-pilot while holding wires together to operate the air conditioner. John and I worried about whether our vehicle would get us back to Merida, but while we sweated it out, Norm and MaryAnn laughed away merrily in the back seat. John and I never let them forget it.

Three days after returning to Seattle, I was flying first class to Beijing with a group from People to People International, all of us guests of the Chinese government in a promotional plan to reestablish the tourism industry after the Tiananmen Square crackdown. Our new high-rise Beijing hotel was such a contrast to my first visit in 1980; the city had exploded with new structures and cars. I'm sure we were the only guests in our twentieth-floor deluxe accommodations with staff everywhere to push elevator buttons, open doors and provide whatever they thought we needed. We were treated as royalty for six days.

There was food, food, and more food—plus a grand banquet in the Great Hall of the People—meetings with the heads of the engineers, women administrators, and design institute, and tours to many great local sites. The best day included a private tour with a Chinese friend to the botanical gardens, where I requested a detour to see the rose garden. She assured me that the roses were finished blooming for the year so there would be nothing to see; however, I insisted, thinking about the roses in Seattle that bloom into autumn. So, we detoured and just around the corner I saw an enormous bed of peonies—the "China Rose." Indeed, they were long through blooming.

Next, we were off to see I.M. Pei's award-winning Fragrant Hill Hotel. The local structural engineer who worked with Pei joined us for lunch and talked about his experience with the project. It was a beautiful building with lovely gardens but too isolated from Beijing to be a commercial success, so it became a center for retreats.

Finally, the grand finale event brought a million Chinese performers dancing in unison in Tiananmen Square and the area around it. We watched from our grandstand seats with foreign ambassadors and dignitaries, and the organization to get the performers in place was a spectacle in itself. As darkness fell, fireworks lit up the city for a good hour. I had never seen such a display before, or since, and I could not help but think how all those funds could have been put toward some better use.

November brought our twentieth wedding anniversary, and for once, Norman's surprise romantic retreat was easy to guess: back to the ocean and our first honeymoon spot.

❖

IN 1990, MY OFFICE WAS WORKING on a major residential addition for former State Sen. Nita Rinehart, and I could hardly wait for the framing to be topped out so I could see the view that this project was all about. Some years earlier, the roof on the Rineharts' house had caught fire from fireworks. They remembered the firemen raving about the best view they had ever seen. The rambler was in the highest part of Laurelhurst but lacked the view that the owners of houses across the street enjoyed. Our work would put them above it all, with views of the Cascade Mountains and Lake Washington to the east; downtown Seattle and Lake Union to the south; the university, Puget Sound, and the Olympic Mountains to the west; and Green Lake and Edmonds to the north. The new master bedroom was the room on the top. Who would ever want to leave it?

In June, my West Seattle High School Class of 1945 marked its very first class reunion. Because we had departed school before World War II ended and many classmates had been in the military, it took forever to organize. Norm thought the girls I went to school with were all beauties, and I had to agree with him. Certainly, the boys had not held up as well! It was fun to catch up with their adventures, careers, and families.

It was Alaska's turn to host the AIA Northwest regional meeting—an opportunity to visit Juneau, the state capital. We took a cable car up to a mountaintop for dinner, where we enjoyed a grand view and watched several large cruise ships move out on their way to the next port. Our program included a short trip to Mendenhall Glacier and a fishing trip for all the participants. Norm and I were guests on a former classmate's yacht, which had a small greenhouse for growing fresh herbs at sea.

Soon after, I traveled back to China with the tour of woman architects postponed from summer 1989. Our three weeks included Beijing, Xi'an, Guilin, Suchow, Shanghai, and Hong Kong. This was now my third visit to Beijing, and I knew it well. However, Guilin was no longer the quaint town in the valley of the giant rock pinnacles that I had fallen in love with in 1980. Before that, I thought these mystical rocks only existed in stylized Chinese paintings. The beautiful valley was still there, but the village had sprouted high-rise hotels—one with a revolving restaurant on the nineteenth floor—and it was overflowing with tourists. We did not recognize Shanghai with its forest of skyscrapers, and it was hard to believe that only ten years had elapsed since my first visit.

After only three days home in Seattle, Norm and I flew to Honolulu for an AIA International Relations Committee meeting, where we would meet with a Japanese delegation. Ben Brewer, our former AIA President, believed we needed a course in cultural protocols. He emphasized that we should not shake hands or have physical contact with any of the Japanese people. I assured him I was friends with their current architectural organization president, but Ben repeated, "No touching." Of course, when President Shoji Hayashi arrived, he greeted me with a huge hug. Ben was horrified. "I told you that he was a friend," I said.

❖

THE UNIVERSITY'S SPRING BREAK had always been our time to squeeze in a trip to discover a new part of the world. However, after Norm retired in 1989, we had no pressure to get back in time to start classes. In 1991, we learned our favorite ship, the *Stella Solaris,* was sailing from the Mediterranean Sea for a run from Buenos Aires to Valparaiso, Chile. A cruise around the southern tip of South America and through the Strait of Magellan was a must. My sister-in-law Norma, her friend Bill, my niece Laurie, and my friend Betty Wagner, who had just lost her husband, Ron, decided to join our adventure.

We talk a lot about how the U.S. is a country of immigrants. South America has a similar history, so I should not have been surprised to step into a Welsh village on the coast of Argentina. In Chile, rain and fog shrouded the beautiful coastline, and the most scenic part of the fjords had to be left to our imaginations. The navigation was by sound, and I was very aware how close we were to the rocks or cliffs as we crept along. I felt like I could have reached out and touched whatever the horn blasts were reverberating from. I found this experience far more unsettling than our passage from the quiet Atlantic Ocean into the wild Pacific.

That transition happened early in the morning. When we tucked into bed that night, we all commented on the smooth waters, but about 2:30 a.m. things began to change. I took the liquor bottles down from the shelf over my bunk. About an hour later I was up again removing all our books from the shelves. Back in bed, I was almost asleep when suddenly the ship rolled over on its starboard side, and we heard crashing sounds throughout our vessel. Would the ship roll over? Those seconds felt like the longest minutes ever! The ship righted itself at approximately 5 a.m., and we were all up. The interior of the ship was a disaster with furniture, file drawers, broken glass, and china everywhere. Amazingly, only one person was seriously hurt: the morning chef, who was scalded by boiling water. After a day of cold food, we recovered and our ship operations returned to normal.

We ended our ocean adventure in Valparaiso, transferring to buses for a drive to charming Santiago to enjoy its old-world buildings and squares, and a grand view from the top of a mountain.

❖

AFTER THIS ADVENTURE, I was ready for a rest and checked into Swedish Hospital for surgery on my right hand, which was almost useless due to an old injury. A surgeon who worked with football players repaired my pesky right thumb. When I awoke after the procedure, the staff were all focused on my left arm, which was huge. The IV tube had been pumping under the skin and not into my vein. But I wanted to know about my thumb: Did they clean up my joints or give me new ones? I had two new joints that were "made from me." I could not find any sore spots on my body where they had removed repair material, so I was very curious. They had split tendons in my arm, using them to make new joints, and I would be in a cast up to my elbow while the tendons grew back. Even with this obstacle I could draw better than before.

When we were home in the summers, of course we had to attend the annual local production of the Wagner *Ring* cycle. Then, in mid-August we traveled to Copenhagen for the Danish-sponsored UIFA Congress. I had forwarded the funds left over from our 1988 Congress in D.C. for their seed money. The gathering was filled with wonderful Scandinavian hospitality, great meetings, delicious food, and special tours over a full two weeks, including a tour of an old castle that had been converted into a modern museum. Co-housing exhibits gave us an insight into the pros and cons of this housing movement, which the Danes had been leading for years. Would this be our future in the U.S.? I was skeptical.

That fall Norm taught at the Tokyo Institute of Technology, and I visited him there. My first experience in Japan had been with the AWIU women, when automobile companies competed over us, lavishing our group with the finest hotels, food, and tours. My second trip connected me with friends and colleagues, who took me into their homes. This time, I was a real tourist. However, we did start off this trip as Thanksgiving dinner guests at the home of one of Norm's former Japanese students, who also invited other former UW students who lived in the area. We dined on salmon in puff pastry that was beautifully prepared by our hostess. The cook, per tradition, remained in the kitchen, and I felt like a queen with my eight male companions.

Our time there in November coincided with our wedding anniversary. I told Norm that a stay in a *ryokan*, a traditional inn, was required for the full Japanese experience. So we took the train to Kyoto to spend two nights in a luxurious little inn that was an oasis from the street noise. Leaving our shoes outside our room, we stepped up onto a mat floor with a few pillows and a television in the alcove that had served as the *tokonoma*, or alcove, for flowers in earlier times. The only door, other than the shoji screen entrance, was to the bathroom with a soaking tub and the toilet, which provided the only seat in the unit.

Our first evening included a wonderful dinner and the quiet opportunity to rest. We were experienced backpackers so sleeping on the floor was not a problem, but the lack of a chair was a challenge. (When camping, we could usually at least find a place to sit on a log or a rock.) The second night a bachelorette party next door went on into the wee hours, and we longed for the street noise over the shrill giggles. Our knees were complaining, and two breakfasts of dried seaweed and fish, no matter how magnificent to look at, were enough. Back in Tokyo we went to McDonald's for a cheeseburger, fries, and a milkshake. In twenty-seven years of marriage, this was our first McDonald's date.

❖

AT THE END OF NOVEMBER, I kissed Norm goodbye, leaving him with his students while I returned to get ready for a big event in Washington D.C.: my installation as the 1992 COF Chancellor. I would be the first woman to hold a top national architectural office.

At this time, there were only about fifty women among the College of Fellows' two thousand eight hundred members. How my mother would have enjoyed this special occasion! With Norm still in Japan, sister-in-law Norma and niece Laurie came to D.C. to represent my family. My other special guests were Anna Halpin, the person responsible for my election, and Bob and Marge Durham. Bob had been my childhood Sunday School teacher as well as a former AIA President and COF

Chancellor. Bob always carried all his medals to these affairs and would loan one to anyone who forgot theirs. This was a lucky break. In a mix-up, no one had ordered a chancellor's medal for me. Bob took off his chancellor's medal, replaced it with his president's medal, and so I was invested as the new chancellor with the same medal he wore when he welcomed me into the COF in 1980.

The COF honored my position by putting me up in a grand two-story suite at the hotel JW Marriott, which included a full bar. We partied in the suite and on the large terrace overlooking Pennsylvania Avenue for hours.

Norm and I were both back home in time to enjoy the holiday festivities together with family and friends.

❖

FOR MY CHANCELLOR YEAR OF 1992, I took on a big task: the production of the second edition of *A History and Directory of the College*. A soft-cover edition called *The Silver Book* had been published in 1984. I read it and noticed many architects listed with a "deceased" symbol by their names—but I knew they were very much alive. I suspected they had not paid their dues and had disappeared from the membership list. I assumed the author was not an architect but a hired writer working with material he had been given. I decided that my project would be to create a more informative and accurate directory. Norman loved the idea and was eager to help, so it became a joint project. In addition to authenticating the membership list, we wanted to include information such as the date of AIA membership, architectural schools with degree years, current firm addresses, and a code to note the offices held or medals received. The book was to be published by the AIA Press in time to be in Boston for the 1992 investiture. The printing was the hardest part, and through the experience, I learned a lot about publishing.

In June, Norm, Norma, and Laurie joined me in Boston for the AIA Convention and the big show I had planned. The COF investiture was held in the Trinity Church, the first masterpiece of Henry Hobson Richardson, himself an AIA Fellow invested in 1867. The historic structure with great barrel vaults and richly colored mosaics and murals retained its heritage design and had never been disrupted by modernization, such as air conditioning. It was a very hot afternoon, and I was sure there would be a puddle of water at my feet after I stood through the program congratulating nine Honorary Fellows and 124 new Fellows as they received their medals, each with a kiss. That started with the first recipient, a friend from Australia,

Chancellor Jane waiting to receive the 1992 FAIA awardees at Trinity Church, Boston

who demanded a kiss and then continued at the insistence of the remaining one hundred thirty-two.

During the convocation dinner, Arthur C. Holden at 101 was honored as our oldest living Fellow. He had received his medal fifty years earlier, in 1942. Because of his health issues, the program was arranged to let him speak first so he could retire early. However, he stayed through the dinner, the speeches and all the festivities, refusing his nurse's efforts to take him home. He was determined to enjoy every moment.

❖

IN THE MIDDLE OF JULY, we celebrated the opening of the Flaming Geyser Bridge project. The drawings had been in a King County drawer for too many years; finally, they had resurfaced, funding was secured, and the new bridge was constructed. The weather was not kind for the opening affair, but the locals turned out and raved about George Tsutakawa's wrapped pylons—a shimmering glory when the sun shone on them. The residents loved their new river crossing, although many had been apprehensive in the beginning. In 1993, our bridge design won national and state awards.

Jane at Flaming Geyser State Park Bridge dedication with Vic Gray and Norm

Also in July, after several 300-mile round trips to our ocean property, I had a surveyor lined up in preparation to finally design and build a house on the land I had purchased more than thirty years earlier. The lot was located between the peninsula's south water system and the north water system, a no-man's-land of one long block, so we had to drill a well.

This turned out to be a hidden blessing as the local paper was always reporting on the squabbling between the residents and the water districts.

In September, my AIA duties included a historic resource meeting in Lexington, Kentucky—a special treat as it gave me the opportunity to again visit the home of my most famous ancestor, Henry Clay. Our family roots go back to Englishman John Clay's arrival in Jamestown, Virginia, in 1613. For me, that is twelve generations.

A week later I was back in D.C. for the American Architectural Foundation meeting and a long-planned gala auction to support the historic AIA-owned Octagon House. The foundation meeting included a special guest: Dr. Jonas Salk, who developed one of the first successful polio vaccines. He was interested in a new project that explored how architectural settings influence human experience. At lunch, we moved to one of the beautiful State Department rooms. Dr. Salk politely rejected seating invitations from the AIA President and others, saying he wanted to sit next to "the woman." I was often the only woman in the room, but this was a new request. No, Dr. Salk was not a womanizer; he knew I was from Seattle and wanted to talk about the city and the UW Medical School, where one of his sons was studying. Of course, I was happy to share my beloved city and university with him. (This meeting later inspired the Academy of Neuroscience for Architecture, ANFA, a legacy project connected to the AIA, with son Peter L. Salk, M.D., serving as president.)

The foundation's evening event was a grand affair with dignitaries bidding considerable sums on art and treasures donated by our members. My contribution was a piece of Chihuly glass, a donation by artist Dale Chihuly, a former UW architecture student. Norman had a winning bid on a 4-foot-tall birdhouse in the shape of the Washington Monument created by architect Graham Gund, and I returned home with a large antique blue and white Japanese plate.

We ended the year in Washington, D.C. with the chancellor's dinner, where I hung the chancellor's medal around John Busby's neck for his 1993 year. I was now technically retired, but I was still not done. I had been appointed to a new position, the College of Fellows historian. Another lesson learned: Be careful what you write and publish.

❖

IN JANUARY 1993, we went to Deer Valley, Utah, for one of Norm's regular meetings of the NCARB. The schedule was designed so members could take advantage of the wonderful high-end ski resort, and I decided to hit the slopes while Norm worked. I took my ski boots with me because I knew no rental boots would fit my extremely long, extremely narrow feet, but I discovered my older boots would not fit on the new bindings of rental skis. Skiers were using those big plastic boots. My long feet required men's boots, but I floated around in them with my ultra-skinny underpinnings. Four pairs of socks helped, but my feet ached as my toes constantly gripped the insoles. The weather was beautiful and the snow great, but one day was all that my knotted feet could take. I turned in the rented skis and boots. Norm breathed a huge sigh of relief.

In the spring, we planned to travel to Egypt, Yemen, and Ethiopia. These were troubled areas: Tourists were being murdered in Egypt and kidnapped in Yemen, and Ethiopian cities were convulsed by riots. Richard, my office neighbor and hairdresser, begged me not to go as he kissed me goodbye. I told Richard the press was overreporting the issues.

We boarded our flight to New York on March 11, planning to rest overnight before continuing the next day. As we were turning in, an emergency broadcast blared on the New York TV. A major storm was headed for the Eastern seaboard, and everyone was to leave the coast immediately. In the morning, we did our last-minute shopping and continued to the airport for our evening Egyptian Air flight, listening to the news of the storm's progress. At 10 p.m. we boarded our flight—the last plane out before all flights were grounded. We settled down for a nice dinner and a movie in the sky.

After checking into our Cairo hotel, we heard the news of the massive winds and snowstorm that we had narrowly escaped. We had no idea when our fellow travelers would be able to join us. Fortunately, Ralph and Shirley Anderson had used air miles to fly from Seattle to London and then to Cairo, so at least there were four of us rattling around in the hotel. This was my third trip to Egypt, and this time we had the Sphinx just for the four of us—plus two policemen on the tallest camels I have ever seen. There was not another visitor anywhere, a blow to the tourism-dependent economy.

The rest of our group arrived three days late and joined us in Aswan. We had missed our scheduled riverboat, so another boat was called into service just for our contingent of about twenty people. The crew outnumbered us about two to one and we were treated like royalty.

Before we traveled to Luxor, we boarded a flight for Abu Simbel, which we had missed on our earlier visit in 1977 because of a travel agent's error. This time we flew over Lake Nasser, almost to the Sudan border, and finally landed at our goal. These enormous temples were in the middle of nowhere, and unlike the Sphinx, which was guarded, we could go right up to these monuments and touch them. It was an extraordinary, personal experience.

In Yemen, the capital San'a seemed like any other modern city when we were in the center of it—but outside the center, it was like entering through a magic gate to a past world. The old city's buildings were made of tan mud brick, with many seven stories high or taller. They were all decorated as if an artist had wielded a giant pastry tube filled with white paint. Delightful patterns covered the walls, and colorful stained-glass windows glittered on the top floor. The top floor was for the men, who gathered there to socialize and chew their khat, a euphoric plant-based stimulant. We toured some of the taller buildings, which were hotels. They were basic but clean, with the bathroom facilities down the hall. The price range was not indicated with stars; rather, rooms were rated as "Two Sheets," "One Sheet," or "No Sheets."

Our lodging was in the central-city Sheraton Hotel with the diplomats, the businesspeople and the wealthy. At the city limits the paved roads stopped and the desert continued, seemingly into infinity. Only a local would take his vehicle across this dangerous line; foreigners would be immediately held up and the car stolen. Yemen men wore a sash around their waists, which served as a holder for a large dagger. We were told it was a prop for their dances, but of course, it is also a sharp first-class weapon if needed. An automatic machine gun, worn over the shoulder, also seemed to be part of their standard dress. It was hard to relax amid this sea of weapons.

After we had seen the city, we climbed into four-wheel-drive Japanese-made jeeps to travel through the rest of Yemen. Our caravan of six or seven vehicles carried four passengers each, plus drivers, and we drove east over the sand and dry riverbeds to Ma'rib, our first major stop. Our visit to the old world, back to the second millennium B.C., included the old dam, considered the finest ancient masonry structure.

This was believed to be the home of Queen of Sheba, and archaeologists had only scratched the surface of this site.

As we continued east, we had a new leader to take us across the desert. A Bedouin drove a pickup truck loaded with drums of gasoline, leading our caravan through the desert, turning here and there without any visual landmarks we could see. We stopped for a picnic lunch at a small shrub where they checked to make sure we were all consuming our required two two-quart bottles of water per day. Later, in a Bedouin camp, we were offered tea. Other than a camel here and a tuft of grass there—and a flat tire—there were no interruptions to our twelve-hour ride.

Then, what a sight! We came to a cluster of high-rise mud towers, like a mini-Manhattan, in the middle of nowhere. We had reached Shibam, the first city in the world with a vertical master plan. The city was one thousand, seven hundred years old and had a population of seven thousand in its prime. This walled city of 100-foot-high mud and clay structures had been mostly rebuilt after a massive flood in 1532. Most of the towers were set only a few feet apart, with just enough space to walk between them.

Tired and hungry, we checked into what I believe was the only hotel, outside the city walls. It did not have enough rooms for our group, so the singles in our group, along with Norm and me, were bused to the "chalet," which looked like former barracks originally built for Russian workers at a gravel pit. The men in our group would stay in one building, and the women in another. With the sun setting over the grimy site, our friend Anne Gould Hauberg suddenly exclaimed, "Now where is that wealthy oil sheik that I came here to meet?" We all laughed, releasing the tension. When the organizers realized they still had a couple in the group, Norm and I were taken back to the hotel and given the sleeping cots for the cooks, who probably got the kitchen floor. Grime had a new definition, and the chalet seemed almost delightful in comparison.

Our next stop was Al Mukalla on the Gulf of Aden. The pockmarked sandy beach was alive with crabs scurrying about until they sensed our presence, then disappeared into their holes. The modest hotel was a welcome upgrade. Resourceful Ann, who was the eldest in our group, vanished briefly and resurfaced with a British petroleum engineer—and a bottle of scotch in this land of no alcohol. And here we'd been worried about whether she could keep up with the rest of us!

Aden appeared to be the other modern city in this country, with a comfortable hotel and swimming pool, which we very much enjoyed. Then we traveled north to Ta'izz and up a steep mountainside where we were sure the jeeps were going to roll over. We finally arrived at an old city on the mountaintop, only to realize we had to repeat the harrowing journey back down.

When we arrived back in San'a, we invited our drivers into the Sheraton for a party, honoring each with stories and tips. This was a first for them. Our weapons-laden men with multiple wives and many children cried. Our guide told us that no other travelers had ever treated them so kindly.

❖

ETHIOPIA WAS OUR NEXT DESTINATION. After getting settled into Addis Ababa we took in a few local sights before packing an overnight bag, checking our luggage at the hotel and departing for Gonder. Our plane left us at a bombed-out airstrip, where we waited on benches for a small aircraft to take us on to the old capital city. We each carried flashlights because we had been told our hotel would have electricity for only a few hours each day. A grand surprise greeted us: A new lodge had recently been completed in the national park. It was comfortable and filled with beautiful native artwork. No need for flashlights after all.

We enjoyed our time there until it was time to depart. Then, we sat at the airstrip watching our plane make several passes overhead but not landing. If the pilot can't see the ground, he will not land, instead returning to his base for the night, and we went back to our lovely lodge very worried. We were scheduled to fly out the next afternoon, and part of our group was still at the Addis Ababa hotel, along with all our belongings. The next morning the plane finally landed, and we made our transfer, arriving just in time to collect our suitcases and get on the bus to the airport.

❖

THAT SPRING, WE TRAVELED TO CHICAGO for the AIA Convention—finally, just to enjoy with no official responsibilities—and then to Kansas City for Norm's annual NCARB meeting. People had asked me for years why I was spending so much time traveling abroad when I had seen so few of our own states. I reassured them I could do that later when I was older and wouldn't be able to do the more demanding international travel. Well, I guess age had caught up with me. The trip to Kansas

City was a first, and it was hard to believe that it had started out as a lumber milling center. I found the network of underground caves, where so much was stored, a fascinating part of the history and economy.

In October, the Dragon Ladies celebrated our sixty-fifth year. We went back to Kauai to Ralph Anderson's latest masterpiece, on the northeast side of the island by Kilauea. Perched high on a cliff, it appeared to look off into infinity. From the swimming pool edge, we could watch bathers on a sandy beach some two hundred feet below. Each room had a corner window wall that retracted, creating the feeling of a house without walls. After a week the other girls departed, and Ralph and Norm arrived, giving us two couples some time together in this beautiful home. Norm proclaimed that without a doubt this was Ralph's best project ever.

I started 1994 with a new design project: a house for my niece Lynn, who was living in Australia. I assured her I could only do primaries and they would need a local architect to do the actual construction drawings. Then in February, we took off for Indonesia, by way of Singapore. The government was now rebuilding the old section of the city that they had been destroying in 1987, having discovered it was a major tourist attraction. After two days there, we boarded a small cruise ship with about ninety other passengers.

Krakatoa at the tip of Sumatra, famous for its great 1883 eruption, was our first destination. Then we went on to Java and Jakarta. After the tours and museum, we went shopping and Norm couldn't resist a sculpture of a bronze dancer in a ring of fire. It was not very large, but it was a heavy souvenir to carry home. In the center of the island, we explored Borobudur Temple, one of the greatest Buddhist monuments built in the eighth and ninth centuries. The view from the top to the valley and village below remains one of my all-time travel highlights.

Our trip took us through Lombok Island and Sulawesi. The most memorable was the Torajan village where we were bused to the highlands, taking with us a small live pig required as a sacrificial gift to the villagers. The houses on stilts, with their great boat bow-type roofs, soared toward the heavens. They were architectural gems. The island culture is unchanged over hundreds of years and is captured in the beautiful carved wood panels and water buffalo horns that cover the dwellings. A step into another world. When I wear my wood and bone necklace—one of my favorites—mentally I'm back in this special village of fascinating structures.

Komodo, with its dragon residents, was next. We watched them eat their dinner from a safe viewing platform, and guides carefully escorted us on the trail to and from our ship, ensuring we would not encounter the free-roaming residents.

Bali was our final destination. Norm and I decided we wanted to have some time there just for ourselves. We went to the art center Ubud and stayed in a cottage in the jungle. We toured the island on our own, much of the time in bare feet and rolled-up pants legs, navigating a flood from heavy rains. And we found another painting by a local artist for our wall, a beautiful way to commemorate our month away.

❖

IN MARCH, IT WAS TIME to get some work accomplished in my office and address a long-term commitment: I had agreed to be a speaker at the Museum of History & Industry lecture series on Historic Seattle Architecture. I was to cover the years of 1940-1965. I remembered the World War II years well, and because most of the audience had arrived in Seattle after the war, I had an attentive group for my stories about home-front life in Seattle. Boeing gave me photographs of the roofs of its aircraft-assembly buildings camouflaged with images of complete faux neighborhoods, including trees, cars, and people. I remembered admiring it from the hillside to the west.

In the 1940s, Seattle was filled with many buildings that were intended to be temporary, mostly housing, and many of these remained for too many years after the war ended. Then, there was a mass movement toward the suburbs, with bargain land values and cheaper new housing. The postwar university campus was alive with new construction to meet the needs of the large veteran enrollment, while downtown Seattle sprouted new high-rise office buildings. The Seattle of my childhood, of course, never returned.

That May, the Girl Scouts honored me at their Portland banquet, and I was invited to speak on "Architecture as a Career." Each year they honored women from different professions. I was treated like a queen and enjoyed meeting so many other professional women whom I had not met before.

Then our friends from Turkey, the Kubans, arrived in Seattle before we all flew to Los Angeles for the AIA Convention. Dogan, an architectural professor, would be the first from his country to receive an Honorary FAIA, and I had the pleasure of being his escort during the investiture. A party on a major movie studio set wrapped up his special day.

That November we spent four days in Key West, Florida, then traveled to Iron Springs Resort to celebrate our twenty-fifth wedding anniversary. After a large Thanksgiving dinner gathering at our house, we traveled to Los Angeles and embarked on a ten-day cruise along the coast of Central America, returning in time for all the Christmas holiday festivities.

I wonder what my horoscope was for 1995. Certainly, I was not ready for that year.

A Horizon House promotional portrait of Jane and Norm
[Courtesy of Horizon House]

17 | A NEW HOME AT HORIZON HOUSE

AT THE BEGINNING OF 1995, Norm and I were back to our frequent-flier routine. In between AIA meetings for me and NCARB meetings for him, I made time to give a lecture at the Seattle Art Museum on our recent travels in Yemen, a country that was still a mystery to most of our audience. I also wrapped up my duties on an advisory committee to interim UW Architecture Dean Paul Schell, who made a confession: "I really did not believe you when you told me that working with Professor Astra Zarina would not be easy." This was a man who had been a port commissioner, a lawyer, a real estate developer, a city agency director, and would soon become Seattle's mayor. My old classmate Astra's demanding, inflexible style and strong opinions were a challenge, even for him. "She has to be the most difficult person I have ever had to deal with," he said.

That March, we were preparing for our upcoming adventure to Tibet, Nepal, and Bhutan when Norm called to interrupt a busy workday. He wanted me to meet him to look at apartments at Horizon House, a continuing care living facility just up the hill from downtown Seattle. We had been on the waitlist for some time, even though we were not yet ready to leave our Laurelhurst home. But Horizon House had called, and Norm said we needed to act interested or they would not call us again.

When we arrived, we were surprised to be escorted to the West Wing, our preferred location in the complex. We had thought those units were all occupied by the original residents. We were shown unit A-U, a two-bedroom, two-bath apartment on the north side of the building with windows looking into Freeway Park and the convention center gardens, which were filled with white magnolias and pink cherry blossoms. "You mean we could live in the heart of the city and never see a rooftop or a street, just gardens?" Norm asked. Yes, the unit was at the right level. We had three days to decide if we wanted it. On the drive home I said, "If you want to do it, let's do it." "But what about your garden?" he asked. If it had been August, I might have felt differently, but I had planted only peas and lettuce so far.

As soon as we arrived home, Norm called Horizon House. We would take A-U. This was the realization of a decision we had made together years earlier when we agreed that we would eventually retire to a life care facility and not depend on nieces or nephews as caregivers in our golden years.

We had only two weeks before we would leave for Asia. In that time, we sold our lot near Port Orchard, contacted a real-estate agent about selling our Laurelhurst home, and met a contractor at Horizon House so he could start renovations as soon as we returned. We planned a major remodel that would remove false ceilings and install a hardwood floor and beautiful cabinets. This would be our final home together, and we intended to live there for many years.

❖

BUT BEFORE WE BEGAN FOCUSING our energies on the pending move, we set off to enjoy our grand adventure into the Himalayas. In Darjeeling, we discovered the Everest Museum featuring famous ascents, climbers, and gear. I felt right at home when I saw the photo of two famous Seattleites: Jim Whittaker, my friend since grade school who was the first American to reach the summit of Mount Everest; and Pete Schoening, who was renowned for saving a group of climbers in a tragic accident on K2 in 1953. Pete was often in The Hastings Group office working with Carolyn Geise, his sister-in-law, on projects. Schoening's company sold Chemgrate, a molded fiberglass grating system we incorporated into the driveways of homes in rainy locations like Kodiak and Seattle.

As we traveled through the majestic peaks, my mind was often far away—designing my newest project, making a list of contacts for our remodeling plans, and sorting out how to sell our Laurelhurst house. However, early one morning my focus was jolted back to Darjeeling when we were rousted at 2 a.m. We were told to leave immediately or be detained for days by a government strike that was about to close the only road and the border. In a whiteout fog, our small caravan of a bus and two cars—one without lights—crawled down the steep mountain roads. We couldn't see the edge, but we knew the cliff did not have any guardrails. We beat the deadline with five minutes to spare, bolting from our vehicles for the closest shrubs to relieve ourselves, men to the left and women to the right. The road closed at 6:30 a.m., blocked with huge logs.

When our group drove up another mountain to Thimphu, Bhutan, the narrow road was suddenly blocked by an accident. As we waited, children from the local village crowded around to see this bus full of strangers with white hair—a sight they rarely saw because people in Bhutan typically did not survive past their forties. They all spoke English, which they were taught in school, and asked us, "How old?" Soon, we had a children's chorus serenading our group of tall elders. We answered with our own songs, which they did their best to learn. A whole new world opened up for all of us.

This tiny country admitted only a handful of visitors each year, and guest accommodations among the soaring mountaintops were limited. Tourists' visits typically coincided with a celebration that included a giant 350-year-old thangka scroll known as a thongdrel, which was unrolled early in the morning so it could be rerolled before any direct sunlight damaged it. It seemed like the entire population of the town and valley was there, watching in the cold mountain air. After the ceremony, village wares were spread across the meadow on blankets for purchase. I was fascinated by the coat-type dress worn by the men, with variations available to suit many temperatures and occasions. I was also impressed by the high-tech archery equipment and the archers' skill as they demonstrated the national sport of Bhutan.

While traveling throughout India, I made note of the road signs—their version of our "Burma Shave" signs. Some of my favorites:

Don't lose your nerve on sharp curve.

When you are hot, keep cool.

It's better to be fifteen minutes late in this life than fifteen minutes early in the next.

Over takers will meet undertakers.

Drink and drive, you don't survive.

If you go to sleep your family will weep.

Certainly, all good messages to take home.

We left beautiful Bhutan and flew to Kathmandu, Nepal. My heart broke as we descended into the Shangri-la valley I had first visited in 1979. Now it was thick with the pollution—exhaust and noise—from three-wheeled motorcycles. When I think of this magical place, I prefer to remember my first visit when we dropped down between snow-topped peaks into a tropical garden.

Several in our group stayed behind to avoid the stress of the 12,000-foot altitude ahead. The rest of us traveled to Lhasa, the former capital of Tibet, where the air was indeed very thin. At first, we were disappointed that we were on the third floor of the hotel instead of the fifth—until we discovered the elevator was often out of order. Three flights of stairs were plenty. The people, like the scenery, were both beautiful and wonderful.

❖

BY MAY 1, WE WERE HOME. We were soon fully absorbed with getting our Horizon House apartment ready and deciding where our collection of books and art would go. We had originally planned to build our beach house before selling our Laurelhurst house so it could absorb much of our collection, but the house sold May 13 to the first prospective buyers who saw it! So we divided our furnishings, art, books, and clothing among five friends and clients who stored them until our beach house was ready. Some of our collection went to the Museum of History & Industry, as well as the university costume shop. Downsizing was the word of the month. In the middle of all the moving bustle, we greeted the incoming national AIA President at our local meeting, where I was awarded the Seattle Chapter Gold Medal at the Museum of Flight.

Moving day was July 15. Our new apartment was still unfinished, and our large dining table stood in the middle of the living room, with a mountain of boxes piled on the table and around the room, awaiting the kitchen cabinets. Our summer influx of visitors started arriving before we were fully unpacked.

We escaped our clutter of boxes that fall by traveling with friends to Turkey's southwest coast. We stayed for a week in the owner's villa at a resort designed by Ralph Anderson and enjoyed its private pool suspended over the Aegean Sea.

In Istanbul, we boarded the *Song of Flower* for a cruise through the islands and the Suez Canal before disembarking in Jordan and busing to the temples of Petra, which we had all to ourselves. Then, in Amman, we discovered wonderful Roman ruins that were not included in our architectural history books. "The best trip yet!" Norm proclaimed.

❖

AT THE END OF OCTOBER, we finally felt settled in our new home. However, I was not done packing boxes. In January 1996, I would move to an office that was an easy walk from Horizon House, closing my East Olive Way office, with its twenty-five years of memories and forty years' worth of architectural drawings and documents. In cleaning out my office, I became a master recycler. Almost everything found a potential use somewhere—either at Goodwill, a senior center art program or the offices of young architects just starting out.

As we celebrated the new year, I realized I was completing the final moves for my two great loves. Norman and I were now settled into a wonderful retirement community, and I was about to move into my last architectural office, just a seven-block walk away. These would be two important places for us to share the joys of life and work with our remaining family, friends, and clients.

Office moving day arrived January 2. Some of the oak cabinetry was destined for our home at Horizon House, so my favorite contractor, Walter Toth, was on hand to help. I looked forward to working in my new office in the bustle of downtown. I had the space all to myself—no more employees, just like at the beginning—and several ongoing projects, including drawing up the plans for our new beach house.

Norm, on the other hand, was now a full-time retiree after more than thirty years as a UW architecture professor, and he was always ready to sign us up for new adventures. We spent a week on Maui with a couple who were close friends of his from high school, and two weeks later, we were off to New York for his Wagner fix at the Met. This time we also had two full days for museum visits. I always enjoyed our annual visits to the big city and the chance to catch up on current art and architecture, as well as the opera.

In May, it was time to get our new Horizon House garden plot in shape. We had been assigned a long, narrow bed along the edge of the terrace that could be seen from our apartment, and we replaced an old hedge-type planting with more colorful plants. I took over chairing the garden committee, which was a bit like a monthly circus act. The committee had never held meetings until we moved in, and they were wary of newcomers. The part-time gardener was probably the only one on the committee happy with the change because I rescued him from several demanding residents.

❖

AFTER NORM'S SUMMERTIME DUTIES grading the design section of the national architect's examination in Scottsdale, we packed for Europe. The 1996 UIFA Congress was scheduled for Budapest, and we joined friends in renting a small van with a driver and a guide for sightseeing before the meeting. Our first stop was

Prague, where we wound through the streets until we reached a sight that made us groan: "Oh no, Frank Gehry has been here!" The new building was nicknamed the "Ginger and Fred Building" because it resembled one of the great Hollywood pair's dance moves. For years all the great cities had cultivated their own distinct personalities and design characteristics, but now they were all starting to look the same. To me, that diminishes the joy of traveling.

In Krakow, Poland, we reflected on its devastating World War II history and Nazi treatment of the Jews—a somber moment in our travels. The local castle had become a museum, and we bought a delightful folk tapestry of the king and queen riding in their carriage during a parade. It would later be hung in our beach house, and this colorful, cheery piece always made me feel better about Poland.

When we reached Budapest and the UIFA gathering, it was time for me and fellow architect and friend Joyce Rutherford to go to work while our traveling companions went off to play. At least one of our meetings was in the beautiful high chamber of the Parliament Building. The building's head engineer was a woman architect who took us on a tour from the basement to the rooftop. Completed in 1902, the original heating and cooling system was still working flawlessly. In the winter, a huge bin was filled with coal for the furnace. In the summer, large ice blocks came down the coal chute and filled the bin for the air conditioning, a simple process that forced recirculating air over the ice. The rooftop was a thrill; we crawled around flying buttresses and over gargoyles, and we slid down slate roof tiles between pediments with nothing around to grasp. U.S. safety rules make this kind of experience impossible at home, but we all made it through without injury. The Hungarian Parliament Building is often featured in European travel literature, and I relive that rooftop slide each time I see those photographs.

❖

WE SPENT TWO WEEKS AT HOME before taking off for the ocean, where our beach house was finally under construction. It was a three-plus-hour drive but once off the freeway it took us through farms and forests, along rivers and around coastal bays. On our many trips, we enjoyed watching the planting and harvesting of crops, new calves following their mothers in the pastures, and the budding spring green leaves that eventually turned beautiful fall colors before dropping off until the next year.

We spent a night at an old resort made up of small rustic cabins arranged around a grass parade ground, snuggled behind sand dunes and sheltered from the wind.

Birthday girls on the beach in Mexico, 1996

Protection from the weather was more important than a beach view to older genera-tions. The next morning, I worked with the contractor at our building site while Norman stayed in the car reading a book. "It's your project," he said.

From the coast, we drove south to explore Oregon with friends from Eugene. Our destination was the southeast corner of the state and the Steens Mountain area, known for its huge bird sanctuary and endless miles of open range land. We stayed in a cabin on a working ranch where other visitors participated in a cattle drive. A small one-room school provided local children with an education through sixth grade, and they were then sent to a boarding school through high school. A wealthy rancher would finance their college educations. Many of these cowboys straight out of a Hollywood movie had a degree or two, and perhaps, one day when their horses were all put out to pasture, they would pursue new careers.

At the end of November, it was time for the annual Dragon Ladies' birthday celebration. The six of us, plus Roz Wolfe and Mervane Benoit, met up in Miami for a cruise to the Caribbean. Mervane was using a wheelchair, so we made sure our

Caroling party – Jim and Genevra Gerhart, Geri Lucks, Ron Barclay, Doug and Lorna Fosth, Norm, Morris Jellison (at organ) and Marilyn Mattocks

cabins were all conveniently close together, as well as luxurious. While at sea, we each did our own thing, and on land, we went sightseeing and shopping together. Our happy hours were filled with talk and laughter that lasted through dinner until showtime. This was Mervane's last real travel outing, and we were all grateful for these memories.

Our New Year's 1997 celebration was at the Bellevue home of our retired dentist friend Ron Barclay. A special treat: dining at our old etched brass and oak table that had been designed by Harry Lunstead. The table was too large for our Horizon House apartment, so Ron bought it for his house, and it is always wonderful when a treasured piece resettles in a good home where you can still visit it occasionally.

My two main design projects were our new beachfront house several hours away, and another apartment remodel in Horizon House just five minutes from my door.

The Horizon House remodeling project was for a woman named Lesley Watson, who had been in a terrible automobile accident that had killed her husband and crushed her skull. She was just out of the hospital after almost a year of having her head rebuilt. Even though she could use only her left arm, couldn't really chew, and was left with limited vision, Lesley was the most upbeat person I have ever met. She was a beautiful client to work with and we became very close friends.

Norm, Lesley, Betty, and Jane at a University of Washington Gala

I visited the beach project several times each month. I was impressed with how the contractor, Steve, handled the most challenging parts of the structural work, which had to be built to withstand hurricane-force storms. Steve was especially proud of the eight log columns he carved out of one enormous felled tree that was at least a hundred feet long.

Any problems on the project arose from the less-complicated construction work that Steve left to his workmen, without supervision. When I questioned anything, they always responded, "This is the way it is always done." (Translation: The way they had always done it.) I'm sure this crew had never had a woman architect looking over their shoulders and they probably felt like I was their mother telling them what to do. It's a tricky business to insist on corrections, which cost money, without completely alienating the contractor, but I knew exactly how far to push before they would walk off the job. So, when the crew set all the window heads at 6 feet, 10 inches, including those adjacent to the 6-foot, 8-inch doors, I insisted they redo the windows next to the doors. But in other areas of the house, I lived with the high windows. I simply raised our bed height so we could enjoy the view of the surf. Some errors I hired another contractor to repair later. My good city contractors had spoiled me by following the architectural plans—what they called the "funny papers"—and consulting with me on any questions.

❖

AS CONSTRUCTION PROGRESSED, Norm finally showed some real interest in the beach house, walking around and plotting out where he was going to hang our art.

We had been planning to build this oceanfront escape for years. On one of our anniversary getaways we decided that we should each create a plan for the ideal beach house. Over Champagne, we disclosed our projects, which turned out to be as different as night and day. Norman had designed a little cottage snuggled down behind the dunes out of the wind with a sleeping loft accessed via a set of steep, ladderlike stairs. I proposed a simple two-and-a-half-story vertical box with a roof deck for enjoying the surf and sunsets. I told Norm I was not going to sleep on any floor that did not have a bathroom. Because we were so far apart, we put our drawings away and enjoyed the remainder of that anniversary weekend.

From then on, the beach house had always been referred to as "Jane's folly," and I had been thinking about it and saving for it for years. With Norm covering our

Jane working with the model of Willapad, the ocean house

household bills, I could bank most of my income. In the end, Norm decided we should use peeled logs like I had used in the design for a client's vacation home—the columns that Steve was so proud of—and the remaining design decisions would be mine. The result was a cottage on top of the dunes with decks in front and a small roof deck off the second floor over the dining space. In the kitchen, I had open shelves and counters, and I looked out to the beach through 12-foot-wide sliding glass doors. Don't ever turn your back to the ocean, no matter how far away it is! Barn doors over the glass provided weather protection and security when we were not in residence. With water closets on all three floors—plus the two at our home in Seattle—we had five toilets for the two of us. When I was a child, one toilet had served the six of us in my family.

In June 1997, we were in the final push to make our new ocean home ready, and Norm had decided we should buy a pair of bikes so we could cruise the flat roads along the Long Beach peninsula. After dinner one evening, we found just the right models at REI—a happy find until I fell off my new bike in the store and fractured my collarbone in three places. I spent the night in the Swedish Hospital emergency room, delaying our plans to leave the next morning to make final arrangements with the contractor. We were on the road the following day, with niece Laurie driving and me in my sling, enjoying the scenery and the ride to our new beach home.

18 | WILLAPAD

Willapad, Ocean Park. The oceanside house finally built on property Jane purchased in 1960.

IT WAS THE FOURTH OF JULY 1997, and Norm and his "girls" (Norma, Laurie, and me with my arm in a sling) were celebrating our first holiday weekend at Willapad. Norm had christened the cabin in honor of Willapa Bay on the east side of our peninsula, and he was busy arranging books on the library shelves and hanging and rehanging the artwork until he was satisfied. Screens were installed and the windows washed, and all those dishes in boxes finally had found homes on the kitchen's open shelves. At last, more than thirty-five years after I had purchased the beach lot, we could start enjoying our oceanfront retreat. Here, we would host the family Fourth and Thanksgiving gatherings for years to come.

From the early years of our marriage, Norm had been dismissive of my beach house ambitions. Whenever I brought up the project, he would complain about "that awful west sun," and remind me that the idyllic view in his childhood had faced east to Mount Rainier from his family's summer cabin on Budd Inlet near Olympia. But now, Norm had found a new love at Willapad. We wore out the highway with our weekend trips, entertaining his friends and colleagues. Even people I had never heard him mention before arrived for bed and board, and he had a great time showing off "his" beach house and the surroundings. Men are funny creatures.

Through that summer and fall, we spent more time at the beach than at home or the office. It took a University of Washington trip to Central America to lure us away.

❖

IN NOVEMBER we flew to San Pedro Sula, Honduras, and bused west to Copan where we were thrilled to see the beautiful condition of the early Mayan city. These wonderful ruins, dating from 613 to 738 AD, are treasures, and our time there was far too short.

At the border in Guatemala, we met our security team: three well-armed men who followed our bus through the countryside. Too many tourists had been robbed or kidnapped in recent months; thus, extra protection was required. Or maybe it was just an excuse to provide jobs. They certainly did not appear to be professional guards, and at one stop we had to find them and wake them up when we were ready to leave.

Back on the coast of the Caribbean Sea we boarded a small boat, which would be our hotel for several days. The trip took us north to explore rivers and tramp through the jungle to meet the howling monkeys. Along the way we picked up drinking water, which unfortunately had not been purified. The crew and most of our group were in trouble, but I had been drinking beer as my liquid of choice so I did not suffer like the others.

We disembarked at Dangriga, Belize, for a road trip to Tikal in Guatemala—a destination Norm was eagerly anticipating. During his graduate school years at the University of Pennsylvania, he spent time at the digs with the archaeologist, drawing maps and details of the ruins. Much progress had been made during the thirty-five years since his last visit.

Then we went back to Belize to stay at the Chaa Creek Cottages, which are tucked into the jungle and illuminated by kerosene lanterns. The highlight was the butterfly farm started by scientist Charles Wright. We studied all the stages of the butterflies' short lives and learned they were shipped all over the world to supply butterfly houses.

Willapad, interior view

THAT NOVEMBER, we enjoyed our first family Thanksgiving celebration at the beach. We bought our turkey at the Ocean Park grocery store, which supplied ingredients for most of the menu at better prices than in Seattle. We were back in the city for the holiday parties, then returned to the beach to prepare for New Year's Eve. It was our turn to host and, yes, we would ring in 1998 at Willapad.

We were traveling to fewer national meetings, but returned to one of my favorite cities, San Francisco, in May for the AIA Convention, and to San Diego later that summer for the NCARB convention. Then, a fiftieth anniversary party for my "third brother" Don Wallace took me back to his Gig Harbor beach house for the first time since my Fourth of July accident there eleven years earlier. It was wonderful to see many of my long-ago neighborhood playmates.

From Gig Harbor we continued on to Willapad to welcome our former backpackers' group for a reunion campout on the sand. The plan was to use the conveniences of the house but spend a lovely night on the beach in our sleeping bags, but I guess age was catching up with them. After dinner as we were all sitting by the fire, they decided to put their sleeping bags on top of the beds instead of going out to sleep under the stars. I was a bit disappointed with their choice—but the next day I was fully annoyed when I discovered they did not use their sleeping bags. I had six extra sets of bed linens to wash. Forget about any future campouts!

❖

IN AUGUST, WE TRAVELED TO JUNEAU for the regional AIA meeting hosted by the Alaska chapter. Due to a shortage of hotel rooms, some of the participants were housed in the locals' homes. After a day of introductory sessions, we gathered early one morning to board the ferry for Skagway. Our group included the naval architect who had designed that ferry and his wife, who was an architect, too. In addition to the scenery and wildlife, we were treated to a design tour highlighting the history and workings of our ship.

After historic tours of Skagway, we boarded a train that crept up the mountain alongside the famous Chilkoot Pass trail, which so many gold seekers had endured on foot. We transferred to a bus to cross the Canadian border into the Yukon Territory, where we passed several lakes before arriving in the town of Whitehorse. During World War II, this was the refueling stop for U.S. military planes flying to Alaska, and my brother JC's buddy, Dean, had been stationed there. The photos sent home in wartime showed nothing but tents and an airstrip. Now, we arrived in a small city with nice hotels, a college, and a performance hall—plus a highway connecting it to the rest of the world.

The local museum told the whole story of the gold rush to the north, and we were at the end of our trail. I wondered: What now? But an Alaska architect had put this whole program together, and in true Alaskan fashion, he went big. It took a fleet of small planes to fly us all back to Juneau, where we gathered up our suitcases and flew home.

❖

A WEEK AFTER RETURNING FROM ALASKA, we left for two months in Japan. The UIFA Congress in Tokyo was first with a grand reunion of many friends from around the world. By now, Norm looked forward to these meetings as much as I did. We took the after-Congress tour with many others, traveling to Yokohama, Kyoto, Nara, and Kobe, where we observed their recovery after the city's disastrous 1995 earthquake. The fascinating temporary shelters built from cardboard Sonotube concrete forms provided important lessons in how to quickly construct economical, yet sturdy, structures—a technique later used by other quake-stricken cities around the world.

After the UIFA tour ended in Osaka, Norm and I returned to Tokyo, where he would spend a month teaching at the Tokyo Institute of Technology. He had been a visiting professor there previously in 1991, but this time, the university provided him with an apartment so we could settle in with our own cooking and laundry facilities. We would move in at the end of the month. In the meantime, we left behind our big suitcases while we traveled with smaller ones. Norm had spent a summer in Japan before we were married and had a list of places he wanted to revisit and share, as well as several new sites to explore.

We took advantage of the wonderful train system for most of our travel. We started in Matsumoto, then bused to Takayama through the Alps via many tunnels. Takayama and its beautifully preserved buildings were like stepping back into a past world.

Kanazawa and its famous landscaped gardens were our next stop. As we traveled, we developed a strategy that worked well: When we arrived at each destination, I stayed at the train station with our suitcases while Norm found us a hotel. In Kanazawa, he found lodging near the station, and when we reached our room, we looked out our window at an ominous sky and realized we had taken shelter just in time. Soon, we were experiencing our first typhoon. The wind sent all kinds of things sailing past our window and into the flooded street below. Unfortunately, the next day, we discovered the historic nineteenth-century gardens had suffered considerable damage.

We had one day and night in Fukui before returning to our apartment in Tokyo and preparing for Norm's classroom duties. He had just one class, and it was held two or three days a week, so in between we enjoyed the city's gardens, temples, and contemporary buildings. We had several friends in Tokyo, so we often joined them for dinner out or in their homes. We also enjoyed a day with my former employee Neil and his girlfriend, who held a high position in the local historic preservation office. She arranged for us to visit a park that contained many historic structures but was closed to the public. I felt for the people on the other side of the fence who could see that only the four of us were allowed to enjoy this special site.

I enjoyed the limited cooking that I managed to do at our Tokyo apartment and never got over the fact that the most expensive item of produce I purchased was a single stalk of celery. Onions, eggplants, and other favorites were real bargains, but celery was apparently a luxury.

A week before our departure I discovered at the grocery store that my billfold was missing. I had been pickpocketed in this country of honesty, and my money, passport, credit cards, and travelers' checks were all gone. I had to visit the U.S. Embassy to obtain a new passport, make phone calls to American Express and the credit card bank—and I also had to report to the police department to be finger-printed and file a police report. I had a record for being stopped in Moscow by the KGB in 1971; now in 1998, I had a police record in Tokyo.

This was my fourth trip to Japan, so I knew how strict the country was about immigration. How could I leave when my passport didn't show I had ever entered? Norm and I spent a day at the Japanese immigration department explaining my new passport and its lack of an entrance stamp. Yes, they understood and assured us that the forms I filled out would address the issue. However, once at the airport we were informed that I would not be able to leave, because I had never officially ar-rived. My first thought was: We had wasted a whole day at the immigration offices when we could have enjoyed visiting another interesting site. We were beginning to think we would never make our flight, and then suddenly I was approved, and we were on our way home.

❖

BACK IN SEATTLE we decided that for the last two months of the year, we would travel only between Horizon House and Ocean Park. We returned to the beach for our family Thanksgiving tradition, which now included our neighbor, Caesar. He enjoyed two turkey dinners because his family came later in the weekend for their holiday gathering, and he bragged to his golf buddies about his special treatment.

We started 1999 by celebrating Norm's eightieth birthday a month late. I had asked him whether he wanted a party or a trip to Malta. His response: "Malta!" January in the Mediterranean sun sounded like a perfect adventure, and the tour was a bargain compared to a dinner party. Our travel companions were mostly sun-seekers and bridge-players who never left the hotel, so it was easy for our delightful young guide to take our small group into historical sites. She arranged for special entrance to city buildings and museums, and she took us to the bus terminal filled with wonderful Art Deco buses, which we could take to any place on the island. Each day we explored a new area while others in our group stayed at the card table or complained about the absence of the sun that had been promised on the brochure.

All of Malta's buildings are constructed from blocks cut from the soft yellow local stone, leaving rectangular pits up to ten feet deep all around the countryside. These pits act as reservoirs collecting rainwater. Malta has never had a fresh water source and has always depended on desalinating sea water for drinking water.

An overnight trip to the small north island of Gozo included an extra surprise: snow. Many residents had never seen snow, and their reactions ranged from fear to delight. Breakers crashed over the sea walls, leaving the main roads flooded and dangerous. We Seattleites may have been the only ones enjoying the wild Mediterranean storms.

In Malta, we had time to fully appreciate the survival of its unique architecture. All the structures that were constructed from the same yellow stone had mellowed over many years to beautiful tones of browns, tans, and creams. Plus, we could say we had seen it all—the whole country of two islands, each special site, points of interest and just about every road. It was the first time we could so thoroughly absorb a region and its history.

❖

DURING OUR WILLAPAD SUMMERS, we enjoyed long stretches at the beach with friends from near and far coming and going (and the inevitable linen laundry duties left in their wake). On the Fourth of July, we always made time to enjoy the full local celebration, including the Ocean Park parade highlighted by a wonderful grocery cart drill team from a local store and a flyover by the Coast Guard. All the kids in town were there and even the dogs were dressed up—a wonderful old-fashioned scene. And because fireworks were not restricted on the peninsula, they would start before

Willapad, interior view looking toward the Pacific Ocean

dark and sometimes go all night. From Willapad, we could watch them along a twenty-mile stretch of the beach. It was a real show.

We were still taking every opportunity to travel and in October 1999, we left our beach haven for London. Once again, there was talk of retiring the *Queen Elizabeth 2* ocean liner, so that meant we had to take a sail on her. We flew to London to enjoy a few days there before sailing back to New York.

One day, our tour bus got stuck in a mysterious traffic jam. The cause turned out to be Tacoma glass artist Dale Chihuly with his toddler son on his shoulders; he was in town preparing for an upcoming exhibit of his work at the Victoria and Albert Museum. We thought we'd left him at home!

Then, at dinner that evening, a Scottish couple asked us where we were from. We started to explain about "the other Washington" and Seattle, home to Boeing and Microsoft, when our new friends exclaimed, "You started Medic One!" He was a fireman in town to receive an award from the queen. The next day in the elevator a stocky fellow in a kilt asked the same question. When I started to reply, he said, "Oh, you are from the area with the worst water in the world, where they train the Coast Guard members." Yes, we said, and explained we had a beach house near there. He was a Coast Guardsman from Wales and had just received his medal from the queen. It is indeed a small world.

❖

AT THE END OF NOVEMBER, the whole world's attention turned to Seattle. It was November 30, the day before Norm and I were to leave for the annual AIA meeting in Washington, D.C., and Seattle was hosting the World Trade Organization (WTO). On my walk to work I noticed lines of out-of-town buses parked around the central business core. They had delivered thousands of protesters of all ages. From my office window overlooking Sixth Avenue and Stewart Street, I watched the crowd size increase until late afternoon when protesters started breaking windows at the Starbucks on the corner and a bonfire erupted in the middle of the street. It was time to head home.

I skirted the area where a few protesters were doing the damage while citizens fought with them to protect property. The streets were barricaded with police in riot gear who were trying to contain the chaos. My problem: The only way home was through their barricades. Approaching the first line, I told the police of my predicament and three of them agreed to let me through to the backup line. That group of police decided to allow me to pass as long as I stayed out of the street and went up the alley to reach Freeway Park and the path to my back door. As I walked past, the officer said, "I never thought I would send a lady up a dark alley to keep her safe."

❖

THE DAWN OF THE TWENTY-FIRST CENTURY found me practicing on my own in my small downtown office, loving every day with no business responsibilities beyond myself. I kept busy with a few small jobs that I could schedule around our travels, and I worked on inventorying my project records. I would ship the bulk of them to the International Archive of Women in Architecture (IAWA) at Virginia Tech University but planned to donate the original drawings of projects that had won local and national awards to the Special Collections at the University of Washington Libraries.

I was also collaborating on a new UW project with my best friend Dr. Shirley Cooke Anderson and the miracle lady Lesley Watson of Horizon House. Our beloved doctor was retiring, and we wanted to honor him. We approached Albert Thurmond, the UW's director of planned giving, about starting an endowment for Dr. James J. Lane Jr., who was renowned for his contributions to the field of rheumatology and had been the first fellowship trainee in the UW Medical School Division of Arthritis. Albert smiled at us like we were children and explained that endowments required a $25,000 investment. He warned us that it is difficult to raise that kind of money and told us not to be disappointed. We thanked him and said we would be back.

We went to work and sent out letters to a hundred of Dr. Lane's former patients, describing our endowment plan and encouraging them to participate. Then, Shirley and I jetted off with our spouses to join friends on a monthlong cruise from South Africa to Athens. The replies would go to Lesley while we were traveling.

Our trip started in Cape Town, South Africa, where we thoroughly enjoyed the scenery, the culture, and the people. We then boarded the *Pacific Princess* of television show *Love Boat* fame for a cruise up the west coast of Africa. On our third day of sailing, we disembarked in Luderitz, Namibia, just north of the heavily guarded diamond mining area. We did not see any diamonds, just huge white mountains of salt. A distinguished British professor of African history named Anthony Hopkins lectured on board the ship each day. He soon became part of our Seattle contingent, joining us for cocktails each evening and calling us the "Seattle Mafia."

We spent four days at sea passing along the coasts of Angola, Congo, Gabon, Cameroon, and Nigeria before we next had our feet on land, in Benin. We had been told that we would only stop at "safe ports" and they could possibly change en route. I was sorry to miss Lagos, Nigeria, and the chance to possibly meet up with three architect friends, Fola, Bola and Dada. However, Benin did not disappoint. The dock surface was covered with all types of crafts to tempt us shoppers with ridiculously low prices, and none of us even considered bargaining.

We took a short bus ride, then transferred to boats to visit Ganvie, the largest floating city on the continent. The village was established in the eighteenth century and its structures rest on stilts above the lake—restaurants, boutiques, a school, a hotel, and, of course, the bamboo huts where the eighteen thousand inhabitants live. Fishing is their livelihood, and the women take the harvest to market each day. On the day we visited, boats went about their business between the stilt structures with little attention paid to us.

Lomé, Togo, was a wonderful shopping destination, with Norm chasing bronzes and me searching for masks. Here, I found my favorite souvenir, a butterfly mask. With its three-and-a-half-foot wingspan, I can't imagine how people dance while wearing one.

Shirley, Jane, and Astra at the Andersons' Alki Beach house

At each stop on the cruise, we were treated to local dances and other cultural events, and in Tema, Ghana, our tour enjoyed a group of dancing haystacks. How they could see or breathe under such a mass of straw will remain a mystery. The real highlight was visiting the city's coffin shop, where they could create a coffin in any shape imaginable: an airplane, boat, car, house, temple, or bottle. Why not be laid to rest in a dream fantasy coffin? Funerals in Ghana could be very expensive.

Next, we were in Ivory Coast where an architect friend lived in Abidjan, the capital and our port. I had written her about our trip but had never received a reply, so I thought she could be traveling. But when we were seated in our tour bus, I was told there was a woman on the dock holding a sign with my name on it. Norm and I got off the bus to greet my friend and join her and her colleague for a tour of their hometown, including the contemporary architecture.

I was disappointed that we did not stop in Monrovia, Liberia. Forty-two years earlier, my suitor Nels Johnson, the Texaco Oil executive, had tried to lure me off to his marble palace there. I never doubted I made the right decision not to join him.

Dakar, Senegal, was our next port—a modern city and a sign we were moving back into a world that felt more familiar. We then docked at Casablanca, Morocco, for my third visit to the city made famous by Hollywood and Humphrey Bogart.

Dr. Jim Lane in the late 1970s with the Johnstons and Andersons

Much of the charm I remembered from 1955 seemed to be lost, but the crowds hawking bogus treasures were just the same.

La Goulette, Tunisia, was our gateway to the city of Tunis and the fifth-century B.C. ruins of Carthage—a definite highlight. We enjoyed Tunis's delightful white houses with their blue doors and colorful flowers tumbling from window boxes, all clean and tidy. It would be a great vacation area.

Finally, Malta was our last stop before Athens. The biggest challenge was figuring out how to get all our new treasures onto the flight home. When the flight attendant saw my butterfly mask, she thought I was carrying my surfboard.

Upon our return to Seattle, we received an excited phone call from Lesley about our progress on the endowment honoring Dr. Lane: "We've made it!" Shirley and I went back to Albert to ask about next steps. He was shocked. "You didn't think we could do it," I said. "Frankly, no," he replied.

We had exceeded our goal of $25,000 in one month—all while Shirley and I were traveling. We knew we had a winner before we started. In the years since, the endowment has grown considerably; each year it funds a world-renowned medical leader to lecture and consult with the UW Medical School staff and students.

❖

JUST A WEEK AFTER RETURNING FROM ATHENS, the news that sister-in-law Norma had collapsed sent us rushing to Swedish Hospital in Seattle. We found a shaken niece Laurie, who had stopped by her mother's house in the late morning and found her lying down, saying, "Something is terribly wrong." In the ER, Norma had no pulse, so she was rushed off to surgery, and Laurie had not heard a word since. It was close to midnight when we learned that Norma was being moved into ICU. Her aorta had ruptured, and they did not expect her to survive. If she did, she would probably be paralyzed, brain dead or both.

Nine very quiet days passed as we watched for any movement from Norma in her hospital bed. Easter morning arrived with Laurie and me on watch, and suddenly, Norma opened her eyes. "Hello, everybody," she said. We almost fainted.

When Norma's heart surgeon arrived the next day, she broke down into tears. "I never gave her a ghost of a chance to make it," she said. "She died on me twice on the operating table" during eight hours of surgery. Now, it was time for healing.

❖

AFTER THE AIA CONVENTION IN PHILADELPHIA in May, we hosted Norm's Phoenix cousins and their spouses on their first visit to Seattle. We saw it all: the Space Needle, Mount St. Helens, and the Museum of Flight; we also enjoyed several lively family dinners and capped their visit with three days at Willapad. After they departed, we stayed on at the beach to get ready for the July Fourth holiday, when the rest of our Seattle-based family joined us. It was Norma's first outing since her heart surgery. She spent much of each day napping, but she enjoyed being there with us and watching the fireworks.

In mid-August we flew to Kodiak to meet nephew Jay and his family for an adventure to their "lodge"—really a cabin—on Deadman Bay near the west end of the island. After a few days in town partying with their friends, we loaded a seaplane with our belongings, food, fuel, drinking water, camping equipment, four adults, and two children. I'm sure we hit that small plane's weight limit!

The views were spectacular, and after our short flight we landed in the bay and cozied up to the beach to unload. A small tractor-like vehicle stored under tarps near the beach was uncovered to carry our supplies to the lodge. Whistles on strings were passed out for our hike up the trail so we could announce our presence to any bears that might be in the front yard. A ladder pulled down off the deck became our front porch stairs. Once we were inside, a propane tank was hooked up to the refrigerator to start cooling our perishables. Kerosene lamps were readied, sleeping bags dropped on bunks, a fire lit and we were settled in. An outbuilding housed a sauna, and our fire also heated water in a tank and, eventually, steam for the sauna.

Only one other structure could be seen down the bay. We took a boat ride, stopping at a crab pot that we had permission to raid. Unfortunately, starfish had eaten our dinner and it yielded nothing. We continued up to the river source until it was too shallow to proceed—such a beautiful trip through the lush wild vegetation. The next day we saw the salmon run coming in. The pinks were leaping, and I had never seen so many fish in the air. With rod and reel in hand we began to snag and drag to try and catch them. Spawning fish at this point do not feed, and they jump to loosen their eggs.

On our fourth day, Norm finally caught a few fish: a cod, a small halibut and a giant starfish. Then friends Pete and Margaret arrived in their boat to take us all further west to Camp Cove. From there we would fly back to Kodiak on a larger plane that served the cannery employees. Pete and Margaret and their three young ones spent the summer fishing at Camp Cove, which was considerably more comfortable than Jay's "lodge." The cove harbored four boats most of the time, known as "Pete's fleet." Margaret cooked and cared for her family, along with the hired men and any fishermen who came by. Sometimes she baked bread twice a day. We had planned to stay just one night, but it turned into four nights when poor weather conditions kept the six of us grounded and under Margaret's feet.

For us, the weather didn't seem that bad. We stayed outdoors most of the time, with the men doing chores and the young girls digging for artifacts. This area had been the homeland of Alaska Native people for centuries, and a midden of arrowheads and other small tools was buried there. Eventually, we boated over to the cannery for supplies, and there we spotted some workers with their luggage. The word was the plane was coming in on the backside of the island. We raced to our boat and back to camp to gather our belongings, returning just in time to make the flight. Somehow, only five of us were booked on the flight—all but me. The mix-up was sorted out, and the plane took off with all of us on board. We flew along the bays on the north shoreline, completing our tour of the island. The pilot only flies through conditions he can see so we stayed below the clouds, picking our route back to town. Like Malta, this is one place I can say I have truly completely seen—if only from above.

A quick run to the Kodiak airport, and we were home after midnight and a day late. The office would have to wait.

19 | RETIREMENT

Waiting for the bus in Bergen, Norway (Betty, Jane, Norm, Margaret Morrison, and Martha Young), May 2003

N EARLY 2001, I STARTED PLANNING the final days of my business office. The move to downtown in 1995 had forced me to clean out the bulk of the disposable collection, and now I needed to finish cataloging my work. It had seemed like an easy task when I promised it to the International Archive of Women in Architecture at Virginia Tech. I can still hear Milka Bliznakov's voice reminding me at every AIA meeting that my collection should be on its way. It was time to deliver. I shifted back and forth between design and research, documenting and tossing.

However, I had another side project to distract me at Horizon House. The West Wing had a total of fifty-one apartment units, including ours. Three units had their own private patios, while another thirty-five units had 6-foot-by-6-foot decks. The remaining thirteen units—including our A-U apartment—had sliding doors opening to 18-inch-wide ledges suitable for planted pots. I designed a plan to add decks to the units that didn't have them, while still preserving the exterior design of the building, and most of the affected residents agreed to invest in their own deck additions. On the morning of February 29, I met with the unit owners who would need to invest to discuss and vote on the project. At the end of my presentation someone questioned my proposal, and then the building began to shake. "Earthquake!" The shaking stopped before anyone could get under the table for cover. Later, I told them, "See what happens when you disagree with me?"

As we left our meeting room, we could see the Horizon House's young staff was in a state of shock. Our CEO told us to get out of the building. "No," most of us insisted. "We are safer inside." I was surprised because our CEO was a former Californian and should have known better. Norm and I had to detour out to the street and through the garage to get around the fire doors, which had automatically locked, to get back to our apartment. We expected to find our Iranian tile or the Chihuly blue glass bowl in pieces and could not believe what we found: Our large Christmas cactus perched on top of a 5-foot-tall column had somehow managed to fly 4 feet west, over the harp, without destroying any of its neighboring art pieces. Its soft landing on the rug left the pot intact with dirt everywhere and a severely wounded plant. The only other evidence of the Nisqually earthquake was that some of our drawers were open for inspection. The Johnstons' art treasures had amazing good luck.

❖

IN APRIL WE WERE TRAVELING AGAIN. After our annual New York Metropolitan Opera weekend—featuring Wagner, of course—we were on our way to Greece with sister-in-law Norma, now recovered from her surgery, and our friend Pat Dark. We met more friends, the Connellys, in Athens, where Norm's former student Tim arranged for us to stay in the old city area for a few days before we boarded a cruise ship to tour the Greek islands and enjoy the Mediterranean's beautiful spring wildflowers.

We quickly learned that the Aegean Sea can get just as nasty as the Mediterranean. Our ship was scheduled to stop in another port to pick up additional passengers, but the waters were too rough. So, about 2 a.m. we were awakened when several small fishing boats arrived with those passengers, terribly seasick after bobbing about for several hours trying to reach our ship. They had to board in the middle of the night via a lowered stairway. Cruise ship companies are not about to leave behind paying customers.

The Johnstons with Norma and the Connellys in Greece

After the cruise, we came back to Athens to find our cab could not get within four blocks of our delightful hotel. The pope was about to make his first visit to Greece, and our hotel was next door to the church he was going to visit. Security was tight everywhere, even though the pope had not yet departed Italy. Several of us older women stood guard over our mound of luggage in the street while others in our party dragged suitcases to the hotel, explaining the situation to the guards. It took about three trips before all of us and our bags finally made it to our destination. We figured we would at least get to see the pope. However, we were not allowed to leave the hotel while he was nearby and missed him completely.

Once the pope was gone, Tim took us to places where only the locals go, including a restaurant that served a wonderful lamb dish with fresh lemon juice. It had to be the best lamb I've ever tasted. In the evenings, we gathered on the roof terrace of our little hotel for cocktails while watching the sun set over the Parthenon. Truly, one of my most special memories.

❖

BACK HOME THAT SPRING, before heading to Willapad for much of the summer, I was busy tidying up the report from the state architect selection committee for the Millennium Carillon Bell Tower project in Olympia. The tower had long been a dream of supporters who believed it would enhance our state Capitol campus. It was such a pleasure to review the design submissions, and I enjoyed the discussions among my colleagues. However, the needed funds could not be raised, and the drawings were destined for a file drawer.

Later in the year, I accepted an invitation to serve on another architect selection committee. Pratt Art Institute, just a half-mile from Horizon House, was planning to add a new building. The panel reviewed proposals from some of Seattle's young, promising firms. Oh, what potential! The finalist proposed a terrific design, an assured award-winner if it had ever been executed. But once again, fundraising efforts fell short, and another work of art was placed in a file drawer. There are so many great unbuilt designs, especially in the archives and drawers of governmental agencies.

❖

THROUGH MY LIFE, there have been very few moments when I have been riveted by news, but that September 2001, television cameras brought one of the most unbelievable scenes of destruction into my living room. The World Trade Center towers in New York had been big news in Seattle when they were constructed in the early 1970s because the architect, Minoru Yamasaki, was a University of Washington graduate and the structural engineers were from a well-known Seattle firm. They were on our must-see list on a trip to New York soon after they opened, and indeed, the towers offered sweeping views in all directions on a beautiful day. The dining also was good (and expensive). For days after they were destroyed by terrorists on September 11, it was impossible to comprehend the devastation we saw. These massive high-rise buildings, only twenty-eight years old, had collapsed and were gone, along with thousands of lives.

No more destruction, please. I have seen enough.

❖

AT THE BEGINNING OF 2002, I planned to close my office completely as soon as my materials were all shipped to Virginia Tech's archives. Of course, there was office equipment to move, sell, donate, or dump. Unfortunately, my office closure plans were disrupted when I fell at the swimming pool. I required surgery to repair my right shoulder rotator cuff, and my right arm was in a sling for over a month. This was the first of almost annual dates with my orthopedic surgeon for the next ten years.

With a lot of help from family and friends, the moving and shipping was finally completed. Each evening I sorted through the color slides of my projects, family, and travels, discarding those that weren't worth keeping. I sent several thousand images to the slide library at the UW College of Architecture and Urban Planning. Many of my slides were taken in the 1950s with Kodachrome film, which held its color quality over the decades. Because newer film products were required to be less environmentally toxic, their color faded significantly over time. The UW slide curator was thrilled to receive replacement slides showing many of the historic structures that students are required to study. I was proud of my rigorous weeding-out job and saved only a small collection of personal photos and slides showing favorite projects for myself.

May brought a new opportunity to tour an American city: Charlotte, North Carolina, site of the AIA Convention. I was fascinated by the inner city full of parking garages and modern buildings that seemed to be asleep. Charlotte had become a major banking center for the East Coast, but after working hours, it was a ghost town. I have never been in a big city that was so quiet at night other than La Paz, Bolivia, which had such a strict curfew that violators would be shot after dark.

The next year we met in San Diego where the COF investiture took place at Louis Kahn's Salk Institute. Sixty-two white doves, representing the new Fellows, were released to fly out over the ocean. At the business meeting Norman and I were honored with the Leslie Boney Spirit of Fellowship Award for continuing service to the COF—the first to be awarded to two people. How nice to be recognized for our teamwork!

The year that Frank Gehry's Walt Disney Concert Hall in Los Angeles was selected for the investiture, my AIA colleagues were in absolute awe—not at Gehry's design, but over the beautiful walls made from a type of wood they did not recognize. I answered their question: "It is VG [vertical grain] Douglas fir, the wood we use for our framing lumber." I then realized how truly unique our forests of fir, hemlock and Western red cedar are to our northwest corner of the country.

IN AUGUST 2002, the regional AIA conference was held in neighboring Tacoma, and Norm and I stayed in a hotel so we would not miss a thing. I was the banquet keynote speaker and was pleased to present a surprise to the attendees—a copy of an early Tacoma AIA history I had discovered in a bundle of old documents. The early regional directors kept their own records, which hopefully were passed along to the next director, but this was not always the case. I'm sure the members of

Norman and Jane with the Les Boney Award

the current Southwest Washington chapter, which included Tacoma, were unaware of the chapter history and had never seen the organizational papers that I had found. Of course, I left the old records where they belonged, in Tacoma, as by then they had their own AIA office and staff to take care of them.

My talk was well received, and then we had a drawing for prizes. Somehow both my name and Norm's came out of the bowl. But it turned out there was another surprise in store for me: Ted Gardugue, our regional director from Hawaii, started describing the history of a new Regional AIA Medal. Then, he announced that I was to be the first recipient. It was truly an honor to be recognized by my closest associates.

SEPTEMBER 2002 was a time for family and friends. We traveled to Waukesha, Wisconsin, where Norm's parents grew up. A cousin and her family still lived on part of the old Shultis family farm. With a bit of hunting, we found the remains of the Johnston family quarry a short distance away. It was still summer—warm and very buggy.

We also visited Milwaukee's award-winning lakefront museum and Frank Lloyd Wright's Taliesin in Spring Green, both definite "musts" for any architect. Taliesin was in much need of repair but continued to function as a school and training studio.

Back in Seattle, we celebrated the fiftieth wedding anniversary of a couple of my early clients who were still living in the 1959 house I had designed for them. The event reunited an old group of my fellow Boeing architects and engineers, and we caught up on the many wonderful happenings in our lives since we shared Annex A in 1952-53.

Another big celebration that fall was the fiftieth anniversary of my university graduation, which I had been helping to plan for over a year. The event took place on November 1, the day before the homecoming football game. Norm, of course, led a campus tour highlighting the many changes that had occurred in the years since we graduated. We enjoyed our celebration dinner in Mary Gates Hall, formerly the Physics Building, which brought back memories from classes in the late 1940s and my UW remodeling jobs in 1985.

IN JANUARY 2003, I was back in my orthopedic surgeon's office to discuss my upcoming left knee replacement. For ten years, since the first time my knee had left me on my face in the middle of the street, I had been on guard, catching myself numerous times from falling. It was time! I had heard how nice it was in Horizon House's nursing section, which offered back massages and other pampering for those recovery from surgery. I was ready for some pampering, but when I came home from the hospital, I did not go into nursing care. I was sent to an isolated room in the Supported Living area with no massage or pampering. After three days, I returned to my apartment. What had I done wrong? Unknown to me, the hospital had reported cases of scabies, so I was put in quarantine.

Despite my disappointment with the recovery treatment, I was pleased with Dr. Daniel Flugstad's work. I had overheard several other physicians saying that if they needed joint replacements, he would be their choice. So, he became mine, and I had the opportunity to choose him many times. My left knee surgery was followed by my right hand, which suffered from carpal tunnel syndrome, and then a total right knee replacement was followed by the left hand, a total left shoulder replacement, and a right hip replacement. Dr. F and his staff became like family.

❖

IT WAS THE SEVENTY-FIFTH YEAR for the Dragon Ladies, and we deserved a special celebration. We traveled to Portland by train and checked into a recently remodeled historic hotel where they housed us in the top floor suite, with fireplaces in several rooms, a conference room, meeting room and a small kitchen. We visited museums, bookstores, Lloyd Center, the Chinese Garden, and many restaurants, all via the free downtown transit system. Five days of fun ended when Shirley and Ralph Anderson's son, Ross, met our return train with his toddler daughter on his shoulders. She looked us over and said, "Grandma, your friends are all so old."

In late August I returned to Portland with Norm for the regional AIA meeting. I was back at the same delightful historic hotel, but this time with a group that was almost all men. The desk clerk said, "You're back! How are the other girls?" Norm and my colleagues wondered: What exactly had happened on my previous trip? I assured them that we must have been remembered simply because we had such a good time. After our meetings, we rode south with friends to spend a few days in Eugene visiting the University of Oregon, one of Norm's alma maters.

With my office now fully closed, we decided that a two-week Caribbean cruise, through the Panama Canal and returning up the West Coast, would be a nice way to celebrate our wedding anniversary. My new Horizon House clients, the Eulenbergs, joined us on the trip aboard the *Regal Princess*.

In our stateroom we were greeted with wine from our travel agent, plus Champagne and chocolate-covered strawberries from Norma and Laurie to celebrate our anniversary. We enjoyed a relaxing day in the sun at sea on our way to Jamaica, where we toured gardens and waterfalls. While shopping, Norm found the perfect little painting with vivid colors to add to our wall of artwork from around the world.

Our next stop was Aruba, where the Dutch-influenced architecture made us feel as if we had arrived in Holland. The Natural Bridge made of coral limestone was the main tourist draw on the island, and it was crowded with Spanish-speaking tour groups. The island's natural sparse vegetation was in extreme contrast to the lush

Jane and Norm with Karen Braitmayer, FAIA, and her family

green lawns and plantings around the high-rise tourist hotels, which seemed artificial and out of place.

Traveling through the Panama Canal and locks was the highlight of our travels. We observed the impressive old equipment and passage process, which still functioned well after so many years. The variety of ships, resting or waiting their turn in the reservoir areas, represented countries from all over our world.

We sailed up the west coast of Central and North America to the tip of Baja California and Cabo San Lucas, a small village that had ballooned into a major tourist area. We managed to find the remains of the old town for our last bit of shopping before heading onward to Los Angeles and home.

We returned just in time to empty our suitcases and head to the beach for our family Thanksgiving at Willapad. And then, with our turkey leftovers and home-made stock tucked into the car, we turned right around for home so we could pack for Washington, D.C. This annual trip had started in 1982, and every year we enjoyed exploring new buildings and catching up with our AIA friends and their spouses. And Norm and I always made time to celebrate his early-December birthday, just the two of us, over dinner at Old Ebbitt Grill, one of our favorite restaurants. At one dinner, we noticed that Olympia oysters were on the menu. This was a Pacific Northwest treat that was hard to find even in Seattle. When we ordered a half-dozen for an appetizer, the waiter hesitated, and we assured him we knew that we were getting tiny oysters. He returned with a dozen, billing us just for the half.

❖

BECAUSE 2005 WOULD BE the two hundredth anniversary of the Lewis and Clark Expedition, many Columbia River and coastal sites were gearing up for a grand tourist invasion. Our friend Faye Lindberg was an Astoria, Oregon, native so we decided to plan a trip to the coast's historic sites for our Horizon House neighbors a year ahead of the crowds. I was traveling to Ocean Park regularly, so I did the research and scouting, and made necessary arrangements with a hotel, restaurants, and museums. Risa, who oversaw resident activities, arranged for a chartered bus. We were all set for an August trip, between the kite festival and Labor Day weekend, when local rates and available space would be the best.

With that summer travel plan well in hand, we could focus on enjoying our major international trip of the year: a tour of Iceland and a cruise up the coast of Norway.

Our one full day to see all of Reykjavik was not nearly enough, but we toured the old town and had the chance to peek into the windows of the president's house because the flag was not up, indicating she was not there. We visited the church and the "Pearl"—a water storage tank with a fancy restaurant on top that offered a great city view.

We had a 5 a.m. departure the next morning for our flight to Oslo; there we met up with Shirley and Ralph Anderson, who had arrived days before. It was May 17, Constitution Day, and the whole country seemed to be there for the wonderful parade, everyone in regional costumes with splashes of brilliant colors that glowed in the bright sunlight.

The next day, our train wound through the hills until we descended to the coast and Bergen, our Seattle sister city. We felt right at home in the rain as we rode a cable car to the top of Mount Ulriken to enjoy the misty view of the city. On our list: finding the Seattle Totem Pole. This pole had been part of our wedding reception in Seattle's Pioneer Square thirty-five years earlier, and soon afterward it was gifted to Bergen. We found it in a park, where it greets ships on their way into the harbor.

At last, we were on our way north aboard a mail boat to see the Norwegian coast. The sun set late and rose early, giving us many hours each day to enjoy the spectacular scenery. We only missed a few towns, docking briefly at night. At one stop it was snowing, with ice chunks floating about while 200 passengers disembarked and new passengers boarded. At Trondheim, we had time to tour the home of several skiing friends, and at Tromso we enjoyed the research aquarium, the university, the ski jump, and the church across the bridge. I remembered my 1956 visit when the economy was suffering, and how the Norwegians were in good spirits even though

Jane and Norm in Bergen with the totem pole that they sat on years earlier during their wedding reception, while it was horizontal and still being carved by Duane Pasco.

they had very little. Now, it seemed they really knew how to invest their newfound oil wealth. The modern development above the Arctic Circle was so well-executed.

At North Cape, the northernmost city in the world, we were treated with sunshine and no wind. We then sailed on to Kirkenes where we disembarked to meet the Laplanders and their reindeer before flying south to Oslo. We learned that "Rudolph" and teammates were actually female reindeer; they retain their antlers year-round, while the males shed theirs.

THAT AUGUST, IT WAS TIME for our grand Lewis and Clark celebration tour. Norm and I welcomed the Horizon House group at their hotel near Willapad, and the next morning, we were off to the Oregon side of the Columbia River to the Fort Clatsop National Memorial, where a park ranger told the story of the rain-soaked explorers. Then we went back to Astoria and the Flavel House before enjoying lunch on the riverfront and a visit to the wonderful Columbia River Maritime Museum with its Coast Guard exhibit.

The next day we devoted to the Long Beach Peninsula, starting with the Lewis and Clark Interpretive Center at the south end, then traveling north to Leadbetter Point State Park, Oysterville, Ocean Park and Nahcotta. We toured a Willapa Bay exhibit of marine life, then enjoyed a farewell dinner at Nahcotta's famous Ark Restaurant. On the last day, we saw the group off with box lunches from the Cottage Bakery, and Norm and I returned to Willapad to await our next round of guests.

WE RESUMED OUR INTERNATIONAL TRAVELS in April 2005 with a smarTours-organized group trip of the Adriatic coast. Upon arriving in Zagreb, Croatia, we enjoyed a bit of shopping before boarding a bus for a lovely drive into Slovenia and our hotel in Bled. I had been wanting to visit this little town to ski since my time in Germany in the 1950s, but somehow it never worked out. Fifty years later, I had arrived, and it was more beautiful than I had anticipated.

Our Golf Hotel room featured a balcony and a great view of the lake and island with a castle that we would tour the next day. We tried out four of the hotel's five swimming pools. We had them mostly to ourselves, so, like the kids, we played on all the fancy slides. We enjoyed our trip around the lake, visiting the small castle and touring St. Martin Church, but our stay in Bled was far too short.

An all-day bus trip, fueled by lunches we made from the hotel breakfast buffet, took us back to Croatia and Opatija on the sea. We also enjoyed driving around the Istria Peninsula, stopping at sites along the south and western coasts, as well as for a lunch of calamari and fries. We saw luxury yachts and cruise ships moored in this busy corner of the Gulf of Venice, and a few in our group made a quick trip to Venice while we stayed back to soak up the local culture with influences from Croatia, Slovenia, and Italy.

Heading south, Plitvice National Park was a must. For Norman, niece Laurie and me, this was a return visit, but we had more time to enjoy it this time than in 1977 when my mother accompanied us. There were so many breathtaking crossings of waterfalls, all with wet slippery stones and few railings to grab onto for support. Twenty-eight years earlier, I had felt the crush of my mother's hand gripping mine; now it was Norm who gingerly eased his way through the rocks and water, hanging on to my arm. This is a place best visited during one's prime, but no matter how exhausting or scary it is, the beautiful memories are worth it. That night, we all slept well in the fresh mountain air, undisturbed by a thunderstorm.

Our delightful guide, Steve, kept us moving on to Split, where we took in the city, palace, and a great garden show. Then we went inland a bit through Bosnia and Herzegovina, still so war-torn, with vast areas off-limits due to fields of land mines that lingered. Finally, we reached beautiful Dubrovnik. Our new hotel was located outside the old city on the rocky coast. We had a full day to enjoy the views, walk on the old city walls, and visit fascinating little shops and restaurants. The beautiful day ended with a special dinner on a downtown terrace overlooking the city.

Next, we traveled to Montenegro. "Mont" was the important part as our tour took us up, up, and up the mountain. The scenery was spectacular, but we wondered how the residents made a living on what appeared to be such poor land. We were happy to be back in our modern Dubrovnik hotel for the night and to have a free day in the old city to wander and take in the views on our own. The entire trip was a constant series of highlights, and we raved about smarTours to all our friends.

That September, we went back to Kodiak to visit Jay and Steph and check out an old house they had bought in town. He intended to rebuild it and turn it into their retirement home. Enough of outback living! I gave Jay a copy of my office's old "do it yourself" measuring instructions so I would have something to work with to design his new house. It would have to be constructed using the old foundation because a sewer easement restricted expanding the footprint. This new project with many tricky problems to solve would keep me busy.

❖

IN 2006, WE JOINED a smarTours trip to Vietnam and Cambodia, irresistible for both of us and our longtime friends, David and Joyce Park. Colonel David had served in Vietnam and was very interested in returning as a tourist. We would meet them in Los Angeles before joining the tour group. But our easy flight down the West Coast got off to a bad start before even leaving the ground. While I was lifting my carry-on into the overhead bin, we heard a loud pop from my right knee. Seating was rearranged so my leg could stretch out, packed in ice, and as soon as we landed, we went to the closest hospital. Nothing was broken, but I would be in a full-leg splint until the knee could be replaced. We decided to continue on with my stiff leg and a large bottle of pain pills. In Hanoi our first day, we enjoyed a wonderful lunch, then the group went off on a walking tour through the city's old section, while I stayed on the bus. We noted that the city houses were very narrow and tall, many only about twelve feet wide. The larger houses were in the countryside where land was more available. That night, with Norm coming down with a cold and me favoring my knee, we decided to skip the 5:30 a.m. wake-up call for the Halong Bay Excursion and enjoy a day of leisure in the hotel instead. I treated myself to a massage with three people working my body for over an hour—for only $25—and it turned out we hadn't missed much more than a bus ride.

Our early call to catch a flight to Hue required a long walk at the airport, which did both Norm and me in. I was thrilled to be met with a wheelchair when we arrived at the Hue airport. Because I was unable to walk the stairs up and down to the aircraft used for domestic flights, I was wheeled through the baggage area and loaded along with the food carts on their lift, meaning I was on the plane first and off last. Hue was a handsome old city of former French colonial era buildings, and many were nicely remodeled. I am sure the French had considered Hue a choice post. I was taken on a tour by bicycle cab to the main entrance of the Citadel, so I did not miss much, even though I couldn't join the walking tour. During lunch we enjoyed observing a large wedding party with the bride in her traditional bright red dress. I would have liked to spend more time in this lovely city on the Perfume River.

In the morning we traveled by bus to Hoi An, over mountain passes and through numerous tunnels along the rugged coastal route. Da Nang sported a beautiful new bridge, reportedly designed by an Italian engineer. There were many new cars among the thousands of bicycles—all in constant motion, dancing in and out of the traffic as they appeared to change partners along the way. The markets overflowed with brilliant displays of fruits and vegetables arranged as if to win first prize at a county fair. Oh, how we wanted to shop and stock up our own kitchens and cook with that beautiful produce! We would have to be satisfied with our photos and memories.

We went out of the city to China Beach, where seashells did not seem to exist; there would be no treasures for our shell bowl under the coffee table at home. The beach was covered with stacks of semicircular woven grass fishing boats that could hold two people at most, and we admired the balancing skills of these sailors.

Saigon was next, brimming with its three million motor scooters, bicycles, and cars. I marveled at the high school girls dressed all in white, two on a bicycle with their skirts tucked up to keep them out of the wheels. Our tours included rubber plantations and tapioca fields before returning to the city center to see the cathedral, post office, opera house, and shopping district.

We traveled on to the Mekong River Delta, where much of the drainage system of Asia reaches the sea. Small boats carried us up the river's channels to villages that produced many types of food, candies, and crafts for the tourists. Tidal action can back up the natural waterway system more than 70 kilometers, and the people who live in the delta long ago learned to live with Mother Nature's cycles. When a house flooded, the residents often just moved everything up to a higher floor.

Cambodia was our next stop, and I was again sent on a wild wheelchair ride through the bustling backside of the airport—a sight that would be better unseen. The first billboards we saw on the highway on our way into town were asking for blood donations. This was a poor country, but our new hotel was a lovely place for tourists visiting Angkor Wat. I tested my knee with a bit of stiff walking through the ruins in the jungle. The tree roots were above ground, looking as if they were reaching out to secure safe anchorage ahead of the next flood. It was the time of year when hundreds of Buddhist monks gathered at Angkor Wat for a week, disappearing into the jungle at night and returning by day in front of the historic temples. The hike through the complex was more than I could manage, so I stayed with the bus driver, watching the mass of silent monks, male and female, gathering at the entrance to the complex. It's an enormous challenge to preserve these structures in this lush environment where the plants grow so quickly, you can almost see it happen. It is a truly magical world.

After leaving the tourist town of Siem Reap, our bus drove along a terrible road among the locals, who were walking and appeared very poor, as we made our way to the third largest lake in the world. We boarded boats for a tour of the life on the lake, including barges large enough to hold a substantial school building with outdoor space to accommodate sports games. The lake's annual water level can vary by up to eight feet, and the houses were constantly towed around, based on the lake level. Or perhaps they were sometimes moved to a better neighborhood, closer to the school. We wondered if residents ever forgot where their house was moored.

Our route home was through Bangkok, which had transformed from the pleasant city we remembered from prior visits into a metropolis with dirty, noisy clogged streets filled with belching fumes and throngs of people. I cherished my memories of how lovely the city had been in the past, with its river filled with smiling vendors in boats selling colorful vegetables and flowers.

After a long flight home, we called Dr. Flugstad for an appointment the next day. It was time for my next knee replacement surgery.

WE CELEBRATED THANKSGIVING at the beach house as usual. But this year, the weather forecasts warned that an early snowstorm was on the way. The coast seldom gets snow, so we paid attention. Norma and Laurie left early because she needed to be back in the city for work. Norm and I stayed longer and started our drive home in bright sunlight, with our sand and grass covered in a lovely white blanket of snow. We saw people driving to work, so thought it would not be too difficult to get back to Seattle. The lesson learned that day: When you see loggers under their trucks putting on chains, stop and install your own. We faced just one hill, on Highway 101 near Raymond, and I thought my front-wheel-drive car would not have a problem with it. However, it was covered with vehicles all over the place, including many stuck in the ditch. I finally got some help putting on our chains and we were safely on our way. But when I needed to remove them, I could not, and there was no gas station open for help. Those chains really got some wear.

Willapad was our only travel destination until May 2007 and the AIA Convention in San Antonio, where we all enjoyed the River Walk. The investiture of the

Fellows took place in front of the Alamo, and we sought out the few shady spots before we had to march out into the full sun.

Back in Seattle, my Horizon House trip committee decided that a Ride the Ducks tour would be fun, and the "duck" arrived at our front door for our contingent to board. We skipped the city tour and spent our time out in Lake Union viewing the houseboats and yachts. Another time, we bused to Flaming Geyser State Park for a picnic. It was nice to revisit the bridge that I had helped design with three incredible team members years earlier.

❖

THE FIRST OF OCTOBER found Norm and me in Bucharest, Romania, for the UIFA Congress. This was a return visit for me, but so much had changed since my 1972 trip. The madman dictator Nicolai Ceauşescu had destroyed most of downtown to build his palace and its grand approach. The huge palace was a series of empty rooms with great chandeliers and a lot of marble—and now was of little use because sanity had been restored to the country. I was glad that I had seen Bucharest and could remember its treasures from before Ceauşescu's destructive reign.

Five days of meetings were mixed up with visits to museums, a trip to Constanta with a mini-cruise and lunch aboard a naval training tall ship, and an evening show featuring folk dancing and singing. A wonderful pan flute concert was our last night's entertainment. The pan flutes ranged from tiny to so large that they were floor-mounted, and I remembered how enchanted I was the first time I had heard one—on my train ride down from Machu Picchu in 1983.

The after-meeting tour took us north to revisit the unique little painted churches, which I so wanted to share with Norman. When I brought my slides home from my 1972 trip, he was fascinated by them. Unfortunately, some had been destroyed by the dictator before they could be preserved. We spent two nights at a monastery where the beds were as hard and cold as sleeping on the ground on our backpacking trips, but we had a bathroom and could easily visit several of the painted jewels that we had come to see.

On our way north, we passed through a national park where the road along a small river was carved out of the base of a rock cliff several thousand feet tall. The gorge was so narrow we could see just a sliver of daylight above. Once we emerged in full light, we breathed a sigh of relief that we had not been buried within the canyon.

Jane with Norm and Donna Dunay in Romania, November 2007

Next, we traveled to Iași on the Moldova border to visit more churches, and on to Gua, arriving in time for a 10:30 p.m. dinner. The next day, we were up early to visit the six best monasteries in the area. Voroneț is considered the finest of the small fifteenth-century structures built during the era of Prince Stephen the Great of Moldavia in the center of Transylvania, the land of dark legends.

Our last stop was the town of Cluj, the heart of this vampire land and the home base of the Unitarian Church, a contrast to its history.

Norm and I left the tour early and took a train back to Bucharest to join a river cruise going up the Danube to Budapest. It was during a visit to one of the small towns along the way that I realized Norman was starting to suffer from dementia. For a while, we had realized that he was getting confused walking through airport terminals he knew well, wanting to head to the wrong concourse or in the wrong direction. But this was different. He had studied the city plan and noted several sights that he wanted to see. With a bit of free time, we were off to seek them out. I asked him several times about the direction he was taking, but he was adamant in his rebuttals. Fortunately, it was a small, contained area, and we had gone as far as possible in the wrong direction, but we barely made it back in time to catch our bus. I realized that from now on, we would need to handle travel differently. I was going to have to watch him more closely.

We boarded our river boat for a leisurely cruise north. The first stop was Svishtov, Bulgaria, where we boarded buses for a drive to Arbanasi to tour early architecture and historic sites on a high plain. It was a long ride, but it was worth it. The structures gave us a sense of scale because the early residents were so much smaller than the people of today. Our group suffered from sore backs the next day from all the ducking to get under doorways. Fortunately, we had a wonderful lazy day to enjoy the river and countryside. We passed through the Iron Gates, a two-lock series, while soaking up the sun in our shorts.

We spent the next day in Belgrade walking to see the city's many sights, including the grave of Yugoslav President Josip Tito, as well as monuments and parks. When we reached Budapest, we stayed aboard our vessel for another day while docked in the city center. Of course, Norm had to go shopping for his piece of art to commemorate this trip. Once he had his Rosenthal blue and white Art Nouveau vase, he could relax and enjoy our return trip to this beautiful city.

We then went to our Budapest hotel for a two-night stay in a room that made me feel like a fairy princess in a children's book. We had ample time to visit architectural and historical sites, but we were too late to catch the fields of blooming sunflowers, which I always associated with Hungary. We savored the wonderful goulash soup and wiener schnitzel—and the many special memories they recalled—before our journey home.

THE NEW YEAR OF 2008 meant it was time for a new left shoulder, courtesy of Dr. Flugstad. I would be in good shape by gardening time, and until then I would focus on my Horizon House trip committee.

April found me all dressed up, standing up with Betty Wagner at her third marriage. Retirement homes aren't always thought of as places to find romance, but I am no longer surprised at how often it happens. Both the bride and her attendant were eighty years old. It had been many years since I had been part of a wedding party.

Also that April, I was truly caught off guard to be selected by the Women's University Club of Seattle to receive their Brava award, which honored civic leaders. I was the first club member to be so honored, as they looked to recognize women who have made major contributions in different professional fields. The lovely gold and diamond Brava necklace piece became part of my very special gold charm bracelet, joining several other treasured items.

The year of 2008 almost slipped by without a major trip, but we decided to go to China on a Yangtze River cruise with sister-in-law Norma and her recently widowed cousin Bill from Vancouver, B.C. Norm and I had first visited the region with a group of architects in 1980, but we knew it would be different, given the economic progress and expansion of tourism since then.

Our first day in Beijing was full of the usual sights: Tiananmen Square, the Summer Palace, a ride in a dragon boat, and the opera in the evening. This was my fourth trip, and I felt like I could pass as a guide. The next day we focused on the buildings used for the Olympic Games, but the smog was so thick that photography was next to impossible. We were ready for clean air, wherever we might find it.

The air indeed cleared as we traveled southwest to Xi'an. I was amazed at how much had been discovered at the Terra Cotta Warriors site since my 1990 trip. China had also fully embraced tourism and the money it generated. Good hotels, historic sites, magnificent scenery, plus a well-run tourist agency were paying off for the now more open country. Of course, as more archaeological sites had been discovered, security had increased. On previous visits, I had been almost face-to-face with the famous clay men and their mounts.

Next, the Yangtze River was the heart of our tour. Our cruise along this engineering feat explored the dams and locks that had changed the landscape so dramatically. Stops along our way to Shanghai included children's performances at schools on boats that also operated as school buses. Many people had lost their historic villages that were flooded by the construction of dams, forcing them to move to higher land or to cities with crowded housing.

Since our last visit, Shanghai had exploded with the construction of wildly designed high-rise buildings that were shoulder-to-shoulder, lit up in bright colors and seeming to fight each other for attention. Norm could not believe how much had changed since 1980. Our top-floor hotel room provided a great vantage point to enjoy and photograph all this color and excitement.

❖

WE WERE BACK HOME in Seattle just in time for Norman's ninetieth birthday celebration in the Sky Lounge at Horizon House. In addition to all the family members in the area, the room was filled with friends, former UW colleagues and students. Norm had a grand time visiting with people he had not seen for many years. I was grateful that the celebration went so well. It was apparent that Parkinson's disease was slowing him down, along with dementia.

In 2009, I was interviewed by the Museum of History & Industry about my time managing the architect's booth at the 1962 World's Fair. MOHAI was preparing for its upcoming fiftieth anniversary exhibit about the fair, and I enjoyed reminiscing about those busy six months, balancing my new practice with almost daily visits to the fairgrounds. Amazingly, both of Seattle's world's fairs had been financial successes, and I fondly remembered my father telling me about his visit to the 1909 Alaska-Yukon Exposition a full century earlier.

My back had been bothering me, so I had been getting cortisone shots from Dr. Ren, a delightful little Chinese woman who seemed to know exactly the right spot. One day she was not available, and I was assigned to a new male doctor. Norm accompanied me as we walked over to the clinic. On the way home, I suddenly found myself clinging to a telephone pole in the rain, waiting for help to arrive. I had a spinal block and was frozen from the waist down. I recalled seeing drunks grasping poles on their way home during early morning hours, and I am sure that is what people must have thought as they drove by. An ambulance deposited me at a nearby hospital to thaw out, and I arrived home by cab at the same time as my evening dinner guests were arriving. That night we enjoyed a very, very late dinner party.

❖

THIS WAS OUR FORTIETH WEDDING ANNIVERSARY YEAR, and a real trip was due. We joined a Regent Cruise northern segment from Seward, Alaska, to Osaka, Japan. We arrived in Anchorage in the rain and drove south to Seward. We were headed across the Bering Sea and knew we might be in for a rough crossing. Kodiak would be our first port of call, and nephew Jay and his family would join us on board for lunch. I knew the area well from working on several projects there and I assured Norm that once we arrived the rain would stop. We joked that I always brought the sun. Indeed, as we arrived, the rain stopped and the sun came out, just as promised.

This was the beginning of an unbelievable adventure. One couple was traveling as guests of the cruise ship company, and during their prior cruise, the weather had been so bad that the ship never docked at any of the intended ports. This time, the sun stayed out and the sea was flat all the way to Dutch Harbor out in the Aleutian islands, where Norm toured me through the town and sites from his 1940s Army days.

The cocktail party aboard their ship in Tokyo Harbor, 2009

Next, we had four days of traveling west and out to sea before we arrived at Petropavlovsk on the Russian peninsula of Kamchatka, where fishing was the main industry. The sun was still shining, and the sea was so smooth that it didn't feel as if we were traveling on water. Norm would go out on our veranda to check, reporting back that indeed we were on water and the ship was moving. The Bering Sea was as flat as a lake on a calm day. I still had the sun with me.

As we turned south, our portside deck received the morning sun for several days before we arrived in Hakodate on Japan's north island, Hokkaido. This was our first visit to this part of Japan. And there, a brief rainstorm finally caught up with us.

Sendai, our next port of call, will always be perhaps my favorite place in Japan. It was a busy tourist town, even in late September. Norm was no longer the walker he had once been. He found an ideal spot in a coastal park where he could have it all—the scenery, the people, the sunny weather—and chose to stay on a bench while I explored the historic sites. Besides the excellent architecture, the cliffside was a backdrop of ancient sculptural pieces, which I did my best to photograph for Norm to see later. We really did not want to leave, but Tokyo was calling, and we had big plans.

Our wonderful Seattle travel agent had worked with us for months to arrange a Johnston/Hastings Tokyo cocktail party aboard our ship for about two dozen of our special Japanese friends. In the month before we sailed, they all had to provide their passport information to our agent, who emailed back and forth to Japan tracking them all down. We had two groups: my women architect friends and Norm's former students and fellow professors from the Tokyo Institute of Technology. With our ship docked in the heart of Tokyo, our friends in festive party apparel arrived with flowers and gifts to a ship almost emptied of our fellow passengers, who were in the city for the evening. The crew encouraged our guests to explore the ship. They were thrilled as most of them had never been on a luxury cruise ship. Some of our personal connections went back to the mid-1970s, including the students and women I met at the 1976 UIFA Congress in Iran. Best yet, when I asked the cruise director about the bill for our party he replied, "No bill. It's just public relations." Wow!

Our last stop was Osaka, and we enjoyed our last cruise dinner with our new Australian friends, John and Nancy. None of us had visited Osaka before, and we were greeted with a proper Seattle-style rain, preparing us for our return home. A quick tour of the city and the huge Ferris wheel right next to the dock filled our remaining hours in Japan with color and music before we traded sea travel for air travel and our flight home.

❖

WE WERE HOME FOR ONLY A WEEK and then packed up for a four-day cruise to British Columbia with Horizon House friends. These short jaunts were easy with the Horizon House bus transporting us between home and the ship in fifteen minutes, and at just $100 per day for everything, the deal meant we couldn't afford to stay home.

Thanksgiving at the beach followed by our annual jaunt to D.C. for AIA festivities took its toll on Norm, who was hospitalized with a heart issue when we returned to Seattle. December then brought Christmas dinner at our apartment and the traditional caroling party, plus the bustle of more festive dinners and parties to wrap up 2009.

After our New Year's Eve open house, it took me until 4 a.m. on January 1, 2010, to finish the last of the kitchen cleanup. Norm was no longer able to share the load and I had also put up the Christmas tree and decorated our apartment to his standards. I lost count of how many dishwasher loads I ran; how many times I handwashed the crystal, silver and pewter; and how much decorating, cooking, and laundering I had done over this ten-day holiday period. But I knew I was done with it. For good.

I vowed I would never wash the good china, silver, and crystal again. I kept my vow by remembering that I could hardly stand up that next day. Change was in order and fifty-plus years of the caroling party at Jane's house were enough. The solution: a holiday cruise in 2010 and a farewell to our holiday traditions.

20 | THE ROGER YEAR

Roger and Stacey with Norm at University of Washington Gould Hall at the opening of the Johnston-Hastings Gallery, December 2014

THINK OF 2010 as the "Roger Year."

Roger Long had been one of Norm's UW architecture graduate students, and back then, he was married to beautiful Shelley and had a 3-year-old daughter, Kelsey. Roger had lost his father when he was very young, and he came to view Norm as the father he never had. I first met Roger when he invited us to dinner at his rental home, which was designed by award-winning architect Jim Cutler. Roger had the looks and charm of a Hollywood leading man—and a lot of talent—but he lacked direction and discipline. He was very religious and believed God would look after him.

Over the years, Norm tried to help Roger stay focused and encouraged him to finish his thesis before he lost his earned credits. Eventually, when Roger had three children and an unfinished house, his wife left him. She got tired of waiting for him to grow up. After we moved downtown into Horizon House, Roger often stayed overnight on our sofa instead of returning to his Bainbridge Island home.

Roger's sketch of Willapad

In 2010, he was still unemployed and had ample time to spend with Norm, as well as at our dinner table and on our sofa. Fortunately, that year he also had a new romantic interest: Stacey, a former girlfriend from his college days in Oregon. Stacey was the divorced mother of four grown children yet maintained the figure and face of a fashion model. If they had not reconnected, I'm certain Roger would have become a permanent part of our household.

That spring and summer, we were still regularly making the three-and-a-half-hour drive to Willapad, often joined by friends from around the country and, of course, Roger. He sometimes brought his children, and he was always wonderful help with the property. Roger also started staying with Norm to keep him company when I had to be away. He was there when I traveled to the AIA Convention that spring and while I recovered after my hip replacement. By this time, Norm was falling frequently due to Parkinson's disease, and he could no longer drive. He was also becoming more confused. My wonderful husband, my best friend, was gradually slipping away from me.

That Thanksgiving, Roger was working on a new business venture: baking pies. His pies tasted good but at $30 each, they were beyond most family budgets. However, he had many orders for the holiday and was convinced he would make his fortune. Norm and I were celebrating the holiday at the beach with family, and we were hunkered down for a terrible incoming storm, with the bathtub full of water and candles and flashlights at the ready if the power went out. Roger was on

Bainbridge Island with a house full of pies ready for the oven—and no electricity. Somehow, he located a town that still had power and rallied friends to transport all his pies to operating ovens. He managed to get them baked and delivered on time, but that stressful day convinced him that baking was not going to be his future. Perhaps he should return to architecture!

Norm was looking forward to our planned holiday cruise, our first escape from the seasonal hosting duties we'd juggled for more than fifty years. But the day before his ninety-second birthday, Norm was hospitalized with bleeding in his esophagus. After four days he was transferred to a nursing home, where he required 24-hour supervision. I hired Roger for night duty, and family members covered day duty. Norm came home in time for Christmas, but there would be no cruise that year.

On New Year's Day 2011, Roger and Stacey joined us for a delayed birthday at Horizon House, and Norm was so happy to be home, surrounded by his favorite people.

❖

THAT SPRING, I BEGAN WORKING on a history of Horizon House with Molly Cone, an experienced author and Horizon House Resident Council president. I thought I already knew a good deal about our building's history. I remembered when the Plymouth Church created its first retirement home in the center of the city, and I even visited an artist friend who lived in the original Horizon House building before the major additions were constructed. But through the history project, I enjoyed learning about former residents like Myrtle Edwards, a Seattle City Council member who advocated for public parks, and many others who built the special community that continues to thrive at 900 University Street in Seattle.

In May, Roger again stayed with Norm while Norma joined me in New Orleans for the AIA Convention. This was Norma's first visit to the city, and we enjoyed seeing the sights, a jazz concert and the many parties hosted in grand old halls and homes. Soon after our return, Norm and I embarked on a weeklong cruise to Alaska with our Horizon House friends. The communities had changed so much over the years since we first started visiting their ports.

That summer, our Horizon House group bused to Skamania Lodge on the Columbia River—a grand perch with a sweeping view upriver to the east. The lodge appeared to be in its own world without a neighbor in the forest for miles. From there, we took the old Hood River railroad up into the Oregon hills and orchard country where Rainier cherries were at their peak. City prices were $3 per pound, but the local price was a mere 57 cents per pound, so we returned with many ten-pound bags to share.

❖

IN MY HOME OFFICE, I was back at work, designing a new house on an old foundation in Kodiak for our nephew Jay. He had sent me his measurements and an easement dictating that the expansion must be constructed upward rather than outward. He built a large garage platform first, with a sizeable shop underneath. The platform provided a staging area and storage for the major construction work. Jay doubled as his own contractor and worked on the project when he had extra time. Because this was a freebie, my one design request was that he build a shaft space to install an elevator in the future to provide easy access between the garage and the upper three floors of the house. I worked so hard to create a workable design that I thought he owed me this, but I still don't know if he heeded my advice. He's never given me a straight answer!

In October, I had to return to the hospital for a back fusion. My sciatic nerves shot pain down both of my legs all the way to my feet, and it was far worse than any of my complaining joints. When I awoke after the surgery my first words were, "I didn't know I could feel so good." It wasn't the pain meds talking; the surgery provided lasting relief. Of course, Roger moved in to look after Norm while I was in the hospital for four days.

After Thanksgiving, we started looking forward to the holiday cruise we had canceled in 2010. On December 21, we arrived in Fort Lauderdale late in the evening before boarding the ship the next day. But Norm's suitcase was missing and then my largest gold crown came out with the first bite at dinner. We were already off to a rough start.

The next morning, Norm's suitcase arrived just in time to join us on the cruise ship. At dinner, we were seated with two other couples, with both women answering to "Judy," and the Judy and John pair became dear friends over the next few days. John was a retired Michigan policeman and a lake-rescue diver. He and Norm really bonded, and he was so helpful, especially in escorting Norm to the restroom during our evenings together. This saved me from hanging around outside the men's room door, calling out to check if everything was all right inside. John always kept track of Norm out of the corner of his eye, and one day he caught him getting off the ship and heading down to the pier. This was Norm's wandering period, and he could not be left alone.

The ship was decorated with Christmas trees and gingerbread houses, and on Christmas Eve, we had a "block party" in the ship's corridor. At dinner that night, we met a Los Angeles couple who were friends of Norma Sklarek, a talented architect who was the first Black woman to receive an AIA Fellowship; she was honored in 1980, the same year as me. I was delighted to ask Norma's friends to pass along my greetings to her, and it was yet another example of how connections from throughout my life have re-emerged at unexpected moments.

Each day brought a new port of call, but Norm often skipped breakfast and chose to take longer naps. John and Judy helped me get him off the ship in a wheelchair in St. Lucia, where he was determined to purchase a souvenir of this trip. He finally selected a small metal wall hanging of a typical Caribbean house doorway and then returned to the ship for another nap. This was not a promising way to welcome in 2012.

During the cruise, we had noticed several people appeared to have bad colds and were coughing. When we didn't see them about, we assumed they were cabin-bound.

Then one day Norm started having difficulty breathing. The ship's doctor put him on oxygen, and he remained in the ship's hospital overnight. The next morning, I was informed that we would need to be evacuated, and I could only take along one small bag with necessary personal items. John and Judy helped us get Norm in a wheelchair and into a lowered lifeboat, which carried us to a small island where a plane would pick us up. We learned Norm was the seventh person to be taken off the ship for medical reasons—a record. Now we knew what happened to those who were coughing earlier.

As promised, a woman stepped out of what looked like a deserted building and explained that the plane was just landing at the other end of the island. We waited in a lovely resort area that was closed for the season until an ambulance came with a nurse, who would accompany us to a Fort Lauderdale hospital. On the flight, Norm thrashed about on the suspended stretcher while the nurse did her best to calm him in a tight space where we couldn't really move around. Once we reached Broward General Hospital, I decided to stay in Norm's room on a cot. He was totally out of it, wild-eyed and trying to pull out all his medical tubes, and I needed to be there when he became coherent. This would be our home for the next week.

I cannot praise the staff of this rescue operation enough. The only glitch was that our luggage was diverted after the ship docked. For a week, I wore the same clothes I had on when we abandoned the ship and I had to wash out my underwear at night and hope it was dry to wear in the morning. The suitcases arrived the day we flew back to Seattle, with Norm, a nurse and oxygen equipment in first class and me in the back.

When we finally arrived at Horizon House, Norm went to the Supported Living (SL) section, and I gave our traveling nurse a goodbye hug before heading to our own apartment and to bed. The SL would be Norm's home for his remaining years. I was no longer able to take care of him myself.

❖

MY DAILY ROUTINE IN 2012 changed substantially. I went back and forth regularly to SL, taking Norm out in a wheelchair for appointments and to the hospital to visit his younger brother, Ted. On Sundays, I brought him home to our apartment in the late afternoon for dinner together. He was always trying to trick me into letting him lie down for just a bit, but I knew I would not be able to get him back up, so I stood firm that he had to go back upstairs if he needed to rest. He never quit trying.

That May, the AIA Convention was in Washington, D.C. By now, sister-in-law Norma was my regular stand-in for Norm and she knew most of our friends. The convocation ball would be held in the National Building Museum, the old Pension Building with its grand interior space, and it was worth the expensive tickets.

The hall that night was filled with middle-aged and older men, handsome in their tuxedos, plus the wives of the officers in stylish formal dresses. It was really a men's party plus Norma and me—a pair of older women without escorts. We ordered martinis at the bar and as we walked away, the bartender called us back, saying he had forgotten something. Our drinks included the olive and onion, so we were perplexed about what was missing. The dinner went well with lovely wine, and then it was time to head back to the hotel. I remember getting on the bus but absolutely nothing more until we were in the lobby with our friends, who commented on what a happy time we were having. I hadn't had much to drink and was sure I was not drunk. But something was definitely wrong.

In our room I found Norma half-undressed and lying on the floor, completely out of it. I had known my sister-in-law for more than fifty years and this was a first. I helped her undress and somehow got her into bed. Then, it was my turn to dissolve into my bed and sleep. In the morning, we both woke up bright and cheery, feeling fine. What had caused both of us to have mental blackouts from the previous evening? It dawned on me that the bartender must have laced our drinks with a date-rape drug. Perhaps he thought he would give a couple of the old boys in our group a night to remember—and one the two of us would completely forget. It was an unsettling, bizarre experience, and fortunately, my loyal long-term colleagues made sure we got back safely that night.

❖

THE FOURTH OF JULY was just around the corner, and we wondered how we would handle the holiday gathering with Norm needing so much care. Charlie Carley, a caregiver from the Home Instead senior care organization, came to the rescue. He agreed to take Norm and me to the beach for several days to enjoy the festivities and fireworks. He took us on a drive up and down the beach in his four-wheel-drive truck, and while generally, Norm and I had never approved of cars on the beach, this ride was an exception. Norm was delighted and giggled throughout. Where else could you view over twenty miles of fireworks bursting through the night and for several days? Laurie and Norma arrived for our grand party, which included neighbors and numerous friends whose tents covered the back and front lawns. Norm sat in his wheelchair on the deck wrapped up in blankets for hours, taking in the scene. This would be his last trip to Willapad.

At the end of July, Norm's brother, Ted, received the French Legion of Honor Medal from the French consul for his service to France during World War II. As a pilot, Ted flew forty-plus bombing raids from England. The ceremony took place at the Johnstons' Des Moines retirement home and was covered by the evening TV news.

That year, the Horizon House trip committee, which I chaired, decided to repeat the popular 2004 Lewis and Clark trip to the mouth of the Columbia River. Our friend Ron Barclay had moved from Bellevue to a large, delightful house on the bay side of the Long Beach peninsula on the serene property of a former rhododendron nursery. Extensive landscape gardens remained, and our group enjoyed a picnic served from the dining room table that had been ours until we downsized and moved into Horizon House. After this trip, all our committee heard was, "When will you do it again?"

With the SL staff taking care of Norm, I was able to join the Horizon House Salt Spring Island trip, which we had been planning for some time. Norma agreed to be my roommate, and we looked forward to finally dining at the island's famous Hastings House. Our last name had always raised the question, were we related? Of course we weren't, but we had to visit our renowned namesake.

Four of us, including Betty and Roz, decided to splurge on the to-die-for meal. Our experience stretched from the moment the dining room opened to closing time, a good five hours. We had it all, from cocktails to after-dinner drinks, plus all the wonderful courses in between. Then Norma announced that the dinner was Eileen's treat. Eileen was Norma's Canadian mother, who would have wholeheartedly supported our folly. We were just sorry she was no longer with us to enjoy the grand evening.

In October, we planned to rest up before the holidays. But then the doctor decided to move Norm's catheter connection into his bladder. On the day of the simple surgery, Norm felt fine. Four days later he was in emergency surgery because his colon had been punctured during the previous operation. Norm was in critical condition and remained in the hospital and nursing care until well into December. The doctor responsible will always be remembered for his negligence. There would be no Washington, D.C., trip for either of us that year.

After a few small, quiet holiday celebrations, I spent New Year's Eve packing up Christmas decorations and hoping 2013 would be a better year for Norm and for me.

❖

THAT YEAR, the Horizon House trip committee planned another Alaska cruise. It was so easy with the bus dropping us off and picking us up at the dock, and Norm wanted badly to make one more trip. I considered what it would take to pay a caregiver to accompany us. If I went through a nursing agency, that would require paying for three people to rotate through eight-hour shifts—a staggering cost. Our Horizon House staff were ineligible, so I asked Charlie if he knew anyone. The answer: "Yes. Me." He had never been on a cruise and had always wanted the experience. Perfect! Norm was thrilled. Our group of approximately twenty people included two other residents in wheelchairs.

Jane and Norm's last cruise to Alaska, accompanied by Charlie Carley

Our accessible stateroom was a double cabin and provided a real bonus—a double deck. Norm and Charlie had the king bed while I took the sofa bed, and a butler came in with snacks and extra service. What an arrangement: three men and extra service! Norm loved the time on the deck in his wheelchair. After dinner he went to bed, while Charlie and I took in the shows. We had visited all the ports on previous trips, so Norm and I stayed on board to enjoy the deck while Charlie took in the sights. In Skagway, I insisted that Charlie should leave early for the famous train ride up the mountainside. That afternoon we wheeled Norm into town so he could shop for small gifts for his "girlfriends." He had always brought back mementos from our many trips over the years to give the women on his UW staff; now the gifts were for his nurses and caregivers. He never forgot the women.

One special moment came on deck when we went up Tracy Arm into a sea of floating ice breaking off the glacier at the head. Over our many Alaska cruises, this was our first visit to Tracy Arm. The weather for this early June sailing was unusually warm and sunny—even hot in Skagway. The whole trip was a great success and Norm could hardly wait to give his report to his new friends in SL upon our return.

❖

WE MUST TAKE A MOMENT to shine a light on Charlie Carley, who became so important in our lives. He grew up in Boston and came west with his partner, Lane, who had family in Eastern Washington. Charlie was an MIT grad with a Ph.D., a computer nerd, a diabetic who watched his diet carefully, and a successful businessman who had sold his company to his employees. After moving to the Seattle area, he managed several businesses on his computer, including Lane's family farms, but he needed an activity to get him out of the house. So he took up caregiving.

He started working at Horizon House as a caregiver for Pat, who kept him on his toes with her wit and challenges, and he quickly became as much a part of Horizon House as any staff or resident. When we discovered his computer skills, his popularity exploded. He was a dream come true for Norm, who enjoyed every conversation as well as Charlie's thoughtful care. We introduced him to the University of Washington and other Seattle landmarks, and he became a part of our extended Hastings family. To complete our circle of connections, he purchased a house in West Seattle just one door down from my first home, where I had lived as an infant.

❖

THAT SUMMER, after Norma and I attended the AIA Convention in Denver, our family regrouped for the July Fourth holiday week at Willapad—this time without Norm. We called him daily to tell him about our activities, but we missed him. It was time to make decisions about the future of our beloved beach house.

And our surrogate son Roger was finally marrying Stacey, the girl who had lost him to another in college and waited many years to reclaim him. Roger, with three grown children, and Stacey, with four, made their commitment in an outdoor waterfront wedding on the Kitsap Peninsula. It was too difficult to get Norm to the celebration, but the important thing was that Stacey had relieved Norm of the responsibility of looking after this talented man-child. Stacey would keep Roger focused on his career for the good of their family, and Norm could rest easy about Roger's future.

Then in early August we lost Lesley Watson, the most positive person I have ever known. She was our miracle woman, and like sister-in-law Norma, she beat all the odds, refusing to give up and living on for more adventures. At our age, we are used to people leaving us, but some of them will forever be part of our daily lives. The memories of Lesley's beautiful smile and her "There is nothing wrong with me—life is wonderful!" attitude continue to brighten my days.

That fall, our Horizon House group enjoyed a trip to Eastern Washington wine country, glowing with sunny days that lit up the leaves turning all shades of reds and golds. My old friend Mable Buller from the Daly firm days joined us for the jaunt over the Cascade Mountains to check out the tasting rooms and museums.

And we had one more wedding to celebrate that year: Charlie and his long-time love, Lane, decided to make it official. Their Horizon House friends insisted the ceremony should be held in our Sky Lounge so we could meet their extended families. What a handsome couple they were in their tuxes, polished shoes, and boutonnieres!

The year wrapped up on a sad note with Norm's younger brother, Ted, leaving us in November. Ted's memorial service was just before Christmas. Our holiday dinner in 2013 was a small gathering at Horizon House, with Norma, Laurie, and my longtime good friend Shirley Anderson joining Norm and me.

❖

THE WINTER OLYMPICS brought an exciting distraction at the beginning of 2014, with some of my favorite sports—ice skating and skiing—keeping me close to the TV. But I knew I needed to turn my focus to saying goodbye to Willapad. Our beach neighbors' spring garage sale gave us a good start at getting it ready to sell.

Norma and I took time out from beach-house cleanup in June to attend the AIA Convention in Chicago, which included an architectural tour via river boat through the city's downtown core. It was a great way to see and photograph the city's architecture on a beautiful day and gave me a new perspective on Chicago.

All of us girls were at the ocean for July Fourth, but it didn't fully sink in that this celebration would be our last at Willapad. We picked through items that family members wanted, and I selected a real estate agent. Her initial suggested asking price was low because the house did not have granite counters or carpeted floors, but I kept reminding her, "This is a beach house." It was never meant to be a city house in the sand. It was not going to appeal to everyone, but I knew the right person would come along and appreciate it for what it was. I held firm on my price.

I was not in a hurry and didn't list it until after Labor Day, assuming it would not move until the next summer.

❖

NORMA AND I CONTINUED TO ENJOY traveling together, and we joined the Horizon House tour to the Broken Islands on the west coast of Vancouver Island. This trip took us back to the town where Norma had lived as a teenager working a summer in a salmon cannery. In the many decades since, the area had become more of a place to play than to work. Retirees built dream vacation homes on these tiny islands that are served by a mail boat, and kayakers came to explore and camp during the summer. We enjoyed visiting the wildlife parks—including a parrot sanctuary of over a thousand birds (and an unbelievable noise level)—and a logging camp accessed by a little steam railroad.

Also in 2014, the second edition of *Shaping Seattle Architecture* was published by University of Washington Press. Years earlier, I had been interviewed for inclusion in this new edition. Because the first edition in 1994 included essays on only deceased architects, I was interested to see how large the second edition would be after adding some living architects important to Seattle design history. When I finally received a published copy, I was stunned to find that only three of us had been included: Fred Bassetti, who unfortunately passed away before the book was published; landscape architect Richard Haag; and me. My first thought was, what would my good friend Arne Bystrom think? In the end, I decided that many of the legendary male architects were still making contributions to the built environment, while I was retired and getting up in years. The book included so many colleagues who had been supportive friends throughout my career, and I was honored to be recognized among them.

The year had one more exciting moment in store for us: On December 2, the day before Norm's ninety-sixth birthday, the Johnston-Hastings families attended the ribbon-cutting ceremony at the University of Washington Gould Hall for the opening of three new galleries honoring UW alums. The center gallery carried our names, Johnston and Hastings, with the Jim Olson gallery to the left and the George Suyama gallery on the right. Charlie and Todd, our great-nephew visiting from Australia, helped get Norm there, lifting him from the car into his wheelchair. Back on campus, Norm held court, greeting and visiting with many former students and colleagues. This would be Norm's last outing.

21 | THE HARD GOODBYES

Portraits of Norm and Jane created by architect Gerry Pomeroy, a UW alum

THE NEW YEAR OF 2015 brought welcome, yet bittersweet, news: Willapad had sold for the price I had insisted on, and it sold for cash. It would take a lot of work in a very short time to move everything out, but Norman gladly accepted the change. He would no longer need to worry about me maintaining the property or traveling back and forth on my own. His two biggest concerns were resolved: Roger Long was happily married and in Stacey's good care, and with the beach house sold, I could settle in to enjoy life at Horizon House with our many friends.

Now, he could just relax and go to sleep, which is what he did on the sixteenth of March, two days after the sale was final. I spent the last six hours of his life with him, holding his hand and reminiscing about our wonderful times together. We shared so many special moments all over the world—far more than could be contained in any book. I especially cherished the travels that were just for us, like our fortieth anniversary cruise across a Bering Sea as smooth as glass, and the places that were "ours," like Old Ebbitt Grill in Washington, D.C., the setting for many happy birthday celebrations. That last night, Norm's lovely blue eyes were wide open, and I like to think that he heard me. At 10:30 p.m., they closed his eyes, and I stayed until midnight when the mortuary staff arrived to take him on his last ride. Norman was finally at rest. We had shared forty-six and a half years of a great partnership, in all arenas of our lives.

❖

IT WOULD TAKE TIME to prepare memorials to honor Norm in his beloved Horizon House and University of Washington communities, and we scheduled the events for the end of May. In the meantime, I had only a month to clean out Willapad for its new owners—a project that required a lot of help.

Charlie and Lane drove their truck to the beach to haul the artwork and other items back to Seattle. Laurie and I used her car over three days to deliver books and household items to the local library, senior center, and nonprofit thrift shops. Brenda Hill and her crew took several truckloads to her Trading Post antique store in Ocean Park. Over the years she had purchased many of my treasures, including my doll collection, linens, cookware, and jewelry. Now I had to part with some of my most precious items, including my beautiful basket collection and grandmother BB's cast iron skillets and Dutch oven, which had prepared my meals from day one. Without the skillets, there would be no more Dutch babies for breakfast. With the truck and car full, we said goodbye to our oceanfront escape and headed back to Seattle.

Just two days after I had to give up Willapad, my Seattle home was disrupted, too, as Horizon House prepared to install a new north wall building skin. While scaffolding went up outside my windows, two women removed everything on the inside of the exterior walls, as well as many items on the floor nearby, and packed them up to store during the construction. Then came the plastic, wrapped inside and outside, and I started a year of life in a sort of summer igloo. I knew what to expect, but many residents were convinced they could not survive the experience. The exterior surface was essentially removed down to the interior plasterboard, and new insulation, windows and exterior cladding were installed. The contractor learned a lot during the work, and the subsequent south wall project would be completed much more quickly.

In mid-May, Laurie accompanied me to the AIA Convention in Atlanta, where I met Donna Dunay to offer assistance, or at least moral support, for the upcoming eighteenth UIFA Congress in Washington, D.C., and Blacksburg, Virginia. Yes, I would be there to celebrate the thirtieth anniversary of the International Archive of

Women in Architecture (IAWA). UW architectural librarian Betty Wagner planned to go with me because she wanted to see what she could learn from the archive to apply to a future UW program.

But first, it was time to say a proper goodbye to Norm.

❖

AT HORIZON HOUSE on Saturday, May 30, Norm's first memorial gathering brought together a room full of his closest family and friends. Former fellow UW architecture professor and Horizon House resident Grant Hildebrand spoke first about his long friendship with Norm. Then nephew Jay Johnston of Kodiak spoke for the Johnston family, and niece Laurie shared memories for the Hastings family. Norm's former student Roger, who spent so many nights on our sofa, came up from his San Francisco home and spoke deep from his heart, filling eyes and cheeks around the room with tears. Charlie curated the slideshow and Norma baked about 600 of Norm's favorite coconut butter cookies for the reception.

The next day, we moved the beautiful flower arrangement designed by Horizon House caregiver Tomasi to the UW Faculty Club on the UW campus for the second service. The Architecture School dean spoke of Norm's contributions to the university, which spanned more than thirty years of teaching and produced five books, including *Washington's Audacious State Capitol and its Builders*, an award-winning history of Norm's hometown, where his father supervised the construction of the state Capitol. Norm also wrote a book celebrating the campus centennial: *The Fountain & the Mountain: The University of Washington Campus, 1895-1995*. Lawyer and colleague Allen Miller remembered Norm's Olympia connections and military service. Our good friend Betty Wagner spoke about his love and support of the UW Libraries, and Allied Arts of Seattle's Alice Rooney spoke of Norm's role in founding the organization.

Finally, I said a few words about the real Norm. A lot of people at the UW service probably didn't know that Norm had many cherished women friends throughout his life—from his earliest school days, from his time in the Army in Nome, and through his career—and he kept in touch with most of them. He was adored by the AIA women spouses, whom he treated to memorable tours and lectures in Seattle and in cities around the country, and most importantly, he was adored by my mother. He was certainly her most appreciative son. Of course, I was surrounded by male friends throughout my life, and so this was just another one of the many ways we complemented each other in our long and beautiful partnership.

There was so much lovely food, and our friend Dan Streissguth said, "It was the nicest memorial service I have ever attended." The new Gould Hall gallery also featured a monthlong exhibit of Norm's work and writings, with a special Sunday opening for those attending the service.

At a family dinner party at Horizon House afterward, thirteen of us enjoyed a lovely evening telling Norm stories celebrating his almost ninety-seven years, the longest life of anyone in the Johnston family.

❖

IN JULY, BETTY AND I TRAVELED to Washington, D.C., for the eighteenth UIFA Congress. We first toured Union Station near our hotel, and then set off for Old Ebbitt Grill, which was packed. We ate perched on stools at the end of the bar, where the excellent bartender entertained us for hours. I wanted to introduce Betty to my D.C. haunts, and our next stop was the roof deck of the Hotel Washington for an after-dinner drink and view of the city lights. But too many changes over the years had taken away the charm of the place. I've never been back, preferring to enjoy my memories from the early 1980s.

During the event, we enjoyed touring the National Museum of American History, the National Portrait Gallery, and the Library of Congress, where we saw early Charles and Ray Eames designs. At the evening receptions, I greeted old friends from around the world, and made new ones like sisters Misti and Rose, young women architects from D.C. who we enjoyed visiting with throughout the week. Almost every evening after dinner, we joined them at the bar for a nightcap. One dinner was at the AIA headquarters, where Linda Banks and I had hosted UIFA more than twenty-five years earlier.

After the D.C. festivities, our group boarded a bus for Blacksburg, with a stop in Charlottesville to tour University of Virginia buildings designed by Thomas Jefferson. That night, we enjoyed a reception and program at Virginia Tech highlighting thirty women architects, including me and fellow Seattleite Jean Young. The next day, we visited the Special Collections in the college library, which housed thirty years of UIFA-accumulated records from women architects. Betty and I were blown away by the large space, the flat files, and the special care in managing this collection. I felt good about my materials being archived there. Virginia Tech set a high bar for the UW to aspire to.

Our last day at Virginia Tech included breakfast in the Architecture School building, a walk to the horticulture garden for lunch—interrupted by a cloudburst that sent us scampering for buses—and a stop by the international award-winning solar Lumen Haus. That night, we enjoyed a special showing of the movie *Lilia!*, which tells the story of Lilia Sofer Skala, an Austrian stage actress who fled the Nazis, labored in a New York zipper factory, studied and practiced architecture, and finally worked her way back to the stage and silver screen to collect Oscar and Emmy award nominations. Her portfolio as an architecture student is in the IAWA. Dinner with Misti and Rose plus our evening bar ritual completed our last day, and then we had to say our goodbyes to the girls.

The next day, we joined a smaller group on a bus that traveled north through West Virginia, stopping at the New River Gorge Bridge, the longest and highest steel arch bridge in the Western Hemisphere. It brought back memories of my childhood fascination watching the construction of Seattle's Aurora Bridge from my grandparents' porch.

After meandering through narrow backroads, we arrived at the Seven Springs Mountain Resort. We were in the Pennsylvania mountains, so we were told, but that was a hard sell for us Northwesterners used to the heights of the Cascade Range.

Our first outing was to the Flight 93 National Memorial, the crash site of the plane that passengers took over during the 9/11 attacks, saving the U.S. Capitol, which was the terrorists' intended target. The visitors' center was unfinished but the rest of the exhibit was complete, highlighting stories of the lost heroes. The design was handsome and created an emotional experience; it demanded quiet time in the expansive open field. It was impossible to leave without feeling changed by the visit.

We also toured Frank Lloyd Wright's last work, the Kentuck Knob house built in the mid-1950s, where we noted several deviations from the master's touch. Apparently, the owner succeeded on a few design points or FLW was just too tired to fight. It was in beautiful condition but certainly not a place I would choose to live.

The next day, we traveled to our main destination, Fallingwater, where we toured the main building and the recently refurbished guesthouse and pool. I could have enjoyed a few nights in that guesthouse! Of course, changes had been made since my last visit almost thirty years earlier during a formal dinner, and we were no longer allowed along the stream to take in the full impact of looking up at the structure.

Our trip continued through Maryland and West Virginia to our final stop: Winchester, Virginia, a lovely town with a rich history. Across from our hotel stood a statue of George Washington as a young man next to the little building where he worked as a surveyor. Local architects toured us through several old structures plus a wonderful new children's museum before plying us with food and drink. We thanked our excursion's hosts: Donna Dunay, her husband, Bob, and Paola Zellner, who I was delighted to discover was a former student and employee of my own former student and employee Norm Millar. Yet another example of how old connections resurface and renew throughout life.

❖

MY NEXT TASK was to establish an endowment at the University of Washington Libraries in Norman's honor for the preservation of historic architectural drawings and other materials in the collection. Our gift would support an archivist to document and organize the materials already in the collection that Norm and Betty had encouraged architects to donate over the years. I was sure Norman would approve.

That fall, former AIA Executive Director Marga Rose Hancock and several UW students decided to honor the women AIA Fellows. Our local chapter wanted to create a presentation for the AIA Women's Summit in Seattle, and Sue Alden, Karen Braitmayer, Jenny Sue Brown, Janet Donelson, Carolyn Geise, Sharon Sutton, and I were selected to record oral-history interviews. This was a great opportunity for our group of elders to catch up and reconnect.

The summit reunited me with women from the UIFA Congress, as well as an AIA staff member and friend of over 30 years, Beverly Willis, FAIA, who was sponsoring a foundation for women designers in New York. I had not seen Bev since we became fellows together in 1980. The most impressive part of the summit was all the talented young women in attendance. They will ultimately shape our future.

❖

THE FINAL ACT TO HONOR NORM that year was a holiday cruise up the Amazon River. Norm and I had wanted to do this trip, but we didn't make it. Norma and Laurie were happy to join me, and my luggage included small packages of his ashes, destined for a famous opera house that he never got to visit. On December 22, we flew to Rio de Janeiro, where we enjoyed a bus tour of the city before boarding our ship. The next year, Brazil would host the Summer Olympic Games, and it seemed impossible that the facilities would be ready in time for the opening.

Our first two days at sea were Christmas Eve and Christmas Day, relaxing and festive before our first port call at Recife. I was sorry our cruise skipped Salvador because it was one of my favorites when I visited in 1983, but Recife was rich in history from its 1588 convent's Golden Chapel, finished in gold leaf, to a reconstructed 1640 synagogue used for weddings. Next, we traveled to Olinda, founded by the Portuguese in 1535 and now a UNESCO World Heritage site, where we toured the old slave market, the cathedral and colonial houses. At the beach, a natural breakwater formed a lovely endless swimming pool, which the whole town seemed to be enjoying on the holiday.

We spent two more days at sea along the coast before starting up the Amazon, and then several days traveling up the muddy river to reach our destination on New Year's Day, 2016: Manaus at the intersection of the Black and Amazon rivers. The Black River is a completely different water system in color, aquatic inhabitants, and acidity, with an insect-free environment that makes it a desirable and hospitable location for the city of Manaus, which included many high-rise buildings.

The city tour included the residential district, modern buildings, and most importantly the 125-year-old Amazon Theatre, the opera house in Manaus. Inside, I felt like I was right back in Europe. It was uncomfortably warm, but I had a great time photographing the ceiling, floor, boxes, seats, stage, foyer, and views out the windows. Then we went out to the garden, a generous space around the building, where I photographed the exterior of this special building in the middle of the jungle. I imagined the European opera singers who boarded the old ships without stabilizers for a rough crossing across the Atlantic, then traveled up the river to sing in productions, only to then reverse their journey. Opera demands strong, healthy singers, and the life of a traveling opera singer was not an easy one. Before we left, we worked Norm's ashes into the soil around the garden's roses and other plants. We hoped he would be able to hear the music.

Our second day, while our ship was docked, we took small boats down the river to see lily pads so enormous that people can stand on them. In the river, the black water did not mix with the muddy water from the Amazon, so the surface was striped. We transferred to canoe-like boats with small outboard motors and canvas awnings for our trip through smaller winding channels to a restaurant barge structure close to the lily pads. The rainy season was about to start, which would refill the river like a major flood, and we experienced the season premiere, which quickly soaked us to the skin. Before long, we had to take turns bailing out water as the boat filled up, and they ferried us back in larger boats for our return. One woman was wearing an expensive safari outfit, and the blouse became transparent in the rain. She laughed and said, "I'm certainly glad I wore a bra today." It took days in the hot sun for my water-soaked shoes to dry out.

We worked our way down the river, which often had a depth of only four feet, and I was surprised we made it. I overhead a conversation with the river pilot who had changed our schedule because he refused to sail through one area at night. The striped water, which became narrower, continued toward the Atlantic Ocean.

Back at sea, our next ports were St. Lucia, St. Barts, and Puerto Rico. With rain behind us, we could enjoy our tours and history lessons. Our last call was at Nassau in the Bahamas, where we could see the resort towns were suffering—overbuilt and dealing with an overabundance of competition. It clearly wasn't all wonderful in paradise.

❖

AT HOME IN SEATTLE, I learned that my dear longtime friend Gretchen had passed away the night before I returned. I had seen her before I left to give her a Christmas gift and my itinerary so she could follow our travels. I knew her health was failing, but she had been alert and cheery as we chatted. I'm sure she willed her departure so she would not be an inconvenience to others. We had enjoyed so many fun experiences together during our single years, swimming and skiing together starting in our university days. Her marriage and the years afterward had not been easy, while I enjoyed a long and happy marriage. I couldn't help but feel badly because she deserved better.

The staff had cleaned out her apartment quickly to make way for the next resident and called me to pick up a box of her belongings. What a trip down memory lane! There were pictures of my smiling friend in her ice-skating costume, receiving awards or posing for publicity shots. This is how I first knew her, through these splashy photos, before we met in our Architecture Appreciation class. I put some items aside for the university collection, and saved special photos and knick-knacks for myself. It was wintertime, and the TV sports featured ice-skating competitions, which we had often watched together, with Gretchen always explaining the difference between the jumps.

❖

THAT SPRING, A BARGAIN TRIP TO DUBAI was impossible to resist, and Betty and Mable agreed to join me. We flew to Los Angeles to board a sixteen-hour nonstop flight to Dubai. What a contrast to the multiple stops on my first cross-country flight to New York in 1952! The time passed quickly as we traveled across the globe watching our favorite old movies starring Spencer Tracy, Katharine Hepburn, Gary Cooper, and Cary Grant.

In Dubai, we landed at the huge new airport, sparkling clean and nearly empty of people. Our long flight was followed by a bus ride to Abu Dhabi, the capital of the United Arab Emirates and a city that was just fifty years old.

The next day, our tour of the city included the magnificent Sheikh Zayed Grand Mosque, built of white marble and designed to accommodate forty thousand worshipers. On the long marble approach to the building, Betty stepped aside for a photo and fell flat on her face. She hadn't noticed the 2-inch difference in levels, and her two front teeth were knocked out by the impact, her scarlet blood a stark contrast on the white marble. An attendant rushed to her rescue and took her to the infirmary while the rest of us stayed to take in the architectural wonder. Back at the hotel, I was surprised to find Betty ready to join our evening dinner cruise. She was determined not to miss another event.

On our own the next day, we visited the new islands constructed from rubble collected from the demolition of many buildings that were only twenty years old. The local sand in the concrete was leaching salt, making the older buildings unattractive. As one building was torn down, a new high-rise would take its place. Money was certainly not an obstacle in this oil-rich country. Lofty cultural ambitions included museums, concert halls, and a visitor center featuring the future of the UAE—all designed by the leading world architects.

The next day we drove back to Dubai though miles of carefully planted small trees, each with their own water nipple intended to make the capital the greenest city in the world. I doubt this will happen in my lifetime. Dubai's buildings feature wild designs, with curves, twists, slopes, slants, projections, voids—just about any unusual design element imaginable. Each building seemed to scream, "Look at me!" We visited the top of the tallest building in the world, or at least it was at that moment.

On the other extreme, we took the Musandam Cruise across to Oman, traveling through the old world of stone houses and fishing villages along a shoreline lined with caves, mountains, and beaches. Oman, like Yemen, provided a study of contrasts between the oldest parts of civilization and the shiny glitz of the nearby modern cities.

Betty still had one small bag of Norman's ashes, which we scattered in the Gulf of Oman. This completed twelve deposits: Norm's Montlake house, the four homes we had shared (the 1891 Fremont house, our Laurelhurst home, Willapad on the ocean and Horizon House), several of his favorite spots on the University of Washington campus, the state Capitol campus in Olympia, Alaska (representing his World War II years), and the Manaus Opera House in Brazil. It was fitting that Norm's final resting places reflected the far-reaching experiences, interests, and contributions he had throughout his long life.

Jane with former women AIA Chancellors and Presidents at the National AIA Convention in New York City, St. Patrick's Cathedral, 2018.

22 | MY NINTH DECADE

FOR MANY YEARS, one of my holiday traditions has been to write a Christmas letter, sharing work and travel adventures, as well as the joys and sorrows of each year, with family and friends. And while I have let go of the work of hosting caroling parties around a candlelit tree, I still give myself the annual holiday assignment of drafting a letter.

In writing this book, I have drawn on this archive of letters, along with letters I wrote from Germany in the 1950s to my family (my mother saved almost all of them). I did not realize when I wrote them, of course, that these letters to loved ones would become such a valuable archive of memories, allowing me to recall people, places and events in near real-time detail. In my younger years, my discipline allowed me to achieve my goals of becoming an architect and traveling the globe. Now, halfway through my ninth decade, it turns out the discipline of writing and saving these letters has helped me share my story with the world.

Looking back on these most recent years before and after my ninetieth birthday in 2018, here are a few more treasured memories from the archive to share:

❖

2016

PAOLA FROM VIRGINIA TECH arrived in mid-March for the national meeting of the Schools of Architecture, where she presented the program on women architects from the 2015 UIFA Congress. Betty and I made sure Paola saw some of the most interesting local architectural sights: the Space Needle, the UW campus, Stephen Holl's chapel at Seattle University, and the Monorail. And during the event, Betty and I crashed lectures, caught up with local friends, and got reacquainted with faculty friends who had moved on to other institutions. It was like going back to school. Unfortunately, Paola's former teacher/boss and my former student/employee

Norm Millar from Woodbury University could not attend the conference, and soon after, he passed away. Such a great loss for the architectural profession.

In May, Betty and I were roommates again, this time at the AIA Convention in Philadelphia, a city with so much history. The convention took over an old railroad station, which required miles and miles of walking. It seemed like each year, the conventions got more crowded and required more walking, but perhaps that is just a sign of my getting older.

Unfortunately, these gatherings were followed by a great loss: My closest and longest friend, Shirley Cooke Anderson, suffered a massive stroke. At least we knew she had been happy her last morning; she simply checked out after breakfast, going to sleep in her chair. I was in her hospital room with Betty and her son, Ross, to say goodbye.

Shirley and I met during high school in 1944 and became roommates in 1948 when we were both working our way through university. We were two Depression-era girls with big dreams—medicine and architecture—and came from families who could not afford to pay for college. We had a bond that lasted for life, and we were always there for each other at a moment's notice, no questions asked.

Later in life, we enjoyed many trips around the world with our husbands and friends. In my more recent trips, I've thought often of my fellow travelers who have made their last journeys—how Shirley would have loved this town, or Norm would have enjoyed a special walk or historic site. Yes, I do miss you!

That summer, we set aside time to remember Shirley. In July, the remaining five Dragon Ladies—Sue Harris Alden, Connie Ritter, Betty Wagner, sister-in-law Norma and I—met up with other friends for a Crab Louie dinner and lots of conversation. We couldn't help but wonder: Who would be the next one to drop out? The Anderson family also hosted a dinner celebration for their mother's longtime friends. I spoke as the person who had known Shirley the longest, and several of us shared wonderful stories about our summer adventures on the *Principia*, the Andersons' 96-foot yacht. The ten or so of us on board always competed to prepare the most exotic meals on our long weekends cruising the Salish Sea.

In fall 2016, I attended UW's Recognition Gala, an annual event where the sight of everyone in party dress in the beautiful Suzzallo Library reading room was the real attraction. A couple of days later Betty and I joined our Horizon House friends on a weeklong cruise to San Francisco and back by way of Victoria, B.C.

Donald Hanberg and Jane during Don's last visit to Seattle

We passed by our old beach house along the way. After we docked in San Francisco, we met up with Roger and Stacey Long in a little neighborhood Italian restaurant for a memorable meal and long conversation about their new life in the city. They both seemed very happy with their jobs and with each other, and still acted like newly-weds. Norman, they are just fine; you do not need to worry about Roger as Stacey has it all under control.

Later that fall, Betty joined the three Hastings girls—Norma, Laurie and me—on an East Coast cruise to enjoy the fall colors. We flew to Newark, where we were supposed to be picked up and transported to our ship, but we found ourselves forgotten for hours in a New Jersey station. It was almost time for the ship to sail when a van finally arrived to take us to New York. We went on a wild ride through the streets of Newark and other towns to reach the waiting ship, and we were practically thrown aboard.

We arrived in Newport, Rhode Island, the next morning. Earlier in the summer, I had reached out to old friend Donald Hanberg, who was living in Connecticut and no longer well enough to make his annual trip to the West Coast. He had a driver who could bring him to Newport for lunch. Betty, Donald, and I had a great time laughing about our past adventures. It was a special afternoon, and we knew we probably would never see Donald again. Oh, this aging process is not fun.

Boston was our next port of call, and the best sight was revisiting H.H. Richardson's Trinity Church, where I had presided over the 1992 Investiture of AIA Fellows when I was Chancellor. Laurie, Norma, and I all groaned, remembering the high heat and humidity that made us feel as if we had stepped out of a lake.

Our ship stopped in Halifax, Nova Scotia, and then cruised along the coast and into the mouth of the St. Lawrence River to visit Charlottetown, Prince Edward Island; Gaspe, Quebec; and up an inlet to Saguenay. There we enjoyed an elaborate stage production telling the story of Quebec, starting with the First Nations, then the immigrants, and through two world wars to present. Horses, chickens, ducks, goats, cows, cars, tanks, and cannons were just some of the props, with guns and explosions punctuating the events on the stage. This unforgettable community program is presented year-round in French and English, and the child performers are all home-schooled to keep school schedules from interfering with the production.

Our tour finished with stops in Quebec City and Montreal. Norma especially enjoyed the trip back to this eastern part of her homeland, where her Irish family had started out in Canada before making their way west to Vancouver.

Back in Seattle, there was another memorial service to attend, in honor of longtime architect friend Morris Jellison. Morris had arrived at UW with five other transfer students from Montana about 1949 and upon graduation in '52 he became my coworker at Boeing and a fellow carpooler. I had advised him on his house remodeling, and he was a regular on our backpacking trips. Morris was always smiling and he loved to sing, be it in the church choir, around a campfire or next to a Christmas tree. He played my little reed organ for fifty years at our annual caroling party. At his service, I was again the one who had known Morris the longest, and his family thanked me for sharing stories they had never heard Morris tell.

For Thanksgiving, our group of six widows and niece Laurie embraced a new tradition, trading kitchen prep work for a carefree dinner at the Women's University Club. We even got to go home with leftovers just like before.

In December, Laurie traveled with me to Washington, D.C., for the annual AIA meeting. We arrived a day early because we wanted to see the newly opened National Museum of African American History & Culture on the Mall. I had been told that tickets wouldn't be available until March, but I decided to try anyway. The morning we arrived, there was no line in sight. When a guard asked if we had tickets, we said "no," and he handed us two. We were in. My hip was bothering me, so we got a wheelchair and went to the top of the building to do the exhibit in reverse, which worked out well. While we were enjoying lunch, a large group of students arrived and went straight to the top floor for exhibits on Michael Jackson and other pop-culture figures. We had the lower floors mostly to ourselves.

❖

2017

AS THE NEW YEAR BEGAN, I was planning for both hip surgery and the centennial anniversary of Fauntleroy School, my alma mater. Early in the year, Betty and I

Fauntleroy grads (Jane '39, Jim & Lou Whittaker '41, Laurie '65) at the school's centennial celebration

enjoyed a lecture by architect Maya Lin and we were invited to join her at a special reception beforehand.

The hip replacement surgery was a piece of cake, and the real benefit was that the good Dr. Flugstad lengthened my leg. I was eighty-nine years old and "even" at last. Best of all, the improvement to my back allowed me to stand longer for chorale performances.

While recovering, I focused on planning for the speakers at our Fauntleroy School centennial celebration in May. Three of us old Fauntleroy kids—Jim Whittaker, Robert Skotheim, and me—had been inducted into the West Seattle High School Hall of Fame, so we were to be the main attraction. (We didn't know it yet, but Lou Whittaker would also be inducted to the hall of fame that year.) A local historian had challenged me to get the Whittaker twins together at any event. No problem! Jim of Mount Everest fame arrived from Port Townsend and Lou came from Mount Rainier. Their older brother, Barney, in his 90s, had planned to attend but didn't feel up to it. Only we locals ever seemed to know that there were actually three Whittaker boys.

On May 21 the sun shone as several hundred of us gathered in the front yard of Fauntleroy School for a group-hug photo. When Jim and I went to the stage, he called Lou up to join us, and the three of us told many stories from the 1930s. Old school photos, architecture plans, and memorabilia filled the former classrooms and hall, and the event was a great success, reuniting families and friends for a magical day. Once it was over, I would miss my monthly planning meetings with many childhood friends, as well as the new ones I made through the project.

In September, Mable Buller, Betty, and I flew to Kalispell, Montana, to depart on a tour of the Canadian Rockies. Our group took a bus to enjoy the views on the Going to the Sun Road in Glacier National Park, then retraced our route to avoid wildfires and crossed the Canadian border to Banff and Lake Louise. My previous visit had been fifty-some years earlier, so I was not surprised that there were many changes. This was another bad year for forest fires and the smell was always with us. After a long drive through scorched land, we arrived in the small town of Jasper, where we joined in the glacier walk on the way to our modest housing. Mount Robson was visible in full sun—a rare treat. We left some of Herb Buller's ashes there in honor of all the mountains he loved and climbed.

In December, Laurie joined me again for the changing of the AIA officers in Washington D.C., where we visited the Spy Museum for the first time and revisited other Smithsonian favorites. Then it was time for another Christmas cruise for the three Hastings girls. This time, we shared a stateroom large enough to accommodate Norma's wheelchair and walker. We noted several families with children, but we only saw the young ones during mealtimes, and we commented on their good behavior. There is hope in this complicated world for the future generations now growing up.

❖

2018

AS I ENTERED MY NINETIETH YEAR, I noted how much Seattle has changed over the decades. In recent years, it became a sea of construction cranes, and with so many new buildings, our city has lost many landmarks, and familiar routes have become harder to find. The year's highlights included visiting the new Nordic Heritage Museum and the new University of Washington Burke Museum while they were still under construction; both will be recipients of our art collection someday.

The lowlights included losing two very close friends. Horizon House was also placed in quarantine for several weeks. It only requires three cases of flu among our five hundred fifty residents for the county health department to make this restriction. We were not entirely confined to our building, but we could not gather in groups for dining, exercise classes, or programs.

But I stayed focused on the positives: working in my garden, singing in the Okay Chorale and managing a small group that sang in Supported Living every two months. I also enjoyed receiving regular inquiries about my contemporary fellow architects from writers and researchers looking for insights. I'm the one with good memories about the architects who were active during the late 1940s and the ensuing decades. For years, my fellow architect and friend Sue Harris Alden and I encouraged writers to document our prominent colleagues while there were still former employees alive to tell their stories. We were not heeded for a long time, but now a younger generation of authors has decided these histories are important. I thoroughly enjoy sharing my recollections of friendships, good times, and funny stories, and I hope I paint a reasonably honest picture of their personalities and contributions to the architectural profession.

And yes, I found time for more travel. I started in May with a four-day cruise to British Columbia. Soon after, I was off to Iceland with our group of traveling widows and niece Laurie. The weather gods forgot it was almost June, and served up 42-degree weather, pouring rain and wild winds, but it was still a wonderful trip led by a knowledgeable geologist guide. We enjoyed a clear day when we took a ferry to an island that was rebuilt after a volcano eruption had buried much of the town, and a highlight was sipping a cocktail while soaking in the heavenly warm waters of the Blue Lagoon. In the fourteen years since my last visit to Iceland, tourism had become the lifeblood of the country, and the charming little fishing village of Reykjavik with its modest homes had been swallowed by a city full of glass high-rise hotels and apartments.

That June, I attended the National AIA Convention in New York City—more than six decades after my first visit to the city in 1954. The four former female AIA Presidents and the four former women Chancellors, all in our robes and medals after the Fellowship Investiture, gathered for a group photo in front of St. Patrick's Cathedral; the portrait would be added to the IAWA collection at Virginia Tech.

Jane addressing the Chancellors group at the last AIA annual December meeting she attended, Kennedy Caucus Room, Washington, D.C., 2018

At the final AIA meeting of the year in Washington, D.C., I played a small role in the installation of the 2019 Chancellor. I was the oldest former Chancellor attending.

❖

2019

AT THE BEGINNING OF THE YEAR, I was amazed to learn that the Johnston-Hastings House had been included in the Society of Architectural Historians' Archipedia among Washington's Classic Buildings. Of two hundred thirty-five entries across the state, fifty-eight were from Seattle, and Norm's and my house was the only residence. What an honor!

I was puzzled by the sole selection of the Johnston house when Seattle has several other nationally and internationally renowned residential architects, so I looked up the nomination form. It highlighted the use of natural light, passive solar gain, energy efficiency, regional materials, and site sensitivity—concerns I always addressed on my projects and approaches rooted in my earliest design experiences. Even in my junior high school sewing class, the instructor commented on my use of an expensive cotton fabric for a dress (29 cents per yard vs. the 15 cents-per-yard fabric that most girls used). As my mother always said: "If you are going to spend time making something, use good material. It will look better and last longer." This became part of my code.

As an architect, I also learned to avoid materials that are expensive mostly because they are popular, and I found great savings by choosing alternatives. For example, during the 1950s and '60s, when carpet was in style, I found warehouses of hardwood flooring at a better price than plywood, which had been in high demand during World War II. So, I installed the hardwood under carpeting instead of plywood. I assured my clients that when wood floors came back in style, they would simply need to remove the carpet and finish the floor. Years later, I received thank yous when my prediction came true.

I also was an early adopter of insulated glazing, which had to be custom-fabricated until it became mass-produced and widely used in sliding glass doors. Many of my projects had window walls created by insulated door blanks made from safety glass, which made for comfortable window seating even during cold weather. Insulated glass cut heat expenses; thus, it was more cost-effective for owners. My heating engineer often remarked on my good sense and wondered why my colleagues didn't use insulated glass.

I had the reputation of getting a lot of house out of a budget, and I embraced the savings that came when clients gathered their own stones for their fireplaces or when old telephone poles that were free for the taking could be used for structural columns. My goal was to produce the most comfortable dwelling for the client's lifestyle within their budget. Hopefully I was successful.

I THOUGHT MY PUBLIC SPEAKING DAYS were over, but that March, I found myself sharing the stage at the Women's University Club of Seattle with a young woman. She spoke about the future of women leaders and I told the stories of the past. Then, Historic Seattle asked me to present an oral history for the Docomomo US/ WEWA group on Midcentury Modern architecture. Former employee and architectural historian Kate Krafft interviewed me about my career in the Johnston/ Hastings Gallery at UW's Gould Hall. In November, I gave another oral history for the Southwest Seattle Historical Society, describing high-school life during World War II. Those two presentations, along with my older oral history at the Museum of History & Industry about Seattle world fairs, made me feel like I was becoming a part of the history of my own city. We grew up together, and I must admit that it is becoming a city I hardly recognize. One enormous change to the face of the city came this same year: A new highway tunnel opened on the waterfront, and the concrete viaduct that had separated downtown from Elliott Bay for seventy years was torn down. Many of us miss the spectacular views of Mount Rainier to the south and the Olympic Mountains to the west from that double-deck structure.

In July, I was able to check off three countries on my must-see list when Laurie and I embarked on a Baltic cruise. Back in grade school I had been fascinated by the three little countries of Estonia, Latvia, and Lithuania that were established after World War I. Norm and I had never managed to visit these European villages with their old town halls and cobblestone squares left untouched by World War II. Our cruise also included stops in many cities I was familiar with: St. Petersburg, Stockholm, Helsinki, Berlin, Copenhagen, and Amsterdam. I found these old metropolitan friends had changed, and their historic features were now surrounded by new glass towers. Soon cities will all look the same, distinguished only by their geographic location.

I kept promising myself that I would not get involved with any new organizations, but when I was asked to join the Allied Arts Board, I said yes. Norm had been one of its founders, and I had to do this for him. I donated many art pieces to the 2019 auction supporting their program sponsoring local young talent in all the arts.

And I finally wrapped up one very important project: A little Le Corbusier watercolor drawing that Tony Canlis had given Norm in 2005 needed to complete its journey. When Norm could no longer enjoy this Picasso-style work, it was to be delivered to the University of Washington in his memory and displayed for the architecture students to enjoy. However, a Seattle Art Museum curator insisted the Le Corbusier had to go to the university's Henry Art Gallery because it was too valuable to be placed where it could be stolen or damaged by improper lighting. I sought advice from former faculty members and friends: Should the valuable artwork be sold, with a copy hung in Gould Hall with its history, or should it be stored away in the art museum? Albert Thurmond from the university's Office of Planned Giving and a lawyer assured me that it was legally mine and I could do whatever I liked, but what appeared to be a simple task of delivering it to the university became a major project.

Albert joked with me about selling it and keeping the money, but I told him Norm would haunt both of us forever. I decided the Le Corbusier should go to New York for auction, with the proceeds going to the university scholarships and endowments we supported. I gave the little gem to the university, and Albert was now in the art business. He would let me know how many dollars I could distribute when he received the funds. I had grand plans in my head until the word came from New York that it was a fake. The paper was not old enough for the signed 1930s date, and the work would be returned.

I like to bring closure to projects, so I wondered where "Corbu" was hanging out. And was it still in the lovely frame that Tony had made? The university received it so it must be somewhere on campus. Josh Polansky from the College of Built Environments, the slide curator who had worked with Norm, finally located the wandering piece. One day Josh called to say he had it in his office, so I went to visit. Yes, there it was, covered with yards of bubble-wrap. Where to hang it? I left that to the university.

My attention in recent years had turned to the project I call "This is for you, Laurie": disposing of old records and routing memorabilia to permanent homes. My sixth-grade baseball award and my winning high-school essay—along with the war bond first prize—are now at the Southwest Seattle Historical Society. My 1944 Honor Girl Camper paddle went to Camp Colman. I've gradually given artwork to museums and a collection of books to the university. I hope to take care of as much as possible so Laurie is not overwhelmed when the day arrives that she must clear out my apartment.

❖
2020

THIS BECAME AN IMPORTANT YEAR in the world history books. I started out the year hoping the election would bring in a new administration to "right our ship" after four destructive years of Donald Trump. Then, just as I was looking forward to early March and birthday parties, everything was canceled due to the COVID-19 virus newly discovered in our state. Horizon House went into a complete lockdown. We had been accustomed to occasional short quarantines during flu season, but this became our new way of life. Meals and mail were delivered to our doors, and we could leave our apartments only to visit the trash and laundry rooms next door, or for emergency medical care.

In April, I found an escape route: a massive uncontrollable nosebleed that required an ambulance ride to the ER. I repeated this experience for three days and required a hospital stay for a blood transfusion after my fourth trip. I begged for the vascular embolization that would solve the issue but was told I was too old. It was finally granted only when my doctor insisted, "Forget her age; she is healthy as a horse."

During those first months of the pandemic, Seattle became a ghost city with schools and businesses closed. The car-free freeway gave us fresher air, which our gardens loved, but we were not allowed out to tend them and I watched the weeds grow from my window.

After May 25, people poured out of their homes and into the streets to protest the police killing of Minneapolis resident George Floyd, a Black man. "Black Lives Matter" banners filled U.S. cities of all sizes and spread to protests around the world. It took just one cellphone video captured by a young woman to tell the story. Around the country, more stories of police brutality were surfaced and resurfaced, and citizens demanded that police departments be held accountable. We needed major changes, and I hoped the presidential election and a new administration could lead the country in a new direction, both with the pandemic and social justice.

The "Black Lives Matter" movement brought memories of good friends throughout my life who would have appreciated the protests and the changes they advocated. From my childhood I remembered the Rev. Mary McKee Chester, protector of all young people regardless of color or background. She ensured that Fauntleroy Church members hosted segregated Black soldiers stationed locally during World War II. From my university years, I remembered Dick Yarbrough, the only Black student in the UW Architecture School and a friend who joined our group at the Blue Moon Tavern for beers, as well as at basketball games, and on skiing and backpacking trips. When Dick said he would skip a gathering to study, it often meant we were headed to a place where he felt uncomfortable. Arne Bystrom was usually the one to suggest a better alternative so Dick would join our group. Dick, always a joyful man, moved to California after school but returned for gatherings in our retirement years even after he lost both his legs due to diabetes.

I remembered Jack Blount, a Black Army veteran who was in charge of the Seattle YMCA swimming pool where our water ballet trained. The love of his life was Ivana, an Italian girl in Rome he met while serving our country. The ballet girls were all in on the plan to help Jack bring Ivana to Seattle as his wife, but they eventually returned to Rome, where Jack went to medical school. We stayed in touch, and in 1954 I reconnected with them in Italy. And of course, I remembered Gertrude

Meriwether, the Washington state native and superb Black director of the model Service Club who helped train the new arrivals each month. She was a wonderful administrator, and I drew on her lessons when I started my own business. When the armed forces integrated after the war, there were often protests among the troops; Meriwether, known for her evenhanded approach, was assigned to problem areas. When she retired, she returned to Seattle, got another degree, and worked with troubled youths. We stayed in touch for years. Lastly, I remembered my dates in Germany with Air Force Gen. Noel Parrish, who had fought for the Tuskegee Airmen's right to fly.

My friends, you have all departed this troubled world, but I think of you knowing you would approve of the changes the masses have insisted take place.

LATER THAT SUMMER, we were finally able to enjoy outdoor activities, tending our gardens and having cocktails with friends, separated by the required six feet. Just as we were feeling a bit liberated, we were pushed back indoors by the wildfire smoke from Canada that settled into the Puget Sound basin, giving us the worst air quality in the country. For a few days, the dense, mustard-colored air reduced our visibility to almost zero.

Christmas 2020 was the first holiday in my life that I celebrated alone, with no family members or friends—a solitary experience and yet shared by millions that season. It was a time to reflect on the ones missed. I'm grateful that Norm selected 2015 for his departure, missing both the Trump years and the pandemic. My two other longtime male friends, Don the sailor and Dan the gardener, departed in 2020, leaving without the opportunity to look toward a more promising future for our country, even with a good deal of work required to achieve it.

AT THE END OF THE YEAR, when the holiday season arrived, I settled down to write my annual letter with Joe Biden the president-elect—and Donald Trump still insisting he won. The country braced for what damage he would do in his remaining six weeks in office. Looking back, I realize that the bookends of my life will be the 1930s Great Depression and the 2020s Great Pandemic. Or on a more somber note, the bookends will be Adolf Hitler and Donald Trump, two narcissistic leaders of destruction and death. If one believes in reincarnation, Trump certainly followed the elder's footprint.

Unfortunately, Hitler's demise did not stop the hate. I remember that shortly after my 1954 arrival in Germany, a smiling little boy ran up asking if I was an American. When I said "yes," he spat in my face and ran away. Years later, when Norm and I were driving through England in 1970, we took a side road to photograph the little company town of Port Sunlight, site of the former Lever soap factory and supposedly abandoned. We were surprised to find a large encampment of young men with swastikas on their clothing who surrounded our car. "Do you know who we are?" they asked. Norman replied, "I believe you are skinheads." Then they said, "If you value your lives, leave now," which we did without any photos. Back home a neo-Nazi group in northern Idaho was often in the news until the FBI took them on.

There is one thing I'll give Trump credit for: He brought these movements to the surface. There would be no more hiding in the shadows. I think back on my teacher Belle McKenzie's statement in 1944: "Remember, only the ignorant are prejudiced." I have decided we have a huge educational problem.

Donald Trump will do anything to get his way, and the violence that ensued when his followers stormed the U.S. Capitol on January 6, 2021, proved it. More than two years later, Trump and his followers still insist he won, and he plans to run for president again in 2024, despite lawsuits, and state and federal cases pending against him. I can only hope he will be in jail in 2024.

Three predictions made to me in 1943 came true, accurately describing the fate of President Roosevelt and the end of the war in Europe and Japan. I have not forgotten the fourth, which foretold that I would live into my nineties and experience the end of the United States as a world power, with Asia replacing it.

I'm beginning to believe that going to war with a foreign country will not be necessary. War within our own people may be responsible for bringing this to pass.

❖

AS I LOOK BACK, the bookends of my life may be notable for hardship and tragedy, but the years in between have been extraordinary, full of adventure and joyful experiences. I achieved my goals: I became an architect, owned a cabin on the ocean shore, and traveled the world, visiting one hundred fourteen countries at last count. And I had a very special partner for more than forty-six years.

Of course, there were times long after I was a child in Mrs. S's Fauntleroy kitchen when I had to pretend something was "pink," but I never stopped loving the great outdoors of Western Washington, the place I have always called home. I'm forever thankful that my parents met in Seattle, created our wonderful family, and stayed together here to raise us. I agree wholeheartedly with the New Zealand architect I met more than thirty-five years ago: Yes, I do live in the most beautiful place in the world.

WITH GRATITUDE

Jane's parents, Harry and Camille Hastings, 1961

BACK IN THE FOURTH GRADE, when I declared my intention to become an architect, I had no idea how many doors my decision would open for me. Architecture is a very respected profession, and to some, it is almost mysterious. Architects are often welcomed into a building closed to the general public because we appreciate, honor, and respect the structure, its design, its history and its contents. Owners are usually flattered that we have requested entrance and trust us to respect their special places.

In my extensive travel experiences throughout my own country and around the world, I have had the privilege to meet and share the hospitality of people from all walks of life—some who have very little and some who have more than most of us can fathom. Often, regardless of background, these hosts were much the same, sharing their love of country, warmth, kindness, and friendship.

I started carrying packets of flower seeds as gifts in the early 1970s while traveling. They were small, easy to carry, and no real loss if removed at country borders. I gave them to gardeners while walking through villages in China, Iran, Russia, Yemen, Bhutan, and many other countries where I found someone caring for a little patch of soil. They were often elders, sometimes disabled, and always returned the warmest smiles. No words were ever exchanged; the picture on the package told the story. I still remember their wonderful faces, and hope the seeds brought color and joy to their lives.

I have had the honor of sharing meals in homes all over the world—in South Africa, Italy, Greece, Germany, France, Russia, Turkey, Sweden, the Netherlands, Spain, Israel, Denmark, Moldova, England, Ecuador, Paraguay, Australia, Guam, New Zealand, Philippines, Malaysia, China, South Korea, and Japan. I enjoyed tea in a Bedouin tent in the middle of the Yemen desert, and lunch in a German herder's mountain cabin. One meal in Tokyo was in a modern all-concrete structure with concrete furniture, and the only unattached pieces were four chairs at the table. I have attended embassy parties in Egypt, Israel, the Soviet Union, and Paraguay, and I was hosted by our Japanese ambassador at a party in their private residence.

The hosts who presumably had the most included Her Royal Highness Princess Grace in her Monaco palace, the Empress of Iran, and our own First Lady Pat Nixon. How could I—a girl born in Depression-era Seattle—have been so privileged to be part of so many marvelous and different lives? Truly, I have led a Cinderella-like life.

I have had the opportunity to appreciate many different cultures, beautiful natural wonders, and striking architectural structures constructed over many centuries. And I do believe we are making progress solving many of the world's problems, however slowly, thanks to new technology and our improved abilities to communicate and understand each other. In the past, the truth was too often hidden or misunderstood.

By now, I have spoken at too many memorial services for friends and loved ones, and I am often the one who knew them the longest. I was there with my two closest friends, Shirley and Gretchen, at the very end, as I was with my devoted, loving husband, Norman Johnston—the man who was my lover, best friend and favorite traveling companion. And when it's my turn to depart, my ashes will join my brother Jim's ashes in the Salish Sea, reuniting with our beloved brother Art, the fisherman of the family, who was lost on his boat so many years ago. The three of us Hastings kids, raised on the water, sailors and swimmers, together again. That is my last bit of planning.

To my wonderful family, my dear friends, my clients, employees, students, and colleagues who have been part of my story—I thank you all. I want to especially thank my devoted niece, Laurie, and former student/employee Kate Hills Krafft for their help in reviewing this memoir and my effort to record my very special life.

And finally, thank you to my teacher, Miss Belle McKenzie, who long ago argued that I should become a writer. Yes, it took some time. This book is also for you.

I have lived my childhood dream and so much, much more.

APPENDIX | WORLD TRAVELS

COUNTRIES AND YEARS Jane visited between 1954 and 2019. Does not include western Canada or the Lower 48 states in the United States.

AFRICA: Benin 2000; Egypt 1971, 1977, and 1993; Ethiopia 1993; Ghana 2000; Ivory Coast 2000; Morocco 1955, 1977, and 2000; Namibia 2000; Senegal 2000; South Africa 2000; Spanish Morocco 1954; Togo 2000; and Tunisia 2000.

AMERICAS: Alaska 1972, 1981, 1982, 1984, 1990, 1998, 2000, 2002, 2005, 2009, 2011, and 2013; Antigua 2016; Argentina 1991; Aruba 2003; Bahamas 1992, 2011, and 2016; Barbados 2016; Belize 1997; Bolivia 1982; Brazil 1982 and 2015; Canada (eastern) 1967, 1976, 1983, 1990 and 2016; Chile 1991; Costa Rica 2003; Dominican Republic 1996; Ecuador 1982; French Guiana 2016; Grand Cayman 1996; Guatemala 1997; Haiti 1992; Hawaii 1965, 1968, 1979, 1981, 1982, 1984, 1988, 1989, 1993, and 1996; Honduras 1997; Jamaica 2003; Mexico 1956, 1984, 1989, 1994, and 1996; Panama 2003; Paraguay 1982; Peru 1982; Puerto Rico 1996, 2011, and 2016; St. Lucia 2011 and 2016; and the Virgin Islands 1992.

ASIA/MIDDLE EAST: Bhutan 1995; Burma (Myanmar) 1985; Cambodia 2006; China 1980, 1989, 1990, and 2008; Cyprus 1971 and 1995; Hong Kong 1980, 1987, and 1990; India 1979 and 1995; Indonesia 1994; Iran 1976; Iraq 1976; Israel 1971; Japan 1979, 1984, 1991, 1998, and 2009; Jordan 1995; Lebanon 1972; Malaysia 1994; Nepal 1979 and 1995; Oman 2016; Philippines 1980; Saudi Arabia 1993; Siberia 2009; Singapore 1987, 1994, and 1995; South Korea 1979; Thailand 1985, 1995 and 2006; Tibet 1995; Turkey 1977, 1995, and 2003; United Arab Emirates 2016; Vietnam 2006; and Yemen 1993.

EUROPE: Austria 1954-56, 1969, 1977, 1980, and 1987; Belgium 1955 and 1977; Bulgaria 2007; Croatia 2005; Czech Republic 1996; Denmark 1955, 1956, 1969, 1977, 1991, and 2019; England 1955, 1970, 1972, 1980, and 1999; Estonia 2019; Finland 1976, 2004, and 2019; France 1955-56, 1969, 1977, 1980, 1983, 1984, and 1987; Georgia 1971 and 1976; Germany 1954-56, 1969, 1976-77, 1980, 1984, 1987, 1991, and 2019; Gibraltar 1955 and 1977; Greece 1977, 1995, 2000, 2001 and 2003; Hungary 1996 and 2007; Iceland 2004 and 2018; Ireland 1970; Italy 1954-56, 1969, 1977 and 1980; Latvia 2019; Liechtenstein 1955; Lithuania 2019; Luxembourg 1955 and 1977; Malta 1999 and 2000; Moldova 1983; Monaco 1969; Montenegro 2005; Netherlands 1955-56, 1977, 1991, and 2019; Norway 1956, 1977, and 2004; Poland 1996; Portugal 1990; Romania 1972 and 2007; Russia 1971, 1976, 1983 and 2019; San Marino 1977; Scotland 1970; Sicily 1977; Serbia 2007; Slovak Republic 1996; Slovenia 1977 and 2005; Spain 1955, 1976, and 1990; Sweden 1956, 1969, and 2019; Switzerland 1954-55, 1977, and 1980; Ukraine 1971 and 1976; Vatican City 1955 and 1977; and Wales 1970.

OCEANIA: Australia (including Tasmania) 1986; Guam 1984; and New Zealand 1986.

AN INDEX OF PEOPLE AND PLACES

ABOUT THE AUTHOR

*Jane Hastings
in the mid-1980s*

L. JANE HASTINGS is an acclaimed Seattle architect whose career spans seven decades, more than 500 building projects, and dozens of regional and national honors. Born in 1928 and raised in Seattle's Fauntleroy community, Jane is a proud graduate of West Seattle High School (1945) and the University of Washington (1952). In 1959, she became the principal of one of Washington's first women-owned architecture firms, and she was an influential member of the International Union of Women Architects during its formative years. Since the 1950s, she has held multiple offices in the American Institute of Architects, both in the Seattle Chapter and in the national organization, and she was named a Fellow of the AIA in 1980. And while her many career "firsts" include being named the first woman Chancellor of the AIA's prestigious College of Fellows, Jane also cherishes her "Honor Girl Camper" award earned at Horsehead Bay in 1944. Jane's friendships and travels have taken her around the world, but she has always returned to the beautiful Pacific Northwest and Seattle, which she continues to call home.